T0332814

Pioneering Approaches in Data Management

Kanak Kalita
Vel Tech Rangarajan Dr. Sagunthala R&D Institute of Science and Technology, India

Diego Alberto Oliva
Universidad de Guadalajara, Mexico

Xiao-Zhi Gao
University of Eastern Finland, Finland

Rishi Dwivedi
Xavier Institute of Social Service, India

IGI Global
Scientific Publishing
Publishing Tomorrow's Research Today

Vice President of Editorial	Melissa Wagner
Managing Editor of Acquisitions	Mikaela Felty
Managing Editor of Book Development	Jocelynn Hessler
Production Manager	Mike Brehm
Cover Design	Phillip Shickler

Published in the United States of America by
IGI Global Scientific Publishing
701 East Chocolate Avenue
Hershey, PA, 17033, USA
Tel: 717-533-8845
Fax: 717-533-8661
E-mail: cust@igi-global.com
Website: https://www.igi-global.com

Library of Congress Cataloging-in-Publication Data

Names: Kalita, Kanak, 1988- editor. | Oliva, Diego, editor. | Gao,
    Xiao-Zhi, 1972- editor. | Dwivedi, Rishi, 1988- editor.
Title: Pioneering approaches in data management / edited by Kanak Kalita,
    Diego Oliva, Xiao-Zhi Gao, Rishi Dwivedi.
Description: Hershey, PA : Engineering Science Reference, [2025] | Includes
    bibliographical references and index. | Summary: "This publication is
    poised to make a significant contribution to both academic and
    professional spheres. It will serve as a pivotal resource for
    researchers, educators, and practitioners, offering fresh insights and
    comprehensive guidance on the latest developments in data analytics. The
    book's emphasis on real-world applications and case studies will foster
    a deeper understanding of how data analytics can be effectively
    integrated into management strategies, thereby influencing the future
    direction of research and practice in this rapidly evolving field"--
    Provided by publisher.
Identifiers: LCCN 2024038954 (print) | LCCN 2024038955 (ebook) | ISBN
    9798369355633 (hardcover) | ISBN 9798369355640 (paperback) | ISBN
    9798369355657 (ebook)
Subjects: LCSH: Big data. | Business--Data processing. | Management--Data
    processing.
Classification: LCC QA76.9.B45 P56 2024 (print) | LCC QA76.9.B45 (ebook)
    | DDC 005.7--dc23/eng/20241102
LC record available at https://lccn.loc.gov/2024038954
LC ebook record available at https://lccn.loc.gov/2024038955

British Cataloguing in Publication Data
A Cataloguing in Publication record for this book is available from the British Library.

Table of Contents

Section 1
Introduction to Data Analytics in Management

*R. Bhuvanya, Sri Ramachandra Institute of Higher Education and
    Research, India*
B. Yamini, SRM Institute of Science and Technology, India
K. Sivakumar, Nehru Institute of Engineering and Technology, India
Gobinath V. M., Rajalakshmi Institute of Technology, India
*V. Sathya, Vel Tech Rangarajan Dr. Sagunthala R&D Institute of
    Science and Technology, India*
*R. Siva Subramanian, R.M.K. College of Engineering and Technology,
    India*

Ayush Gupta, IIM Bodhgaya, India
Saikonda Vaishnavi, IIM Bodhgaya, India

Section 2
Applications of Data Analytics in Business

*Satadruti Chakraborty, Indian Institute of Social Welfare and Business
    Management, India*
*Dipa Mitra, Indian Institute of Social Welfare and Business
    Management, India*

Section 3
Data Analytics in Specific Domains

Detailed Table of Contents

Section 1
Introduction to Data Analytics in Management

Chapter 1

    R. Bhuvanya, Sri Ramachandra Institute of Higher Education and
        Research, India
    B. Yamini, SRM Institute of Science and Technology, India
    K. Sivakumar, Nehru Institute of Engineering and Technology, India
    Gobinath V. M., Rajalakshmi Institute of Technology, India
    V. Sathya, Vel Tech Rangarajan Dr. Sagunthala R&D Institute of
        Science and Technology, India
    R. Siva Subramanian, R.M.K. College of Engineering and Technology,
        India

Data analytics, which is critical in today's decision-making, is driving the rapidly changing corporate environment. Its management, growth, and strategic objective transformation are explored in this article. Strategic choices, innovation, and competitiveness are enabled by data analytics. Big data values huge data kinds, recognises patterns, anticipates trends, and real-time possibilities, decision-making and helping companies grow. For market leadership, predictive analytics improves operational efficiency and resource allocation by forecasting trends, client demands, and simplifying processes. AI and ML automate activities, find patterns, and propose ways to enhance judgements, revolutionising industry and e-commerce. Data-driven marketing improves expenditure, engagement, and campaigns. Responsible data use and transparency address privacy and ethics. Examples demonstrate how data analytics supports innovation, solves business problems, and provides outcomes. Finally, data analytics integration trends, challenges, and possibilities emphasise the need for a data-centric culture.

Ayush Gupta, IIM Bodhgaya, India
Saikonda Vaishnavi, IIM Bodhgaya, India

This chapter delves into the rising prominence of big data in driving strategy decisions.
It establishes a definition for big data and its defining features, elaborating how it
contributes to the functioning of the corporate world. This chapter introduces the idea
of strategic decision-making as a necessity for favorable outcomes. Soon after, the
chapter treads into depths of data-driven objectivity preferred over qualitative analysis.
The chapter also unveils how big data aids in serving customer insights, benefitting
organizational operations and overall performance. The benefit of significant data
insights offering predictive analyses and control over the consequences of business
decisions is also explained in great detail. Finally, to provide an understanding of
the practical application of data analytics, the chapter discusses working of big data
in a chosen business domain.In summary, this chapter introduces Big Data and its
functioning, the benefits of using data-driven insights during decision-making, and
the applicability of big data in business operations.

Section 2
Applications of Data Analytics in Business

Chapter 3

Satadruti Chakraborty, Indian Institute of Social Welfare and Business
Management, India
Dipa Mitra, Indian Institute of Social Welfare and Business
Management, India

This study aims to determine the critical components of high-quality travel website services that have a substantial impact on Indian consumers' purchase intentions as well as use the 'Importance Performance Analysis' matrix to assess the competitive qualities of service in terms of their specific significance and relevance to business success. The research here is based on Exploratory Research approach using Quantitative Research Techniques. Data for the study is collected by framing questionnaires. There are two phases to the examination of this study: Structural evaluation of the scale using SPSS and AMOS and IPA matrix. The study is the first of its kind in the area of online travel behavior research because it not only unifies all factors that influence decisions into a single framework but also assesses the effectiveness of the attributes by conducting further survey research to ascertain where they rank for five of India's top travel agencies. The study's conclusions will give travel industry marketers information they can use to enhance their internet marketing strategies.

Chapter 4

Gurleen Kaur, Xavier Institute of Social Service, India
Amar Eron Tigga, Xavier Institute of Social Service, India

The non-banking financial companies (NBFCs) sector in India has undergone a significant transformation and are playing a critical role for the development of core infrastructure and financing economically weaker sections. Social media plays a multifaceted role in this industry in building trust, shaping brand identity, educating stakeholders and connecting with broader audiences through media channels. This study delves into how social media presence in five major NBFCs of India differs. The data is collected from the company's official social media handles and social media monitoring tools. Employing a mixed-methods approach, the research combines quantitative data analysis of social media engagement with qualitative insights gleaned from social media coverage themes. The paper analyses the wide set of strategies to find the competitive strategies which would be helpful for competitive advantage to the companies. Strategies focused on content, engagement and platform specific strategies could be used to gain a competitive edge in the non-banking financial sector.

The improvement of companies' innovation capability is one of their foremost strategic objectives. To achieve this goal, companies allocate significant resources. Analyzing the current situations of companies and controlling for the enhancement of innovation capabilities based on this analysis ensures the efficient utilization of resources. Companies should focus on improving their innovation capability while also concentrating on how to elevate their innovation maturity levels. This focus will guarantee leadership in the industry and exports in the future. In this study, the innovation capabilities of four companies operating in different sectors are compared. Additionally, the innovation maturity levels of the companies are determined. The companies operate in the information technology, food, plastic, and aviation sectors. Significant differences in innovation capabilities among the companies have been observed. To determine these differences, the Mann-Whitney U test is conducted.

Geo-marketing integrates traditional marketing with GIS to support companies in identifying target markets and strategically positioning themselves. This chapter explores OSM data utilization for competitor analysis, demographic insights, amenity evaluation, market segmentation, site selection, and store optimization. Extracting POI data from OSM, such as retail stores and supermarkets using different can inform strategic decisions. Spatial analysis techniques like distance calculations and buffer analysis can assess competitor proximity and identify potential store sites. Demographic analysis can infer population characteristics, complemented by external datasets. Amenities can be evaluated using density and hotspot analyses to pinpoint prime locations. Market segmentation can cluster areas with similar POI distributions for targeted strategies. Site selection overlays POI layers to optimize accessibility and meet market demand. Store optimization enhances performance through foot traffic analysis and POI data, enhancing customer satisfaction and profitability.

Chapter 7

Mukesh Kumar Sharma, Arka Jain University, India
Kanika Prasad, National Institute of Technology, Jamshedpur, India
Dinesh Kumar, National Institute of Technology, Jamshedpur, India

In circular economy (CE), the significance of waste collection and segregation cannot be overstated, as these practices play a key role in diminishing environmental impact and fostering resource efficiency. It is expected that the waste generation would raise manifolds by the next decade. The shift to CE has the potential to result in annual savings amounting to billions in material costs. Thus, strategic waste practices play a crucial role in fostering sustainability and economic benefits. This article focuses on addressing multifaceted challenges to enhance the efficiency and sustainability of waste management practices. Hence, it introduces a framework utilising the IF-TOPSIS methodology to assess impediments in the execution of waste collection and segregation strategies. Thirteen barriers have been discerned through literature reviews and expert evaluations. The study highlights that lack of public awareness as significant obstacle. These findings offer valuable insights to industries, academia, and government bodies, guiding them towards proper implementation.

Section 3
Data Analytics in Specific Domains

    K. Lavanya, Vellore Institute of Technology, India
    B. N. Dorendra, Vellore Institute of Technology, India
    Sweta Chopdar, Vellore Institute of Technology, India
    Akshay Mahantshetti, Vellore Institute of Technology, India

The Spotify Recommendation System represents a cutting-edge application of data science and streaming technology, harnessing the power of PySpark and Kafka to deliver highly personalized music recommendations to users. Music streaming platforms use collaborative-based filtering methods, which has a Sparsity Problem leading to pressing demand for even more personalized recommendations, delivered in real-time, leaning on implicit feedback collaborative filtering techniques. The foundation of our recommendation engine is Alternating Least Squares (ALS) Implicit Collaborative Filtering. It enables data scientists and engineers to process enormous amounts of user data, such as listening history, track information, and user preferences, in an effective manner. The algorithm assists in the discovery of significant insights that improve the precision of music recommendations through data transformation and feature engineering. Kafka, a high-performance event streaming platform, is essential for assuring real-time data acquisition and processing.

    N. Bhanu Prakash Reddy, Saveetha University, India
    W. Deva Priya, Saveetha University, India

The major focus of this research work is to improve the accuracy of rice quality in real-time images using Support Vector Machine and Convolutional Neural Network. The recommended algorithm for Rice Quality Prediction. The Rice Quality Prediction dataset used in this study contain 356 rice samples (273 for for training 83 for testing) are Support Vector Machine with sample size N=10 and Convolutional Neural Network with sample size N=10 with the G-power of 80% and information units are gathered from more than a few internet sources with the latest learn about findings and threshold 0.05. The rice dataset is utilized for experimental work, and it is carried out with the assistance of the Jupyter software program tool. The end result of the Rice Quality Prediction is the usage of Support Vector Machine in contrast with Convolutional Neural Network.

Chapter 10

Balaji Pavan, Saveetha University, India
Kalimuddin Mondal, Saveetha University, India

The purpose of this work is to improve the Fake logo prediction Through CNN Over KNN. A novel method has been developed to detect fake logos using K-Nearest Neighbors (KNN) and Convolutional Neural Networks (CNN), which were trained and tested with varying splits. The CNN model outperformed KNN in terms of accuracy and speed, owing to its ability to extract complex features from images. However, CNN models may require significant resources, especially for large datasets. To enhance the system's accuracy and efficiency, the CNN model can be optimized and combined with a KNN model. The system is designed to detect fake logos in real-time and adapt quickly to new logos with minimal training, offering an effective and efficient approach for identifying fraudulent logos. The Gpower test was used with a significance level of $\alpha=0.05$ and power of 0.85, resulting in an accuracy rate of approximately 85%.

Chapter 11

Shailendra Kumar Mishra, REVA University, India
R. Sreelakshmy, Vel Tech Rangarajan Dr. Sagunthala R&D Institute of
*   Science and Technology, India*
Gaurav Kumar, Wipro Limited, Canada
Dheeraj Kumar, Cognizant Technology Solutions, India
Sujeet Kumar, Intenim Technologies Pvt. Ltd., India

Cardiac arrest is one of the most frequently occurring causes of death worldwide. In this disease, the heart normally fails to provide enough blood to other regions of the body to allow them to perform their regular functions. It is tough for doctors to forecast cardiac arrest because various medical and physical habits are taken into consideration for forecasting cardiac arrest. Because the list of parameters is large, it is important to automate the procedure to avoid manual mistake, enhance medical efficiency, and reduce costs. The paper presents Explanatory Data Analysis (EDA) and feature engineering of a data set on the basis of observations. The model uses various Machine Learning (ML) algorithms such as catBoost, Logistic regression, k-Nearest Neighbors, etc. to predict heart failure. In this comparison study, the research paper examines the performance of various machine learning algorithms. The model's performance is best on catboost. Analysing tools such as f-1 score and ROC-curve are drawn to evaluate the algorithm's efficiency.

The expansion of digital infrastructure has prompted the establishment of data centers, which need efficient cooling systems to operate reliably. This chapter digs into the complicated world of cooling technologies, as well as the issues they face and the novel solutions they provide. It highlights the need of effective cooling in data centers, as well as the relevance of balancing efficiency and energy consumption, scalability, and environmental concerns. The chapter goes over different cooling methods, such as conventional air cooling, sophisticated liquid cooling, and phase-change solutions. It also emphasizes the use of innovative materials for increased heat transmission and thermal management, such as graphene and carbon nanotubes. In addition, the chapter covers the use of Artificial Intelligence in cooling systems, providing real-time monitoring and predictive analytics. Modular data centers, rack-level cooling, and improved free cooling solutions will be continuous advances in data center cooling in the future.

Section 4
Special Topics in Data Analytics and Emerging Trends

The study explores the impact of Emotional Intelligence (EI) on Financial Literacy(FL) of individuals belonging to Gen Z. Using a two-wave research design method,136 respondents from the Bihar -Jharkhand Region of India were studied. Empirical evidences suggested that EI significantly impacts FL amongst Gen Z. Further, Sociability and Wellbeing in Gen Z were found to be the factors related to EI impacting their FL. Importance of developing behavioural, cognitive and non-traditional forms of intelligence such as EI and its impact on FL have been discussed. Training programmes and focused interventions on developing EI have also been highlighted. The relationship between EI and FL in the chosen context has remained unexplored in context of India. The field of FL has not provided enough attention to the role of emotions and emotional intelligence in decision making and the study tries to study this gap.

    Bhabani Prasad Mahapatra, Xavier Institute of Social Service, India
    Vartika Banerjee, Xavier Institute of Social Service, India
    Gurleen Kaur, Xavier Institute of Social Service, India

As Generation Z constitutes a significant demographic within the user base of dating apps, a thorough understanding of their priorities, values, and relationship approaches becomes imperative. Drawing upon secondary data sources, including official reports from dating apps and pertinent literature, this research presents a comprehensive analysis of global dating trends, discernible shifts in user behaviour, and prevailing market dynamics. Moreover, the study endeavours to contribute to the refinement of dating platforms by offering actionable insights. The engagements of GenZ in OKCupid- a popular online dating app has been analysed. The findings derived from this research are poised to facilitate user interface modifications, and guide the development of novel features that resonate with the authentic, self-growth-oriented, and inclusive values of Generation Z. By unravelling these intricate layers, the research aspires to empower dating platforms to engage with the dating landscape more meaningfully and adapt proactively to the evolving dynamics of Generation Z's dating preferences.

    P. Kritee Rao, National Institute of Technology, Jamshedpur, India
    Akanksha Shukla, National Institute of Technology, Jamshedpur, India

Strategic Management assists in optimization of business resources. It is a long term plan that is thought and executed at higher levels of an organization to derive striving and sustainable outcome. It is vital to manage the finances, especially for a developing economy. There is dearth of research in this context, especially for the state of Jharkhand. Considering this, the study analyses the factors of strategic management for higher level of authorities of the banking industry in Jharkhand. The banking industry of this state is often called as economically and strategically less-developed regarding the financial inclusion. Hence, this paper identifies the factors for strategic management in banking industry and prioritizes them based on a weightage determination method Logarithmic Percentage Change-driven Objective Weighting (LOPCOW). The analysis results staff development as the foremost factor for strategic management, followed by staff retention and team orientation. The factor technological superiority have been ranked the lowest.

This study explores the relationship between education, religion, and family size in Bihar, India. Bihar is an interesting case for examining fertility rates due to its traditionally high levels of natalism and low levels of literacy. Various literature on this topic was reviewed to identify gaps in the research. Data obtained from the National Family Health Survey (NFHS) was then used to analyze how a woman's education and religious beliefs affect the number of children she has. Finally, ANOVA tests, Chi-square tests, and other relevant analyses were utilized to further investigate all areas of interest. The findings show that education plays a more significant role than religion in achieving a lower and more sustainable replacement fertility rate for women in Bihar. However, incorporating a religious perspective in educational interventions can help make them more effective for broader societal development.

A specialized smart calculator designed for small industries offers advanced functionalities beyond mathematical operations. It incorporates point-of-sale (POS) capabilities, streamlining billing processes. Users access their accounts via a user-friendly website, gaining access to features like sales and purchase analytics. The calculator simplifies inventory management by providing insights into stock levels and sales patterns, enabling data-driven decisions. Leveraging machine learning, it generates accurate sales predictions, empowering businesses to optimize operations. The software component includes an accessible web platform for account management and analytics. This integrated solution equips small industries with tools for efficient sales management, inventory control, and informed decision-making, fostering growth and success.

Chapter 18

To compare the efficiency of pattern matching password method and digital signature method for secure cloud computing, and to propose an improved efficiency solution. To ensure data security, it is essential to employ suitable methods such as the Novel Pattern Matching Password algorithm and Digital Signature methods, which offer varying levels of security. Data security involves protecting data from unauthorized access, use, modification, intrusion, change, examination, recording, or destruction. Cloud computing is an Internet-based computing model that provides shared computing resources and data to computers and other devices as required. In this study, the pre-test power value was determined using G Power 3.1 software, with a set of statistical parameters, including $\alpha=0.05$, power=0.80 10 iterations for each group, and difference between two independent means. Technical Analysis software was utilized to implement and compare the two algorithms, PMP and DS.

Preface

The rapid advancement of data analytics is reshaping the landscape of business management and decision-making. As editors of *Pioneering Approaches in Data Management*, we have sought to curate a collection of insights that not only encapsulate the current state of data analytics but also project its future potential to revolutionize various sectors. This book aims to bridge the gap between complex theoretical foundations and real-world applications, offering readers a comprehensive view of how data analytics can drive strategic innovation and performance.

Our contributors bring together a wealth of expertise from across academia and industry, presenting novel methodologies, practical tools, and detailed case studies that underscore the transformative potential of data-driven practices. Each chapter is crafted to provide both foundational knowledge and actionable strategies, making this book relevant to a broad audience of researchers, educators, and practitioners alike. By exploring both the technical aspects and practical implications of data management, *Pioneering Approaches in Data Management* serves as a foundational resource for those seeking to navigate and harness the power of data in today's complex business environment.

We envision this book as a pivotal resource for academic researchers, data science students, and business analytics professionals, as well as for consultants and industry leaders eager to adopt data-centric strategies. With a blend of practical case studies and theoretical insights, this book equips readers with the tools and perspectives needed to drive data-powered decision-making and fosters a deeper understanding of data analytics' role in contemporary management.

We are grateful to all contributing authors for their commitment to advancing knowledge in data analytics and for their invaluable insights that make this volume both comprehensive and forward-looking. We hope this work inspires readers to embrace the potential of data-driven approaches and to be at the forefront of innovation in data management.

ORGANIZATION OF THE BOOK

Chapter 1: Data Analytics in Management Empowering Decision-Making through Insights

The first chapter explores the transformative impact of data analytics in modern management. The authors delve into how data analytics reshapes strategic decision-making, fostering innovation and market competitiveness by extracting meaningful insights from big data. This chapter discusses the use of predictive analytics for improved operational efficiency, resource allocation, and client demand forecasting, as well as the role of AI and machine learning in automating tasks and enhancing decision-making processes. Moreover, it emphasizes the ethical use of data, advocating for responsible practices and transparency. Through real-world examples, the chapter demonstrates the role of data analytics in solving business challenges, illustrating the importance of a data-centric culture within organizations.

Chapter 2: Big Data and its Impact on Strategic Business Operations and Decision-Making

In this chapter, the authors focus on the rising influence of big data in shaping corporate strategies and enhancing decision-making processes. The authors provide a comprehensive definition of big data, examining its role in improving operational efficiencies and organizational performance. This chapter underscores the shift towards data-driven decision-making, highlighting how big data contributes to predictive insights, customer intelligence, and risk management. Concluding with an in-depth case study, Gupta and Vaishnavi illustrate the practical applications of big data analytics, providing insights into the strategic benefits of data-informed decisions in a competitive business landscape.

Chapter 3: Competitiveness and Sustainability of Online Travel Agencies in India

This chapter analyzes the competitive landscape of five prominent online travel agencies in India, examining key service factors that drive consumer purchasing decisions. Utilizing an exploratory research approach with quantitative methods, the chapter applies the Importance Performance Analysis (IPA) matrix to evaluate the service qualities critical for business success. By synthesizing user feedback and service metrics, this chapter offers valuable insights for travel marketers seeking to enhance their digital presence and customer engagement strategies in the online travel industry.

Chapter 4: Assessment of Social Media Presence and its Effectiveness to Achieve Business Goals in NBFCs

Chapter 4 examines the role of social media in the non-banking financial companies (NBFCs) sector in India, focusing on its impact on branding, stakeholder engagement, and customer trust. Through a mixed-methods analysis, the authors compare social media engagement strategies of five leading NBFCs. This chapter highlights key content and platform-specific strategies that contribute to competitive advantages, offering a strategic framework for NBFCs to leverage social media as a vital tool for audience connection and brand development.

Chapter 5: Data-Driven Comparison of Companies' Ability to Innovate

In this chapter, the author investigates how companies in diverse sectors—information technology, food, plastic, and aviation—differ in their capacities for innovation. Using the Mann-Whitney U test, the study quantifies the disparities in innovation capabilities and maturity levels, illustrating how each company's strategic allocation of resources affects its innovation outcomes. This comparative analysis provides a roadmap for businesses seeking to strengthen their competitive edge through enhanced innovation capabilities and maturity.

Chapter 6: Using OpenStreetMap Data for Geomarketing Insights and Business Growth

Chapter 6 explores the integration of geo-marketing with GIS to optimize business growth strategies. The chapter details how OpenStreetMap (OSM) data can support competitor analysis, demographic segmentation, site selection, and store optimization. Through spatial and demographic analyses, the authors demonstrate how businesses can leverage OSM data to make data-driven decisions on store placement, customer targeting, and market demand assessment, thus maximizing both reach and profitability.

Chapter 7: Analysis of Barriers in Waste Collection and Segregation for Circular Economy Using IF-TOPSIS Approach

This chapter addresses the critical role of waste management in achieving circular economy objectives, highlighting the challenges faced in waste collection and segregation. The authors utilize the IF-TOPSIS methodology to identify 13 key barriers, including public awareness, to sustainable waste practices. This chapter offers strategic recommendations for industries, government bodies, and academic institutions, providing a valuable framework to overcome these challenges and foster resource efficiency.

Chapter 8: Real-time Music Recommendation System Integrating PySpark and Kafka for Enhanced User Experience

This chapter presents an advanced music recommendation system for Spotify, leveraging PySpark and Kafka for real-time, personalized recommendations. Using collaborative filtering and the ALS Implicit Collaborative Filtering model, the system processes extensive user data to enhance recommendation accuracy. The integration of Kafka enables efficient real-time data processing, marking a significant advancement in delivering tailored user experiences in music streaming platforms.

Chapter 9: An Efficient Rice Quality Prediction Using Convolutional Neural Network in Comparison with Support Vector Machine

Chapter 9 presents an innovative approach to rice quality prediction using Convolutional Neural Networks (CNN) alongside Support Vector Machine (SVM) models. Analyzing a dataset of 356 rice samples, the study reveals that CNN outperforms SVM in terms of accuracy for real-time quality assessment. This chapter offers valuable insights for agricultural quality control, showcasing how deep learning techniques can be effectively applied to enhance food quality evaluation processes.

Chapter 10: Efficient Fake Logo Prediction Through Convolutional Neural Networks Over K-Nearest Neighbors

This chapter introduces a novel method for detecting fake logos using CNN and K-Nearest Neighbors (KNN), with CNN demonstrating superior accuracy in identifying counterfeit logos. The chapter highlights how CNN's ability to extract complex image features provides a robust framework for real-time fraud detection. This work has practical implications for brand protection, offering a scalable solution for companies to mitigate logo counterfeiting.

Chapter 11: Advancing Heart Attack Prediction: Machine Learning for Enhanced Cardiac Risk Analysis

Chapter 11 explores machine learning models for predicting cardiac risk, comparing algorithms such as catBoost, logistic regression, and k-Nearest Neighbors. The chapter highlights catBoost as the most effective model based on f-1 scores and ROC curve analysis. This study demonstrates the potential of automated ML models to assist healthcare providers in risk assessment and early intervention for cardiac conditions.

Chapter 12: Electronic Cooler Technologies and Superior Data Center Cooling Techniques

This chapter discusses the growing need for advanced cooling solutions in data centers, reviewing conventional and emerging technologies. The chapter covers methods such as air cooling, liquid cooling, and phase-change materials, alongside the integration of AI for predictive cooling management. The insights provided are critical for maintaining data center reliability while balancing energy efficiency and environmental concerns.

Chapter 13: Exploring the Influence of Emotional Intelligence on Financial Literacy Amongst Gen Z

In this chapter, the authors examine the influence of emotional intelligence (EI) on financial literacy (FL) in Gen Z, revealing that attributes such as sociability and well-being are pivotal. Using a two-wave research design, the study highlights the significance of behavioral and cognitive intelligence in financial decision-making. The chapter underscores the value of targeted interventions to improve EI, ultimately enhancing financial literacy and promoting sound financial behaviors in Gen Z. EI and FL is explored in light of Gen Z's unique financial behavior and values. This chapter emphasizes the importance of fostering EI to improve financial literacy and decision-making skills in young adults, recommending structured educational interventions that can positively shape Gen Z's financial future.

Chapter 14: Assessment of Gen Z's Behaviors and Preferences on Online Dating App OKCupid

This chapter examines the behaviors, values, and preferences of Generation Z users on the popular online dating app, OKCupid. Through a comprehensive analysis of secondary data, including dating app reports and relevant literature, the study identifies key trends and behavioral shifts among Gen Z users in the global dating market. The findings provide insights into the priorities of this demographic, such as authenticity, self-growth, and inclusivity. The authors suggest that these insights could guide interface adjustments and the development of new features that align with Gen Z's distinct values, enabling dating platforms to better connect with and retain this influential user group.

Chapter 15: An Analysis of Strategic Management Factors for the Banking Industry in Jharkhand

In this chapter, the authors explore strategic management factors for the banking industry in Jharkhand, focusing on the unique challenges faced by financial institutions in this developing region. Using the Logarithmic Percentage Change-driven Objective Weighting (LOPCOW) method, the study identifies and ranks key strategic factors such as staff development, retention, team orientation, and technological advancement. Results highlight staff development as the most critical factor for sustainable growth in Jharkhand's banking sector, underscoring the need for targeted strategies to strengthen and modernize this essential industry in an economically underdeveloped region.

Chapter 16: The Triadic Relationship Between Fertility, Education, and Religion Among Women in Bihar

This study investigates the complex relationships between fertility rates, education levels, and religious beliefs among women in Bihar, a region with high natalist tendencies and low literacy. Using data from the National Family Health Survey (NFHS), the authors analyze how education and religion influence family size, employing statistical methods such as ANOVA and Chi-square tests. The findings suggest that education plays a more significant role than religion in reducing fertility rates, but integrating religious perspectives into educational initiatives could enhance their effectiveness, promoting sustainable development and broader societal progress.

Chapter 17: Industry 5.0 and Small-Scale Enterprises: Developing a Smart Calculator

This chapter presents the development of a smart calculator tailored for small-scale enterprises, designed to streamline sales management and inventory control. The calculator integrates point-of-sale (POS) capabilities, allowing for efficient billing and real-time access to sales and purchase data. Enhanced with machine learning, it offers predictive analytics for sales forecasting and inventory management, providing small businesses with tools for informed decision-making. The calculator's web platform enables user-friendly access to account management, facilitating operational efficiency and supporting the growth of small enterprises in an Industry 5.0 context.

Chapter 18: Comparing the Accuracy of Pattern Matching and Digital Signature for Secure Cloud Computing

In this chapter, the author compares the security and efficiency of two authentication methods—pattern matching password (PMP) and digital signatures (DS)—in cloud computing environments. Using G Power 3.1 software to assess pre-test power values and Technical Analysis software to implement the algorithms, the study evaluates each method's ability to secure data against unauthorized access, modification, and intrusion. The results highlight the strengths and limitations of PMP and DS, offering insights into their applicability and suggesting improvements for enhanced data protection in cloud computing applications.

CONCLUSION

As we conclude this edited reference work, we reflect on the dynamic and interdisciplinary insights each chapter has contributed to advancing our understanding of contemporary challenges and innovations across diverse fields. The collaborative effort displayed here underscores not only the breadth of current research but also the interconnectedness of emerging technologies, shifting societal values, and evolving organizational strategies that shape our world today.

The authors represented in this volume have explored a wide spectrum of topics, ranging from the behavioral nuances of Generation Z in digital spaces and strategic management in evolving economies, to the intricate relationships between social demographics and development, and the applications of machine learning and data security in cloud environments. Each chapter is a testament to the growing need for specialized knowledge that is both adaptable and inclusive. The insights presented here are designed to equip scholars, practitioners, and policy-makers with practical tools and theoretical frameworks that can inform future innovations and interventions within their respective fields.

Our aim as editors has been to curate a collection that not only addresses immediate questions but also inspires long-term, critical reflections on the broader implications of these findings. The case studies and analyses presented are not merely academic inquiries; they are blueprints for meaningful change, fostering a future that is better equipped to handle the complexities of a digitally interconnected, data-driven world.

We hope that this volume serves as a valuable resource, prompting further inquiry and fostering continued collaboration across disciplines.

In closing, we extend our deepest gratitude to the contributing authors for their dedication and insight, and to our readers for engaging with this work. We trust that the ideas shared here will ignite fresh discussions, spark new research, and ultimately, lead to actionable solutions that resonate beyond the pages of this book.

Section 1
Introduction to Data Analytics in Management

Chapter 1
Data Analytics in Management Empowering Decision–Making Through Insights

R. Bhuvanya
https://orcid.org/0000-0003-4399-0617
Sri Ramachandra Institute of Higher Education and Research, India

B. Yamini
https://orcid.org/0000-0003-3531-108X
SRM Institute of Science and Technology, India

K. Sivakumar
Nehru Institute of Engineering and Technology, India

Gobinath V. M.
https://orcid.org/0000-0002-9132-4910
Rajalakshmi Institute of Technology, India

V. Sathya
https://orcid.org/0000-0002-0355-1401
Vel Tech Rangarajan Dr. Sagunthala R&D Institute of Science and Technology, India

R. Siva Subramanian
https://orcid.org/0000-0002-7509-9223
R.M.K. College of Engineering and Technology, India

ABSTRACT

Data analytics, which is critical in today's decision-making, is driving the rapidly changing corporate environment. Its management, growth, and strategic objective transformation are explored in this article. Strategic choices, innovation, and competitiveness are enabled by data analytics. Big data values huge data kinds,

DOI: 10.4018/979-8-3693-5563-3.ch001

recognises patterns, anticipates trends, and real-time possibilities, decision-making and helping companies grow. For market leadership, predictive analytics improves operational efficiency and resource allocation by forecasting trends, client demands, and simplifying processes. AI and ML automate activities, find patterns, and propose ways to enhance judgements, revolutionising industry and e-commerce. Data-driven marketing improves expenditure, engagement, and campaigns. Responsible data use and transparency address privacy and ethics. Examples demonstrate how data analytics supports innovation, solves business problems, and provides outcomes. Finally, data analytics integration trends, challenges, and possibilities emphasise the need for a data-centric culture.

1. INTRODUCTION TO DATA ANALYTICS IN MANAGEMENT

Data analytics is the new phenomenon which allows organizations to gain the knowledge from the bulk of data and thus making the best decisions. This part gives a summary of the basic principles of data analytics, follows its development in corporations, and points out its importance in the decision-making processes (Vashisht, P., & Gupta, V 2015).

A. Fundamentals of Data Analytics

Basically, data analytics is the activity of analysing raw data to make inferences that are applicable and helping in the decision making (Prasanth, N. N., & Devi, K. V 2023). The reason why data analysis is used is to find patterns, trends, and correlations in data, which is done by various methods and instruments for data collection, processing, analysis, and interpretation. Among the essential elements of data analytics are:

1. **Data collection**: This means of course getting the needed information from a variety of sources, like IoT devices, external sources, and internal databases. It is determined by the objectives of the research and the type of data; several techniques of data collection can be applied.
2. **Data Processing:** Upon being brought after the completing of the collection, the data gets its dirty parts removed, changed and finally ready for the analysis by the procedures which are employed to clean, transform, and make the data ready for the analysis. To make sure that the data is of a high quality and consistent, this may involve getting rid of the duplicates, managing the missing information, and the formats to be standardised.

3. **Data Analysis**: There are various techniques for data analysis, among which descriptive analytics is the one that provides background on the previous patterns and performance, predictive analytics, which predicts the future based on past data, and prescriptive analytics, which advises on the best way to make decisions

4. **Data Visualisation:** The dashboards, graphs, and charts that are used for visualising data are helpful for stakeholders to understand the huge, complicated datasets and also to communicate the insights to them. Through the means of data visualisation tools, the users could interactively go through the data and find out the trends or anomalies in the data very quickly (Shi-Nash, A., & Hardoon, D. R 2017).

B. The Development of Business Data Analytics

The computer technology and the digitization of data have precipitated the emergence of data analytics in business. Originally the function of the organisations to obtain the significant insights from the data was limited because of their dependence on the manual techniques and the primitive instruments for data analysis.

With the computers becoming more popular and software technology being developed, organisations started to apply databases and spreadsheets for data analysis and storage. The introduction of business intelligence (BI) tools in the 1990s was the beginning of the possibility of looking at the data, making reports, and carrying out simple analytics operations. The demand for data analytics skills increased as the e-commerce and the internet boom started to take place. Businesses were looking for a way to outshine their competitors by using data to analyse the behaviour of their consumers, to improve their processes, and to encourage innovation. The new age of data analytics was ushered in by the appearance of the big data technology in the first decade of this century, which made possible the handling and analysis of huge amounts of data on a large scale by enterprises. The firms have now been in data infrastructure, analytics platforms, and personneling to take the full advantage of data for strategic decision-making, and thus, data analytics has become a mainstream component of the contemporary corporate operations.

C. Data Analytics' Significance in Decision-Making

All the various levels of the organisation count on data analytics to assist them in the making of their tactical, operational, and strategic decisions. There are various primary factors that show the significance of data analytics when it comes to decision making. These include:

1. **Data-Driven Insights**: Organisations can get important data about consumer demands, the market situation, and their own performance by looking at the past data and finding out the patterns and trends. Through the provision of realistic information, these insights allow businesses to make informed decisions which in turn, help them to be on top of the competitive field.
2. **Performance Optimisation:** Data analytics help businesses to find those areas where they can be more effective, to remove the bottlenecks, and to improve the processes and products and services. With the help of the data-driven insights to optimise performance, the organisations are able to improve their productivity, profitability and efficiency.
3. **Risk Management:** Through the use of data analytics, businesses may find out risks connected to supply chain interruptions, market volatility, and cybersecurity threats and will be able to evaluate them proactively. The employment of the predictive modelling tools and the analysis of the historical data, aids the organisations to predict the possible hazards and to come up with the mitigation plans that would reduce the effects of these hazards.
4. **Innovation and Growth:** Data analytics encourages innovation by making businesses aware of and understand the unseen opportunities, hence, they can create new and innovative goods and services as well as enter the untapped markets. Companies can promote the growth and build a competitive advantage for the long term by the means of data analytics to foster innovation.

In summary, data analytics has turned into a critical tool for companies to extract data insights and make sensible decisions. Businesses may utilize data to come up with the strategic, operational, and organisational success hashing to the data analysis principles, tracking its development in the business world, and knowing about its importance in the decision-making process, (Elgendy, N., & Elragal, A 2016).

II. BIG DATA AND STRATEGIC DECISION-MAKING

A. Understanding Big Data

Once the huge amounts of organized and unstructured data produced quickly from various sources, such as social media, sensors, mobile devices, and commercial transactions, are called big data. These datasets are a real problem for the traditional data processing and analysis techniques since of their mass, velocity, diversity, and authenticity (Taylor-Sakyi, K. 2016). The first thing that is realized in the process of understanding big data is the huge amount of data that is produced; then the second thing that comes up is the variety of data sources and formats. Conventional relational database management systems may be utilized to categorize and analyse structured data which could be the sales transactions and customer demographics. To get the ideas from the unstructured data like the emails, photos and the postings on social media, the more advanced methods such as machine learning and natural language processing are needed (Siva Subramanian et al 2023).

B. Big Data's Effect on Corporate Strategy

Big data has a profound effect on corporate strategy, thus transforming the way businesses operate, compete, and even develop in the digital era. The big data has enabled the businesses to have more insight into the consumer behaviour, the industry trends, and the rivalry dynamics, which in turn helps them to make the right strategies.

The possible of big data to make better customer experience and engagement is one of the main impacts on the company plans. Companies may design goods, services, and promotional campaigns to suit the particular needs and tastes of each client by analyzing consumer data from the various touchpoints. Thus, the final product of this personalized strategy is the enhancement of the revenue and the profit margin since it is the creation of customer satisfaction and the loyalty of the clients and their retention.

Organisations could also maximise the usage of resources and the operational efficiency by the use of big data. Many operational data, for instance, production output, supply chain performance, and equipment maintenance records may be studied by the organisations in order to discover the inefficiencies, optimise the workflows, and to allocate the resources better. The operation improvement raises the general performance of the firm, cuts the costs, and also increases the productivity.

Through big data analytics, businesses are able to identify new opportunities and risks in their sector, by having detailed information about market trends and competitive dynamics of the industry. Organisations can foresee the transformations in customer preferences, the emergence of market trends and the competitor threats by means of social media discussions, the observation of competitor actions and the market trend evaluations. Companies may maintain their competitive edge in the market by being foresighted, altering their plans, taking the opportunities, and reducing the risks, which will be the consequence of their foresight.

C. Using Analytics from Big Data to Make Decisions

Employing complex analysis methods to acquire the pertinent information from large and complex datasets is a must for using big data analytics for the decision-making process. This process is based on the data mining techniques to identify the

5

patterns, sentiment analysis to analyse consumer sentiment and machine learning algorithms for predictive modelling (Nithya et al 2023). Organisations may now use the big data analytics to make data-driven choices instead of gut instinct or intuition. Organisations may make suitable, fact-based decisions by looking at the past data to find the trends, correlations, and patterns. Big data analytics provides the businesses with the data they need to confidently make the strategic choices whether they are introducing new goods, expanding into new areas, or optimizing pricing tactics. In short, big data has a huge impact on the business strategy, it helps the companies to improve customer satisfaction, to make the processes more efficient and to realize the market possibilities. At the current time, when data is used as a tool for decision-making, companies may get a competitive advantage by applying big data analytics.

III. PREDICTIVE ANALYTICS IN BUSINESS OPERATIONS

A. Overview of Predictive Analytics

Predictive analytics, a specific branch of the advanced analytics, is able to make very accurate predictions about the future using both historical and present data (Lee et al 2022). The term machine learning, data mining, and statistical algorithms that are used to analyse big datasets and discover linkages, trends, and correlations that are then used to generate predictions is the process of this technology. The other two, in addition to descriptive analytics which is about data summarization and diagnostic analytics which is about the reasons for certain events, are predictive analytics. Rather, predictive analytics by the way of coming to conclusions from the past and predicting the future events tries to give an answer to the question "what is likely to happen next".

B. Predictive Analytics Applications in Operations

Various sectors and corporate activities including governance, marketing, and sales can gain from the use of predictive analytics, which can be used to achieve its targeted objectives, improve decision-making, and make the processes more efficient. Predictive analytics is often used in operations for the following reasons: Predictive analytics is often used in operations for the following reasons:

Figure 1. Predictive analytics applications in operations

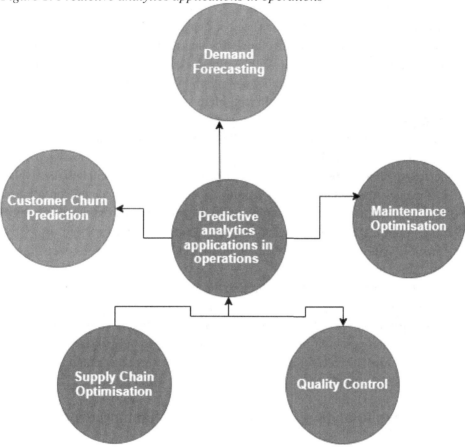

1. **Demand Forecasting**: Data from previous sales, industry trends, and the external factors such as seasonal patterns and economic indicators may be used to make the prediction of future demand for goods and services through predictive analytics. Organisations can drop the inventory surplus, enhance the level of customer satisfaction, and eliminate the stockouts by the optimization of the supply chain logistics, production planning, and inventory management through the precise demand prediction.

2. **Maintenance Optimisation:** Predictive maintenance is a technique that proactively schedules maintenance tasks by using sensor data, equipment telemetry and past maintenance records in order to prevent equipment failure and thus, to save downtime and the cost of repairs. Companies could cut the costs of main-

tenance, extend the life of their assets, and avoid sudden failures by looking for the trends that signal the equipment is going to break down soon.

3. **Quality Control:** Prediction of flaws or departures from specified standards can be done by using predictive analytics that finds trends and abnormalities in production process data as well as product quality data. Organisations can improve the whole product quality and reliability by the adoption of the remedial measures, detection of quality problems early and using of the real-time monitoring and predictive modelling tools.

4. **Customer Churn Prediction**: By utilizing the transaction history, the engagement indicators, and the data on customer behaviour, predictive analytics may be able to identify the customers who are likely to leave or switch to the rivals. Companies may reduce customer turnover and keep their valuable customers by developing the focused retention program which would include the loyalty programmes, the proactive customer service, and the personalised offers by forecasting the customer turnover and identifying the main reasons of customer attrition (Yamini et al 2024).

5. **Supply Chain Optimisation:** Through the anticipation of changes in demand, the supply chain risks' recognition, and the inventory levels, shipping routes, and distribution networks' optimization, predictive analytics may enhance the supply chain operation. Predictive analytics may help businesses to cut down costs, to be on the alert for the changing market circumstances, and to improve the suppliers' efficiency.

C. Predictive Analytics' Advantages for Enhancing Productivity

Predictive analytics use in company operations provides a number of advantages for companies looking to boost productivity and competitiveness:

1. **Better Decision-Making:** Through the process of predictive analytics, decision-makers get practical insights and understanding of the future events which helps them to make decisions based on data-driven forecasts rather than their thoughts or guesses.

2. **Cost Reduction:** Predictive analytics helps businesses to trim their operating expenses and improve resource utilisation, which finally leads to large cost savings by optimizing workflows, reducing waste, and cutting downtime.

3. **Increased Productivity**: Companies may boost productivity and focus on value-added activities by using predictive analytics to eliminate the repetitive tasks, automate the operations, and discover the opportunities for the process optimisation

4. **Competitive Advantage:** With the help of predictive analytics, businesses are able to see what trends are coming, find opportunities, and reduce risks before their competitors do, thus, they get a competitive edge which in turn helps them to innovate, adapt, and beat their rivals in the constantly changing market conditions.
5. **Customer happiness:** Businesses may boost the customer's happiness, loyalty, and retention rates by the means of the predictive analytics that will allow the provision of the goods, services, and the experiences tailored, timely, and relevant to the customer.

To conclude, predictive analytics is the key to the modern corporate world, which, in turn, helps to streamline the processes and increase the productivity of the companies and provides the strategic insights that help the businesses to prosper in the current competitive environment. Organisations, on the one hand, will be on the way of sustainable development and success while on the other hand, they will be able to do the data-driven decisions and forecast the future trends by using predictive analytics.

IV. MACHINE LEARNING AND AI IN MANAGEMENT

A. Introduction to Machine Learning and AI

The artificial intelligence (AI) and the machine learning (ML) are the game-changing technologies that might totally alter the management in various sectors.

1. Machine Learning: The part of the AI that focuses on teaching the systems to recognize the patterns and to anticipate or to decide without the explicit programming is called the branch of the AI. ML algorithms acquire the knowledge over time by going through the history of the data and thus, they are able to get better and more efficient. Mainly, the common ML methods are reinforcement learning, supervised learning and unsupervised learning.
2. Artificial intelligence: This is the making of computer system that can perform tasks like voice recognition, visual perception, decision-making and language translation that normally require human intellect. AI is a technology which comprises of a broader range of technologies like robots, machine learning (ML), natural language processing (NLP), and computer vision, etc (Gracious et al 2023).

B. Machine Learning's Function in Automating Management Procedures

The process is made efficient through the combination of new technologies such as machine learning that see to the streamlining of processes, the creation of a leaner environment, the automation of different management procedures.

1. **Data Analysis and Insights:** Machine learning algorithms can go through large volumes of data in order to find trends, patterns, and insights which will later guide the decision making for strategic purposes. ML will make managers acquire new knowledge about the consumer behaviour, market dynamics, and corporate performance, they will be able to do it automatically, and all the processes like the sentiment analysis, the anomaly identification, and the predictive modelling will be done automatically (Sudha et al 2024).
2. **Process Automation:** Managers will be able to direct their time and energy to higher-value duties by using machine learning algorithms to automate the repetitive jobs and processes like the data input, document processing, and customer service. Automation is a procedure which makes work very fast, decreases the errors as well as the error rates, and the overall organisational efficiency is one of the biggest gains.
3. **Predictive Analytics:** Managers may have a view of the future events, such as demand shifts, sales patterns, and consumer preferences, by means of machine learning techniques such as predictive modelling and forecasting. The managers might be able to easily manage risks, allocate resources appropriately, and make the right decisions by means of predictive analytics (Balbin et al 2020).
4. **Personalised Recommendations:** Support-recommended products, content suggestions and marketing offer to the clients which are based on their tastes, behaviour and previous interactions are given by the machine learning algorithms. Customisation is a tool to build brand loyalty, boost conversion and to enhance consumer engagement.
5. **Risk management:** Machine learning algorithms are in a position to analyze past data and discover the patterns that indicate possible dangers such as fraud, cyber attacks, and irregularities in the financial system. Machine Learning (ML) boosts the risk management and strengthens the organizational resilience to the attacks by the same time it automatically detects the distortions and reports the suspicious activities.

C. Using AI to Optimise the Process of Making Decisions

Artificial intelligence has the capability to understand, analyze and talk in natural language with humans which in turn makes computers to do the things that are impossible for machine learning. The AI-driven decision-making systems fasten the decision-making processes by way of the latest methods among which are computer vision, robotics, and natural language processing.

1. **Natural Language Processing (NLP):** To derive sentiment, intention, and insights from unstructured text data such as emails, social media postings, and customer reviews, AI-powered NLP systems analyse the data. Managers could be well-informed about the customers' inquiries, new trends, and consumer feedback by the use of NLP (Pajila et al 2023).
2. **Computer Vision:** For a system to be able to extract information, to identify objects and to detect patterns from visual data, mainly photos and videos, computer vision systems of AI driven nature are used for the analysis and interpretation of the data. Managers may apply computer vision to make operations such as quality control, object detection, and picture recognition automated which is a vital for industrial settings.
3. **Robotic Process Automation (RPA):** The skill of understanding how people operate with software applications is simulated by the AI-driven RPA solutions, which consequently automate the monotonous jobs and processes. Through the usage of raw data input, invoice processing and inventory management, RPA makes these processes more efficient by lowering manual labour and hence, improving the operational effectiveness.
4. **Decision Support Systems:** ML algorithms and AI approaches are employed by AI-based DSSs in order to assist managers in facing the challenging decision-making. These gadgets assist managers to make the right decisions faster by analysing data, deriving insights, and proposing courses of action based on certain criteria.

To sum up, automation of chores, enhanced decision-making, and the opportunity for businesses to bring new chances for development and innovation are the several ways that artificial intelligence and machine learning are changing the management methods. Managers can thus, boost productivity, obtain a competitive edge and enhance efficiency by employing ML and AI technologies in the light of the modern corporate environment that changes very fast.

V. DATA-DRIVEN MARKETING STRATEGIES

A. Importance of Data-Driven Marketing

A planned scheme, which is called "data-driven marketing", uses the knowledge from the data analysis to guide the campaign decisions. Nowadays, the digital companies have to employ data-based marketing in order to stay ahead of the competition and to attain the desired target audience. This is mainly because customers generate countless amounts of data by means of their online activities.

Figure 2. Importance of data-driven marketing

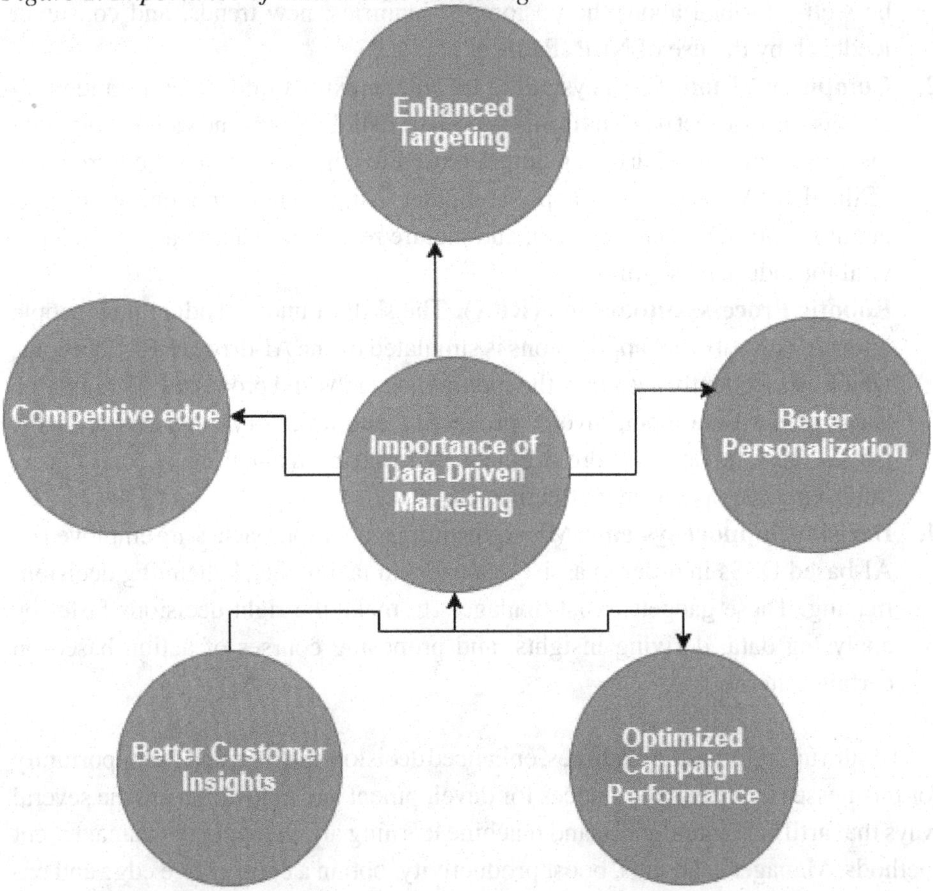

1. **Enhanced Targeting:** Companies may split up their target group in the following ways; demographics, behaviour, interests and so on, among other relevant variables using data-driven marketing. Companies may find out about the customers who are of high value to them and change their products and marketing messages to suit the needs of the certain customer segments by looking at customer data. Thus, the fact that they are not disturbed by things affecting their target audience results in more concentrated and successful advertising campaigns.

2. **Better Personalization:** It is necessary for clients to be provided with experiences that are both on the point and interesting and thus, the differentiation of such experiences is personalisation. Nowadays companies can customize their promotions, content, and message to each individual customer based on his or her browsing habits, past purchases, and preferences thanks to data-driven marketing. Personalized marketing strategies have the possibility to create a bond with the customers and increase their loyalty to a brand at the same time as the brand connects more with the customers and has more conversions.

3. **Optimized Campaign Performance:** Businesses may evaluate the outcome of their marketing activities on the go and make data-based decisions to optimize their activities by using data analytics and performance indicators. Through this method, businesses can essentially improve the return on investment (ROI) of their marketing initiatives, the way of targeting techniques can be enhanced, and resources can be more budgeted efficiently.

4. **Better Customer Insights:** Through data-driven marketing, companies are able to get useful information about the tastes, behavior and buying habits of their target audience. The research of the consumer data from different channels will help the companies to get to know the target market and thus, they will be able to improve their products, services and customer interactions(Subramanian, R. S. et al 2023).

5. **Competitive edge:** Owners of companies that have used the data-driven marketing potential have a major advantage over competitors in the present-day competitive market. Companies that are still on the carpet may give way to the market trend prediction, the beating of their rivals that depend on the traditional and less data-driven methods to marketing, thus the use of data to be the decision making of the strategic business.

B. Techniques for Segmentation and Personalisation

Data-driven marketing policies should always incorporate segmentation and personalisation so that firms can tailor their campaigns to the specific needs and preferences of each customer.

1. **Segmentation:** The target audience is the separate groups that are created on the basis of the shared characteristics like behavioural tendencies, psychographics, or demographics. Through tailoring the products and the advertising to the specific criteria and the tastes of each group, segmentation allows the companies to put their marketing efforts in the right direction.

2. **Personalisation:** Through the process of sending personalized messages, information, and offers to the clients that are determined by their past interactions, interests, and behaviours, personalisation goes beyond the segmentation. Through the supply of every consumer with the right and the exact material at the right time, personalization strategies such as dynamic content, product suggestions and personalized email marketing campaigns are the way to increase the engagement and the conversion.

C. Using Analytics to Assess Marketing Effectiveness

Evaluating the achievements of marketing campaigns, the way resources are used as efficiently as possible and getting the best return on investment all depend on the measurement of marketing effectiveness. Analytics are employed in the data-driven marketing to monitor the key performance indicators (KPI) and to measure how marketing initiatives impact on company results.

1. **Key Performance Indicators (KPIs):** The statistics in question are taken into consideration to evaluate the achievement of marketing campaigns and projects. Among the common marketing KPIs are the conversion rate, customer lifetime value (CLV), return on advertising spend (ROAS), customer acquisition cost (CAC), and marketing attribution metrics which include first-touch and multi-touch attribution.

2. **Marketing Analytics Platforms:** Companies can monitor, analyse, and visualise the marketing performance data of their campaigns with the assistance of marketing analytics platforms like HubSpot, Adobe Analytics, and Google Analytics. These systems enable the data-driven decision-making and the optimization by the organization of data on the metrics such as the campaign success, user engagement, conversion funnels and the website traffic in real-time.

3. **A/B Testing and Experimentation:** Besides, A/B testing or the technique of comparing the effectiveness of multiple creative versions or marketing methods to find out which one results in the best outcome, is also termed as split testing. Through the businesses; the most effective marketing techniques will be found and the plans will be adapted by doing controlled experiments and examining the outcomes.

4. **Attribution Modelling:** Here, the contact points of the customer journey are connected to the sales or conversions. The businesses can even go for channel mix optimization to get the best out of the return on investment and also redistribute the marketing resources in a more efficient way by knowing how various marketing channels and interactions impact conversions.

Therefore, in summary, companies can employ the use of consumer data to enhance the campaign success, personalisation and targeting by utilizing data-driven marketing strategies. By dividing the audience into segments, adapting the message to each audience, and using analytics for marketing performance measurement, companies can increase engagement, conversions and build closer relationships with their customers.

VI. RISK MANAGEMENT AND ANALYTICS

A. Risks in Business Operations

Every business operation has some risk either from the inside or the outside that may be the reason for the failure. A sound risk management is based on the multiple hazards that organisations encounter.

1. **Operational Risks:** These dangers are brought about by people's mistakes, internal procedures and systems. Supply chain disruptions, vehicle breakdowns, employee errors, and issues with the regulatory compliance are a few examples of these dangers.
2. **Financial Risks:** The danger is predicated by the time and market volatilities of the financial operations and markets. Market risk, credit risk, liquidity risk and currency risk are the four types of financial hazards that are among the financial risks.

Figure 3. Risks in business operations

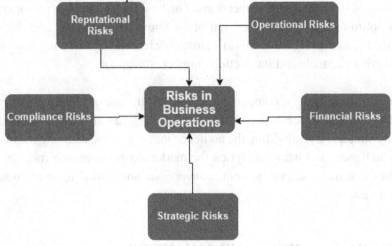

3. **Strategic Risks:** As a result, the whole accomplishment of the strategic goals of a company can be affected by a lot of factors. These dangers might be the unpredictability of the customers' behavior, the competitive pressure, technological glitches, and the market trends.
4. **Compliance Risks:** Doing what they are not supposed to, disobeying laws, rules, and industry standards, is the sure way to be noncompliant, which is dangerous. Among the different ways that the noncompliance is preventing the individual from the after the legal consequences, the financial penalties, the damage to the one's reputation and the lost commercial opportunities is the way.
5. **Reputational Risks:** The good name and image of a firm can be spoiled by the bad comments or the media coverage. The products that get recalled, the immoral acts of the companies, the data breaches, and the public controversies are some of the dangers of these.

B. Applying Analytics to Risk Evaluation

The analytics tool is one of the ways through which organizations can detect potential threats and vulnerabilities which is the first step to the identification, evaluation, and management of risks. Companies can be the first to discover any new hazards and thus come up with measures to diminish them by studying data from various sources.

1. **Data Collection and Aggregation:** The first step in the risk analysis is the information collection from both internal and external sources. The changes in the efficiency, productivity, accuracy, reach, and customer base that are the outcome of the data that is harvested from the financial data, operational indicators, market data, client feedback, and industry reports are the main reasons for the improvements.
2. **Risk Identification:** The trends, pattern, and anomalies that might be interpreted as hazards are discovered by applying the methods of data mining, machine learning, and statistical analysis. Companies can establish and rank risks by their degree of impact and their probability of happening by studying the relationships in the past data.
3. **Risk Quantification:** The analytical techniques enable the organisations to analyse and measure the potential impacts of the hazardous situations on the value of the stakeholders, the financial performance and the business goals. The different results of various risk scenarios can be simulated and their probability and the severity of the result can be evaluated by means of methods such as scenario analysis, stress testing, and Monte Carlo simulations.
4. **Predictive Modelling:** Through analysis of historical data and patterns, the predictive analytics methods such as forecasting and predictive modelling may be used to help the organisations to predict the future hazards. The organisations might be able to avert dangers from turning into crises by being watchful of the leading indicators and early warning signs(Brooks, C., & Thompson, C 2017).

C. Data-Driven Risk Mitigation Strategies

With the identification and assessment of risks it is possible that the organisations will make the mitigation and management plans. Companies will be able to make the right decisions and use the resources more effectively using the data-driven risk mitigation strategies to tackle the major risks.

1. **Risk Prevention:** Data analytics can reveal the causes and factors that contribute to the risks and hence, the organisations can use it for the prevention of possible problems by setting the preventive measures in place. The regular basis of the upgrades of the processes, the reinforcement of the controls, and the staff training are some of the examples of this.
2. **Early Detection:** Through the identification of important risk factors and performance metrics, analytics assists companies in solving the problems while they are still in the process of occurrence. Corporations can control the impact of hazards before they become unavoidable by introducing corrective measures and taking actions right after the early discovery.

3. **Scenario Planning:** Modelling the various risk scenarios and analysing their possible impacts on the company's operational and result are the activities of the data-driven scenario planning. Based on the modelling of different situations, organisations can come up with the risk management techniques and the backup plans.

4. **Constant Monitoring and Review:** Risk management is a continuous process that has to be monitored, adjusted and reviewed in line with the ever-changing risks and business situations. Though, organizations can utilize data analytics to monitor mitigation activities, have a check on the risk indicators at any given time, and measure the efficiency of the risk management techniques.

To sum up, analytics is the key to risk management as it aids businesses in the detection, assessment, and the most effective decrease of risks. Organisations can, on their own, handle risks, defend from possible threats and, therefore, secure their business processes and stakeholders through the use of data-driven insights.

VII. ETHICAL CONSIDERATIONS AND DATA PRIVACY

A. Ethical Implications of Data Analytics

Organizations have to tackle a lot of ethical problems that arise from data analytics in order to ensure the right and responsible use of data.

1. **Privacy and Consent:** The protection of people's personal information is one of the fundamental ethical issues. Before getting, using or giving out a person's personal information to other organizations, one must have the permission of that person. In order to honor people's privacy, the opt-in/opt-out procedures and the transparent privacy rules should be put in place.

2. **Data Bias and Fairness:** Whenever the data analytics algorithms are trained on biassed datasets or the algorithm has a built in biases, they will show bias. Unjust results from biassed algorithms could make the existing injustice and inequality more severe. Prejudice can be cut down by the organisations through the following means: making sure that datasets are diverse, the algorithmic decision-making procedures are transparent, and the algorithmic fairness is continuously monitored and assessed.

3. **Accountability and Transparency:** Businesses should be transparent and straightforward about their data practices, that is, the collection, management, and the utilization of data. They should design the algorithmic decision-making processes to be clear and easy to understand and hence enable people to question

and contest the computer-made judgments. The organizations should be held accountable for any abuse or unethical behaviour with data analytics by the way of accountability measures.

4. **Data Security and Protection:** The trust and confidence of the people are kept safe by the safeguarding of the confidential data from unauthorized access, breaches, and cyberattacks. Institutions should, to an extreme for the sake of the data protection, have solid security policies, encryption methods, and access restrictions, only to avoid the possible risks. Techniques like data anonymization and pseudonymization will be able to protect the privacy of people, while on the other hand, they can be used for data analysis.

B. Privacy Issues with Collecting Data and Utilisation

The collection, the storing, and the use of personal data brings the privacy issues, especially when the data analytics is involved.

1. **Data Collection Practices:** First of all organizations should ask for the ethical permission of people before collecting any of their personal information and then make sure that they are only getting the data that they need for their stated objectives. All the people should be told about the ways in which their data will be used and collected in a way that can be easily comprehended and should be done legally and in a transparent way.

2. **Data Storage and Retention:** The organizations should have the regulations for the safe storage of the data, thus the theft of data, identity theft, and the leaks will be prevented. A public should be knowledgeable about the data retention laws, and data should be kept for the required time so that it can be used to achieve its objectives.

3. **Data Usage and Sharing:** Private data should be used by organisations only for the reasons that were given for its collection and then be available to people. The sharing of data and selling of data to other parties are not allowed, unless it is for legal or regulatory reasons and the consent of the people concerned is obtained. Data minimization techniques are the tools that should be adopted by the organisations to guarantee that personal data is collected and used only when necessary.

C. Making Sure Organisations Adhere to Ethical Data Practices

Organisations should come up with a comprehensive strategy that encompasses not only the policies, processes and cultural norms but also guarantees the ethical data practices.

1. **Ethical Policies and Guidelines:** The first step in this process is to set up the appropriate procedures for the collection, management, and utilization of data. The organization's approach to moral conduct and the use of data that is in line with the current situation should be reflected in these policies which should also be in line with the legal and regulatory standards.

2. **Ethics Education and Training:** The employees should be, in fact, the ones being taught about the ethical data practices, which include the compliance standards, the privacy principles, and the data security procedures. The training programs must be planned for the training of the workers and their roles and responsibilities and the real-world examples and case studies should be included.

3. **Ethics Oversight and Governance:** To verify and inspect the data practices and to make sure that they are in accordance with the ethical norms, organizations should establish the systems of oversight such as ethics committees or data ethics boards. These watchdog groups should be able to investigate unethical activities, give out penalties, and suggest solutions.

4. **Ethical Leadership and Culture:** The conception and the ideology of an organization are framed by its ethical leadership. Leaders should be the examples of moral behavior and honesty, put moral issues at the starting point when making decisions, and foster a culture of openness, responsibility, and trust.

5. **Ethical Data Design and Engineering:** Data scientists and engineers, who are the professionals responsible for the creation of data analytics systems and algorithms, should take into account ethics while designing them. Thus, you have to be always on your toes when it comes to the ethical issues that appear in the whole data cycle and think about the possible effects on people's rights, autonomy and privacy.

Corporations can get a good image among the stakeholders, secure the privacy and rights of the people, and cut the risks that are related to data analytics by starting with the ethical data practices. The data world is getting more and more than ever, and so the data practices are being more and more regulated. The data practices are not just required by the laws and rules but also by the moral foundations of the organizations to respect the principles and to keep their good credibility and reputation.

VIII. THE FUTURE OF DATA ANALYTICS IN MANAGEMENT

A. Emerging Trends in Data Analytics

Data analytics is a field that always changes because of the change in customer demands, technological breakthroughs, and the change in consumer habits. undefined

1. **AI-Powered Analytics:** AI and machine learning technologies are being increasingly used to automate procedures, find out insights, and provide predictive capabilities, hence, this is being done in the data analytics systems. The AI-enabled analytics tools assist the businesses in making the correct decisions by analysing the big data fast, detecting the trends and generating useful insights(Agarwal et al 2021).

Figure 4. Emerging trends in data analytics

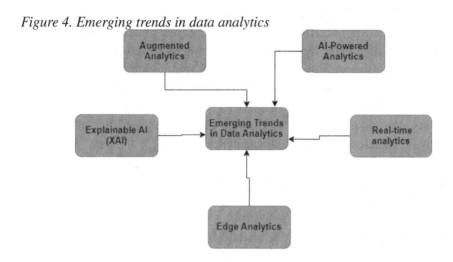

2. **Real-time analytics:** Real-time analytics lets organisations be able to get the instant insights and thus be able to adapt quickly to the changing circumstances. Companies can now record and evaluate streaming data in real time, thus, the risk management can be proactive, customers can be easily targeted, and decisions can be dynamic. This is done by the large scale of the Internet of Things (IoT) devices and sensors.
3. **Edge Analytics:** On the other hand, edge analytics processes and analyses data at the network's edge, which is nearer to the data source, rather than in central data centres or cloud environments. By cutting the data transport and storage in centralised places, edge analytics boosts data security and privacy, accelerates data processing, and shortens latency. Applications such as remote monitoring systems, industrial IoT, and autonomous cars whose need for real-time insights and low-latency responses is very important should hence, pay special attention to edge analytics.

4. **Explainable AI (XAI):** The aim of Explainable AI is to enhance the transparency and the interpretability of the AI and ML models so that the users can understand the decision-making process and the variables that affect it. Through XAI approaches, model behaviours, and decision-making processes are revealed, therefore regulatory compliance, trust, and accountability are improved. Explainable AI is a must for the sensitive areas where the fairness and openness are of major importance, e.g., criminal justice, healthcare, and finance.

5. **Augmented Analytics:** To make human decision-making better, augmented analytics applies ML and AI to the analytics tools and thus, the analytics tools become super intelligent. Augmented analytics supports the automation of the processes related to preparing, finding of insights, and report production enabling business users to access and analyse data more easily without the need for having highly technical skills. Augmented analytics will empower the business people to get insights and take action based on the data suggestions that are given to them by the democratization of data analytics.

B. Challenges and Opportunities in Data-Driven Decision-Making

1. **Data Integrity and Quality:** The main difficulties to data-driven decision-making are the maintaining of data consistency and quality across numerous sources. Data silos, inconsistencies, and errors that may have a negative effect on the decision-making processes impose the need for the organisations to engage in data governance, data quality management, and data integration solutions.

2. **Privacy and Security Issues:** Due to the fact that, in most cases, a lot of private and personal data are collected and processed, the problems of privacy and security are becoming more crucial in data-driven decision-making. Organisations have to comply with data protection regulations, install stringent security measures, and have well-defined policies and processes for data management in order to protect the privacy of people and avoid data breaches.

3. **Skills and Talent Gap:** A wide variety of skills, including domain knowledge, data analytics, data science, and machine learning, are required for the decision making based on the data. Companies are frequently having a hard time in finding and keeping the knowledgeable and expert employees who know how to use data and provide the insights that are relevant.

4. **Ethical and Regulatory Compliance:** In the process of decision-making based on data ethics factors which are bias, justice and openness are of great importance. To safeguard the credibility and trust, organizations need to be sure that

their models and algorithms are bias-free, respect people's rights and privacy, and conform to the legal and ethical requirements.

No matter how tough these challenges seem, the fact is that the data-driven decision-making gives organisations a great opportunity to enhance client experiences, to improve their performance, and to encourage innovation:

1. **Better Understanding and judgement:** Organisations may access and analyse enormous volumes of data to find patterns, get insights, and make well-informed choices via data-driven decision-making. Companies can be certain about their markets, customers, and methods through the use of data analytics which will make them make their processes efficient, reduce the risks and take advantage of the opportunities.

2. **Improved Customer Experiences:** Firms can create products, services and experiences that suit the customers' likes, needs and Groups can in return give the customer a personalized experience, a one-to-one advice and the custom-made marketing strategies which are the outcome of the customer data analysis(Divya et al 2023).

3. **Innovation and Competitive Advantage**: By the means of data analytics, firms can create new products, services, and businesses, and at the same time, find the ways to differentiate themselves in the market and innovate. This is achieved through the data-enabled way of decision-making. By using organised companies can spot new patterns, foresee clients' needs, and be the first in the race against the rivals in the market and the changing market by making the decisions based on the data.

4. **Cost savings and operational effectiveness:** Data-driven decision-making assists organizations to find inefficiencies, cut waste, and, at the same time, manage processes, operations and finances. Businesses can possibly reduce the extra expenses through the whole company, raise the speed of operation and the productivity with the help of data analytics.

C. The Role of Data Governance and Privacy Regulations

For data-driven decision-making to be conducted in an ethical and responsible manner, data governance and privacy laws are essential. The future data-driven decision-making can be done in an ethical and responsible way only if the data governance and privacy laws are in place:

1. **Data Governance:** The below measures are done by organisations to make sure the data, which are the availability, accuracy, and security of that data, are following procedures, rules and controls. Data governance is the phrase for this activity. The roles and duties are clearly defined, data standards and regulations are in place, and the regulatory compliance and the industry best practices are promoted through the smooth functioning of the data governance frameworks. Companies could manage data as a strategic asset, reduce the risks and increase data value for innovation and decision-making through the use of data governance.

2. **Regulations Concerning Privacy:** The privacy instructions such as the General Data Protection Regulation (GDPR) are a illustration of a law that establishes the privacy standards on websites. Businesses should comply with the regulations of the gathering, that are related to the California Consumer Privacy Act (CCPA) and the European Union. These laws demand the businesses to get the people's informed consent before collecting their personal data, to tell the truth and be honest about their data practices, and to establish some measures to protect people's privacy. Mainly, consumer trust, the avoidance of legal and reputational issues, and ethical data practices in data-driven decision-making are the three things that depend on by whom data-driven decision-making is being done.

To conclude, the new trends like AI-powered analytics, real-time analytics, edge analytics, explainable AI, and augmented analytics will be the ones that will lead the way to the analytics in management in the future. Apart from this, businesses can get a competitive advantage and the innovation can be stimulated by data-driven decision-making, but there are also the problem of data privacy, quality, expertise, and ethics. Organisations could use data analytics for the decision making, customer satisfaction improvement and sustainable development and success in the tackling of these issues and also use data governance and privacy legislation.

IX. BUILDING A DATA-CENTRIC ORGANIZATIONAL CULTURE

A. Importance of a Data-Driven Culture

Organisations that want to thrive in the present digital times when data is viewed as a strategic asset, must have a data-driven culture:

Figure 5. Importance of a data-driven culture

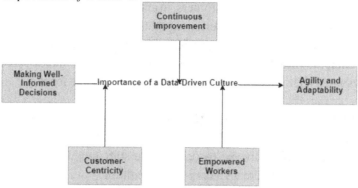

1. **Making Well-Informed Decisions:** The leaders at all levels of the organizations are advised to make their choices not on the instinct or gut feeling but on the facts and evidence in a culture where decisions are based on data. Businesses could be the ones to stimulate the innovation and corporate success by the usage of data analytics and insights to make more objective, evidence-based, and well-informed decisions.

2. **Continuous Improvement:** The staff is, to be precise, instructed to try, modify and adjust according to the evidence-based information and feedback, and thus, a data-driven culture is created where a continuous improvement and learning is conducted. Companies can be the innovators, improvers and efficiency factors through the data-driven techniques, which will make them on the way to the lasting competitive advantage.

3. **Agility and Adaptability:** These two qualities which are the main reasons for the success in the modern, fast-paced and dynamic corporate world are these two qualities. By the use of data and analytics, which are the tools of the organizations to make proactive decisions and modifications, they are able to respond quickly to the changes in the market, consumer preferences, and new trends.

4. **Empowered Workers:** The data-centered culture creates workers at all levels to be data-conscious and to participate in the projects and the decision-making processes which are based on data. Organisations can boost the employees' skills in data analysis, drawing conclusions and achieving positive change in their teams and departments by making them accessible to information, resources and training.

5. **Customer-Centricity**: The businesses that have a data-driven culture are more successful in acquiring their customers, in anticipating their needs and in providing them with services and experiences that are tailored to them. Corporations may change their goods, services, and marketing campaigns as the customers' needs alter, thus attracting the customer, making the customer loyal and raising customer satisfaction by using the customer data and feedback.

B. Methods for Promoting Data Adoption and Literacy

Companies may apply diverse tactics to urge staff members to embrace their data literacy skills so as to create a data-driven culture.

1. **Training and Education:** The courses and materials that will be offered to the staff members should be in detail and comprehensive to help them be more data literate and analytically skilled. Besides, the students will also have the opportunity of performing actual practical learning and experimentation as well as giving them the instruction on data analysis tools, strategies, and best practices.
2. **Role-Based Training:** Training programs should be modified to match the particular jobs and duties of the staff members, and at the same time, one should give useful and practical examples of how data can be a tool to influence the decisions and the results of the corporation.
3. **Data Champions and Advocates:** Select the people within the organization who are the experts in data-driven projects and can be the voice of this concept, telling about the successful experiences of the organization and suggesting the use of data in all the team and department to make important decisions.
4. **Data Transparency and Access:** Let us make sure that the staff members are the ones who have the necessary tools and data to be able to do their daily duties and also to make decisions. The greater the people are knowing about the sources, uses, and processing of data, the more they are willing to data governance and decision-making.
5. **Promote Collaboration:** The departmental silo must be eliminated to enable the sharing of group knowledge and thus to promote the cross-functional cooperation and the exchange of information across the teams and the departments. Establish communities of practice, forums, or data laboratories where the staff members can interact, exchange ideas, and in this way, they will know from each other.

C. The Function of Leadership in Fostering a Data-Centric Perspective

To cultivate a data-driven mindset and mentor the cultural transformation inside the company, the leadership is of the utmost importance.

1. **Set the Tone:** Leaders have to demonstrate their dedication to making the decisions that are fact-based by being themselves. Thus, they should start with the number of data projects on the agenda, allocate the resources and make the investments in people and technology to have such a data-driven culture.
2. **Communicate the Vision:** Indeed, the company's data strategy goals and the benefits of the shift to a data-oriented approach should be detailed. The promotion of innovation, lifelong learning and data literacy is to achieve strategic goals and to create a good company.
3. **Empower Staff:** Give the employees the chance of being the ones who drive the data projects and to make the decisions. Encourage the employees to be the initiators of their own work, to try new things and to take the calculated risks. Then provide them the required tools and resources so that they can be achievers in their data-based projects.
4. **Acknowledge and Reward:** Workers that are rational and that assist the company in accomplishing of its data projects and objectives should be applauded and awarded. We should be happy with the achievements, pass on the good practices and the environment that respects and appreciates the accomplishments be data-driven.
5. **Promote Accountability:** The staff members are supposed to be responsible for the accuracy, honesty, and legitimate use of data. Through the assistance of workers in their data driven projects, set the goals and targets that are specific for data driven success. They should always be with you and you should ask them for their opinion all the time.

Organisations may develop an environment that will foster creativity, improve decision-making, and, thus, create long-term value for the stakeholders and the public by recommending data literacy and adoption, encouraging collaboration, and allowing people to decide on their own. The leadership embraces the cultural change by talking to the flow of the change, creating the right tone, outlining the vision, and letting the staff to accept the data as a tactical advantage and a success driver for the company.

X. CONCLUSION

To sum up, the study of data analytics in management has proved that the data-driven methods are the revolutionary ones in the way of operational excellence, strategy development, and organisational decision-making. Acquiring the knowledge about the background of data analytics, and the new trends and problems to find out how data has gone from a simple information tool to a strategic asset which companies in many sectors can use. Creating a culture in which data is the supreme value is the key for businesses since they are the ones dealing with the difficulties of the digital world. Organisations may both inspire innovation, open up new possibilities, and acquire a competitive edge in the market by adopting innovative technologies, promoting the collaboration, and above all, putting a high value on data literacy. Leadership is the key factor that drives the cultural shift, creates the tone, and makes the staff use data to its fullest advantage, thus, becoming the most powerful engine of the organization's success. Besides, data-driven decision-making which is the basis of all processes of ethical considerations and regulatory compliance is also the fundamental pillars of responsible decision-making. Focusing on data governance, privacy protection, and ethical data usage will be the key to the organisations to respect individual rights, to earn the customer's trust and to be responsible and open in their data deal. The field of data analytics in management is on the fast track to become more valuable because of the new technologies like AI, real-time analytics, and edge computing. To reach sustainable development, the innovation and increase of the value of the stakeholders and consumers, organizations should be the ones that embrace the data-driven attitude and use data as a strategic asset and in changing to the changing data environment. The whole of the data analytics in management journey highlights how essential it is to accept data as a power of gaining the competitive advantage and organizational change. Organisations can get new ideas, make well-informed decisions and be successful in the future by the culture of data which is based on the data that is important for the tasks.

REFERENCES

Agarwal, A., Singhal, C., & Thomas, R. (2021). *AI-powered decision making for the bank of the future*. McKinsey & Company.

Balbin, P. P. F., Barker, J. C., Leung, C. K., Tran, M., Wall, R. P., & Cuzzocrea, A. (2020). Predictive analytics on open big data for supporting smart transportation services. *Procedia Computer Science*, 176, 3009–3018. DOI: 10.1016/j.procs.2020.09.202 PMID: 33042316

Brooks, C., & Thompson, C. (2017). Predictive modelling in teaching and learning. Handbook of learning analytics, 61-68. DOI: 10.18608/hla17.005

Divya, P., Girija, P., Anuradha, M., Dinesh, M. G., & Aswini, J. (2023). Heterogeneous Ensemble Variable Selection To Improve Customer Prediction Using Naive Bayes Model. *International Journal on Recent and Innovation Trends in Computing and Communication*, 11(5s), 64–71. DOI: 10.17762/ijritcc.v11i5s.6599

Elgendy, N., & Elragal, A. (2016). Big data analytics in support of the decision making process. *Procedia Computer Science*, 100, 1071–1084. DOI: 10.1016/j.procs.2016.09.251

Gracious, L. A., Jasmine, R. M., Pooja, E., Anish, T. P., Johncy, G., & Subramanian, R. S. (2023, October). Machine Learning and Deep Learning Transforming Healthcare: An Extensive Exploration of Applications, Algorithms, and Prospects. In 2023 4th IEEE Global Conference for Advancement in Technology (GCAT) (pp. 1-6). IEEE.

Lee, C. S., Cheang, P. Y. S., & Moslehpour, M. (2022). Predictive analytics in business analytics: Decision tree. *Advances in Decision Sciences*, 26(1), 1–29. DOI: 10.47654/v26y2022i1p1-29

Nithya, T., Kumar, V. N., Gayathri, S., Deepa, S., Varun, C. M., & Subramanian, R. S. (2023, August). A comprehensive survey of machine learning: Advancements, applications, and challenges. In *2023 Second International Conference on Augmented Intelligence and Sustainable Systems (ICAISS)* (pp. 354-361). IEEE. DOI: 10.1109/ICAISS58487.2023.10250547

Pajila, P. B., Sudha, K., Selvi, D. K., Kumar, V. N., Gayathri, S., & R. S. (2023, July). A Survey on Natural Language Processing and its Applications. In 2023 4th International Conference on Electronics and Sustainable Communication Systems (ICESC) (pp. 996-1001). IEEE.

Prasanth, N. N., & Devi, K. V. (2023). *Fundamental Of Data Science And Big Data Analytics*. Academic Guru Publishing House.

Shi-Nash, A., & Hardoon, D. R. (2017). Data analytics and predictive analytics in the era of big data. Internet of things and data analytics handbook, 329-345.

Siva Subramanian, R., Maheswari, B., Nikkath Bushra, S., Nirmala, G., & Anita, M. (2023). Enhancing Customer Prediction Using Machine Learning with Feature Selection Approaches. In Inventive Computation and Information Technologies [Singapore: Springer Nature Singapore.]. *Proceedings of ICICIT*, 2022, 45–57.

Subramanian, R. S., Maheswari, B., Bushra, S. N., Nirmala, G., & Anita, M. (2023). Enhancing Customer Prediction Using Machine Learning with Feature Selection Approaches. Inventive Computation and Information Technologies: Proceedings of ICICIT 2022, 563, 45. DOI: 10.1007/978-981-19-7402-1_4

Sudha, K., Balakrishnan, C., Anish, T. P., Nithya, T., Yamini, B., Subramanian, R. S., & Nalini, M. (2024). Data Insight Unveiled: Navigating Critical Approaches and Challenges in Diverse Domains Through Advanced Data Analysis. Critical Approaches to Data Engineering Systems and Analysis, 90-114.

Taylor-Sakyi, K. (2016). Big data: Understanding big data. arXiv preprint arXiv:1601.04602.

Vashisht, P., & Gupta, V. (2015, October). Big data analytics techniques: A survey. In *2015 International Conference on Green Computing and Internet of Things (ICGCIoT)* (pp. 264-269). IEEE. DOI: 10.1109/ICGCIoT.2015.7380470

Yamini, B., Ramana, K. V., Nalini, M., Devi, D. C., & Maheswari, B. (2024). Customer churn prediction model in enterprises using machine learning. *International Journal of Advanced Technology and Engineering Exploration.*, 11(110), 94–107.

Chapter 2
Big Data and Its Impact on Strategic Business Operations and Decision-Making:
Exploring How Big Data Influences Corporate Strategies and Decision-Making Processes

Ayush Gupta
IIM Bodhgaya, India

Saikonda Vaishnavi
IIM Bodhgaya, India

ABSTRACT

This chapter delves into the rising prominence of big data in driving strategy decisions. It establishes a definition for big data and its defining features, elaborating how it contributes to the functioning of the corporate world. This chapter introduces the idea of strategic decision-making as a necessity for favorable outcomes. Soon after, the chapter treads into depths of data-driven objectivity preferred over qualitative analysis. The chapter also unveils how big data aids in serving customer insights, benefitting organizational operations and overall performance. The benefit of significant data insights offering predictive analyses and control over the consequences of business decisions is also explained in great detail. Finally, to provide an understanding of the practical application of data analytics, the chapter discusses working of big data in a chosen business domain.In summary, this chapter

DOI: 10.4018/979-8-3693-5563-3.ch002

introduces Big Data and its functioning, the benefits of using data-driven insights during decision-making, and the applicability of big data in business operations.

INTRODUCTION

Understanding the relationship between Big Data and Strategic decision-making is essential for anyone delving into the business world. The role of big data in influencing strategies revolving around the corporate world is vast. Before understanding the relationship, the chapter will provide a glimpse of big data and strategic management.

Consider the example of Netflix to understand how data-driven insights can benefit an organization. Netflix is known for leveraging consumer data to enhance user experience and make bold decisions. The OTT Platform performed rigorous data analytics on consumer usage data of over 30 million plays, 4 million subscriber ratings, and 3 million searches before deciding to produce successful series like The House of Cards, Arrested Development, etc. Analyzing different parameters of consumer usage data like customer watch time, repeat watches, location, interests, and other demographics, the company was able to bet on the success of the production of these series.

The above exemplifies how data can increase a company's profitability. It aids decision-making, decreasing the probability of failures and increasing risk aversion, factors directly linked to the company's financial performance. This chapter will introduce Big Data and its attributes, then delve into its applicability in various domains of an organization's operations. This is followed by more significant details of how data analytics can aid decision-making by reducing risks and uncertainties. The chapter ends with a few case studies to provide practical knowledge.

Literature Review

What is "Big data"? According to (Jindal et al., 2022), Big Data refers to a large volume of data. When joined together, this data is beyond the reach of technology to be stored, managed, and processed. This data is pervasive around us, even in our day-to-day lives, and with this information age, it will continuously increase. Nevertheless, our traditional tools and methods must be revised to meet our requirements. Big data is based on significant impact factors, namely value, velocity, volume, veracity, and variety, also known as the 5 V's of big data. (Robinson and Gillis, 2023) Big data has been commonly discussed in the past century regarding three key factors: volume, velocity, and variety. Over time, two additional V's, namely value and veracity, were incorporated to enhance the ability of data scientists to express and convey the significant attributes of big data more effectively.

5Vs:

- Velocity relates to the rate at which data is generated and the speed at which it is sent. Efficient data flow is crucial for firms that want timely access to their data to make optimal business decisions.
- Volume is the quantitative measure of the total amount of data that is present. Volume is analogous to the foundational aspect of big data, representing the original magnitude and quantity of collected data. When the amount of data reaches a significant size, it qualifies as big data. Nevertheless, the definition of big data is subjective and will vary based on the prevailing computing capabilities in the market.
- Value pertains to the advantages that big data can offer and is closely linked to the actions businesses can take with the gathered data. Extracting value from big data is essential, as the value of extensive data dramatically depends on the insights that can be derived from it.
- Variety pertains to the multitude of different data types. An organization may acquire data from multiple data sources, each of which may differ in usefulness. Data can be obtained from both internal and external sources inside an organization. The issue in achieving variety lies in the standardization and distribution of all the acquired data.
- Veracity pertains to data's inherent quality, precision, honesty, and trustworthiness. The collected data may contain missing elements, inaccuracies, or fail to offer genuine and relevant insights. Veracity generally pertains to the degree of confidence in the gathered data.

Likewise, the implications of big data are explored in (Charles and Gherman's 2013) research, which contends that the key to its power is not data processing but rather data conversion into helpful knowledge for wise decision-making. They stress that for big data to become a competitive advantage, one must adopt a new mentality and recognize its many characteristics, such as context, connection, and complexity.

The next big word is "Strategic Decision-Making." According to (Alhawamdeh, 2019), decision-making is recognizing and skillfully choosing from various options according to one's tendencies. It consists of a range of processes that are all necessary transitions from thinking to action or the building blocks of behavior. Strategic decision-making is an effort to prepare for an organization's long-term future and raise the likelihood that the company will succeed.

Strategic management aims to identify methods to enhance the organization's performance. This contributes to the strategic decision-making process of a company and helps decide its capacity to maintain its position in a predictable environment. (Tatum et al., 2003) assert that managers are responsible for making operational decisions and addressing immediate issues. Furthermore, they explained that managers had distinct decision-making styles due to varying levels of information, alternative options, and efforts to combine and synchronize diverse input sources. However, managers can make effective strategic decisions by following the decision-making process, which ensures the efficiency of those decisions.

The coalition of the above parts results in Data-Driven Decision (DDD) Making. (Jindal et al., 2022) DDD is the process of making judgments based on the study of data rather than relying just on intuition. For instance, an advertiser may select advertisements based on their extensive industry expertise and past experiences. Alternatively, he can make his decisions by utilizing data analysis to examine how consumers react to various advertisements. Additionally, he has the option to utilize a combination of these strategies. DDD does not adhere to an all-or-nothing approach, and many companies engage in DDD to varying extents. All the benefits of using data to guide autonomous decision-making are fully represented. Erik Brynjolfsson, a financial analyst, along with collaborators from MIT and Penn's Wharton School, has conducted a study on the impact of DDD on performance. They have implemented a Data-Driven Decision (DDD) scale that evaluates how effectively organizations utilize data to make informed choices. They demonstrate convincingly that when an organization processes data, it generates a significant amount and manages a substantial amount of potential confusion. Furthermore, the crucial factor is minimal: just one standard deviation increase on the DDD scale corresponds to a 4-6% advancement in progress. DDD is also associated with higher productivity, profitability, usage of goods, and market value.

The chapter will now discuss the relationship between big data and strategic decision-making. For reference, (Turner & Atkinson, 2018) investigated how Big Data is starting to impact various company operations and how that impact affects business strategy. Their research revealed a need for more knowledge regarding big data, especially its uses outside marketing campaigns. The study pinpointed possible obstacles to extensive data integration in enterprises. It offered targeted comprehension strategies to close the knowledge gap between firms that have embraced big data and those that have not.

When discussing the relationship between the two parts, the inclusion of real-time case scenarios in retail, marketing, and finance will be highlighted, and the role of data analytics in making critical strategic decisions will be discussed to ensure practical understanding. The learnings from case studies aim to include the utilization of purchase data to understand risk mitigation in the retail sector, usage of data analytics in the manufacturing sector for predictive maintenance through surveillance of sensor data, and finally, utilization of data for risk assessment in the finance sector.

How Big Data is Changing Strategic Decision-Making?

Every company is entailed in situations requiring decision-making, whether in the manufacturing sector, marketing, finance, or human resource segment. The decision-making process is based on numerous assumptions, premises, and context. While the assumptions and context are externally gained, the premise of a decision is built with solid evidence. Moreover, this evidence is formed by studying data and reaching conclusions. According to (*The Advantages of Data-Driven Decision-Making | HBS Online*, 2019), data-driven decision-making uses data to validate a course of action before committing to it. Today's companies face complex situations and must react quickly to the changing scenarios. Data understanding and data-based decisions are practical tools to deal with these environments and their requirements for problem-solving (Özemre & Kabadurmuş, 2020).

Big Data Analytics is uncovering trends, patterns, and correlations in large amounts of raw data to help make data-informed decisions. According to (Özemre Kabadurmuş, 2020), Big Data Analytics can be applied to interdisciplinary fields like medical and pharmaceutical segments, financial market prediction, and customer churn prediction. With the new age AI methodologies of data analysis, thanks to the availability of large chunks of data, companies have eased their data analysis process, inputting way more efficiency and effectiveness than before. However, according to (Akter et al., 2019), company performance differences can only be seen when these conclusions drawn from data analysis are included in the decision-making process.

(Turner & Atkinson, 2021) explored the emerging effects of Big Data on companies across different business functions and their influence on strategic decision-making. However, they found a lack of understanding of BDA (Big Data Analytics) beyond short-term benefits derived for a company. They emphasize that understanding Big Data's dimensions, including complexity, connectedness, and context, is much more important to turn it into a competitive advantage for a company. They also claim that the devil lies in the detail-applying focused understanding, meaning that broad analytics performed almost prove to be of little use because of the wastage of resources, especially in the context of costs. Therefore, focusing on certain required aspects will ensure cost-saving and increased effectiveness.

In entirety, according to (Turner & Atkinson, 2021), data analytics performs a notable job in aiding corporations with trustable decision-making, therefore reducing the risk of failures. However, the decisions based on this data could prove detrimental, given the data is highly manipulated or deviates from actuality. Therefore, companies must ensure the rightness of their data, just as it is crucial for them to support their decisions with conclusions drawn from data.

Below are the different roles of a company in which data analytics, specifically Big Data Analytics, can provide meaningful help.

BDA and Market Research

Big Data analysis can provide an in-depth insight into the market by understanding data and finding consumer patterns and behavior trends, thus providing a competitive edge over forming marketing strategies. Marketing strategies are long-term goals to achieve a company's targets in sales or revenue and profit generation, which directly affects the company's performance. Hence, it is of utmost importance to develop the right strategies, bearing in mind the negative consequences if done wrong.

According to (Liu, Wan, & Yu, 2023), the theoretical frameworks supporting Big Data analysis in forming marketing strategies by performing market research lie in Personalized Market Theory. It believes that consumers have individual preferences and tastes, so a company trying to sell something to them needs to form personalized strategies to appeal to them. This is precisely where BDA steps in, with its capability to provide details of large chunks of consumer patterns, thus helping the marketer reach very useful conclusions, providing them with the ability to create personalized product recommendations, Pricing, and marketing communication, and improve customer satisfaction and loyalty. Another theory that (Liu, Wan, & Yu, 2023) mention is the Market Segmentation theory, which believes that the market can be divided into several segments, each with different characteristics, and studying these characteristics is crucial to coming up with suitable marketing strategies, which undoubtedly BDA claims to do. Another helpful feature of BDA is that it can provide more precision while identifying target markets and potential customer groups, thus providing help in forming targeting positioning strategies.

An example that (Liu, Wan, & Yu, 2023) provides is how regression analysis, a simple technique to find the strength of relationships between independent and dependent variables, can help a marketer understand how much one independent variable affects the dependent variable, thus allowing him to make improvements. This also helps ensure cost-effectiveness by providing hints on where the resources should be allocated while improving.

A recent article in Forbes said that 87% of enterprises believe that Big Data will redefine the competitive landscape of most different industries within as little as just three years (Columbus, 2014). Eighty-nine percent also believe companies not adopting Big Data strategies may risk losing their momentum alongside market share (Columbus, 2014).

According to (Barutçu, 2017), BDA also eases customer retention. By collecting data on the customers' behavior pre- and post-purchasing, along with up-to-date technologies that give access to their browsing activity, a marketer can understand their experience and expectations and thus form personally tailored suggestions alongside recommendations to retain them. Retaining customers simultaneously involves dividing or clustering customers based on their lifestyle, age, working professions, etc. It allows for understanding these clusters' buying behavior patterns. Even newer products now have better profitability because they no longer just rely on the creator's intuition but are backed by strong data collection, data curation, and data analysis, allowing more control over results than ever before, thus, fortunately, reducing risks to a great extent, especially for new age companies and startups.

Operational Efficiency with BDA

Operational efficiency can be described as reducing waste generation, effort, and material usage as much as possible to cut down on costs. In brief, it is the ratio of output gained over inputs used for a business. Businesswire talks about how data analytics is highly required for food industry companies. Big data management increases operational efficiency by utilizing shopping data to analyze customer behavior. It supports the application of predictive analytics to find out or determine the average wait time at checkout. This helps businesses in the food sector provide the greatest services possible to their clients and increase the effectiveness of their operations. Large data and analytics also help businesses analyze market trends and recommend the ideal inventory levels that food sector businesses should have at various locations.

Even in today's global economy, supply chains are called a business's artery. The supply chain is simply the network of companies and businesses producing a product or service. While the definition might seem simple, the process stands quite complex. As per (Shabbir & Gardezi, 2020), in the modern world, where supply chains increasingly compete, information gathering and understanding about SC partners have become crucial. This step is mentioned as knowledge management. And to no surprise, knowledge management can be acquired through access to a tool called Big Data analytics. (Arunachalam et al., 2018) reports that the huge demand fluctuation requires companies to leverage themselves with ready solutions, which can fortunately be formed from data understanding, collected through previous such incidents. Supply Chain analytics also reduces risks, allowing them to be better alert and equipped with information, which makes (Davenport and O'dwyer, 2011; Shafiq et al., 2020) believe it to be the core reason for several companies to flock towards incorporating BDA for operational efficiency.

(Mani et al., 2017) also talks about the importance of BDA when it comes to practicing sustainability in supply chain networks. Social sustainability can be described as the product or process factors affecting all the stakeholders involved. Although there lies a research gap in building a bridge between sustainability and applying BDA to practice sustainability, there is a clear indication that the application must be performed in all chain segments to reap full benefits. Five overlapping sources of supply chain risk are identified by Mason-Jones and Towill: supply, demand, environmental, process, and control. Any external uncertainties resulting from political (such as fuel crises), natural (such as fires and earthquakes), or social (such as terrorist attacks and strikes) factors are considered environmental risk sources. Taking supply chain risk research a step further, it is contended that supply chain vulnerability—which is defined as "an exposure to disturbances stemming out of supply chain risks and impacting the supply chain ability to serve the end customer market effectively" —is determined by this risk. Predicting to avoid these hazards is necessary for sustainability. (Choi et al., 2018) contend that big data is a useful instrument that may be applied to address operational and supply chain risk issues.

The next question is how to manage operational risk through Big Data analytics. Operational risks, simply put, are the hazards and dangers a company encounters while dealing with day-to-day activities. However, these risks are heavy costs if not obstructed from taking place. According to (Cornwell et al., 2022), given the utility of traditional manual, static, and qualitative risk management strategies, research suggests using BDA for better dynamic management of risks. Through various studies and surveys, the author streamlines the core risk management process steps: identification, analysis, evaluation, treatment, communication, monitoring, and reporting. Risk management is harnessing the value of data analytics to gain timely insights that inform policies and procedures alongside controls and early identification. Artificial Intelligence is increasingly being utilized for quickness and sharpness in the foremost step of the risk mitigation process: identification.

Risk professionals expect data analytics to transform the discipline from three main perspectives. Firstly, the internal data will offer more scientific insights against the more biased views that the company would gain from sample data. Second would be the continuous risk assessment offered by data analytics against the irregular static assessments offered by traditional methods. Third, analytics' predictive power and the ability to form complex relationships between real-time variables would allow for a forward-looking approach, which is not offered by non-dynamic methods (Aven et al., 2016). Working together, these three characteristics will make risk management a valued component of decision-making and the soul of every organization, as discussed above.

Another major cost driver for an organization is risk quantification. With risks identified, the organization knows its potential losses, but with risk quantification, it can know how much the potential loss can precisely be. Fortunately, BDA entails quantification methodologies that combine the estimates of the frequency and severity of events. A quantitative study of cost-effective risk reduction solutions is made possible by empirically quantifying the frequency, effects, and overall risk of loss of containment from LNG carriers utilizing PRA on marine traffic, ship operating, and environmental data. However, due in large part to regulatory constraints, risk quantification is most frequently used in the banking industry to estimate capital (Aven et al., 2016)

Dividing risk into two broad types, financial and operational, it can be understood that a larger part of the financial segment involves much of fraud and information security threats, seeking themselves to micro-diagnostic predictive analyses. Across both sectors, research entailing a multi-risk perspective is largely theoretical and qualitative, with subjective data obtained from experts. (Cornwell et al., 2022) The COVID-19 pandemic is an example of how a single event can affect different dimensions of an organization's operational risk profile.

BDA and Predictive Analyses

Predictive analysis is a term often used in statistical and analytics techniques. It essentially means to predict or forecast the future based on current data and information. This chapter discussed risk reduction and aversion, briefly touching upon predictive analysis. It is time to delve deeper into understanding why it is important and how it affects strategic business decision-making.

In a broad summary, predictive analysis works by judging based on a score derived from predictive analytical models (Kumar & L., 2018). In most cases, a higher score indicates a higher chance of the occurrence of a situation for which the analysis is being performed, and a lower score indicates a lesser chance of the event happening. These models essentially help identify risks and opportunities and, therefore, aid businesses and organizations in making better decisions, equipped with the knowledge of the fruits it might and might not bear. An important feature for which BDA is used in predictive analysis is proactiveness. It helps organizations become proactive and not reactive, thus helping them have better control over the consequences of their decisions (Kumar & L., 2018).

Here is an example to better understand how predictive analysis might help companies. Consider an XYZ company that sells a variety of items through its online e-commerce platforms. With every purchase made by its customers, data is collected. It is observed from data collection that geysers have better demand in winter and coolers in summer. Now, the application will collect more data on the price ranges that are opted for by the customers, what their reactions entail on seeing offers regarding these products, what other products are brought in combination with geysers and coolers, etc. The XYZ company will perform BDA analytics with the collected data and identify better requirements of the customers. With these conclusions and findings, the application will understand and predict what recommendations will attract different types of customers and will proceed to make these recommendations catering to individual customers' preferences. This will undoubtedly result in better sales, which leads to better revenue and final profits, thus increasing the performance of a company or organization (Kumar & L., 2018).

Predictive analysis is not just limited to the above-mentioned e-retailing and e-commerce purposes. It in fact has a wide range of applications in a number of domains. An insurance company collects data from a professional third party to perform analytics and predict which type of profession might prefer a certain kind of insurance. Banking companies might be interested in using predictive analyses to identify risky customers or those who are more prone to being fraudulent customers. Pharmaceutical companies might be interested in finding and predicting the areas that are prone to fewer sales of a certain type of medicine, thus making sure they have fewer supplies with longer expiry dates, creating efficiency in the distribution part of their decision-making (Kumar & L., 2018).

The next topic to explore is the various steps involved in the predictive analysis process, through which a data analyst can try to understand future outcomes by studying the present scenarios.

According to (Kumar & L., 2018), there are six steps involved in the process, the first being requirement collection. To develop a predictive model, the organization must decide what the aim of the prediction is. In brief, the data analysts will try to understand the requirements for a prediction and how the projections will affect their target customers.

The next step is data collection. After identifying the requirements of the client organization, the analyst will collect data from different sources meeting the aforementioned requirements. The collected data might be in a structured or unstructured form that requires verification before performing any kind of analysis on it.

The third step is data analysis and massaging. Firstly, the collected data is prepared and made fit before its utilization. Once the data is skimmed through, the quality is tested, which is essential to determine that the data is not biased or misleading in any way. The possibilities of erroneous data presence and missing attributes must be removed to ensure that the procedures performed on it only ensure accurate results. This directly means that the effectiveness depends on the quality of the data. This analysis segment of the procedure is also referred to as data mugging or massaging.

The fourth step in the process is statistics. Across many statistical and machine learning techniques used to derive meaningful conclusions and findings, regression and probability theory are popularly used. Similar to this, machine learning methods like artificial neural networks, decision trees, and support vector machines are frequently employed in a variety of predictive analytics applications. Every predictive analytics model is built using machine learning and/or statistical methods. To create predictive models, the analysts then apply the ideas of machine learning as well as statistics. Machine learning approaches are very well superior to traditional statistical techniques and any predictive model development process requires the use of statistical techniques.

Next comes predictive modeling. In this step, a model is developed with machine learning techniques. After the development procedure, it is tested on the dataset that has been collected. Following development, the model is evaluated using a test dataset that is a subset of the primary dataset to ensure that it is valid; if this is accomplished, the model is deemed fit. When fitted, the model may accurately forecast newly entered data into the system. The multi-model solution is chosen for a problem in many situations.

The final step is prediction and monitoring. After successful utilization, the model is deployed for everyday practices. The model is then continuously monitored to ensure that the predictions and results are accurate. Here, it can be seen that the predictive process is not a step process but a multi-step process that requires circumspect at every stage to ensure that the process ends successfully. Any error at one of the stages might result in false results, which are dangerous because of the consequences they might bring both financially and operationally to an organization (Kumar & L., 2018).

Case Studies

Applying the theoretical to practical understanding will help us understand the real-life scenarios that companies face and how big data analytics is being explored. Below, strategic decision making through leveraging data analytics is discussed through the domain of supply chain.

Supply Chain

Organizations leverage Big Data to their advantage and personalize customer interactions, fostering enduring and loyal relationships (Chen et al., 2012). Big Data enables organizations to anticipate client preferences, often preempting their requests accurately. Both consciously and, in some cases, subconsciously, our fascination with technology has instilled in us a desire to access and utilize data.

For example, the popularity of Nike+ FuelBand and Jawbone's UP, devices that monitor daily physical activity, along with the MyFitness Pal app, which tracks food intake, has given users unprecedented access to detailed information about their health and eating habits. Ben Arnold, the Executive Director and Industry Analyst for Consumer Technology at the NPD Group, stated that the $330 million in sales generated by digital fitness devices encompasses the entire category, including pedometers, sports watches, and heart rate monitors. However, digital fitness trackers accounted for the highest percentage of these sales, at 72 percent. This amounts to approximately $238 million. According to (Barutçu, 2017), Consumers increasingly find value in Big Data as they become more interested in their personal data. This curiosity motivates them to log in and consistently use products that collect such data.

According to (Jindal et al., 2022), the expenditure on digital advertisements reached over $283 billion in 2018 and is projected to increase to $517 billion by 2023. Nevertheless, in a survey conducted by Rakuten, advertisers determined that they wasted approximately 26% of their advertising budget due to using incorrect strategies or channels. By utilizing information and analytics, marketing teams can effectively target the appropriate audience with tailored promotions, enabling firms to enhance the return on investment of their advertising campaigns.

Let's take the example of Coca-Cola. The company has over 2.7 million on Instagram and 0.1 billion followers on Facebook; as a result, it possesses a substantial amount of information it can analyze. This includes brand mentions and the photographs shared by its fans. Coca-Cola strategically leverages data analytics and image processing to precisely target customers based on the images they upload on social platforms. This enables them to gain insights into the individuals consuming their products, their geographical origins, and the context in which their image is associated. The personalized advertisements presented this way resulted in a 4 times higher click-through rate than other targeted advertising methods.

According to (Ejuma Martha Adaga et al., 2024), there is a huge significance of Big Data in improving customer experience and engagement as it improves customer experience and engagement, a crucial aspect of emphasis in the contemporary company landscape. (Vakhariya and Khanzode, 2018) investigated the function of big data analytics in the UAE retail sector. They highlighted its significance in comprehending consumer behavior and enhancing recommendation systems. Through interviews and observation, their research uncovered that Big Data empowers merchants to gain a deeper understanding of individual needs, resulting in more precise and impactful consumer interaction initiatives.

(Atal, 2020) investigated the implementation of a Big Data analytics framework in the field of e-commerce, with a specific emphasis on enhancing the online customer experience. The study analyzed online product reviews and ratings to identify significant customer concerns, including product size, fit, and quality. The study emphasized that the utilization of Big Data analytics has the potential to offer significant insights into customer preferences and areas of dissatisfaction, hence allowing e-commerce platforms to customize their offerings and enhance customer satisfaction.

According to (Ejuma Martha Adaga et al., 2024), utilizing Big Data to enhance consumer experience goes beyond the scope of retail and e-commerce. It includes a range of businesses where having a deep grasp of customer behavior and preferences is essential. Big Data analytics technologies facilitate the gathering and examination of consumer data from many origins, allowing businesses to have a comprehensive understanding of customer interactions and experiences. Firms can customize their services and products using a data-driven strategy, creating a more immersive and gratifying consumer experience. Furthermore, Big Data plays a crucial part in client interaction by empowering firms to anticipate customer requirements and inclinations. By analyzing customer data, firms can predict forthcoming trends and customer behaviors, enabling them to respond to customer requirements actively. Forecasting customer behavior is highly beneficial for developing tailored marketing tactics and product offerings that effectively connect with customers. Big Data greatly improves customer experience and engagement by providing organizations profound insights into customer behavior and preferences. By leveraging Big Data analytics, firms can customize their services to align with client wants, forecast future trends, and ultimately cultivate more robust customer connections. Adopting a data-driven approach is crucial for firms aiming to be competitive and adaptable in the current dynamic market landscape.

According to (Barutçu, 2017), Big data further facilitates customizing. The utilization of Big Data enables us to gain a more comprehensive comprehension of our environment and a more profound insight into customers, encompassing not only a limited number of individuals but billions. As the data gathered is utilized to ascertain consumer preferences, further methods will be modified to discern how to influence their purchasing behavior toward the products they prefer (Tirunillai and Tellis, 2014). Just like online shoppers can be tracked through their IP address, which allows them to receive personalized offers through ads or emails related to their browsing history or purchases, consumers also enable this personalized advertising based on their purchases and social interactions, both online and offline. In his book The Formula, Luke Dormehl illustrates how even a simple mention of "Cape Town" in an email can prompt airlines to send promotional emails for "Affordable flights to Africa" directly to your inbox (Dormehl, 2014). Airlines and other travel corporations utilize algorithms to analyze data and identify individuals more likely to be interested in future travel to South Africa. Despite the email's unrelated context to flying, utilizing Big Data enables more effective marketing campaigns through enhanced predictive capabilities.

Courier businesses have used a system that uses the real-time geographical location of their trucks and traffic data to determine the most efficient route for delivering packages to consumers. UPS has dedicated a decade to developing its On-Road Integrated Optimization and Navigation system (Orion) to optimize the 55,000 routes within its network. According to the company's CEO, David Abney, implementing the new system is expected to result in annual cost savings of $300 million to $400 million. Trucking businesses are currently using analytics to enhance their operations. For instance, they employ fuel consumption analytics to enhance vehicle efficiency and utilize GPS technologies to minimize waiting times by allocating real-time storage spaces. (Big Data and the Supply Chain: The Big-supply-chain Analytics Landscape (Part 1), 2016)

Retailers can now leverage emerging data sources to enhance their planning processes and augment their ability to sense and anticipate demand. For example, Blue Yonder has developed advanced forecasting techniques for the retail industry. These techniques handle large amounts of data, including 130,000 products and 200 factors influencing sales. Every day, these techniques generate 150,000,000 different probability distributions. This has significantly enhanced the precision of predictions, provided a clearer understanding of the company's requirements for logistical capacity, and decreased obsolescence, inventory levels, and instances of stockouts. The recent expansion of third-party cloud-based platforms, such as Blue Yonder, is also increasing the availability of these activities for other shops.

IBM has facilitated the integration of production planning and weather forecasts for bakeries. Baking companies can enhance demand forecasting for several product categories by integrating temperature and sunshine data, key elements in shaping consumer preferences. Amazon has obtained a patent for a method called "anticipatory shipping," where orders are prepared and sent into the delivery system before customers place them.

Advanced analytics can also empower logistics firms to reduce the number of delivery attempts for goods by utilizing their data to forecast when a specific consumer is more likely to be present at their residence. Companies can reduce expenses and decrease carbon emissions by strategically choosing appropriate transportation methods. A prominent consumer packaged goods (CPG) company is allocating resources toward analytics to gain insights into the optimal mode of transportation for goods, whether it requires expedited truck delivery or allows for slower barge or rail shipment. (Big Data and the Supply Chain: The Big-supply-chain Analytics Landscape (Part 1), 2016)

Traditional retailers, who face strong competition from online stores that excel in data analysis, have recognized the benefits of using data-driven optimization to gain a competitive edge. These strategies are currently employed to carry out tasks such as optimizing shelf space and determining mark-down prices. Advanced analytics can assist merchants in determining the optimal selection of products to place in high-value areas, such as aisle ends, and the ideal duration for their placement. Additionally, it can empower them to investigate the sales advantages obtained by grouping together connected products.

The prominent search engine company Google has purchased Skybox, which offers high-resolution satellite images. These images may be used to monitor parking lot vehicles and predict customer demand in physical stores. Previous studies have investigated using drones outfitted with cameras to surveil and assess the quantities of products available on store shelves. Equivalent technologies can be implemented immediately at the location of utilization. Amazon's Dash service offers clients wireless buttons that can conveniently reorder household supplies, such as laundry detergent or shaving blades, with a single press. Ultimately, retailers may connect with the data collected from consumers' internet-connected refrigerators to predict demand accurately in real-time. (Big Data and the Supply Chain: The Big-supply-chain Analytics Landscape (Part 1), 2016)

Other examples:

Uber: According to (Jindal et al., 2022), enhancing speed and efficiency of transportation through data analysis whenever customers utilize Uber to request a ride, we envision a surplus of drivers congregating in our vicinity and anticipate being able to secure a car quickly. Although we have been accustomed to this convenience, Uber's significant challenge regularly is bridging the demand-supply mismatch. Fortunately, predictive analytics allows the business to analyze important metrics and historical data that include the number of completed trips and ride requests in different areas of a location and the specific time and day when these activities occur. This data helps Uber gain an understanding of areas experiencing a shortage of drivers, allowing them to proactively notify drivers to relocate to those areas in advance to take advantage of the inevitable increase in demand.

Starbucks: According to (Chitkara University, 2023), Starbucks determines its optimal shopping locations via big data analytics. Starbucks strategically selects optimal locations for new stores by analyzing foot traffic patterns, demographic data, and local habits. This strategic approach guarantees enhanced customer footfall, revenue generation, and brand recognition, implying the significance of big data analytics in the evolution of the retail sector.

General Electric: According to (Chitkara University, 2023), GE enhances the functionality of industrial gear via big data analytics. It employs predictive maintenance techniques by gathering and analyzing data from sensors embcddcd in machines, enabling them to schedule maintenance proactively before any issues occur. This predictive maintenance technique reduces the time that equipment is not functioning, cuts the expenses associated with the operation, and extends the lifespan of crucial equipment, showcasing the potential of big data in the industrial sector.

PepsiCo: According to (Kopanakis, 2024), the consumer-packaged goods firm depends on vast amounts of data to ensure effective supply chain management. The company is dedicated to restocking the shops' shelves with suitable quantities and varieties of products. The company's clientele submits reports containing their warehouse inventory and point of sale (POS) inventory to the company. This data is utilized to reconcile and predict production and shipment requirements. By doing so, the corporation guarantees that shops possess the appropriate products in the correct quantities and during the specified timeframe. Attend this webinar featuring the Customer Supply Chain Analyst from the organization as they discuss the significance of big data analytics in the PepsiCo Supply chain.

Finance

According to (Dutta, n.d.), IBM's 2023 data breach report reveals that the average cost of a data breach globally in 2023 was $4.45 million. This is a 15% increase compared to the previous three years. The report gathered data from 550 businesses that had a data breach. One contributing factor to the high expenses is the time-consuming process of identifying and containing a breach. Fortunately, big data analysis enables firms to proactively discover vulnerabilities before malicious individuals exploit them. In the event of a breach, doing a data analytics risk assessment can assist in identifying the most effective method to address the security vulnerability and restore your business operations promptly.

DBS Bank: According to (Jindal et al., 2022), Utilizing Artificial Intelligence and Analytics to Enhance Customer Service, DBS Bank, a prominent financial institution in Singapore, is well-acquainted with competition. In the face of increasing fintech rivals, the brand must prioritize innovation. DBS has invested heavily in data analytics and AI, allocating more than SGS 44 billion in recent years. This investment aims to provide their clients with highly personalized experiences and recommendations, enabling them to make more informed financial decisions.

This entails offering sophisticated banking services that encompass the following:

- Providing investment suggestions on financial products and instruments
- Offering stock recommendations based on an investor's portfolio
- Sending notifications about favorable foreign exchange rates
- Alerting users about unusual transactions

DBS is endeavoring to alter the way clients bank and transform their perception from being solely a bank to that of a reliable financial advisor by scrutinizing their sources of information. To ensure the success and longevity of this progress, the bank trained over 16,000 employees in big data and data analytics to transform the business into a data-driven enterprise. Employees within the bank will actively seek to leverage information to address business difficulties, identify opportunities, and create more intuitive experiences and products for their customers.

BlackRock: According to (Dutta, n.d.), BlackRock is a prominent global asset management company that utilizes big data to create more efficient asset management techniques. BlackRock uses this groundbreaking strategy to identify superior investment prospects, optimize portfolio returns, make well-informed choices, and provide added value to its clientele. The investment management organization employs big data in finance to scrutinize extensive financial data, economic indicators, and market movements. This enables them to acquire valuable knowledge about potential investment prospects and hazards. By employing data-driven strategies, BlackRock can make well-informed investment decisions and enhance the performance of its portfolio.

American Express: According to (Chitkara University, 2023), the organization uses big data analytics to identify fraudulent transactions. Algorithms have the ability to identify unusual patterns and bring attention to potentially deceitful actions by analyzing extensive databases in real-time. This proactive approach safeguards clients and maintains the brand's trust and reputation in the tightly regulated financial industry.

UOB Bank: According to (Kopanakis, 2024), the Singaporean corporation consists of a brand that facilitates risk management via big data. As a financial institution, there is a significant risk of incurring losses if risk management is not carefully considered. UOB bank recently inculcated big data into a trial of a risk management system. Consequently, the bank decreased the time required to calculate the value at risk. Originally, the process required almost 18 hours, but implementing a risk management system that utilizes big data has reduced the duration to only a few minutes. With this endeavor, the bank may soon be capable of conducting real-time risk analysis.

Societe Generale: According to (Dutta, n.d.), Societe Generale is a prominent French bank with a history spanning over 150 years. The investment banking firm caters to a vast clientele of 25 million individuals across 66 nations. The financial services organization has prioritized adopting data-driven strategies, taking technologies such as AI, big data, and ML to enhance the experiences of its consumers, regulators, and staff. Their objective is to utilize data to enhance the efficiency of current business models and identify novel prospects. Since 2014, the corporation has invested in big data and AI, recognizing their crucial role in its digital transformation. The bank employs a workforce of more than 1,000 data experts who utilize big data to inform investment choices and continuously monitor real-time risk exposures. This strategy enables businesses to decrease uncertainty and improve the performance of their investment portfolio.

CONCLUSION

Clearly, in today's age, data is King. However, without the right resources acting as a key to unlocking it, it remains an untapped source. This is where data analytics transforms raw data into actionable insights that can be used during strategic decision-making in an organization. Data analytics can be likened to acquiring a powerful weapon, allowing organizations to find their way through uncertainty after gaining a much-needed edge when competing in the business arena.

According to (Christenson Jr. & Goldstein, 2022), the innovation of data analytics is that it eliminates subjectivity where intuition and experience can fall short due to bias. Instead of relying on such subjective factors, businesses base their strategic planning on a quantitative basis provided by data analytics. The ability of data analytics to identify patterns and trends within datasets means that businesses can see what others cannot— both in opportunities and risks hidden behind numbers. This empowers organizations to make choices based on concrete evidence, not just a feeling in their gut that may or may not pan out.

Imagine a company seeking to broaden its market share. Typically, this would entail generalized marketing efforts— casting the net wide and crossing fingers for good luck. But data analytics presents an alternative path: a more focused one. Through the study of the age group, gender, geographical location, and purchase frequency plus mode, in addition to clients' online activities, businesses can zero in on the most receptive audience— without leaving it to chance.

(Christenson Jr. & Goldstein, 2022) says that another component is predictive analytics. This entails using historical data plus other variables in the analysis to give an idea of what is coming in the future. With this foresight, organizations can proactively adjust their strategies, staying relevant and competitive as markets evolve. For example, a retail store might forecast seasonal demand patterns through data analytics and adjust its stock levels.

In conclusion, data analytics takes center stage as a strategic decision-making tool. By making sense of the data and acting on it, organizations stand to make informed choices, streamline operations, and steer through uncertainty with more confidence. In this era where the amount and intricacy of data are always on the rise— those who turn to data analytics find themselves best placed not only to survive but also to thrive amidst today's dynamic business environments.

REFERENCES

Adaga, E. M., Okorie, G. N., Egieya, Z. E., Ikwue, U., Udeh, C. A., DaraOjimba, D. O., & Oriekhoe, O. I. (2023). The role of big data in business strategy: a critical review. Computer Science & IT Research Journal, 4(3), 327-350.

Akter, S., Bandara, H. M. R. J., Hani, U., Wamba, S. F., Foropon, C., & Papadopoulos, T. (n.d.). Analytics-based decision-making for service systems: A qualitative study and agenda for future research. Research Online. https://ro.uow.edu.au/gsbpapers/562/

Arunachalam, D., Kumar, N., & Kawalek, J. P. (2018, June). Understanding big data analytics capabilities in supply chain management: Unravelling the issues, challenges and implications for practice. *Transportation Research Part E, Logistics and Transportation Review*, 114, 416–436. DOI: 10.1016/j.tre.2017.04.001

Aven, T. (2016). Risk assessment and risk management: Review of recent advances on their foundation. *European Journal of Operational Research*, 253(1), 1–13. DOI: 10.1016/j.ejor.2015.12.023

Barutçu, M. T. (2017, September 10). Big Data Analytics for Marketing Revolution. *Journal of Media Critiques*, 3(11), 163–171. DOI: 10.17349/jmc117314

Barutçu, M. T. (2017, September 10). Big Data Analytics for Marketing Revolution. *Journal of Media Critiques*, 3(11), 163–171. DOI: 10.17349/jmc117314

Big data and the supply chain: The big-supply-chain analytics landscape (Part 1). (2016, February 16). McKinsey & Company. https://www.mckinsey.com/capabilities/operations/our-insights/big-data-and-the-supply-chain-the-big-supply-chain-analytics-landscape-part-1

Choi, T., Wallace, S. W., & Wang, Y. (2018, October). Big Data Analytics in Operations Management. *Production and Operations Management*, 27(10), 1868–1883. DOI: 10.1111/poms.12838

Christenson, A. P.Jr, & Goldstein, W. S. (2022). Impact of data analytics in transforming the decision-making process. *BIT Numerical Mathematics*, XII(1), 74–82. DOI: 10.14311/bit.2022.01.09

Columbus, L. (2014, October 21). 84% of enterprises see big data analytics changing their industries' competitive landscapes in the next year. Forbes. https://www.forbes.com/sites/louiscolumbus/2014/10/19/84-of-enterprises-see-big-data-analytics-changing-their-industries-competitive-landscapes-in-the-next-year/?sh=a61492417de1

Cornwell, N., Bilson, C., Gepp, A., Stern, S., & Vanstone, B. J. (2022, February 27). The role of data analytics within operational risk management: A systematic review from the financial services and energy sectors. *The Journal of the Operational Research Society*, 74(1), 374–402. DOI: 10.1080/01605682.2022.2041373

Cornwell, N., Bilson, C., Gepp, A., Stern, S., & Vanstone, B. J. (2022, February 27). The role of data analytics within operational risk management: A systematic review from the financial services and energy sectors. *The Journal of the Operational Research Society*, 74(1), 374–402. DOI: 10.1080/01605682.2022.2041373

Jindal, R., Bharadwaj, M., & Mishra, V. (2022). IMPACT OF BIG DATA ON BUSINESS DECISIONS THROUGH THE VIEW OF DATA SCIENCE-BASED DECISION MAKING.

Kopanakis, J. (2024, February 29). *5 Real-World Examples of How Brands Are Using Big Data Analytics*. Mentionlytics. https://www.mentionlytics.com/blog/5-real-world-examples-of-how-brands-are-using-big-data-analytics/

Kumar, V., & L, M. (2018, July 16). Predictive Analytics: A Review of Trends and Techniques. *International Journal of Computer Applications*, 182(1), 31–37. DOI: 10.5120/ijca2018917434

Liu, Q., Wan, H., & Yu, H. (2023, June 28). Application and Influence of Big data Analysis in Marketing Strategy. *Frontiers in Business. Economics and Management*, 9(3), 168–171. DOI: 10.54097/fbem.v9i3.9580

Liu, Q., Wu, H., & Yu, H. (2023, June 28). *Application and Influence of Big Data Analysis in Marketing Strategy*. Frontiers in Business, Economics and Management. https://doi.org/DOI: 10.54097/fbem.v9i3.9580

Mani, V., Delgado, C., Hazen, B., & Patel, P. (2017, April 14). Mitigating Supply Chain Risk via Sustainability Using Big Data Analytics: Evidence from the Manufacturing Supply Chain. *Sustainability (Basel)*, 9(4), 608. DOI: 10.3390/su9040608

Özemre, M., & Kabadurmus, O. (2020, May 26). A big data analytics based methodology for strategic decision making. *Journal of Enterprise Information Management*, 33(6), 1467–1490. DOI: 10.1108/JEIM-08-2019-0222

Robinson, S., & Gillis, A. S. (2023, November 17). *5V's of big data*. Data Management. https://www.techtarget.com/searchdatamanagement/definition/5-Vs-of-big-data#:~:text=The%205%20V's%20of%20big%20data%20%2D%2D%20velocity%2C%20volume%2C%20value,innate%20characteristics%20of%20big%20data

Shabbir, M. Q., & Gardezi, S. B. W. (2020, July 8). Application of big data analytics and organizational performance: The mediating role of knowledge management practices. *Journal of Big Data*, 7(1), 47. Advance online publication. DOI: 10.1186/s40537-020-00317-6

Shafiq, A., Ahmed, M. U., & Mahmoodi, F. (2020, July). Impact of supply chain analytics and customer pressure for ethical conduct on socially responsible practices and performance: An exploratory study. *International Journal of Production Economics*, 225, 107571. DOI: 10.1016/j.ijpe.2019.107571

The Advantages of Data-Driven Decision-Making | HBS Online. (2019, August 26). Business Insights Blog. https://online.hbs.edu/blog/post/data-driven-decision-making

Turner, C. (2021). Strategic Decision Making: The Effects of Big Data. *International Journal of Operations Management*, 1(2), 38–45. DOI: 10.18775/ijom.2757-0509.2020.12.4005

Section 2
Applications of Data Analytics in Business

Chapter 3
Competitiveness and Sustainability of Online Travel Agencies in India:
A Case Study on Five Leading Online Travel Agencies in India

Satadruti Chakraborty
https://orcid.org/0000-0001-5147-022X
Indian Institute of Social Welfare and Business Management, India

Dipa Mitra
https://orcid.org/0000-0002-7639-0098
Indian Institute of Social Welfare and Business Management, India

ABSTRACT

This study aims to determine the critical components of high-quality travel website services that have a substantial impact on Indian consumers' purchase intentions as well as use the 'Importance Performance Analysis' matrix to assess the competitive qualities of service in terms of their specific significance and relevance to business success. The research here is based on Exploratory Research approach using Quantitative Research Techniques. Data for the study is collected by framing questionnaires. There are two phases to the examination of this study: Structural evaluation of the scale using SPSS and AMOS and IPA matrix. The study is the first of its kind in the area of online travel behavior research because it not only unifies all factors that influence decisions into a single framework but also assesses the effectiveness of the attributes by conducting further survey research to ascertain where they rank for five of India's top travel agencies. The study's conclusions will give travel industry marketers information they can use to enhance their internet

DOI: 10.4018/979-8-3693-5563-3.ch003

marketing strategies.

INTRODUCTION

In India's service economy, the travel and tourism sector has been a key engine of growth. The Indian online travel industry has been greatly impacted by the development of the internet and information technology research. According to a *Statista* (*2023*) report, the Indian internet travel market is anticipated to be valued at 31 billion US dollars by the financial year 2025. The Indian internet travel market is expected to be valued USD 17.24 billion in 2024 and increase at a compound annual growth rate (CAGR) of 10.5% to reach USD 28.40 billion by 2029, according to a different survey conducted by Mordor Intelligence (2023). Travellers from all over the globe use the internet to find fascinating locations to visit, so having a good online presence is vital for the hotel industry. Notwithstanding the fact that the internet has become a boon for the travel industry, the online travel agencies are now engaged in intense competition as a result of certain e-commerce features. The switching cost is also low; hence, it has become hard for the OTAs to retain customer loyalty. Therefore, the only means of surviving in this very competitive industry is to differentiate and create a place in the consumer's mind by providing a superior quality of service.

To succeed in the online market, an e-service company has to develop the approach of seeing things from the customer's perspective and design the system in such a way that it can meet and fulfil customer expectations. The key to this is to understand how clients interpret and define e-service quality. The primary objective of this study is to develop an instrument in order to determine the components that define the overall quality of service of tourism websites in India. However, a thorough assessment of the literature revealed that performance indicators must also be provided to the items examined in addition to importance on satisfaction levels. In order to solve this issue, customers of five of India's biggest online travel agencies are surveyed to understand consumer satisfaction as well as identify areas of improvement. The Importance-Performance Analysis matrix, which is created using the scale's items as a starting point, serve as the survey's foundation.

LITERATURE REVIEW

Assessment of 'Online service quality' and 'Purchase Intention' is an essential criterion in the world of digitisation, and it plays a critical part in the success or failure of travel web service providers. The implications of evaluating the effectiveness of a website have long been debated by academicians. Several authors have concluded that travel websites with good design and quality have the ability to engage more potential travellers than poorly designed websites. Therefore, websites of travel service providers are extremely crucial for their business. According to Park and Gretzel (2007), in order to improve the online trip planning experience, online travel companies should concentrate on building operational and conceptual characteristics of websites that will meet the expectations of future voyagers seeking information. The last two decades have seen a boom in the online travel market in India. Dhingra et al. (2022), investigated the influence of 'e-commerce website online service quality' on 'Customer satisfaction' and 'Purchase intent'. According to Taryadi & Miftahuddin (2021), evaluating 'Service quality' is a crucial component in customer 'Travel decisions'. In the Indian online tourist business, Kumra & Singh (2018) sought to evaluate the effects of four elements of 'e-service quality' on 'Consumer Satisfaction'. The findings reveal that 'Information', 'Responsiveness' and 'Security' are the primary factors that strongly lead to 'Satisfaction' of customers who perform online travel bookings in India. Several studies have been conducted from the viewpoint of consumers in Western nations on the aforementioned subject (Ref- Table-1), but there has been hardly any research from the point of view of Indian customers.

Table 1. A summary of different dimensions used by various authors to measure service quality of online travel websites or online travel agents

Researcher	Country/ Location	Dimensions
Wen (2012)	United States	"Information Quality", "Service Quality" and "System Quality"
Mohammed et al. (2016)	China	"Interactivity", "Reliability", "Privacy" and "Efficiency"
Elci et al. (2017)	Turkey	"System Quality" and "E-Service Quality"
Li (2018)	China	"Information Content", "Safety", "Website Structure" and "Usability"
Kumra and Singh (2018)	India	"Website Design", "Information", "Responsiveness" and "Security"
Pham (2019)	Vietnam	"Interactive Service Quality", "Ease of Use", "Information Quality" and "Visual Appeal"
Muzakir et al. (2021)	Indonesia	"Website Design", "Fulfilment", "Customer service", "Security/ Privacy", "Efficiency" and "Incentives"

Among the research strategies most frequently implemented in travel literature is Importance-Performance Analysis (Boley et al., 2017; Wong et al., 2011). It is frequently utilised to identify the divergence between stakeholders' perceived importance of a specific matter and the actual effectiveness in managing that issue.

Martilla and James (1977) established the IPA matrix for the first time in the marketing field to assist target audiences in identifying and evaluating specific features of a product or service by considering their importance to the evaluator and their impact on the overall success of the organisation. This matrix allows managers to ascertain which characteristics need and merit improvement and which ones have drained too many resources with little return on customer satisfaction. Fahrurrozi (2022) as well as Saggaf et al. (2018) used IPA matrix to evaluate academic services, while Boley et al. (2017) assessed 'Sustainable Tourism Projects' using IPA.Lai and Hitchcock (2015) examined 59 distinct publications that used the technique and showed how adaptable IPA is. While IPA is widely used in the tourism and hospitality literature, its application to online tourism website quality has been confined to a few researches (Kim et al., 2007; Chiou et al., 2011; Ramirez-Hurtado et al., 2017; Wong et al., 2020).

RESEARCH GAP

As far as the knowledge of the researcher, the bulk of research in this subject are undertaken from the standpoint of Western customers in developed countries, with empirical studies in developing countries, notably India, being uncommon. Given India's rapidly rising Internet population, which is on track to overtake China as the world's second-largest e-commerce industry, study into the factors that influence Indian customers' purchasing decisions is long overdue. This study's goal is to fill that gap by examining the variables that affect 'Online purchase intentions' or 'Travel intentions', with a focus on the effects of 'Website service quality'. Another principal goal of this study is to determine whether the online purchasing process for travel-related items meets customer needs and expectations. . Recognizing the IPA's limited application in the field of online service quality of Travel websites, the study intends to apply IPA to users of top five travel websites in India in order to identify which parameters are essential to consumers and which are not.

RESEARCH OBJECTIVE

- To ascertain the essential aspects of travel website service quality that have a substantial impact on Indian consumers' purchase intentions.
- To analyse the competitive aspects of services in terms of their relative importance and contribution to business success.

RESEARCH HYPOTHESES

The term "hypothesis" refers to a notion that has to be tested. In the previous unit, a thorough literature review was given. The study here proposes the following hypothesis:-

H1: Purchase Intention is significantly influenced by the dimensions of e-travel site quality.

RESEARCH METHODOLOGY

The research here is based on Exploratory Research approach using Quantitative Research Techniques. Data for the study is collected by framing questionnaires.

There are two phases in this study:

Phase 1: Structural evaluation of the scale using SPSS and AMOS

A scale on 'E-Travel Website Service Quality' comprising 29 items has been constructed on the basis of the following seven constructs- 'Functionality', 'Ease of use', 'Design', 'Information accuracy', 'Responsiveness and fulfilment', 'Customer relationships' and 'Financial incentives'. The constructs - 'Functionality' comprising 4 items, 'Ease of Use' comprising 3 items, 'Website Design' comprising 2 items and the construct 'Information Accuracy' comprising 3 items have been adapted from Chen and Kao (2010). The construct 'Responsiveness and Fulfilment' comprises 7 items, out of which the first 3 items have been adapted from Ho and Lee (2007) and the rest 4 items have been taken from Jou and Day (2021). The construct 'Customer Relationship' comprises 5 items, out of which the first 3 items have been adapted from Ho and Lee (2007) and the rest 2 items have been taken from Jou and Day (2021). The construct 'Financial Incentives' consisting of 5 items have been adapted from Lin (2010). The response format for all these statements are measured with a 5 point Likert scale ranging from 1 = Extremely Unimportant to 5 = Extremely Important. The construct 'Travel Purchase Intention' comprising 3 items has been adapted from several researches (Chen and Kao, 2010; Hsu, Chang and Chen, 2012; Puspitasari et al., 2021). They are also measured with a 5 point Likert scale ranging from 1 = Strongly Disagree to 5 = Strongly Agree.

The questionnaire is designed using Google form and circulated through emails and social media channels like Facebook, Whatsapp and Linkedin. Respondents are included mostly from educational institutions, offices and households. Around 800 questionnaires are distributed. The study analyses cross-sectional data from customers of online travel services in India who are geographically scattered. 552 responses are collected in this phase.

Phase 2: Using IPA Matrix to identify the gap between Importance and Performance measures

In the next phase of the research, once the scale is generated, the scale is used to take surveys from several customers who are familiar with online travel websites like MakeMyTrip, GoIbibo, Cleartrip, Yatra and Booking.com. Several of them have also participated in the first phase of the survey. Total number of respondents for this survey is 455.

Both the questionnaires are presented in the Appendix section.

DATA ANALYSIS AND INTERPRETATION

In the first phase, the data is collected to identify the dimensions that affect service quality perception. The response rate was 79% (n=421). Males make up 56% of the responses, while females make up 44%. The age range 26–40 has the highest percentage of responses (49.6 percent), followed by the 40–55 age range with 28% of respondents. 10 percent of respondents are over 55, compared to 12.4 percent who are under 25. Postgraduates make up 48% of the total, followed by graduates (36%) and undergraduates (16%). 50.8% of respondents has an annual salary of more than 10 lacs, while 35% make between 5 and 7 lacs and the rest earns less than 5 lacs per annum.

The main survey's returned data is filtered out in the first stage of analysis using statistical techniques for 'missing data', 'outliers', 'normality', 'homoscedasticity', and 'common method biasness'. Since Google Forms automatically flags incomplete responses at the time of form submission, there is practically no missing data. There were 19 multivariate outliers, as determined by the Mahalanobis D^2 score. They were taken out of the sample of data. The 'P-P plot', the 'skewness and kurtosis' results as well as insignificance of 'Mardia's coefficient' indicate that the data is normal. 'Bivariate Pearson Correlation' and 'Multiple Regression' are used to test the assumption of multicollinearity, and the results show that r, VIF, and tolerance effects are all within acceptable limits, indicating that multicollinearity is not present. Finally, 'Harman's single factor test' is used to examine the data for 'Common Method Biasness'. The result indicate that there is no 'Common Method Bias' in the model. The data is further analysed using SPSS and AMOS.

Exploratory Factor Analysis

The initial answers for the 'EFA' are produced using 'Principal Component Analysis' and 'Orthogonal Varimax Rotation'. The 'Kaiser-Meyer-Olkin' (KMO) test for 'Sample Adequacy' and the 'Bartlett's Test for Sphericity' both reveal statistically significant relationships between the items, indicating that they are suitable for EFA. Individual dimensions of the suggested instrument explains more than 79 percent of total variation. The next step is to check the factor loadings and remove those items whose loadings are less than 0.5 (Hair et al., 2011). Four items are removed with factor loadings of 0.464, 0.486, 0.391 and 0.474 respectively. The items are: ETWSQ_5, ETWSQ_13, ETWSQ_24 and ETWSQ_27. A Composite table (Table 2) is presented with the loadings for better clarity. Based on shared meaning on the items of each factor they are named as- Fulfilment, User Interface and Interactivity, Reliability, Incentives, Functionality and Complaint handling.

Table 2. Composite Table with items and loadings

Factors	Construct items	FACTOR LOADINGS					
		1	2	3	4	5	6
Fulfilment	ETWSQ_2	0.651					
	ETWSQ_10	0.566					
	ETWSQ_11	0.712					
	ETWSQ_12	0.602					
	ETWSQ_14	0.667					
	ETWSQ_15	0.794					
	ETWSQ_16	0.774					
	ETWSQ_18	0.518					
	ETWSQ_19	0.506					
User Interface and Interactivity	ETWSQ_8		0.609				
	ETWSQ_9		0.558				
	ETWSQ_20		0.542				
	ETWSQ_21		0.704				
	ETWSQ_22		0.700				
	ETWSQ_23		0.501				

continued on following page

Table 2. Continued

Factors	Construct items	FACTOR LOADINGS					
		1	2	3	4	5	6
Reliability	ETWSQ_3			0.544			
	ETWSQ_4			0.602			
	ETWSQ_7			0.725			
	ETWSQ_25			0.606			
Incentives	ETWSQ_26				0.711		
	ETWSQ_28				0.804		
	ETWSQ_29				0.525		
Functionality	ETWSQ_1					0.691	
	ETWSQ_6					0.700	
Complaint Handling	ETWSQ_17						0.615

However, for the research purpose, only the first four factors are retained. The reason being that the last two factors have only two and one item respectively, which is bound to create identification problems in the Confirmatory Factor Analysis stage. Another reason is that reliability for such factors will be low.

STRUCTURAL EQUATION MODELLING

Measurement Model Analysis

Using 'Confirmatory Factor Analysis', the 'Measurement Model's' overall performance is evaluated. Table 2 presents the 'Factor Loadings', 'Cronbach's Alpha', 'AVE' and 'CR' for all the factors. According to Bagozzi and Yi (1988), the spectrum of acceptable 'Factor loadings' ranged from 0.50 to 0.95. On the other hand, the 'Average Variance Extracted' (AVE) is over 0.50 and the acceptable value of 'Composite Reliability' (CR) is above 0.70. (Fornell & Larcker, 1981;Hair et al., 2011). When the Cronbach alpha value is 0.70 or more, the measurement is considered reliable. (Hair et al., 2011). Each factor loading falls within the range of 0.59-0.82. Cronbach alpha scores ranges from 0.71 to 0.88, surpassing 0.70, indicating reliable measurements. The latent constructs' AVE ranges from 0.51 to 0.63 and is greater than 0.5, indicating high 'Convergent Validity'. The confidence intervals (CRs) for all constructs fall between 0.71 and 0.89, above the 0.70 requirement, which indicates that the measurement items for each construct has good internal consistency.

Table 3. 'CFA' and 'measurement reliability' (n=421)

CONSTRUCTS	'Factor Loadings'	'Cronbach's Alpha'	'CR'	'AVE'
FULFILMENT	0.63-0.78	0.882	0.886	0.57
INTERFACE	0.63-0.69	0.825	0.825	0.54
RELIABILITY	0.59-0.63	0.71	0.715	0.51
INCENTIVES	0.65-0.70	0.713	0.715	0.55
PURCHASE INTENTION	0.76-0.82	0.84	0.841	0.63

Notes: Fit indices: 'χ^2' = 943.4; 'df' = 265; 'χ^2/df' = 3.56; 'AGFI' = 0.885; 'GFI' = 0.89, 'CFI' = 0.892, 'RMSEA' = 0.056

According to Table 4, 'Discriminant Validity' is indicated by the projected inter-correlations between all variables being smaller than the square roots of the 'AVE' for each construct (Fornell & Larcker, 1981). The 'Measurement Model' produced a 'Chi-square' of 943.4 (d.f.=265, p<0.01) which violates the assumption of Model fitness according to Hoelter (1983). However, additional fit indices are advised when evaluating Model fitness because 'Chi-square' is significantly impacted by sample size. The 'Normed Chi-square' (χ^2/df = 3.56) is expected to lie in the 2.0–5.0 range (Tabachnick & Fidell, 2007), the 'Root Mean Square Error of Approximation' (RMSEA=0.056), with a cut-off point being <0.08 (Hu & Bentler, 1999), the 'Comparative Fit Index' (CFI=0.892) and the 'Goodness of Fit Index' (GFI=0.89) which is at the threshold i.e. > 0.90 (Hair et al., 2011), imply that the data somehow satisfactorily fits the measuring model (Bagozzi and Yi, 1988).

Table 4. 'Discriminant validity' measures

	AVE	FULFILMENT	INTERFACE	RELIABILITY	INCENTIVES	PURCHASE INTENTION
FULFILMENT	0.57	**0.754**				
INTERFACE	0.54	0.598	**0.734**			
RELIABILITY	0.51	0.649	0.707	**0.714**		
INCENTIVES	0.55	0.253	0.736	0.588	**0.74**	
PURCHASE INTENTION	0.63	0.363	0.33	0.33	0.535	**0.793**

'Structural Model Analysis' and 'Testing of Hypotheses'

AMOS is used for the investigation of the 'Structural Model' and 'hypotheses testing' after the accuracy of the 'Measurement Model' has been verified. The 'Squared Multiple Correlation' is 0.48 for Purchase Intention, this shows that 48% variance in Purchase Intention is accounted by the four dimensions of Travel Website

Quality – Fulfilment, Interface Design, Reliability and Incentives. It should be noted that even if the 'Squared Multiple Correlation' value is low, like in behavioural science prediction models, it is absolutely appropriate to employ this structural model; as often, 'R-squared values' are less than 50%. The logical argument is that people are more difficult to predict than physical systems (Frost, 2009). It is also stated that significant conclusions can be drawn even in cases when the R-squared value is low and the predictors are statistically significant. All the four factors here are found to be statistically significant predictors. The results are presented in Table 5. The influence of Fulfilment on Purchase Intention is positive and significant (b= 0.22, t = 6.52, p < 0.05). The influence of Interface on Purchase Intention is also positive and significant (b= 0.71, t = 8.83, p < 0.05). Similar findings are observed for the other two dimensions as well. Reliability as a construct is observed to be a significant predictor of Purchase Intention (b= 0.55, t = 4.85, p < 0.05) as well as Incentives (b= 0.28, t = 6.34, p < 0.05).

Table 5. 'Structural path relations' using AMOS

'Path Relations'	'Estimate'	'Standard Error'	'C.R'.	P
FULFILMENT -> PI	0.22	0.069	6.52	***
USER INTERFACE->PI	0.71	0.082	8.83	***
RELIABILITY -> PI	0.55	0.196	4.85	***
INCENTIVES ->PI	0.28	0.096	6.34	***

The overview of model fitting criteria is shown in Table 6. All the values are observed to be between acceptable levels. Fit matrices demonstrate how well the model fits the data. ('CMIN/DF' = 3.56, 'GFI'=0.91, 'CFI'=0.95, 'TLI'=0.94, 'RMSEA' = 0.042, 'SRMR'= 0.06). The entire model is depicted in Figure-1. Thus, we can conclude that the study supports the hypothesis H1 which states that Purchase intentions for travel-related products from travel websites are largely influenced by the quality dimensions of the travel website.

Table 6. 'Model fit indices' using AMOS

Fit indices	Acceptable fit	Value obtained using AMOS
'CMIN/DF' ($\chi 2$ /df)	2-5	943.4/265=3.56, p<0.000
'Goodness-Of-Fit Index' (GFI)	"Value >0.95 good fit; value 0.90-0.95 adequate fit"	0.91
'Comparative Fit Index' (CFI)	"Value >0.95 good fit; value 0.90-0.95 adequate fit"	.958
'Tucker Lewis Index' (TLI)	"Value >0.95 good fit; value 0.90-0.95 adequate fit"	.949
Approximation Residual ('RMSEA')	"Value<0.05 goodfit; value 0.08-0.05 adequate fit"	.042
'SRMR';	<0.08	0.06

Figure 1. Full structural model using AMOS (Researcher's analysis)

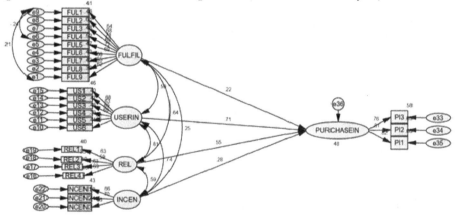

IPA MATRIX

In the second phase of the analysis, users of e-travel websites are asked to complete the scale that was established in the study in order to gauge how well they think the travel websites are performing. Based on their scores, Importance Performance Gap Analysis charts are prepared for five travel websites (MakeMyTrip, GoIbibo, Cleartrip, Yatra and Booking.com). The demographic profile of the data collected (455 responses) during the second phase of the study is presented in Table 7.

Table 7. Demographic profile of the data (Survey Phase 2)

CHARACTERISTICS		NO. OF RESPONDENTS	% OF RESPONDENTS
GENDER	MALE	246	54
	FEMALE	209	46
AGE (In Years)	<25	91	20
	25-55	318	70
	>55	46	10
EDUCATION	UNDER-GRADUATE	55	12
	GRADUATE	191	42
	POST-GRADUATE	209	46
INCOME RANGE/ANNUM (In Rs.)	<5 LACS	91	20
	5 LACS-10 LACS	200	44
	>10 LACS	164	36
AVG TRIPS/YEAR	2 OR LESS (Occasional Traveller)	250	55
	>2 (Regular Traveller)	205	45
TRAVEL WEBSITE MOST FREQUENTLY USED	MakeMyTrip	118	23
	GoIbibo	107	21
	Booking.com	106	20.5
	Yatra.com	98	19
	Cleartrip.com	60	11.5
	Other (e.g. Ixigo, Musafir, Via.com, etc.)	26	5

Case Study I- MakeMyTrip (No. of customers surveyed-118)

Table 8. Mean importance performance scores of MakeMyTrip

DIMENSIONS	Mean Imp	Mean Perf
INTERFACE	4.4	3.90
RELIABILITY	2.45	2.45
FULFILMENT	3.30	1.30
INCENTIVES	1.30	3.0

These numbers are plotted on the IPA grid using MS EXCEL. (Refer Fig- 2)

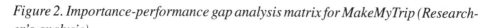

Figure 2. Importance-performance gap analysis matrix for MakeMyTrip (Research-er's analysis)

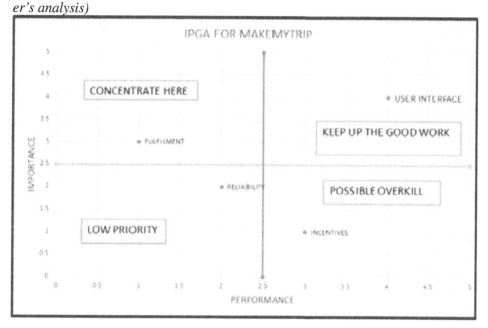

The IPA matrix for MakeMyTrip shows the areas that should be prioritised in contrast to the ones that are performing remarkably well. The firm clearly needs to concentrate on the Fulfilment dimension which comprises of items like customer responsiveness and information accuracy. The users gave the highest rating for the Interface dimension which they found interesting and interactive. The Reliability dimension scores low on both Performance as well as Importance factors while Incentives are one area where the firm is going for overkill with too many unnecessary deals and offers.

Case Study II- Golbibo (Number of customers surveyed-107)

Table 9. Mean importance performance scores of Golbibo users

DIMENSIONS	Mean Imp	Mean Perf
USER INTERFACE	4.40	4.00
RELIABILITY	2.45	2.45
FULFILMENT	3.30	1.30
INCENTIVES	1.30	3.30

These numbers are plotted on the IPA grid using MS EXCEL. (Refer Figure 3)

Figure 3. Importance-performance gap analysis matrix for GoIbibo (Researcher's analysis)

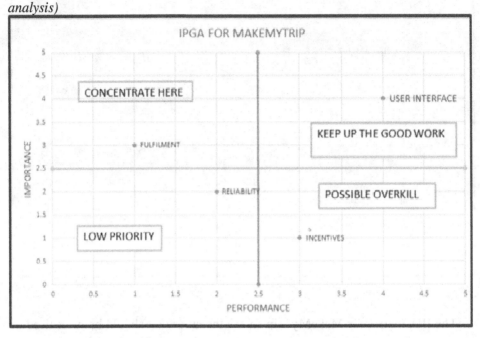

The IPA matrix for GoIbibo is pretty similar to that of MakeMyTrip. This is not surprising as the company is a wholly owned subsidiary of MakeMyTrip Limited which owns 100 percent stake in GoIbibo. The users gave the highest rating for the User Interface and Interactivity dimension which is comparatively the best among all the websites studied. GoIbibo app has a Community forum where travellers can easily interact with fellow travellers for any query. However, the company can work on the Fulfilment dimension which comprises Information Accuracy. The company focuses too much on incentives to capture the market which sometimes confuses potential buyers.

Case study -III Yatra.com (No. of customers surveyed – 98)

Table 10. Mean importance performance scores of Yatra.com

DIMENSIONS	Mean Imp	Mean Perf
INTERFACE	4.4	3.90
RELIABILITY	2.45	2.45
FULFILMENT	3.30	1.30
INCENTIVES	1.30	3.0

Figure 4 presents the IPA matrix for Yatra.com.

Figure 4. Importance-performance gap analysis matrix for Yatra.com (Researcher's Analysis)

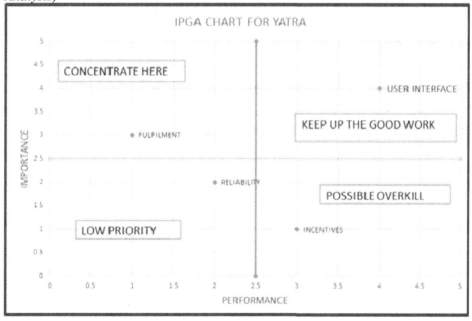

The IPA Chart for Yatra is similar to that of MakeMyTrip. The company needs to work on the Fulfilment dimension especially in areas related to payment security, information accuracy and responsiveness to customers. The customers of Yatra are happy with the website Interface which they reported were fun, interesting, and easy to understand and have several customisable features. Factors like having a dedicated

69

FAQ page, providing price-comparison functions and showing a running total of purchases scored low on both Importance as well as Performance criteria, while a common problem is seen again in the Incentives dimension where respondents felt that the company is focusing too much on unnecessary discounts and deals.

Case study IV - Booking.com (No. of customers surveyed – 106)

Table 11. Mean importance performance scores of Booking.com

DIMENSIONS	Mean Imp	Mean Perf
INTERFACE	4.4	3.90
RELIABILITY	2.45	4.30
FULFILMENT	3.30	2.10
INCENTIVES	1.30	1.0

Figure 5 presents the IPA matrix for Booking.com.

Figure 5. Importance-performance gap analysis matrix for Booking.com (Researcher's Analysis)

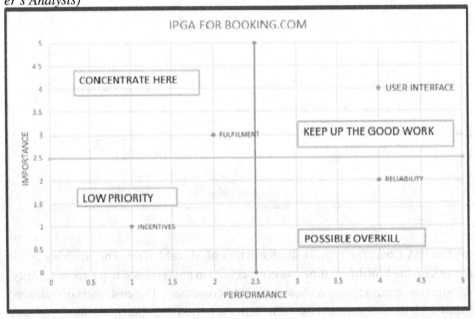

It was observed that Booking.com's IPA Chart was distinct from the others. Here, the website must improve on the Fulfilment dimension, particularly in terms of payment security, information accuracy, and customer responsiveness. Having a dedicated FAQ page, providing price-comparison functions, and displaying a running total of purchases are examples of areas where the company is placing too much emphasis. Customers of Booking.com are pleased with the website's Interface, which they deemed to be engaging, interesting, simple to comprehend, and equipped with a number of configurable features, however respondents rated the Incentives component poorly.

Case study V - Cleartrip (Number of customers surveyed – 60)

Table 12. Mean importance performance scores of Cleartrip users

DIMENSIONS	Mean Imp	Mean Perf
INTERFACE	4.4	1.3
RELIABILITY	2.45	2.3
FULFILMENT	3.3	2.45
INCENTIVES	1.30	3.0

These figures are plotted on the IPA grid using MS EXCEL. (Refer Figure 6)

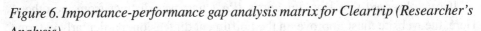

Figure 6. Importance-performance gap analysis matrix for Cleartrip (Researcher's Analysis)

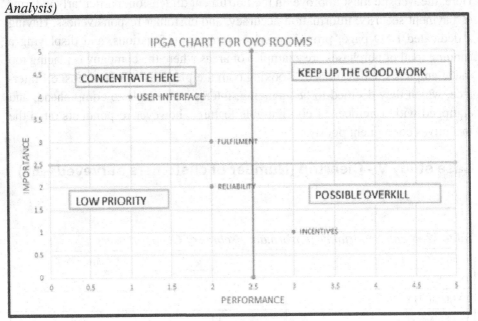

The IPA matrix for Cleartrip illustrates the areas that should be prioritised vs those that are working well. The firm clearly needs to concentrate on both Fulfilment as well as User Interface dimension which comprises items like customer responsiveness, information accuracy and website design. The Reliability dimension also scores poorly on both the Performance and Importance elements, while Incentives is an area where again the company is overcompensating with excessive deals and incentives.

DISCUSSION

A growing percentage of travellers are planning their trips online (including tickets, hotel reservations, travel insurance, and other services). As a result, the number of services offered by India's e-Travel portals have increased. These portals are developing into "one-stop shops" for all of a traveller's needs rather than being distinct entities.

The findings from the study can be taken as an important frame of reference by online travel agents who could identify quality-of-site attributes that might help them in developing appropriate business strategies and sustain their competitive position.

The study here proposed a scale based on prior literature review and the structural model developed using AMOS showed good model fit indices and significant relationships between the 'exogenous' and 'endogenous variables'. The Interface dimension, which includes website design, customisable features, providing a platform to share personal experiences, a chat box option, and providing individual and personalised attention to users, has been identified as the most influential factor affecting online travel purchase intention. It is discovered that the second most crucial element is the 'Reliability' dimension comprising of factors like showing confirmation of items and running total of purchases, having a dedicated FAQ page and providing price comparison functions. The third significant dimension is found to be 'Incentives' comprising of items like membership bonus, special offers, instalment payments, etc. 'Fulfilment' comprising of factors like security of payment, information accuracy and reliability and customer responsiveness is observed to be the fourth significant dimension.

RECOMMENDATION

The following specific recommendations are suggested for the companies studied in this research. For MakeMyTrip, the firm clearly needs to concentrate on the Fulfilment dimension which comprises items like Customer Responsiveness and Information Accuracy. Online clients want their questions and concerns to be answered and handled fast; therefore responsiveness is a service trait that gets a lot of attention. The company over performs on Incentives, offering far too many pointless promotions and incentives. GoIbibo needs to focus on Information Accuracy as several customers conveyed that many times the information portrayed on the website does not match the real picture. The Interactivity feature present on the GoIbibo App which allows potential travellers to communicate with fellow travellers has been highly appreciated by the traveller communities, however most of the Incentives provided by the company are targeted towards Frequent travellers and not towards Occasional Travellers. For Booking.com, the company is observed to be putting too much attention in some areas, such as having a separate FAQ page, offering price-comparison features, and showing a running tally of transactions. But the company has to work on the Incentives dimension, which is almost non-existent. The Incentives dimension should include elements like instalment payments, exclusive offers for credit card customers, discounts, and bargains. Yatra needs to improve in the areas of Payment Security, Information Correctness and Customer Responsiveness. Customers of Yatra are pleased with the Website Interface, which they described as having a variety of customizable features and being entertaining, fascinating, and simple to use. For Cleartrip, the company must explicitly focus on both the Fulfilment as well as the User Interface dimensions, which include factors like Customer Responsiveness, Information Correctness and Website Design. The business like several others overcompensates in the area of Incentives. Therefore, Online Travel Agents should constantly monitor and re-examine their sites to check whether any updation is required or whether any feature is lacking.

CONCLUSION

This study contributes to the expanding corpus of research on the standard of online tourist services. It outlines the defining features of e-travel service quality and provides appropriate metrics for evaluating each aspect. The indicators serve as a reliable and credible measuring tool. E-travel service companies may use a scale similar to this as a management tool to assess the effectiveness of their online services and implement pertinent procedures meant to raise the calibre of their offerings. The study's findings are applicable to marketing managers and practitioners who build strategic plans and implement solutions to increase tourist online shopping through B2C e-commerce and sustain in this highly competitive world.

LIMITATIONS AND FUTURE SCOPE OF THE STUDY

The current research is an initial attempt to obtain a better knowledge of online purchasing decisions from e-travel sites and the elements that impact them. The study's findings should be interpreted in context of its limitations, some of which can be utilised to drive future research.

First, in order to boost statistical power and more firmly demonstrate the robustness of the findings examined in this study—particularly with regard to enhancing the predictive usefulness of the model—further research is required with a larger sample size.

Second, the e-service quality elements for evaluating travel website quality are selected after a thorough analysis of literature in the relevant area. Despite the fact that multiple studies' findings in the fields of computer technology, consumption patterns or consumer behaviour, psychology, and marketing serve as the foundation for the model, there may always be unaddressed factors that influence customers' online purchase intentions. If alternate items or scales are used, the findings could be different. Other elements that may influence buying decisions include trust, product differentiation, brand reputation, hotel laws, etc., which might all be researched in the future. Since the goal of this study is to look at how potential travellers choose to book trips online, future research may also look into the relationship between risk and purchase decisions.

Notwithstanding the aforementioned drawbacks, the main research provides valuable understanding of how online travel agencies should construct their websites according to these specific standards to influence visitor recommendations, purchase intents, and industry sustainability.

REFERENCES

Bagozzi, R. P., & Yi, Y. (1988). On the evaluation of structural equation models. *Journal of the Academy of Marketing Science*, 16(1), 74–94. DOI: 10.1007/BF02723327

Boley, B. B., McGehee, N. G., & Hammett, A. T. (2017). Importance-performance analysis (IPA) of sustainable tourism initiatives: The resident perspective. *Tourism Management*, 58, 66–77. DOI: 10.1016/j.tourman.2016.10.002

Chen, C. F., & Kao, Y. L. (2010). Relationships between process quality, outcome quality, satisfaction, and behavioural intentions for online travel agencies - evidence from Taiwan. *Service Industries Journal*, 30(12), 2081–2092. DOI: 10.1080/02642060903191108

Chiou, W. C., Lin, C. C., & Perng, C. (2011). A strategic website evaluation of online travel agencies. *Tourism Management*, 32(6), 1463–1473. DOI: 10.1016/j.tourman.2010.12.007

Dhingra, S., Gupta, S., & Bhatt, R. (2022). Comparison of e-service quality of Indian e- commerce websites. *International Journal of Indian Culture and Business Management*, 26(3), 407–426. DOI: 10.1504/IJICBM.2022.124595

Elci, A., Abubakar, A. M., Ilkan, M., Kolawole, E. K., & Lasisi, T. T. (2017). The Impact of Travel 2.0 on Travelers Booking and Reservation Behaviors. *Business Perspectives and Research*, 5(2), 124–136. DOI: 10.1177/2278533717692909

Fahrurrozi, M. (2022). Evaluation of Educational Service Quality of Vocational High School (VHS) Based on Importance Performance Analysis (IPA) Quadrant. *Eurasian Journal of Educational Research*, 97(97), 27–42.

Fornell, C., & Larcker, D. F. (1981). Evaluating structural equation models with unobservable variables and measurement error. *JMR, Journal of Marketing Research*, 18(1), 39–50. DOI: 10.1177/002224378101800104

Frost, J. (2019). "Regression Analysis: An Intuitive Guide". e-book. https://statisticsbyjim.com/regression/

Hair, J. F., Ringle, C. M., & Sarstedt, M. (2011). PLS-SEM: Indeed a silver bullet. *Journal of Marketing Theory and Practice*, 19(2), 139–152. DOI: 10.2753/MTP1069-6679190202

Ho, C. I., & Lee, Y. L. (2007). The development of an e-travel service quality scale. *Tourism Management*, 28(6), 1434–1449. DOI: 10.1016/j.tourman.2006.12.002

Hoelter, J. W. (1983). The analysis of covariance structures: Goodness of fit indices. *Sociological Methods & Research*, 11(3), 325–344. DOI: 10.1177/0049124183011003003

Hsu, C. L., Chang, K. C., & Chen, M. C. (2012). The impact of website quality on customer satisfaction and purchase intention: Perceived playfulness and perceived flow as mediators. *Information Systems and e-Business Management*, 10(4), 549–570. DOI: 10.1007/s10257-011-0181-5

Hu, L., & Bentler, P. M. (1999). Cutoff criteria for fit indexes in covariance structure analysis: Conventional criteria versus new alternatives. *Structural Equation Modeling*, 6(1), 1–55. DOI: 10.1080/10705519909540118

Intelligence, M. (2023). *India Online Travel Market Size & Share Analysis - Growth Trends & Forecasts (2024 - 2029)*https://www.mordorintelligence.com/industry-reports/online-travel-market-in-india

Jou, R. C., & Day, Y. J. (2021). Application of revised importance–performance analysis to investigate critical service quality of hotel online booking. *Sustainability (Basel)*, 13(4), 2043. DOI: 10.3390/su13042043

Kim, D. J., Kim, W. G., & Han, J. S. (2007). A perceptual mapping of online travel agencies and preference attributes. *Tourism Management*, 28(2), 591–603. DOI: 10.1016/j.tourman.2006.04.022

Kumra, P., & Singh, M. (2018). Factors Influencing E-Service Quality in Indian Tourism Industry. *Research World*, 9(1), 99–110.

Lai, I. K. W., & Hitchcock, M. (2015). Importance–performance analysis in tourism: A framework for researchers. *Tourism Management*, 48, 242–267. DOI: 10.1016/j.tourman.2014.11.008

Li, Y. (2018). A Study on E-service Quality Dimensions for Online Travel Agencies. In *MATEC Web of Conferences* (Vol. 228, p. 05011). EDP Sciences. DOI: 10.1051/matecconf/201822805011

Lin, C.-T. (2010). Examining e-travel sites: An empirical study in Taiwan. *Online Information Review*, 34(2), 205–228. DOI: 10.1108/14684521011036954

Martilla, J. A., & James, J. C. (1977). Importance-performance analysis. *Journal of Marketing*, 10(1), 13–22.

Mohammed, M. E., Wafik, G. M., Jalil, S. G. A., & El Hassan, Y. A. (2016). The Effects of E-Service Quality Dimensions on Tourist's e-Satisfaction. *International Journal of Hospitality and Tourism Systems*, 9(1).

Muzakir, M., Bachri, S., Adam, R., & Wahyuningsih, W. (2021). The analysis of forming dimensions of e-service quality for online travel services. *International Journal of Data and Network Science*, 5(3), 239–244. DOI: 10.5267/j.ijdns.2021.6.010

Park, Y. A., & Gretzel, U. (2007). Success factors for destination marketing web sites: A qualitative meta-analysis. *Journal of Travel Research*, 46(1), 46–63. DOI: 10.1177/0047287507302381

Pham, L., Limbu, Y. B., Bui, T. K., Nguyen, H. T., & Pham, H. T. (2019). Does e-learning service quality influence e-learning student satisfaction and loyalty? Evidence from Vietnam. *International Journal of Educational Technology in Higher Education*, 16(1), 1–26. DOI: 10.1186/s41239-019-0136-3

Puspitasari, N. B., Purwaningsih, R., Fadlia, N., & Rosyada, Z. F. (2021). Driving Factors of the Intention to Purchase Travel Products through Online Travel Agent (OTA). In *Proceedings of the International Conference on Industrial Engineering and Operations Management* (pp. 1729-1731). DOI: 10.46254/SA02.20210641

Ramirez-Hurtado, J. M. (2017). The use of importance-performance analysis to measure the satisfaction of travel agency franchisees. *RAE*, 57(1), 51–64. DOI: 10.1590/s0034-759020170105

Saggaf, M. S., Aras, M., Akib, H., Salam, R., Baharuddin, A., & Kasmita, M. (2018). *The Quality Analysis of Academic Services Based on Importance Performance Analysis*. IPA.

Statista. (2023). *Online travel market size in India in financial year 2020, with an estimate for 2025, (in billion U.S. dollars)*https://www.statista.com/statistics/1344430/india-online-travel-market-size-by-type/

Tabachnick, B. G., Fidell, L. S., & Ullman, J. B. (2007). *Using multivariate statistics* (Vol. 5, pp. 481-498). Boston, MA: pearson.

Taryadi, A. R., & Miftahuddin, M. A. (2021). The Role of Mediation Electronic Word of Mouth (E-wom) in Relationship Quality of Services and Tourism Products against Visiting Decisions. *Journal of Economics Research and Social Sciences*, 5(1), 64–76. DOI: 10.18196/jerss.v5i1.10948

Wen, I. (2012). An empirical study of an online travel purchase intention model. *Journal of Travel & Tourism Marketing*, 29(1), 18–39. DOI: 10.1080/10548408.2012.638558

Wong, E., Rasoolimanesh, S. M., & Sharif, S. P. (2020). Using online travel agent platforms to determine factors influencing hotel guest satisfaction. *Journal of Hospitality and Tourism Technology*, 11(3), 425–445. DOI: 10.1108/JHTT-07-2019-0099

Wong, M. S., Hideki, N., & George, P. (2011). The use of importance-performance analysis (IPA) in evaluating Japan's e-government services. *Journal of Theoretical and Applied Electronic Commerce Research*, 6(2), 17–30. DOI: 10.4067/S0718-18762011000200003

APPENDIX I

Questionnaire for Survey (Phase 1)

NOTE:-1=Extremely Unimportant, 2=Unimportant, 3=Neutral, 4= Important, 5=Extremely Important

Table 13.

PART-A (E-Travel Website Service Quality)	1	2	3	4	5
1. The site should provide various payment options. (ETWSQ_1)					
2. The site should provide secure payment systems.(ETWSQ_2)					
3. The site should provide a confirmation of items ordered. (ETWSQ_3)					
4. The site should provide a running total of purchases as the order progresses. (ETWSQ_4)					
5. It should be easy to get anywhere on the online travel agent's website. (ETWSQ_5)					
6. One should not get lost on the online travel agent's website. (ETWSQ_6)					
7. The online travel agent should provide a site map. (For example- Home page, Orders, FAQ etc.) (ETWSQ_7)					
8. The online travel agent's website design should be innovative. (ETWSQ_8)					
9. One should be able to see the graphics clearly on the online travel agent's website. (ETWSQ_9)					
10. Prices should be shown with the items on the screen. (ETWSQ_10)					
11. The online travel agent should provide accurate information. (ETWSQ_11)					
12. The online travel agent should update information immediately. (ETWSQ_12)					
13. The online travel agent should provide FAQ information. (ETWSQ_13)					
14. The Online travel agent should respond to users' enquiries promptly. (ETWSQ_14)					
15. The online travel agent should provide help when problems are encountered. (ETWSQ_15)					
16. The customers should be informed immediately when transactions are completed. (ETWSQ_16)					
17. The Online travel agent should provide a message channel for users' complaints. (ETWSQ_17)					
18. Products/Services should be delivered by the time promised. (ETWSQ_18)					
19. Policies for cancelling orders laid out on the site should be customer-friendly. (ETWSQ_19)					
20. The site has features personalised to users. (ETWSQ_20)					
21. The website develops a platform for users to share travel experiences. (ETWSQ_21)					
22. The website makes it easy for users to turn to chat rooms for ease of information. (ETWSQ_22)					
23. Understands specific needs and gives personal attention. (ETWSQ_23)					
24. Easy to track the delivery of products/services purchased. (ETWSQ_24)					
25. The website provides price comparison function. (ETWSQ_25)					
26. The website provides membership bonus collection for free gift. (ETWSQ_26)					

continued on following page

Table 13. Continued

PART-A (E-Travel Website Service Quality)	1	2	3	4	5
27. The website provides special offers. (ETWSQ_27)					
28. The website provides special offers exclusively for credit card holders. (ETWSQ_28)					
29. The travel purchase can be paid by instalments using credit card. (ETWSQ_29)					

Table 14.

(PART B) (Travel Purchase Intention)	1	2	3	4	5
30. If I had to do it over again, I would make the next purchase again from online mode (using sites like Booking.com, MakeMyTrip, Yatra etc).(TPI_1)					
31. I feel buying travel products online has more benefits. (TPI_2)					
32. The choice to purchase from an online medium is a wise one. (TPI_3)					

Table 15.

PART C: DEMOGRAPHIC DETAILS			
GENDER	MALE		FEMALE
AGE	<25	25-55	>55
LEVEL OF EDUCATION	UNDER-GRADUATE	GRADUATE	POST GRADUATE
INCOME RANGE/ANNUM	<5 LACS	5 LACS-10 LACS	>10 LACS
AVERAGE TRIPS / YEAR	2 OR LESS	>2	

Questionnaire for Survey (Phase 2)

Survey on Performance Analysis

Importance (1-Extremely Unimportant to 4-Extremely Important)
Performance (1-Weakest to 4-Strongest)

Table 16.

Questions	IMPORTANCE				PERFORMANCE			
	1	2	3	4	1	2	3	4
The OTA website provides secure payment systems.								
Prices are shown with the items on the screen.								
The OTA website provides accurate information.								
The OTA website updates information immediately.								
The OTA website responds to users' enquiries promptly.								
The OTA website provides help when problems are encountered.								
The customers are informed immediately when transactions are completed.								
Products/Services are delivered by the time promised.								
Policies for cancelling orders laid out on the website are customer-friendly.								
The OTA website design is innovative.								
One is able to see the graphics clearly on the OTA website.								
The OTA website has features personalised to users.								
The website has a platform for users to share travel experiences.								
The website makes it easy for users to turn to chat rooms for ease of information.								
Understands specific needs and gives personal attention.								
The website provides a confirmation of items ordered.								
The website provides a running total of purchases as the order progresses.								
The OTA website should provide a site map. (For example- Home page, Orders, FAQ etc.)								
The website provides price comparison function.								
The website provides membership bonus collection for free gift.								
The website provides special offers exclusively for credit card holders.								
The travel purchase can be paid by instalments using credit card.								

Suggestions, if any? _____

Table 17.

DEMOGRAPHIC DETAILS						
GENDER	**MALE**			**FEMALE**		
AGE	**<25**		**25-55**		**>55**	
LEVEL OF EDUCATION	**UNDER-GRADUATE**		**GRADUATE**		**POST GRADUATE**	
INCOME RANGE/ ANNUM	**<5 LACS**		**5 LACS-10 LACS**		**>10 LACS**	
AVERAGE TRIPS / YEAR	**2 OR LESS**			**>2**		
ONLINE TRAVEL AGGREGATOR (OTA) WEBSITE MOST FREQUENTLY USED (Choose any 1)	MakeMyTrip	Cleartrip	Booking.com	Ibibo	Yatra	Any other (Mention)

Chapter 4
Assessment of Social Media Presence and its Effectiveness to Achieve Business Goals in NBFCs

Gurleen Kaur
https://orcid.org/0009-0008-8238-5130
Xavier Institute of Social Service, India

Amar Eron Tigga
Xavier Institute of Social Service, India

ABSTRACT

The non-banking financial companies (NBFCs) sector in India has undergone a significant transformation and are playing a critical role for the development of core infrastructure and financing economically weaker sections. Social media plays a multifaceted role in this industry in building trust, shaping brand identity, educating stakeholders and connecting with broader audiences through media channels. This study delves into how social media presence in five major NBFCs of India differs. The data is collected from the company's official social media handles and social media monitoring tools. Employing a mixed-methods approach, the research combines quantitative data analysis of social media engagement with qualitative insights gleaned from social media coverage themes. The paper analyses the wide set of strategies to find the competitive strategies which would be helpful for competitive advantage to the companies. Strategies focused on content, engagement and platform specific strategies could be used to gain a competitive edge in the non-banking financial sector.

DOI: 10.4018/979-8-3693-5563-3.ch004

INTRODUCTION

The financial services sector is characterized by intense competition and a dynamic landscape that demands strategic communication and a robust social media presence. In this context, understanding how financial institutions are portrayed in social media compared to their competitors becomes crucial. For financial organizations, social media presence is multifaceted tool that not only contributes to the external perception of an organization but also plays a critical role in internal communication, stakeholder management, and overall business success. Strategic management of social media presence is essential for organizations looking to thrive in today's competitive and information-centric environment.

Social media presence is a strategic tool for financial organizations. It helps to build and maintain trust, communicate effectively with stakeholders, and position themselves competitively in a dynamic industry. It serves as a powerful means to shape public perception and contribute to the overall success of the organization.

In today's dynamic financial landscape, navigating the social media landscape strategically has become vital for any organization's success. A well-managed social media presence not only bolsters trust and credibility by securing positive coverage in reputable outlets, but also fosters regulatory compliance by mitigating the impact of negative press. Effective social media relations serve as a crucial tool for crisis management, enabling organizations to control the narrative during challenging times and minimize reputational damage.

Beyond image management, a vibrant social media presence empowers financial institutions to differentiate themselves through strategic brand positioning. By showcasing themselves as reliable, transparent, and customer-centric entities, they can attract a wider audience and gain a competitive edge.

Additionally, social media serves as a valuable platform for educating stakeholders. Financial organizations can leverage media channels to demystify complex concepts, provide market insights, and foster financial literacy among clients and investors. Notably, its strong presence also grants access to valuable market insights, keeping organizations abreast of industry trends, regulatory changes, and evolving consumer preferences. Finally, in the digital age, engaging with audiences online through social media has become paramount. By actively participating in social media, financial institutions can connect with broader audiences and adapt to ever-changing communication trends to enhance customer engagement, brand building and educating stakeholders leading to improved business growth.

The assessment of social media presence in non-banking financial companies (NBFCs) involves a multi-faceted approach, including a comparative analysis of the social media strategies of five major NBFCs. This analysis highlights the varying degrees of engagement, content quality, and audience reach among these companies, providing insights into the effectiveness of different social media channels in driving company growth. It also identifies areas of improvement in the current social media presence, such as a strategic approach focused on **content, engagement, and platform-specific nuances**. By addressing these improvement areas, companies can optimize their social media strategies to enhance customer engagement and foster sustained growth.

Literature review

Social media is not just about apps and websites; it's a whole new way to approach marketing in today's digital world. Platforms like Instagram, Facebook and LinkedIn provide a space for a company's brand to connect with its target audience on a deeper level, fostering engagement and growth. The reach of social media is undeniable. Take India, for example. According to Forbes, in early 2023, nearly 40% of the entire population (over 398 million people aged 18 and over) were active users on major social media platforms. This highlights the immense potential of social media marketing for brands looking to connect with a vast and engaged audience (Forbes, Social Media Statistics, 2024).

Studies point to the expanding role of social media in India, where it has transcended its original function of social connection. It has emerged as a society-shaping tool including the economic aspects. The influence of social media remains wide ranging from small businesses to large multinational corporations (Mehta, 2023).

Social networking platforms serve as a cost-effective and user-friendly solution for small and medium enterprises (SMEs) to bridge the gap between themselves and their target audience, be it local or global. This accessibility is particularly advantageous for SMEs, which often face challenges in adopting new technologies due to resource constraints (Vidhyalakshmi and Kumar, 2016).

Social networking sites have transcended their role as mere communication channels, evolving into crucial elements for businesses and individuals to establish their online presence. These platforms now facilitate crucial connections, acting as a matchmaking tool for businesses and potential customers, as well as individuals seeking professional or personal connections (Tiwari, Lane, & Alam, 2019).

Social media empowers individuals with unfettered access to a vast information stream, enriching their knowledge base. Organizations can leverage this phenomenon for knowledge management by strategically harnessing the collective intelligence disseminated on these platforms (Mittal and Kumar, 2019).

According to Siddiqui and Singh (2016), social media acts as a wellspring of knowledge for society through campaigns, advertisements, informative content, and promotions. This keeps users informed about current events and fosters connections by enabling them to share various forms of media, including text, images, audio, and video.

Social media empowers companies to conduct competitive analysis, gleaning valuable insights into their competitors' strategies. Additionally, it helps market research and brand reputation management, enabling companies to understand their target audience and gauge public perception (Kumar and Pradhan, 2016).

Social media platforms have become a critical space for both happy and unhappy customers to share their experiences. Here, customers can voice their opinions and expect prompt responses to their concerns. This real-time feedback loop is invaluable for market researchers. Social media goes beyond just positive recommendations. Unhappy customers can also warn others about potential pitfalls, influencing individual's buying decisions. This social interaction fosters trust and purchase intent among consumers. Essentially, social networks empower customers to become brand advocates, sharing their positive or negative experiences with purchased products, and shaping overall brand perception (Parson, 2013).

Few actions should be kept in mind while using social media for posting content for companies. Ko et al. (2022) found that brand posts with emojis on Instagram elicited more likes (increased by 72%) and comments (increased by 70%) than those without emojis. Agresta and Bonin Bough (2011) emphasize the importance of quality over quantity when it comes to content on the Facebook. They recommend against overwhelming followers with excessive content, which can be perceived as spam and lead to annoyance. Instead, they recommend focusing on creating valuable and engaging content that sparks conversation and encourages interaction among your audience. (Agresta and Bonin Bough, 2011).

Berger and Messerschmidt (2009) highlight a growing trend: consumers are increasingly distrustful of traditional advertising and commercial sources of information. Instead, they turn to online communities to find product reviews and recommendations written by other consumers. These online communities, often consisting of like-minded individuals, provide a valuable platform for consumers to seek trustworthy product information and directly engage with each other to ask questions and share experiences.

Several studies have examined the impact of social media marketing on brand loyalty in the Indian financial industry. One such study by Aggarwal and Singh (2016) found that social media marketing has a significant positive impact on brand loyalty in the Indian financial industry. The study revealed that social media marketing activities such as creating brand pages, sharing informative content, and engaging with customers positively influence brand loyalty. The study also found that customers who engage with banks on social media platforms are more likely to be loyal to the financial company and continue to use their products and services.

The rise of social media has fundamentally transformed the way customers and organizations collaborate, creating a new era of interconnectedness across the globe (Choudhury & Harrigan, 2014; Khadim, Hanan, Arshad & Saleem, 2018). According to Kietzmann, Hermkens, McCarthy, and Silvestre (2011), social media has been depicted as far as its usefulness, including identity, presence, sharing, connections, gatherings, discussions, and reputation. While, in practice, social media refers to those platforms through which individuals convey.

Firms that use social media more often and at a high level adapt to the environment of social media and are also able to achieve more information about the customers, thus increasing organizational performance (Tajudeen, Jaafar & Ainin, 2018; Wang & Kim, 2017). In addition to that organizations using social media can trust earlier than competitors by developing platforms for increasing organization performance in terms of sales growth, profitability, and increase in market share (Garcia-Morales, Martín-Rojas, & Lardón-López, 2018; Kumar & Reinartz, 2018).

According to Mike McGuirk (2021), businesses have been growing as consumers' use of social media platforms and their consumption of digital media has increased. Looking for new approaches to monitor, track, and analyse this online customer activity to support a wide range of business functions including customer assistance, marketing, and customer experience management.

Online Engagement

Online engagement serves as the pivotal agent facilitating the transformation of prospective clientele into patrons, patrons into devoted adherents, and devoted adherents into vocal proponents of a brand. Within the framework of online customer engagement, a plethora of manifestations exist, ranging from the mere act of favoring a Tweet to the elaborate creation of video content on platforms such as YouTube. Nonetheless, the underlying motivations compelling individuals to interact with brands exhibit a remarkable consistency across these diverse modalities. (DuffAgency, n.d.)

Online engagement serves as the bridge between brands and their audiences, fostering deeper connections and building long-term relationships. It is not merely about attracting attention but about sustaining meaningful interactions that resonate with customers on a personal level. This engagement, whether through a simple like on a Tweet or the creation of a detailed YouTube video, cultivates a sense of loyalty and advocacy among consumers. By strategically leveraging online engagement, companies can transform casual observers into loyal customers and loyal customers into vocal brand advocates. This seamless connection between engagement and brand loyalty underscores the importance of selecting the right platforms for marketing efforts, as seen with Instagram, LinkedIn, Facebook, and Twitter(X), each offering unique advantages for different aspects of business growth.

Why Market on Instagram

Instagram presents a distinctive advantage over its counterparts in the realm of social media owing to its inherent emphasis on visual content. For businesses leveraging products with strong design attributes or services yielding visually discernible outcomes, Instagram emerges as the preeminent platform for content exhibition. Within this milieu, various forms of content such as video, imagery, and illustration find fitting resonance. Nevertheless, the efficacy of content dissemination hinges upon the strategic underpinning of marketing endeavors. Prudent delineation of a comprehensive strategy prior to immersion in a new social media platform, irrespective of its universal efficacy, serves to maintain alignment with organizational objectives and, crucially, audience preferences. (Hubspot, n.d.)

Why Market on LinkedIn

LinkedIn emerges as a formidable platform within the domain of financial services, as evidenced by empirical studies. Analytic Partners' research underscores its efficacy, revealing a staggering sevenfold increase in incremental customer sign-ups compared to traditional display media. Moreover, Nielsen's investigation underscores LinkedIn Ads' superior prowess in driving Brand Lift, positioning it as the premier choice for both business-to-business (B2B) and business-to-consumer (B2C) brands. Crucially, the platform fosters a perception of heightened professionalism, intelligence, quality, and respectability among audiences, as elucidated by Nielsen's findings. LinkedIn's pervasive global presence, with over 850 million members across 200 countries and territories, amplifies its reach and impact. Additionally, marketers benefit from unprecedented access to up to nine times more monthly touch points, particularly for engaged LinkedIn members leveraging the LinkedIn Audience Network. These collective insights substantiate LinkedIn's indispensable role in social media marketing strategies, particularly within the financial services sector. (Why you should be marketing on LinkedIn right now, 2023)

Why Market on Facebook

Meta's suite of apps, including Facebook, has facilitated over 200 million businesses in transitioning online, particularly during the COVID-19 pandemic. Notably, more than 70% of Facebook users engage with local business pages weekly, underscoring the platform's significance for local commerce. Messaging capabilities significantly enhance commerce, with individuals being 53% more inclined to shop from businesses they can message. Facebook Shops, catering to the burgeoning e-commerce sector, boasts over 1 million monthly global users, emphasizing its pivotal role in facilitating online retail. Marketers harness Facebook's extensive advertising reach, with the potential to engage over 2.2 billion users. Furthermore, the platform's advertising ecosystem exhibits a promising trajectory, with a notable 28% increase in ad impressions and a 9% decrease in average ad costs year-over-year. (Pilot, 2024)

Why Market on Twitter(X)

Direct messaging on Twitter fosters authentic connections by requiring mutual followings, ensuring conversations are meaningful and personalized. Utilizing tags facilitates engagement and content discovery, as tweets receive notifications and may appear in users' feeds based on network interactions. Twitter's chronological feed necessitates frequent posting, up to 15 times daily, to maintain relevance. Marketers leverage diverse content formats to entertain and educate followers, fostering engagement. Moreover, Twitter offers a platform for brands to cultivate their unique voice, whether authoritative or playful, contributing to brand identity development. (Marq.com, n.d.)

This literature review addresses the significant role of social media in modern marketing, particularly within the non-banking financial sector, where it has evolved from mere communication platforms to essential tools for business growth and customer engagement. Despite extensive research on the benefits and usage of social media platforms like Instagram, Facebook, LinkedIn, and Twitter, there is still a gap in understanding their specific impact on non-banking financial companies. While studies have explored social media's influence on brand loyalty and customer interaction in broader industries, there is limited analysis on how these platforms contribute to the competitive positioning and growth of NBFCs. This study is needed to fill this gap, offering insights into how NBFCs can use social media more effectively to enhance their market presence, engage with customers, and improve overall business performance and drive business growth.

METHODOLOGY

Research Methodology

The research methodology for this study employs a mixed-methods approach, combining quantitative data analysis with qualitative insights to provide a holistic understanding of the social media presence of NBFCs in India. The methodology is divided into several key components:

1. **Research Design**: This study employs a mixed-methods research design to analyze the social media activities of five major NBFCs. The research aims to understand the strategies employed by these companies, their effectiveness, and areas for improvement. The study is structured to provide both quantitative and qualitative insights, ensuring a comprehensive analysis of social media presence and its impact on business goals.

2. **Data Collection**: Secondary data is collected from the official social media handles of Bajaj Finserv, L&T Finance, Cholamandalam Finance, Shriram Finance, and Mahindra Finance. Social media monitoring tools, such as Keyhole, are used to track metrics like follower count, engagement rates, post reach, and the frequency of posts. The data collection process spans a specific period, ensuring a consistent and reliable dataset for analysis.

3. **Descriptive Analysis**: The descriptive analysis focuses on measuring and comparing the social media presence, reach, and visibility of the NBFCs across various platforms, including Instagram, LinkedIn, Facebook, and Twitter. Key performance indicators (KPIs) such as follower count, engagement rates, and post frequency are analyzed to provide a clear picture of each company's social media performance. Statistical tools and techniques are used to analyze the data, ensuring accuracy and reliability.

4. **Qualitative Analysis**: The qualitative analysis involves examining the content and themes of social media posts and user comments to gain insights into the sentiment and perception of the NBFCs. This analysis helps identify the key themes and patterns in social media conversations, providing a deeper understanding of how these companies are perceived by their audience. Thematic analysis is employed to categorize and interpret the qualitative data, ensuring a systematic and thorough examination.

5. **Data Analysis Tools**: Various data analysis tools and techniques are used to analyze the collected data. Social media monitoring tools like Keyhole provide real-time data and analytics, helping to track and measure social media performance. Statistical software is used to perform quantitative analysis, ensuring

accurate and reliable results. Thematic analysis software aids in the qualitative analysis, helping to categorize and interpret the data systematically.

6. **Comparative Analysis**: The study includes a comparative analysis of the social media strategies employed by the five NBFCs. This involves comparing their social media presence, engagement rates, content strategies, and overall effectiveness. The comparative analysis helps identify the strengths and weaknesses of each company's social media approach, providing valuable insights for strategic recommendations.

7. **Strategic Recommendations**: Based on the findings of the quantitative and qualitative analyses, strategic recommendations are developed to enhance the social media presence and effectiveness of the NBFCs. These recommendations focus on improving engagement rates, optimizing content strategies, and leveraging social media as a tool for competitive advantage. The recommendations are tailored to address the specific needs and goals of each NBFC, ensuring practical and actionable guidance.

Results

Insights on how on different social media channels, different companies differ in their strategy giving them the competitive advantage over other companies is listed below.

Figure 1. Follower count as key performance indicator: February 27, 2024

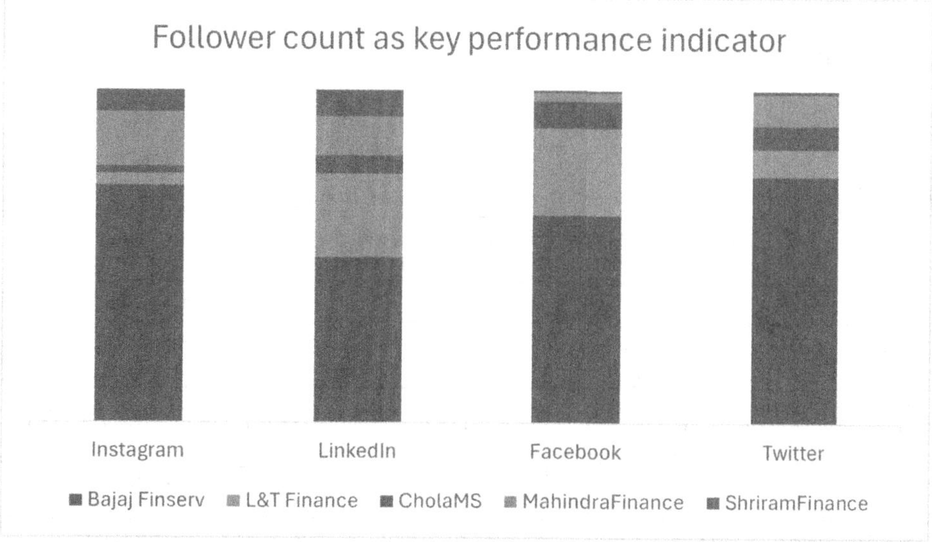

Follower count as key performance indicator

Instagram   LinkedIn   Facebook   Twitter

■ Bajaj Finserv   ■ L&T Finance   ■ CholaMS   ■ MahindraFinance   ■ ShriramFinance

Instagram Insights:

Figure 2. Frequency of Instagram posts and engagement rates (Keyhole for the period January 28- February 28, 2024)

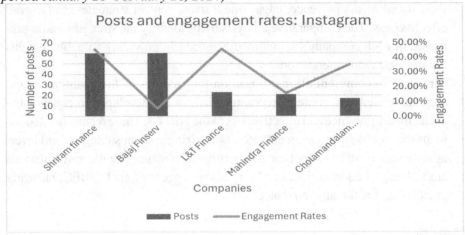

The top posts of the companies varied in their content strategy. Bajaj Finserv's top posts were focused on building healthy credit scores and its product (Bajajwaa-lidigitalFD), Mahindra Finance emphasized on its contests approach, Cholamanda-lam Finance focused on its CSR Strategy while Shriram Finance and L&T Finance focused on its product.

LinkedIn insights

Table 1. Snapshot of companies' performance on LinkedIn

Company	Followers	Articles	Events	Pop-up tab to visit website	Cover image
L&T Finance	503 K	☒	☒	☒	Planet App
Bajaj Finserv	995 K				"Savdhaanrahein, safe rahein" campaign
Cholamandalam Finance	110 K	☒	☒		Company's tagline "We fund it"
Mahindra Finance	235 K	☒	☒		"Money gyaan se Jeevan asaan" campaign
Shriram Finance	157 K	☒	☒		Company's tagline "Celebrating relationships"

(LinkedIn handles, dated 27 February 2024)

Facebook Insights

Table 2. Comparative analysis for their follower count on Facebook (dated February 27, 2024)

Company	Followers	Comment option
Bajaj Finserv	24 L	No
Mahindra Finance	10 L	Yes
Cholamandalam	310 K	Yes
Shriram finance	98 K	Yes
L&T Finance	24 K	Yes

Twitter insights

Figure 3. Frequency of Twitter posts and engagement rates (Keyhole for the period January 28- February 28, 2024)

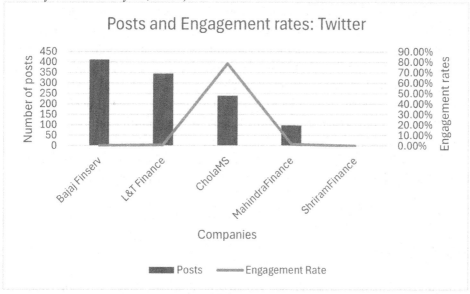

The top posts of the companies varied in their emphasis on content strategy. L&T Finance focused on its microfinance summit, Bajaj Finserv focused on its products with the hashtag #HarKadamAapkeSang, Mahindra Finance focused on its CSR campaigns and Cholamandalam Finance emphasised on its Chola MS App.

Discussion

For Instagram, Bajaj Finserv had the majority of followers followed by Mahindra Finance and Shriram Finance. Average engagement rates were highest for carousel followed by reels and images for L&T Finance during January 28- February 28, 2024, period.

For LinkedIn, Bajaj Finserv had the maximum followers (957 K) followed by Mahindra finance (177 K), Shriram Finance (104 K), Cholamandalam Finance(87 K) and L&T Finance. Bajaj Finserv had articles while all other companies lacked them in their LinkedIn posts. Headings were present in all companies (Bajaj Finserv, Cholamandalam finance, Shriram finance and Mahindra finance) except L&T finance. Tab to visit website was present in all companies (Bajaj Finserv, Cholamandalam finance, Shriram finance and Mahindra finance) except L&T finance. Bajaj Finserv had events posted while all other companies lacked them in their LinkedIn posts. For cover image, L&T Finance focused on its Planet App, Bajaj Finserv focused on its "SavadhaanRahein, SurakshitRahein" campaign, Mahindra Finance focused on "Money gyaan se Jeevan asan campaign", Shriram Finance focused on company's tagline: Celebrating relationships and Cholamandalam finance focused on "Company's tagline: We fund it".

For Facebook, BajajFinserv had the highest follower count (24 L), followed by Mahindra Finance (10 L), Cholamandalam Finance (310 K), Shriram Finance(98K) and L&T Finance (24 K). Bajaj Finserv had disabled comment option for its posts on Facebook whereas other competitors had the option enabled. Contests were being used by Mahindra Finance to attract an audience. Cholamandalam's CSR Activities were shown in the form of a grid which helped in clear depiction. Bajaj Finserv had a comprehensive cover image illustrating Bajaj Finserv's multiple service-providing channels (through SMS, Calls, Mobile apps, etc).

For Twitter, the follower count was maximum for Bajaj Finserv followed by Mahindra Finance and L&T Finance. The engagement rate by followers was the highest for Cholamandalam Finance.

CONCLUSION

In NBFCs, media presence plays a pivotal role for it to succeed. It helps them to build brand awareness, lead management, and competitive advantage.

The comparative analysis of the social media presence of five major companies in the NBFC Space has revealed some key insights. All companies have avenues to learn from each other in different domains of social media marketing.

Digital marketing includes an essential part of AIDA Model (Attention, Interest, Desire, Action) which helps in crafting a well-knit social media strategy. This research delved into the online presence of various non-banking financial companies (NBFCs) to identify key strategies for enhancing social media engagement. The analysis revealed crucial areas where NBFCs can optimize their online strategies to attract a wider audience and achieve their business goals.

Building a captivating social media presence is crucial for NBFCs in today's digital landscape. However, simply "being there" isn't enough. A strategic approach focused on **content, engagement, and platform-specific nuances** is key to unlocking the full potential of social media. The two important factors to be kept in mind are:

- **Functionality Factors -**

Know your audience: Conduct thorough research to understand your target demographics, their interests, and pain points. Tailor content, accordingly, focusing on topics relevant to their financial needs and aspirations.

Informative and engaging: Strike a balance between informative content that builds trust and engaging formats that captivate attention. Experiment with explainer videos, infographics, interactive quizzes, and user-generated content.

Regularity in posting: Analyse best posting times for each platform to maximize reach and engagement and use scheduling tools to ensure consistent posting even during busy periods.

- **Sharing factors:**

Call to action (CTA): Clearly tell your audience what you want them to do, whether it's visiting your website, subscribing to your newsletter, or engaging in a poll.

Social listening: Actively monitor mentions, comments, and messages to understand audience sentiment and respond promptly. Address concerns, answer questions, and show appreciation for positive interactions.

Platform-Specific Strategies

The "Platform-Specific Strategies" section serves to provide a focused approach to social media marketing by outlining tailored strategies for different platforms. Recognizing that each social media platform offers unique features and caters to distinct audiences, this section emphasizes the importance of adapting marketing tactics to align with the strengths and user behaviors of each platform. By detailing strategies specific to Facebook, Instagram, YouTube, Twitter, and LinkedIn, the section offers actionable insights for businesses to effectively engage their target audience, enhance brand visibility, and drive customer interaction. This tailored approach ensures that marketing efforts are not only comprehensive but also optimized for maximum impact across various social media channels, aligning with the broader goal of integrating social media into overall business strategies.

- **Facebook:** Create groups for specific financial topics or demographics to foster deeper community engagement. Utilize Facebook Live for webinars, Q&A sessions, or financial literacy workshops. Run targeted ads to reach relevant audiences based on demographics and interests.
- **Instagram:** Partner with relevant micro-influencers for authentic endorsements and wider reach. Utilize Instagram Stories for behind-the-scenes glimpses, educational tips, and product promotions. Leverage Reels and IGTV for engaging short-form video content.
- **YouTube:** Create valuable content like explainer videos, product demonstrations, and expert interviews. Collaborate with finance and lifestyle YouTubers for wider audience reach. Improve video titles, descriptions, and thumbnails for better search visibility.
- **Twitter:** Host Twitter chats and polls to encourage audience participation and generate discussions. Utilize Twitter hashtags strategically to join relevant conversations and increase discoverability. Pin important tweets like FAQs or promotional offers for easy access.
- **LinkedIn:** Showcase industry expertise by sharing thought leadership articles, research reports, and white papers. Participate in relevant LinkedIn groups and discussions to set up credibility and network with potential clients. Share employee stories and company culture to create a more humanized brand image.

By implementing these platform-specific strategies and focusing on content, engagement, and sharing factors, NBFCs can craft a social media presence that resonates with their target audience, builds brand loyalty, and ultimately drives business growth. Social media is a dynamic landscape, so continuous monitoring, adaptation, and a commitment to audience engagement are essential for long-term success.

Future Scope of Work

The future scope of work for the analysis of social media presence and its effectiveness as a strategy to achieve business goals in Non-Banking Financial Companies (NBFCs) includes the following areas:

1. **Expansion to Additional NBFCs**: Extending the research to include a larger number of NBFCs beyond the initial five companies studied. This will provide a more comprehensive understanding of industry-wide social media practices and strategies, allowing for broader insights and more robust conclusions.

2. **Longitudinal Studies**: Conducting longitudinal studies to track changes in social media strategies and their effectiveness over time. This will help identify trends, the impact of evolving social media platforms, and shifts in consumer behavior, providing a dynamic perspective on the role of social media in the NBFC sector.

3. **Integration of Emerging Social Media Platforms**: Analyzing the impact of emerging social media platforms such as TikTok, Snapchat, and new niche platforms that may gain popularity. This will help understand how NBFCs can leverage these platforms to reach younger and more diverse audiences.

4. **Advanced Analytics and AI Integration**: Utilizing advanced analytics and artificial intelligence (AI) tools to gain deeper insights into social media data. This includes sentiment analysis, predictive analytics, and machine learning models to forecast trends and consumer behavior, enhancing the strategic decision-making process.

5. **Customer Segmentation and Personalization**: Exploring more granular customer segmentation and personalization strategies based on social media data. This will help NBFCs tailor their content and engagement strategies to different customer segments, improving customer satisfaction and loyalty.

6. **Impact of Regulatory Changes**: Investigating the impact of regulatory changes on social media strategies in the financial sector. Understanding how compliance requirements affect social media practices will help NBFCs navigate regulatory challenges while maintaining effective communication with their audience.

7. **Cross-Channel Integration**: Studying the integration of social media strategies with other digital marketing channels such as email marketing, search engine optimization (SEO), and content marketing. This holistic approach will provide insights into how NBFCs can create cohesive and synergistic marketing campaigns.

8. **User-Generated Content and Community Building**: Exploring the role of user-generated content and community-building initiatives on social media. Understanding how these elements contribute to brand loyalty and customer engagement will help NBFCs foster stronger relationships with their audience.

9. **Crisis Management Strategies**: Developing and analyzing effective social media crisis management strategies. This will help NBFCs prepare for and respond to negative events or feedback, mitigating reputational damage and maintaining customer trust.

10. **Return on Investment (ROI) Analysis**: Conducting detailed ROI analysis of social media activities to measure their financial impact. This will provide NBFCs with a clearer understanding of the cost-effectiveness of their social media strategies and help justify investments in social media marketing.

11. **Cultural and Regional Differences**: Investigating how cultural and regional differences affect social media strategies and audience engagement. This will help NBFCs customize their social media approaches to different geographic markets, enhancing their global reach and effectiveness.

REFERENCES

Aggarwal, M., & Singh, H. (2016). Impact of social media marketing on brand loyalty in Indian banking industry. *Journal of Internet Banking and Commerce*, 21(3), 1–15.

Agresta, S. and Bonin Bough, B. (2011). Perspectives on social media marketing. Boston: Course Technology, a part of Cengage Learning.

Berger, C.S and Messerschmidt, M.C. (2009). Babbling before banking? Online communities and pre-purchase information seeking. International Journal of Bank Marketing [e-journal] 2 (6).

Choudhury, M. M., & Harrigan, P. (2014). CRM to social CRM: The integration of new technologies into customer relationship management. *Journal of Strategic Marketing*, 22(2), 149–176. DOI: 10.1080/0965254X.2013.876069

DuffAgency. (n.d.). What is online engagement. Retrieved February 26, 2024, from Duff Agency Website: https://duffy.agency/insight/what-is-online-engagement/.

Forbes. (2024, February 6). Social Media Statistics. Retrieved February 15, 2024, from Forbes: https://www.forbes.com/advisor/in/business/social-media-statistics/#:~:text=Social%20Media%20Usage%20Statistics,-The%20average%20person&text=Interestingly%2C%20Indians%2C%20on%20average%2C,spent%20on%20social%20media%20platforms

Garcia-Morales, V. J., Martín-Rojas, R., & Lardón-López, M. E. (2018). Influence of social media technologies on organizational performance through knowledge and innovation. *Baltic Journal of Management*, 13(3), 345–367. DOI: 10.1108/BJM-04-2017-0123

Hubspot. (n.d.). Instagram Marketing. Retrieved 22 2024, February, from Hubspot.com Website: https://www.hubspot.com/instagram-marketing

Kietzmann, J. H., Hermkens, K., McCarthy, I. P., & Silvestre, B. S. (2011). Social media? Get serious! Understanding the functional building blocks of social media. *Business Horizons*, 54(3), 241–251. DOI: 10.1016/j.bushor.2011.01.005

King, B. (2010). *Bank 2.0: How customer behavior and technology will change the future of financial services*. Marshall Cavendish Business.

Ko, E., Kim, D., & Kim, G. (2022). Influence of emojis on user engagement in brand-related user-generated content. Computers in Human Behavior, 136. doi/. DOI: 10.1016/j.chb.2022.107387

Kumar, V., & Pradhan, P. (2016). Reputation management through online feedbacks in e-business environment. [IJEIS]. *International Journal of Enterprise Information Systems*, 12(1), 21–37. DOI: 10.4018/IJEIS.2016010102

Kumari, A., & Singh, A. (2017). Impact of social media marketing on brand loyalty: A study with reference to State Bank of India. *International Journal of Applied Business and Economic Research*, 15(3), 363–374.

Marq.com. (n.d.). 11 reasons your brand should use twitter marketing. Retrieved March 3, 2024, from Marq.com website: https://www.marq.com/blog/11-reasons-your-brand-should-use-twitter-marketing

McGuirk, M. (2021). Performing social media analytics with Brandwatch for Classrooms: A platform review. *Journal of Marketing Analytics*, 9(4), 363.

Mehta, R. (2023, December 23). How social media is playing an important role in Indian GDP. Retrieved 05 2024, January, from Times of India.

Mittal, S., & Kumar, V. (2019). Study of knowledge management models and their relevance in organisations. Int. J. *Knowledge Management Studies*, 10(3), 322–335.

Parson, A. (2013). How Does Social Media Influence the Buying Behavior of Consumers? https://yourbusiness.azcentral.com/social-media-influence-buying-behavior-consumers-17017.html (Accessed 24 January 2024).

Pilot, S. (2024, April 6). Facebook Statistics. Retrieved April 10, 2024, from Social Pilot.co: https://www.socialpilot.co/facebook-marketing/facebook-statistics

Siddiqui, S., & Singh, T. (2016). Social media its impact with positive and negative aspects. *International Journal of Computer Applications Technology and Research*, 5(2), 71–75. DOI: 10.7753/IJCATR0502.1006

Tajudeen, F. P., Jaafar, N. I., & Ainin, S. (2018). Understanding the impact of social media usage among organizations. *Information & Management*, 55(3), 308–321. DOI: 10.1016/j.im.2017.08.004

Tiwari, S., Lane, M., & Alam, K. (2019). Do social networking sites build and maintain social capital online in rural communities? *Journal of Rural Studies*, 66, 1–10. DOI: 10.1016/j.jrurstud.2019.01.029

Vidhyalakshmi, R., & Kumar, V. (2016). Determinants of cloud computing adoption by SMEs. *International Journal of Business Information Systems*, 22(3), 375–395.

Why you should be marketing on LinkedIn right now. (2023, July 6). Retrieved February 20, 2024, from Linkedin.com: https://www.linkedin.com/business/marketing/blog/linkedin-ads/why-you-should-be-marketing-on-linkedin-right-now

Chapter 5
Data–Driven Comparison of Companies' Ability to Innovate

Fatma Altuntas
https://orcid.org/0000-0001-8644-5876
Istanbul Topkapi University, Turkey

ABSTRACT

The improvement of companies' innovation capability is one of their foremost strategic objectives. To achieve this goal, companies allocate significant resources. Analyzing the current situations of companies and controlling for the enhancement of innovation capabilities based on this analysis ensures the efficient utilization of resources. Companies should focus on improving their innovation capability while also concentrating on how to elevate their innovation maturity levels. This focus will guarantee leadership in the industry and exports in the future. In this study, the innovation capabilities of four companies operating in different sectors are compared. Additionally, the innovation maturity levels of the companies are determined. The companies operate in the information technology, food, plastic, and aviation sectors. Significant differences in innovation capabilities among the companies have been observed. To determine these differences, the Mann-Whitney U test is conducted.

1. INTRODUCTION

Companies have been focused on enhancing their innovation capabilities to turn global competition into an opportunity in recent years. The enhancement of companies' innovation capabilities is considered one of their most important competitive tools (Elverdi & Atik, 2020; Mattei et al. 2019). The ability to innovate enhances

DOI: 10.4018/979-8-3693-5563-3.ch005

the success of companies while also supporting their competitive strength (Müller-Prothmann & Stein, 2011; Mendoza-Silva, 2021b). Inków (2019) emphasizes that the concepts of "innovation and innovativeness" are considered as the key to success for all economies. Additionally, Bahrami and Evans (1989) emphasized that approximately 35 years ago, technological uncertainty, market uncertainty, competition uncertainty, and arena uncertainty significantly affected firms. In today's world, as a result of the rapid development of internet-based technologies and the spread of globalization, the pace of change in production, service, and sales dynamics within firms has also accelerated. This acceleration sheds light on even greater uncertainty related to competition in the future. In rapidly changing industries, it is important for companies to respond quickly and timely to market changes (Mendoza-Silva, 2021b). This allows companies to survive in the global competitive environment. Additionally, establishing a culture of innovation within the company, forming long-term partnerships, and ensuring customer satisfaction will enhance the company's reputation within the industry and society (Vlăduț et al. 2018). From another perspective, Sundbo (1997) points out that in the 1900s, the "innovation department" was developed as a Research and Development (R&D) department and was science-based. Recently, in order to manage innovation strategies, companies are trying to make the task of 'innovation' more systematic by rapidly establishing innovation departments. In the literature, innovation capability is explained with different approaches. These approaches are compiled in Table 1 according to the Mendoza-Silva (2021a) study.

Table 1. Definitions of innovation capability

Definition	Author(s) (Year)
It is the capacity of 1) developing new products satisfying market needs, 2) applying appropriate process technologies to produce these new products; 3) developing and adopting new products and processing technologies to satisfy future needs; 4) responding to the accidental technology activities and unexpected opportunities created by competitors.	Adler and Shenbar (1990)
The ability to continuously transform knowledge and ideas into new products, processes, and systems for the benefit of the firm and its stakeholders.	Lawson and Samson (2001)
The skills and knowledge needed to effectively absorb, master, and improve existing technologies, and to create new ones.	Romijn and Albaladejo (2002)
It relates to the firm's capacity to introduce new processes, products, or ideas in the organization.	Hult et al. (2004)
The application of relevant knowledge to the attainment of market value and is the successful implementation of creative ideas within an organization.	Zhao et al. (2000)

continued on following page

Table 1. Continued

Definition	Author(s) (Year)
An important factor that facilitates an innovative organizational culture, characteristics of internal promoting activities and capabilities of understanding and responding appropriately to the external environment	Akman and Yilmaz (2008)
The ability to mobilize the knowledge, possessed by its employees, and combine it to create new knowledge, resulting in product and/or process innovation.	Çakar and Ertürk (2010)
A comprehensive set of organizational capabilities that facilitate firms to recognize, seek out, learn, organize, apply and commercialize innovative new ideas, processes, products, and services	Cahang et al. (2012)
The application of knowledge and skills embedded within the routines and processes of the firm to perform innovation activities pertaining to technical innovations (develop new services, service operations, and technology) and non-technical innovations (managerial, market, and marketing)	Ngo and O'Cass (2013)
It is the firm's ability to generate, accept, and implement new ideas, processes, products, or services, is one of the key resources that drive a firm's success in the marketplace.	Wangs and Dass (2017)

(Source: **Mendoza-Silva, 2021a**)

Moreover, monitoring the developed innovation capability provides significant feedback on whether the company is achieving its innovation goals. Companies to assess the effectiveness of reaching innovation goals in their strategic planning process can use this feedback. An innovation audit is an approach used to evaluate the outputs obtained and their impacts in relation to the results (Viederyte & Abele, 2020). If the expected outputs are obtained from the innovation audit, new strategies can be formed based on the assumption that sufficient performance has been achieved (Viederyte & Abele, 2020). However, if the expected outputs are not obtained from the innovation audit, the anticipated risks of the business should be evaluated. In this scenario, the inability to innovate will push the business towards bankruptcy (Yam et al., 2004). Innovation audit enables the company to evaluate its current potential. This evaluation directs the company to reconsider its innovation strategies and make new plans. Innovation audit enables the organization to identify factors that hinder its creativity and innovativeness, allowing for the management of the innovation process (Attallah et al., 2019). There are many advantages for companies to control their ability to innovate and manage the innovation process. The following benefits are provided below.

✓ The digital maturity level of the company's workflow processes, production-related technologies, and operational management processes is supported (Azhari et al., 2014; Viederyte & Abele, 2020).
✓ Companies that enhance their innovation capabilities provide support for financial goals of cost reduction (Illmeyer et al., 2017).

✓ Efficiency is increased through the management of innovation capabilities (Van Kleef et al., 2007; Cormican & O'Sullivan, 2004).

✓ Increasing the ability to innovate in both production and service processes will facilitate rapid adaptation to changes in customer demand and trends in customer demands (Uyar, 2018; Onağ & Tepeci, 2016).

✓ Customer satisfaction is expected to increase as a result of product diversity, product development, service diversity and improvement of service delivery (Vlăduţ et al. 2018).

✓ Another advantage of managing firms' innovation capabilities is considered to be its enabling companies to identify current and potential risks more ag-ilely (Bowers and Horakian, 2014).

✓ The results of a neutral SWOT analysis add value (Vlăduţ et al. 2018).

✓ All these advantages are considered as long-term investment support for companies.

The subsequent flow of this study consists of three sections.The second section provides a review of the literature, and the conceptual development is discussed. Subsequently, the innovation capabilities of four companies operating in different sectors are analyzed, in the third section. In addition, the innovation maturity levels of the four companies are assessed. In the final section, a comprehensive evaluation is provided.

2. RELATED LITERATURE AND CONCEPTUAL DEVELOPMENT

Components of the innovation concept according to Hussain et al. (2019) study are *"exploiting new ideas," "looking for novel methods to doing things," "being inventive in use procedures,"* and *"marketing novel services and products common-ly"*. In the literature, components of innovation have been approached with different perspectives and methods. Zawislak et al (2012), proposed a framework for innovation capability. Verhaeghe and Kfir (2002) proposed a suggestion named holistic system framework. On the other hand, Giménez-Medina et al. (2023) emphasize that the literature indicates that the recommendations approach innovation from a general perspective and that a holistic approach is adopted throughout the entire process.

In the study by Iddris (2016), a literature review was conducted. Additionally, Idris (2016) provided 51 examples of innovation capability dimensions used in the literature.

Researches mainly focus on the relationship between innovation and firm per-formance. Jin and Choi (2019) empirically investigated the innovation activities and business performance of 160 firms in Korea between 2009 and 2017. Çavusgil et al.

(2003) conducted a study examining the innovation capability, innovation performance, and the effect of knowledge transfer on the firm's innovation capability based on the knowledge theory. Calantone et al. (2022) emphasize the connection between the concept of innovation and organizational learning. Also, Calantone et al. (2022) investigated the relationship between firm innovation and firm performance. In another study, Kızıloglu (2015) emphasizes the importance of the relationship between organizational learning and innovation, arguing that there is a negative relationship between openness to ideas and innovation management. Additionally, Saunila (2020) emphasizes that small businesses can increase their innovation capacity based on characterizations of innovation capability. Achi et al. (2016) provided information on how companies should assess their innovation maturity levels. Verhaeghe and Kfir (2002) identified the innovation profiles of three different companies in South Africa under the headings of main topics and sub-topics.

According to our research, research on firms' innovation capabilities is limited. Zhao et al. (2005) have linked firms' technology resource types with their innovation capabilities. They evaluated the effects of four types of resources on firms' innovative capabilities. Ceylan and Özarı (2018) underscore the need for systematic efforts at the corporate level for a company to be successful in the changing world competitive environment. At the same time, Erol and İnce (2012) have considered it essential for companies to continuously monitor and evaluate both themselves and their competitors as a necessity.

Feedback received by auditing innovation processes and innovation capabilities by an independent auditor is extremely valuable. Corsi and Neau (2015) emphasized the importance of the concepts and words used in firms. They brought a different perspective. In Figure 1, the conceptual differences between innovative approach and innovative project are visually explained. According to Corsi and Neau (2015), Figure 1 highlights that a company can enhance its capabilities by understanding the difference between its innovative approach and innovative project.

Figure 1. The conceptual differences between "innovative approach," "innovative project," and "innovability" (Corsi and Neau, 2015)

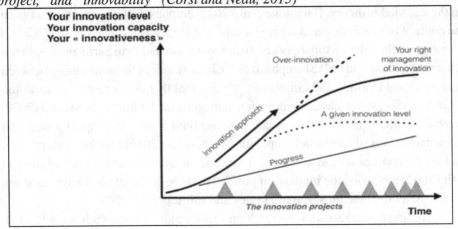

In the literature, along with the evaluation of the innovation capabilities of the companies, the innovation maturity levels of the companies are evaluated. Lookman et al. (2022) states that models within the scope of maturity are the perfection of the companies' goals. Wendler (2012) emphasized the definition of the word 'maturity' according to The Oxford English Dictionary, which is: *"The state of being mature; fullness or perfection of development or growth"*. In the literature, Lookman et al., (2022) evaluated the maturity levels of some companies in Indonesia by measuring their innovation capabilities. Alongside these considerations, Song (2023) notes that the size of businesses also affects their overall innovation capacity. Bley et al. (2021) utilized fuzzy-set qualitative comparative analysis and necessary condition analysis to assess the levels of innovation maturity in small companies. Müller-Prothmann and Stein (2011) proposed an integrated innovation maturity model. Niewöhner et al., (2021) has explained the impact of innovation maturity models on the digitization process. Additionally, Niewöhner et al., (2021) has emphasized the importance of companies evaluating themselves initially and explained that incremental and radical innovations are crucial. Demir (2018) suggests that enhancing strategic management maturity is essential for improving firms' innovation capabilities. Lewrick and Raeside (2010) investigated which skills are needed at which stage in the process of increasing the maturity of companies and explored the challenges that may arise when uncovering the firm's capabilities. According to Essmann and Du Preez (2009), organizational maturity and innovation are traditionally considered as opposites, in the literature. On the contrary, Essmann and Du Preez (2009) emphasize that combining these concepts will ensure prosperity in the future of the organization. There are also studies that evaluate innovation capability from another aspect within the framework of resource-based theory. *"Within resource-based theory, a firm is a strategic entity"* (Barney et al., 2021). According to resource-based theory, analyzing and interpreting companies' resources enables them to achieve sustainable competitive advantages when creating strategies (Madhani, 2010). A company can gain the ability to identify where value is created or destroyed by measuring and tracking the variables that enable the structuring of its resources (Ujwary-Gil and Potoczek, 2020). Additionally, management based on resource-based theory is considered strategically valuable (Freeman et al., 2021). Papatya (2013) asserts that the resources possessed by a company serve as a tool for gaining power over its competitors and emphasizes the importance of this tool in adding value to the company. Innovation capability is also an important resource for companies and it is argued that it will provide competitive advantage based on this resource. In addition to competitive advantage, it is also envisaged to provide sustainable competitive advantage. Madhani (2010) also advocates that a resource's ability to provide competitive advantage should be evaluated within the framework of four items (Valuable, Rare, Imperfect Imitability, Irreplaceability). Innovation capability is also a value for companies. At the same time, innovation is a concept that can be rarely introduced due to its conceptual meaning and supports the ability to imitate imperfectly. There are studies in the literature that evaluate the innovation capability of companies in different dimensions according to the resource-based approach. AlNuaimi et al., (2021) established a resource-based model to reveal the innovation capability of companies with different variables. Bhattacharyya and Jha (2015) conducted a capability assessment of small and medium sized enterprises in terms of resource-based view and dynamic capability theory perspectives. Kim et al. (2015) evaluated the capabilities that reveal service innovation with a resource-based perspective. In this study, H_1 hypothesis was established based on resource-based theory.

H_1: There exists variability in innovation capabilities among companies operating in diverse sectors.

Material and Method

Efforts by companies to enhance their innovation capabilities reflect an awareness that adds value to the company and contributes to changes in the industry's vision and structure. A company's growth is assessed as a development that can be measured by both quantitative and qualitative factors, in addition to financial indicators (Bolek et al., 2021). Therefore, one of the most important goals of many companies today is to improve their innovation capabilities. In this study, companies in 4 different sectors were evaluated. These companies are established in Turkey. An innovation audit tool survey containing a total of 50 statements in 5 different dimensions, developed by Braden Kelley, was applied to each of the companies (Kelley, 2003). Survey questions are presented in Appendix-A. The survey has been conducted in Turkish. The Turkish survey questions were taken from the study by Altuntas and Büyük (2022). The survey questions used a 5-point Likert scale [(1) Strongly Disagree; (2) Disagree; (3) Neither Agree nor Disagree; (4) Agree; (5) Strongly Agree]. The dimensions in the survey questions consist of "strategy", "idea generation", "idea evaluation and idea selection", "idea implementation", "collaboration and infrastructure" (Nada et al., 2012). There are 10 expressions in each dimension. Strategy is symbolized by the questions S1-S10, idea generation, İ1-İ10, idea evaluation and idea selection FD1-FD10, idea implementation Y1-Y10, cooperation and infrastructure FT1-FT10.

Figure 2. Comparing the averages of the total answers given to the survey dimensions (Created by author)

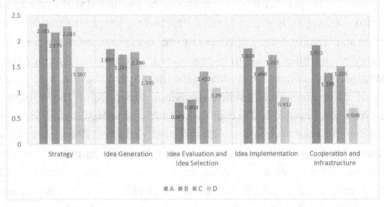

Survey questions are applied to companies operating in different sectors. These companies are named as A, B, C and D. The company A, operates in the information technology sector. The company B, operates in the food sector. The company C, operates in the plastic sector. Lastly, Company D operates in the aviation sector. Comparison of the averages of the answers given for each dimension in the survey is given in Figure 2.

Figure 2 shows the average values of the answers for the strategy dimension. The order of the companies for the strategy dimension is A, C, B and D from largest to smallest. The ranking of companies for the idea generation dimension is A, C, B and D from largest to smallest. The ranking of companies for the idea evaluation and idea selection dimension is C, D, B and A from largest to smallest. The ranking of companies for the idea implementation dimension is A, C, B and D from largest to smallest. The ranking of companies for cooperation and infrastructure dimensions is

A, C, B and D from largest to smallest. Employees of company A evaluate that they are successful in strategy and idea generation. However, the employees of company A evaluate that they need to improve in terms of idea evaluation and idea selection. At the same time, company A employees scored higher in the preparations for co-operation and infrastructure dimensions. The employees of company D have rated lower scores compared to other companies in all stages of innovation. According to Figure 2, the employees of company C scored high in the idea evaluation and idea selection dimensions. Compared to other companies, it ranks first in the dimension of idea evaluation and idea selection. Employees of company C evaluated their idea generation processes with lower scores than the employees of company A. However, the employees of company C evaluate that the process of evaluating and selecting ideas is more successful than the employees of other companies. The totals and averages of the answers given by the respondents in each company are presented in Table [2-4].

Table 2(a). Innovation audit survey values of companies (S1 - S10 and I1 - I10)

Questions	S1	S2	S3	S4	S5	S6	S7	S8	S9	S10
A Firm	2.24	3.16	2.43	2.57	1.81	1.92	2.89	2.35	1.95	2.11
Mean	2.343									
B Firm	1.89	2.21	2.32	2	2.42	1.39	2.79	2.84	1.84	2.05
Mean	2.175									
C Firm	2.18	2.41	2.05	1.77	2.23	2.55	3.14	2.45	1.32	2.77
Mean	2.287									
D Firm	1.3	1.9	1.4	1.73	1.34	1.37	1.7	1.83	1.27	1.23
Mean	1.507									

Table 2(b). Innovation audit survey values of companies (S1 - S10 and I1 - I10)

İ1	İ2	İ3	İ4	İ5	İ6	İ7	İ8	İ9	İ10
2.76	0.59	2.08	0.19	3.14	2.27	2.14	0.73	3	1.59
1.849									
2.53	0.21	2	0.05	2.74	2.61	2	0.44	2.89	1.94
1.741									
2.23	0.32	2.23	0.5	2.27	2.18	1.59	1.27	3.27	2
1.786									
2.06	1.13	1.29	1.16	1.29	1.26	1.26	1.16	1.45	1.29
1.335									

Table 3(a). Innovation audit survey values of companies (FD1 - FD10 and Y1 - Y10)

Questions	FD1	FD2	FD3	FD4	FD5	FD6	FD7	FD8	FD9	FD10
A Firm	2.22	0.68	0.95	0.84	0.59	0.08	0.43	0.86	0.84	0.54
Mean	0.803									
B Firm	1.68	1.63	1	0.78	1.11	0.16	0.39	0.72	0.56	0.56
Mean	0.859									
C Firm	2.09	1.5	1.95	1.95	1.95	0.86	0.91	0.95	0.95	1
Mean	1.411									
D Firm	1.6	1	1.03	1.07	1.1	1	1.03	1	1	1.07
Mean	1.09									

Table 3(b). Innovation audit survey values of companies (FD1 - FD10 and Y1 - Y10)

Y1	Y2	Y3	Y4	Y5	Y6	Y7	Y8	Y9	Y10
1.08	0.62	1.57	2.41	3.24	1.78	2.65	2.05	2.03	1.11
1.854									
1.67	0.67	0.58	1.11	1.63	2.83	2.22	1.53	1.79	0.95
1.498									
1.86	1.5	2.27	2.14	1.41	1.95	1.59	1.14	2.18	1.23
1.727									
1.03	0.87	0.93	0.87	0.9	0.83	0.97	0.9	0.93	0.89
0.912									

Table 4. Innovation audit survey values of companies (FT1 - FT10)

Questions	FT1	FT2	FT3	FT4	FT5	FT6	FT7	FT8	FT9	FT10
A Firm	2.08	1.35	2.16	1.89	2.86	2.89	2.95	0.46	0.46	2.03
Mean	1.913									
B Firm	1.63	1.58	2.16	1.28	0.89	1.63	1.58	1.32	0.89	0.82
Mean	1.378									
C Firm	2.68	1.23	1.18	1.73	1.68	1.64	1.64	0.91	1.09	1.27
Mean	1.505									
D Firm	0.97	0.66	0.62	0.72	0.66	0.69	0.66	0.72	0.66	0.62
Mean	0.698									

Expected results for each company and the distance of the companies from these expected results are given in Figure 3. All companies are seen to be closer to the expected ideal point in the strategy dimension. In companies A, B, and C, the dimension of idea selection and idea evaluation remained furthest from the expected results. In company D, the cooperation and infrastructure dimension fell short of the expected target.

In this study, the differences of companies according to innovation audit survey dimensions are examined. For this purpose, a normality test is conducted. The normality assumption is not met for all dimensions. The Kruskal-Wallis H test is a non-parametric method used to test the significance of differences among the medians of three or more groups when the assumption of normal distribution is not met (Jamil & Khanam, 2024; Clark et al., 2023; Sherwani et al., 2021; Arslan et al., 2018). Therefore, for the comparison of firms, non-parametric tests such as the Kruskal-Wallis test and Mann-Whitney U test are analyzed using IBM SPSS 21.00 package program.

The test statistic (H) for the Kruskal-Wallis variance analysis is provided in Equation 1 (Arslan et al., 2018). Kruskal Wallis H Test results are given in Table 5 R_i is the sum of the ranks of the observed values in each group. N is the total number of observations, n_i is the number of observations in each group and "k" is the number of groups.

$$H = \frac{12}{N(N+1)} \left(\sum_{i=1}^{k} \frac{R_i^2}{n_i} \right) - 3 \left(N + 1 \right)$$
(1)

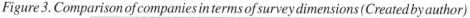

Figure 3. Comparison of companies in terms of survey dimensions (Created by author)

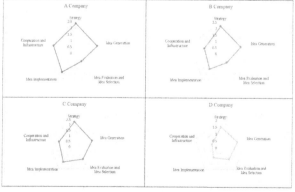

Table 5. Kruskal Wallis H test results

Company	Dimensions	Mean Rank	X^2	p
A	Strategy	34.65	13.486	.009
	Idea Generation	27.50		
	Idea Evaluation and Idea Selection	11.55		
	Idea Implementation	26.55		
	Collaboration and Infrastructure	27.25		
B	Strategy	38.10	16.501	.002
	Idea Generation	30.00		
	Idea Evaluation and Idea Selection	13.00		
	Idea Implementation	24.70		
	Collaboration and Infrastructure	21.70		
C	Strategy	38.40	13.423	.009
	Idea Generation	27.95		
	Idea Evaluation and Idea Selection	16.95		
	Idea Implementation	24.95		
	Collaboration and Infrastructure	19.25		
D	Strategy	42.50	42.244	.000
	Idea Generation	37.00		
	Idea Evaluation and Idea Selection	26.50		
	Idea Implementation	15.15		
	Collaboration and Infrastructure	6.35		

Mann-Whitney U test was used to determine which dimensions caused significant differences in innovation capabilities among companies. In this research, since there are 5 dimensions, 10 pairwise comparisons were made. The comparison was calculated according to Equation (2).

$$c = \frac{n}{r!(n-r)!}$$ (2)

Since 10 comparisons will be made, a new significance level is determined. New level of significance (p/10) was calculated. According to this process, it is determined as 0.005. Mann Whitney U test results of companies' innovation capabilities are given in Table [6-9]. The results of company A are given in Table 6. The results of company B are given in Table 7. The results of company C are given in Table 8. Finally, the results of company D are given in Table 9.

Table 6. The results of the Mann-Whitney U test in terms of the dimensions of Company A

Company	Dimensions	Mean Rank	U	p
A	Strategy	11.70	38.0	0.364
	Idea Generation	9.30		
	Strategy	15.10	4.00	0.001*
	Idea Evaluation and Idea Selection	5.90		
	Strategy	12.50	30.0	0.131
	Idea Implementation	8.50		
	Strategy	11.85	36.5	0.307
	Collaboration and Infrastructure	9.15		
	Idea Generation	13.15	23.5	0.045
	Idea Evaluation and Idea Selection	7.85		
	Idea Generation	10.80	47.0	0.821
	Idea Implementation	10.20		
	Idea Generation	10.75	47.5	0.850
	Collaboration and Infrastructure	10.25		
	Idea Evaluation and Idea Selection	6.70	12.0	0.004*
	Idea Implementation	14.30		
	Idea Evaluation and Idea Selection	7.60	21.0	0.028
	Collaboration and Infrastructure	13.40		
	Idea Implementation	10.05	45.5	0.734
	Collaboration and Infrastructure	10.95		

* < 0.005 There is a significant difference

In company A, innovation capability differed in terms of two groups. These are the dimensions of "strategy" – "idea evaluation and idea selection, idea evaluation and idea selection - idea implementation". Company B shows significant differences in terms of dimensions "strategy" –"collaboration and infrastructure", "strategy" – "idea evaluation and idea selection". Company B should focus on its strategic processes. Company C shows differences in terms of the "strategy" - "idea evaluation and idea selection", "strategy" - "collaboration and infrastructure" dimensions. In the results of company D, there was no significant difference in the comparison of only two dimensions. These are the "strategy" – "idea generation" dimensions. On the contrary, there is a significant difference in the other nine dimension comparisons.

Table 7. The results of the Mann-Whitney U test in terms of the dimensions of Company B

Company	Dimensions	Mean Rank	U	p
B	Strategy	11.10	44.0	0.650
	Idea Generation	9.90		
	Strategy	15.30	2.0	0.000*
	Idea Evaluation and Idea Selection	5.70		
	Strategy	13.60	19.0	0.019
	Idea Implementation	7.40		
	Strategy	14.6	9.0	0.002*
	Collaboration and Infrastructure	6.40		
	Idea Generation	12.80	27.0	0.082
	Idea Evaluation and Idea Selection	8.20		
	Idea Generation	11.60	38.0	0.406
	Idea Implementation	9.40		
	Idea Generation	12.20	33.0	0.198
	Collaboration and Infrastructure	8.80		
	Idea Evaluation and Idea Selection	7.80	23.0	0.041
	Idea Implementation	13.20		
	Idea Evaluation and Idea Selection	7.80	23.0	0.041
	Collaboration and Infrastructure	13.20		
	Idea Implementation	11.20	43.0	0.596
	Collaboration and Infrastructure	9.80		

* < 0.005 There is a significant difference

Table 8. The results of the Mann-Whitney U test in terms of the dimensions of Company C

Company	Dimensions	Mean Rank	U	p
C	Strategy	12.45	30.5	0.140
	Idea Generation	8.55		
	Strategy	14.50	10.0	0.002*
	Idea Evaluation and Idea Selection	6.50		
	Strategy	13.65	18.5	0.017
	Idea Implementation	7.35		
	Strategy	14.30	12.0	0.004*
	Collaboration and Infrastructure	6.70		
	Idea Generation	12.50	30.0	0.130
	Idea Evaluation and Idea Selection	8.50		
	Idea Generation	11.45	40.0	0.472
	Idea Implementation	9.55		
	Idea Generation	11.95	35.5	0.272
	Collaboration and Infrastructure	9.05		
	Idea Evaluation and Idea Selection	8.50	30.0	0.129
	Idea Implementation	12.50		
	Idea Evaluation and Idea Selection	9.95	44.5	0.677
	Collaboration and Infrastructure	11.05		
	Idea Implementation	12.05	34.5	0.241
	Collaboration and Infrastructure	8.95		

* < 0.005 There is a significant difference

Table 9. The results of the Mann-Whitney U test in terms of the dimensions of Company D

Company	Dimensions	Mean Rank	U	p
D	Strategy	13.10	24.0	0.049
	Idea Generation	7.90		
	Strategy	14.90	6.0	0.001*
	Idea Evaluation and Idea Selection	6.10		
	Strategy	15.50	0.00	0.000*
	Idea Implementation	5.50		
	Strategy	15.50	0.000	0.000*
	Collaboration and Infrastructure	5.50		
	Idea Generation	14.60	9.0	0.002*
	Idea Evaluation and Idea Selection	6.40		
	Idea Generation	15.50	0.00	0.000*
	Idea Implementation	5.50		
	Idea Generation	15.50	0.00	0.000*
	Collaboration and Infrastructure	5.50		
	Idea Evaluation and Idea Selection	15.0	5.0	0.001*
	Idea Implementation	6.0		
	Idea Evaluation and Idea Selection	15.50	0.00	0.000*
	Collaboration and Infrastructure	5.50		
	Idea Implementation	14.65	8.50	0.002*
	Collaboration and Infrastructure	6.35		

* < 0.005 There is a significant difference

Teece (2019) conducted research based on the capability theory of firms. Teece (2019) emphasized the differences of the companies, which indicates that distance dimensions such as business model differences, technical feature differences and market distance differences should be addressed in order to realize the transformation. Companies operate in different sectors. We suggest that although the sectors of companies A, B, C, D are different, improvements can be made by benchmarking their business models.

The current situation of the company is evaluated based on the innovation maturity model and the company's innovation audit survey results (Altuntas & Büyük, 2022). In the innovation maturity model developed by Braden Kelley, companies are examined in 5 different categories. These categorical levels are evaluated according to the steps of (Level 1) Reactive, (Level 2) Structured, (Level 3) In Control, (Level 4) Internalized, and (Level 5) Continuously Improving. Companies innovation maturity levels have a score equivalent. If the company gets a value between 0-100, it is Reactive (Level 1). If the company gets a value between 101-130, it is Structured (Level 2). If the company gets a value between 131-150, it is in control (Level 3). If the company gets a value between 151-180, it is Internalized (Level 4). If the company gets a value between 181-200 it is in Continuously Improving (Level 5). According to this research, the score of Company A is 87.62. The score of company B is 77 . The score of company C is 86. Finally, the score of company D is 55.42. Accordingly, the innovation maturity level of companies A, B, C and D is Reactive (Level 1). Innovation maturity levels of companies A, B, C and D are insufficient. Corsi and Neau (2015), emphasize those following questions numbered [1-12] should be evaluated in the company, regardless of the level of the company.

"1- How to define this level?

2- What characterizes this level?

3- What does this level evoke?

4- What are the eligibility criteria for this level?

5- What are the sign that show that the lower level has been abandoned?

6- What are the particular challenges at this level?

7- What are outstanding gains and benefits enjoyed by the organization at this level?

8- What advices can we offer to an organization at his level? (NB. These are tips that can be advised, however, thei implementation depends on the context and the factors specific to the organization: we cannot generalize here).

9- What are the common gaps and weakneses at this level?

10- What are the risk and threats associated with this level?

11- Which evidences of the assimilation of prerequisites leading to this level?

12- Which questions to ask for reaching the next higher level?"

Companies A, B, C, and D are given the following recommendations:

Companies should create an action plan and innovation roadmap to move to the structured level as soon as possible.

Company employees should be knowledgeable not only about the production and operational processes within their own departments but also about those in other departments.

Based on this process knowledge, a definition of collaborative innovation should be formulated.

Just as the mission and vision of companies are unique, their definitions of innovation should also be unique.

The company should continuously encourage its personnel to innovate and support the controlled risk-taking process of the personnel.

Innovation strategies must be included in the company's strategic objectives without fail. Specific objectives such as technological, open, closed, radical, and service innovations should be defined under these strategies.

More collaboration should be established with data analysts who investigate customer demands and requests. Companies should establish data collection departments. Different types of data should be provided to both the R&D center and data analysts.

The view that innovation in companies should only be carried out by authorized departments or individuals is widespread. It is necessary to convey this misconception to employees through training sessions. In addition, companies should take "Google's 20% Time"[1] practice as an example.

Companies should create an innovation incentives section on their websites for external stakeholders. For internal stakeholders, they should develop practical software solutions.

Company employees should be trained on Six Sigma and other techniques that support this approach. Every employee should be trained in time management. Poor time management is a significant factor affecting productivity and performance (Korzynski & Protsiuk, 2024; Tan & Zahdjuki, 2023).

Company employees are highly motivated to continually improve the company, but they are hesitant to present new ideas. To address this, a system should be established to reward and honor employees who innovate, generate ideas, and develop methods, with certificates being awarded.

Companies should encourage and reward not only their employees but also their business partners, customers, and suppliers to generate ideas.

An innovative idea generation club or institution should be established.

Even if an idea produced by a company is useful and feasible, if the current company does not have the opportunity to implement it, the idea can be transferred to another company in exchange for a copyright fee.

Every company should develop a method that allows for the generation of innovative ideas based on its own operational processes. These ideas should be stored as institutional memory.

Company personnel should be provided with innovation training. The training program should cover a wide range of topics, including the definition, various types, processes, and strategies of innovation. Collaboration with university academics can be sought for this training.

Companies should definitely repeat innovation audits at short intervals (Chan & Vasarhelyi, 2018). The audit results obtained over the years should be compared within each period, and these comparisons should be reported.

To understand the company's current level of innovation maturity, the weakest link in the chain is identified (Corsi & Neau, 2015). Strengthening the weakest link will inevitably lead to reaching the next level.

CONCLUSION AND EVALUATION

Assessing companies' innovation capabilities and controlling their innovation capabilities provide a wide range of benefits to the company. The most significant contribution is expected to be ensuring that the company efficiently utilizes its tangible and intangible resources. As a result, sustainable production can be achieved. Additionally, an increase in customer satisfaction, which is one of the most significant outcomes of a well-functioning process, is expected. The assessment of companies' innovation capabilities contributes to their strategic competitive advantage. Furthermore, evaluating companies innovation capabilities has another aspect that affects inter country export potential. Innovation capability is being integrated into the corporate culture of companies. It is believed that sustainable innovation capabilities can develop with the existence of this culture. The innovation ability of companies varies depending on the sector in which they operate. The reason for this variability stems from the nature of the industry ecosystem. The innovation capability of companies is shaped by the dynamics, trends, and relationship with technology of the sector. In recent years, some companies view the development and monitoring of innovation capabilities as a significant vision. This vision should be expanded.

In this study, the innovation capabilities of companies operating in four different sectors have been evaluated based on survey results. The difference between sectors also demonstrates diversity in innovation capability. On the other hand, although the sectors are different, the dimensions of "strategy" and "idea evaluation and idea selection" distinguish the company. Additionally, in the study, the innovation maturity levels of the companies have been determined. All four companies are at (Level 1) Reactive. Recommendations have been provided to the companies.

This study has two limitations. Firstly, the innovation capabilities of companies were evaluated in a general framework. In future studies, it is recommended that companies be examined and compared in more niche areas. These examinations can be conducted in terms of product innovation capability, process innovation capability, organizational innovation capability, marketing innovation capability, resource innovation capability, and green innovation capability. Additionally, it should be considered how technological innovations can be integrated with the concept of sustainability to achieve long term success (Jin & Choi, 2019). The second limitation is that the study is limited to four companies. In the future, sector diversity should be increased by including more companies from different sectors. Furthermore, future researchers are called upon to compare the eco-innovation maturity levels of different companies.

REFERENCES

Achi, A., Salinesi, C., & Viscusi, G. (2016). Information Systems for Innovation: A Comparative Analysis of Maturity Models' Characteristics. CAiSE 2016 International Workshops / [ed] John Krogstie, Haralambos Mouratidis, Jianwen Su, Cham: Springer International Publishing, 2016, Vol. 249, 78-90

Adler, P. S., & Kwon, S. (2002). Social capital: Prospects for a new concept. *Academy of Management Review*, 27(1), 17–40. DOI: 10.2307/4134367

Adler, P. S., & Shenbar, A. (1990). Adapting your technological base: The organizational challenge. *Sloan Management Review*, 32, 25–37.

Akman, G., & Yilmaz, C. (2008). Innovative capability, innovation strategy, and market orientation: An empirical analysis in Turkish software industry. *International Journal of Innovation, Management and Technology*, 12, 69–111.

AlNuaimi, B. K., Singh, S. K., & Harney, B. (2021). Unpacking the role of innovation capability: Exploring the impact of leadership style on green procurement via a natural resource-based perspective. *Journal of Business Research*, 134, 78–88. DOI: 10.1016/j.jbusres.2021.05.026

Altuntaş, F., & Büyük, B. (2022). İnşaat Sektöründe Faaliyet Gösteren Bir Firmada İnovasyon Stratejilerinin Belirlenmesi ve İnovasyon Denetimine Yönelik Uygulama. *Journal of Entrepreneurship and Innovation Management*, 11(1), 59–79.

Arslan, A. K., Yaşar, Ş., Çolak, C., & Yoloğlu, S. (2018). R Shiny paketi ile Kruskal Wallis H testi için interaktif bir web uygulaması. *Annals of Health Sciences Research*, 7(2), 49–55.

Attallah, S. A. A., Mamlook, R., & Al-Jayyousi, O. (2019). A proposed methodology for measuring sme innovation. *Arab Gulf Journal of Scientific Research*, 37(2), 1–22. DOI: 10.51758/AGJSR-02-2019-0005

Azhari, P., Faraby, N., Rossmann, A., Steimel, B., & Wichmann, K. S. (2014). *Digital Transformation Report -2014* (Kalmeyer, N., Ed.). Neuland GmbH & Co. KG.

Barney, J. B., Ketchen, D. J.Jr, & Wright, M. (2021). Resource-based theory and the value creation framework. *Journal of Management*, 47(7), 1936–1955. DOI: 10.1177/01492063211021655

Benavente, S. L. (2017). 20% time in the classroom-bringing Google philosophy and the keys to motivation to your school. In *INTED2017 Proceedings* (pp. 1016-1020). IATED.

Bhattacharyya, S. S., & Jha, S. (2015). Mapping micro small and medium enterprises from the resource-based view and dynamic capability theory perspectives and innovation classification. *International Journal of Entrepreneurship and Small Business*, 25(3), 331–350. DOI: 10.1504/IJESB.2015.069700

Bley, K., Pappas, I. O., & Strahringer, S. (2021). Innovation Capability in Small Industrial Companies-a Set Theoretic Approach to Maturity Models. In ECIS.

Bolek, M., Pietraszewski, P., & Wolski, R. (2021). Companies' growth vs. growth opportunity: Evidence from the regular and alternative stock markets in Poland. *Acta Oeconomica*, 71(2), 279–307. DOI: 10.1556/032.2021.00014

Bowers, J., & Khorakian, A. (2014). Integrating risk management in the innovation project. *European Journal of Innovation Management*, 17(1), 25–40. DOI: 10.1108/EJIM-01-2013-0010

Çakar, N. D., & Ertürk, A. (2010). Comparing innovation capability of small and medium-sized enterprises: Examining the effects of organizational culture and empowerment. *Journal of Small Business Management*, 48(3), 325–359. DOI: 10.1111/j.1540-627X.2010.00297.x

Calantone, R. J., Cavusgil, S. T., & Zhao, Y. (2002). Learning orientation, firm innovation capability, and firm performance. *Industrial Marketing Management*, 31(6), 515–524. DOI: 10.1016/S0019-8501(01)00203-6

Ceylan, A., & Özarı, Ç. (2018). TOPSIS Yöntemiyle Benzer Sektörlerdeki Firmaların Finansal Performans Analizlerinin Karşılaştırılması: BİST 30 Endeksinde İşlem Gören Firmalar Üzerine Bir Araştırma. *Kesit Akademi Dergisi*, 16(16), 421–431. DOI: 10.18020/kesit.1514

Chan, D. Y., & Vasarhelyi, M. A. (2018). Innovation and practice of continuous Auditing1. In *Continuous Auditing* (pp. 271–283). Emerald Publishing Limited. DOI: 10.1108/978-1-78743-413-420181013

Chang, Y. C., Chang, H. T., Chi, H. R., Chen, M. H., & Deng, L. L. (2012). How do established firms improve radical innovation performance? The organizational capabilities view. *Technovation*, 32(7-8), 441–451. DOI: 10.1016/j.technovation.2012.03.001

Clark, J. S., Kulig, P., Podsiadło, K., Rydzewska, K., Arabski, K., Białecka, M., Safranow, K., & Ciechanowicz, A. (2023). Empirical investigations into Kruskal-Wallis power studies utilizing Bernstein fits, simulations and medical study datasets. *Scientific Reports*, 13(1), 2352. DOI: 10.1038/s41598-023-29308-2 PMID: 36759640

Cormican, K., & O'Sullivan, D. (2004). Auditing best practice for effective product innovation management. *Technovation*, 24(10), 819–829. DOI: 10.1016/S0166-4972(03)00013-0

Corsi, P., & Neau, E. (2015). *Innovation Capability Maturity Model. "A Method to Progress"*. John Wiley & Sons. DOI: 10.1002/9781119144335

Demir, F. (2018). A strategic management maturity model for innovation. *Technology Innovation Management Review*, 8(11), 13–21. DOI: 10.22215/timreview/1196

Elverdi, S., & Atik, H., (2020). Türkiye'de inovasyon ölçümüne yönelik bir değerlendirme. IBAD Sosyal Bilimler Dergisi, 695-712.

Erol, Y., & İnce, A. R. (2012). Rekabette Pozisyon Okulu Düşüncesi Ve Kaynak Tabanlı Görüşün Karşılaştırılması. Cumhuriyet Universitesi Journal of Economics & Administrative Sciences (JEAS), 13(1).

Essmann, H., & Du Preez, N. (2009). An innovation capability maturity model–development and initial application. *International Journal of Industrial and Manufacturing Engineering*, 3(5), 382–393.

Freeman, R. E., Dmytriyev, S. D., & Phillips, R. A. (2021). Stakeholder theory and the resource-based view of the firm. *Journal of Management*, 47(7), 1757–1770. DOI: 10.1177/0149206321993576

Giménez-Medina, M., Enríquez, J. G., & Domínguez-Mayo, F. J. (2023). A systematic review of capability and maturity innovation assessment models: Opportunities and challenges. *Expert Systems with Applications*, 213, 118968. DOI: 10.1016/j.eswa.2022.118968

https://www.wiwo.de/downloads/10773004/1/DTA_Report_neu.pdf

Hult, G. T. M., Hurley, R. F., & Knight, G. A. (2004). Innovativeness: Its antecedents and impact on business performance. *Industrial Marketing Management*, 33(5), 429–438. DOI: 10.1016/j.indmarman.2003.08.015

Iddris, F. (2016). Innovation capability: A systematic review and research agenda. *Interdisciplinary Journal of Information, Knowledge, and Management*, 11, 235–260. DOI: 10.28945/3571

Illmeyer, M., Grosch, D., Kittler, M., & Priess, P. (2017). The impact of financial management on innovation. *Entrepreneurship and Sustainability Issues*, 5(1), 58–71. DOI: 10.9770/jesi.2017.5.1(5)

Inków, M. (2019). Measuring innovation maturity–literature review on innovation maturity models. *Informatyka Ekonomiczna*, 1(51), 22–34. DOI: 10.15611/ie.2019.1.02

Jamil, M. A., & Khanam, S. (2024). Influence of one-way ANOVA and Kruskal–Wallis based feature ranking on the performance of ML classifiers for bearing fault diagnosis. *Journal of Vibration Engineering & Technologies*, 12(3), 3101–3132. DOI: 10.1007/s42417-023-01036-x

Jin, S. H., & Choi, S. O. (2019). The effect of innovation capability on business performance: A focus on IT and business service companies. *Sustainability (Basel)*, 11(19), 5246. DOI: 10.3390/su11195246

Juliani, A. J. (2014). *Inquiry and innovation in the classroom: Using 20% time, genius hour, and PBL to drive student success*. Routledge. DOI: 10.4324/9781315813837

Kelley, B. (2003). Innovation, Change and Digital Transformation. from Free Innovation Audit: Braden Kelley's 50 Question Innovation Audit: https:// bradenkelley .com/offerings/innovation-audit/ Date of access: 01.04.2024

Kim, M., Song, J., & Triche, J. (2015). Toward an integrated framework for innovation in service: A resource-based view and dynamic capabilities approach. *Information Systems Frontiers*, 17(3), 533–546. DOI: 10.1007/s10796-014-9505-6

Kiziloglu, M. (2015). The Effect of Organizational Learning on Firm Innovation Capability: An Investigation in the Banking Sector. *Global Business and Management Research*, 7(3).

Korzynski, P., & Protsiuk, O. (2024). What leads to cyberloafing: The empirical study of workload, self-efficacy, time management skills, and mediating effect of job satisfaction. *Behaviour & Information Technology*, 43(1), 200–211. DOI: 10.1080/0144929X.2022.2159525

Lawson, B., & Samson, D. (2001). Developing innovation capability in organisations: A dynamic capabilities approach. *International Journal of Innovation Management*, 5(03), 377–400. DOI: 10.1142/S1363919601000427

Lewrick, M., & Raeside, R. (2010). Transformation and change process in innovation models: Start-up and mature companies. *International Journal of Business Innovation and Research*, 4(6), 515–534. DOI: 10.1504/IJBIR.2010.035711

Lookman, K., Pujawan, N., & Nadlifatin, R. (2022). Measuring innovative capability maturity model of trucking companies in Indonesia. *Cogent Business & Management*, 9(1), 2094854. DOI: 10.1080/23311975.2022.2094854

Madhani, P. M. (2010). Resource based view (RBV) of competitive advantage: an overview. Resource based view: concepts and practices, Pankaj Madhani, ed, 3-22.

Mattei, G., Canetta, L., Sorlini, M., Alberton, S., & Tito, F. (2019, June). Innovation maturity model for new product and services development: a proposal. In *2019 IEEE International Conference on Engineering, Technology and Innovation (ICE/ITMC)* (pp. 1-9). IEEE. DOI: 10.1109/ICE.2019.8792581

Mendoza-Silva, A. (2021a). Innovation capability: A sociometric approach. *Social Networks*, 64, 72–82. DOI: 10.1016/j.socnet.2020.08.004

Mendoza-Silva, A. (2021b). Innovation capability: A systematic literature review. *European Journal of Innovation Management*, 24(3), 707–734. DOI: 10.1108/EJIM-09-2019-0263

Müller-Prothmann, T., & Stein, A. (2011, Haziran). I²MM–İnovasyon yeteneğinin yalın değerlendirmesi için entegre inovasyon olgunluk modeli. XXII ISPIM Konferansında (12-15).

Nada, N., Ghanem, M., Mesbah, S., & Turkyilmaz, A. (2012). İnnovation And Knowledge Management Practice in Turkish SMEs, Journal of Knowledge Management. *Economics and Information Technology*, 2(1), 248–265.

Ngo, L. V., & O'cass, A. (2013). Innovation and business success: The mediating role of customer participation. *Journal of Business Research*, 66(8), 1134–1142. DOI: 10.1016/j.jbusres.2012.03.009

Niewöhner, N., Lang, N., Asmar, L., Röltgen, D., Kühn, A., & Dumitrescu, R. (2021). Towards an ambidextrous innovation management maturity model. *Procedia CIRP*, 100, 289–294. DOI: 10.1016/j.procir.2021.05.068

Onağ, O., & Tepeci, M. (2016). Örgütsel öğrenme kabiliyetinin örgütsel yenilikçilik araciliğiyla yeni ürün ve işletme performansina etkisi. *Isletme Iktisadi Enstitüsü Yönetim Dergisi*, (80), 50.

Papatya, N. (2013). Çokuluslu şirketlerin kaynak-tabanlı biyo-politik üretiminde rekabetçi gücün diyalektiği-eleştirel ve bütünsel bakış. *Süleyman Demirel Üniversitesi İktisadi ve İdari Bilimler Fakültesi Dergisi*, 18(3), 1–23.

Romijn, H., & Albaladejo, M. (2002). Determinants of innovation capability in small electronics and software firms in southeast England. *Research Policy*, 31(7), 1053–1067. DOI: 10.1016/S0048-7333(01)00176-7

Romijn, H., & Albaladejo, M. (2002). Determinants of innovation capability in small electronics and software firms in southeast England. *Research Policy*, 31(7), 1053–1067. DOI: 10.1016/S0048-7333(01)00176-7

Saunila, M. (2020). Innovation capability in SMEs: A systematic review of the literature. Journal of Innovation & knowledge, 5(4), 260-265.

Sherwani, R. A. K., Shakeel, H., Awan, W. B., Faheem, M., & Aslam, M. (2021). Analysis of COVID-19 data using neutrosophic Kruskal Wallis H test. *BMC Medical Research Methodology*, 21(1), 1–7. DOI: 10.1186/s12874-021-01410-x PMID: 34657587

Song, Y. (2023). How do Chinese SMEs enhance technological innovation capability? From the perspective of innovation ecosystem. *European Journal of Innovation Management*, 26(5), 1235–1254. DOI: 10.1108/EJIM-01-2022-0016

Sundbo, J. (1997). Management of innovation in services. *Service Industries Journal*, 17(3), 432–455. DOI: 10.1080/02642069700000028

Tamer Cavusgil, S., Calantone, R. J., & Zhao, Y. (2003). Tacit knowledge transfer and firm innovation capability. *Journal of Business and Industrial Marketing*, 18(1), 6–21. DOI: 10.1108/08858620310458615

Tan, D., & Zahdjuki, D. A. (2023). The Compliance of Limited Liability Companies to Conduct Annual General Meeting of Shareholders. *Journal of Judicial Review*, 25(1), 51–70. DOI: 10.37253/jjr.v25i1.7736

Teece, D. J. (2019). A capability theory of the firm: An economics and (strategic) management perspective. *New Zealand Economic Papers*, 53(1), 1–43. DOI: 10.1080/00779954.2017.1371208

Ujwary-Gil, A., & Potoczek, N. R. (2020). A dynamic, network and resource-based approach to the sustainable business model. *Electronic Markets*, 30(4), 717–733. DOI: 10.1007/s12525-020-00431-6

Uyar, M. (2018). Muhasebe Denetimi ve İç Kontrol Sisteminin İşletmelerde İnovasyon Yapma Yeteneğine Etkileri Üzerine Ampirik Bir İnceleme. İstanbul Gelişim Üniversitesi Sosyal Bilimler Dergisi, 5(1), 149-168.

Van Kleef, J. A., & Roome, N. J. (2007). Developing capabilities and competence for sustainable business management as innovation: A research agenda. *Journal of Cleaner Production*, 15(1), 38–51. DOI: 10.1016/j.jclepro.2005.06.002

Verhaeghe, A., & Kfir, R. (2002). Managing innovation in a knowledge intensive technology organisation (KITO). *Research Management*, 32(5), 409–417.

Viederyte, R., & Abele, L. (2020). Innovations audit of industrial clusters: process and main trends of development. International Multidisciplinary Scientific Geo-Conference: SGEM, 20(4.2), 43-54.

Vlăduţ, G., Tănase, N. M., Caramihai, M., & Purcărea, A. A. (2018). Innovation Audit for business excellence. In *Proceedings of the international conference on business excellence* (Vol. 12, No. 1, pp. 1026-1037). DOI: 10.2478/picbe-2018-0092

Walker, A. (2011). 'Creativity loves constraints': The paradox of Google's twenty percent time. *Ephemera*, 11(4).

Wang, X., & Dass, M. (2017). Building innovation capability: The role of top management innovativeness and relative-exploration orientation. *Journal of Business Research*, 76, 127–135. DOI: 10.1016/j.jbusres.2017.03.019

Yam, R. C., Guan, J. C., Pun, K. F., & Tang, E. P. (2004). An audit of technological innovation capabilities in Chinese firms: Some empirical findings in Beijing, China. *Research Policy*, 33(8), 1123–1140. DOI: 10.1016/j.respol.2004.05.004

Zawislak, P. A., Cherubini Alves, A., Tello-Gamarra, J., Barbieux, D., & Reichert, F. M. (2012). Innovation capability: From technology development to transaction capability. *Journal of Technology Management & Innovation*, 7(2), 14–27. DOI: 10.4067/S0718-27242012000200002

Zhao, H., Tong, X., Wong, P. K., & Zhu, J. (2005). Types of technology sourcing and innovative capability: An exploratory study of Singapore manufacturing firms. *The Journal of High Technology Management Research*, 16(2), 209–224. DOI: 10.1016/j.hitech.2005.10.004

ENDNOTE

[1] See: **Juliani, (2014); Walker, (2011); Benavente, (2017).**

APPENDIX I

(Source: **Kelley, 2003**)

Questions S1-S10

We have a common definition for the word 'innovation'
Innovation is one of our core values
There is support for taking risks
It is okay to fail once in a while
Our company has an innovation strategy
Our innovation strategy is linked to our corporate strategy
Senior executives drive innovation in our organization
We have people focused on identifying key future market, customer, and other insights
Innovation is the job of my boss
Innovation is part of my job

Questions I1-I10

I know how to submit an innovation idea
We have a web site for submitting innovation ideas
I collaborate on innovation ideas with my coworkers
We have software for innovation management in place
We have a new product development process in place
We launch new products on time
We launch new products faster than our competition
Six sigma is well understood and widely distributed in our organization
We are constantly looking to improve as an organization
We have a methodology for generating ideas in our company

Questions FD1-FD10

I know what kinds of innovation ideas the company is looking for
I have been trained on these one or more innovation methodologies
We have a portfolio of innovation projects
Our portfolio of innovation projects is actively managed
We have a formal process for innovation idea selection
We use one or more innovation methodologies
We have a clear set of innovation metrics

We have a process for killing innovation projects
We have a formal process for innovation idea funding
We have a separate pool of funding available for innovation projects

Questions Y1-Y10

We have an innovation idea development process
We have a formal process for staffing innovation idea projects
We have a process for recognizing and rewarding innovators
Our organization is a good home for innovators
Our organization is a good home for intrapreneurs
Marketing and R&D have a good relationship and share information
Knowledge of the customer is shared widely in our organization
People have time to innovate in our organization
People know where to go for funding for an innovation idea
There is more than one funding source available for innovation ideas

Appendix- A (Continued) (Sources: Kelley, 2003)

Questions FT1-FT10

We solicit innovation ideas from employees
We solicit innovation ideas from suppliers
We solicit innovation ideas from partners
We solicit innovation ideas from customers
Suppliers would describe our organization as innovative
Partners would describe our organization as innovative
Customers would describe our organization as innovative
We have a formal process for open innovation
We have a formal innovation public relations strategy
We are considered the partner of first resort for innovation ideas

Chapter 6
Using OpenStreetMap Data for Geomarketing Insights and Business Growth

Munir Ahmad
https://orcid.org/0000-0003-4836-6151
Survey of Pakistan, Pakistan

Sudhair Abbas Bangash
Sarhad University of Science and Information Technology, Pakistan

Maher Ali Rusho
https://orcid.org/0009-0001-5759-7042
University of Colorado, Boulder, USA

Sudipta Halder
https://orcid.org/0009-0007-4095-3948
Atria Institute of Technology, The Netherlands

Iram Shahzadi
Pir Mehr Ali Shah Arid Agriculture University, Pakistan

ABSTRACT

Geo-marketing integrates traditional marketing with GIS to support companies in identifying target markets and strategically positioning themselves. This chapter explores OSM data utilization for competitor analysis, demographic insights, amenity evaluation, market segmentation, site selection, and store optimization. Extracting POI data from OSM, such as retail stores and supermarkets using different can

DOI: 10.4018/979-8-3693-5563-3.ch006

inform strategic decisions. Spatial analysis techniques like distance calculations and buffer analysis can assess competitor proximity and identify potential store sites. Demographic analysis can infer population characteristics, complemented by external datasets. Amenities can be evaluated using density and hotspot analyses to pinpoint prime locations. Market segmentation can cluster areas with similar POI distributions for targeted strategies. Site selection overlays POI layers to optimize accessibility and meet market demand. Store optimization enhances performance through foot traffic analysis and POI data, enhancing customer satisfaction and profitability.

INTRODUCTION

Market identification with census and postal geography is vitally important for companies to be able to position themselves and compete effectively for targeted marketing segments (Beaumont, 1989). Geo-marketing is realized as a strategic approach based on combining the traditional elements of marketing with GIS and the latest technologies. Consequently, it helps to quantify the consumer behaviour, proper selection of the site, the improvement of the advertising and selling methods through the use of sociodemographic and spatial information. Location analysis is most relevant in locations where we have such complexities as the vertical space, for instance, the building which in most cases can affect the consumer's behavior and other market factors. As these factors can be integrated by geo-marketing, this improves decision-making, where the strategies that are used by businesses will fit with the local market environment and consumer habits.

Major strategic marketing goals may include the best locations of the businesses, improving the clients' experiences, analysis of the geographical information for the improvement of the business decisions, and increasing the efficiency of marketing avenues. Geo-marketing also assumes major significance because it helps in understanding the behaviour of the markets thereby helping the companies improve their strategies and make informed decisions regarding the same (Augusto, 2020). Sociodemographic variables and patterns of location are useful in geo-marketing models to assist supermarkets in positioning their locations for optimal market coverage (Baviera-Puig et al., 2016). Thus, geo-marketing helps to enhance selling point location, market reaction, and developing greater tendencies to sales volume, and customer attraction with the enhanced overall market performance (Chaskalovic, 2009).

Geo-marketing is essential for companies that plan further development or choose sites for opening their branches and is particularly relevant for real estate leasing (B. A. Tkhorikov et al., 2020). Geo-marketing systems at an advanced level employ data clustering that helps in sorting and analyzing geospatial information including but not limited to the housing costs, the position of shops marts or any other centers, and the locations for setting up bank branches (Shaitura et al., 2020). Applying micro geo-data in financial services requires the incorporation of geo-marketing information into marketing tools, strengthening the decision makers' utilities (Hertig & Maus, 1998).Such applications establish the relevance and importance of geo-marketing in strategic planning and the improvement of operational efficacy across various industries.

Geospatial data, especially leveraging OpenStreetMap, can potentially revolutionize international marketing research. By harnessing location-based mobile targeting, analyzing store competition, and enhancing city marketing strategies, OpenStreetMap can provide a robust platform for precise spatial insights (Wichmann et al., 2023). Its open-access nature allows businesses to access detailed geographic information, facilitating strategic decisions in market expansion and customer engagement. OpenStreetMap's comprehensive dataset can enable businesses to identify optimal locations for new ventures, understand local market dynamics, and effectively tailor marketing campaigns to specific geographic regions. OpenStreetMap can play a pivotal role in modernizing and optimizing international marketing practices through accessible and accurate geospatial data. Therefore, the chapter aims to explore how OpenStreetMap can provide valuable geo-marketing insights and foster business growth.

This chapter is structured as follows. The second section offers background on OpenStreetMap and its applications in various business aspects. The third section explores the essential components and data sources for successful geo-marketing data analysis. The fourth section delves into utilizing OSM datasets for geo-marketing analysis. Finally, the concluding section summarizes the key points of the chapter.

BACKGROUND INFORMATION

OpenStreetMap (OSM)

OpenStreetMap (OSM) is a wiki for geographic information and an open project for mapping that has global coverage with editable, user-generated, real-time update features (Weber & Haklay, 2008). OSM data can be applied in urban analysis, land cover mapping, routing or navigation, and many other purposes in different application domains. For example, OSM has been used to assess 27000 streets in the United States depending on the metropolitan, municipal, and neighborhood classifications of urban form and features of the street network (Boeing, 2020a). OpenStreetMap data can be utilized to create and compile Open Land Cover (OLC) for Heidelberg,

Germany, while the accuracy is found to be at 87% in general (Schultz et al., 2017). Moreover, geospatial land use and land cover data derived from OpenStreetMap can be applied in the development of urban study areas for London and Paris as argued by (Fonte et al., 2019). The data from OpenStreetMap can be employed in determining the Local Climate Zones, especially the natural ones for the area of interest in Coimbra City in Portugal as noted by (Lopes et al., 2017).

OSM-based navigation can involve textual and cartographic interfaces and augmented images to guide the target object along a planned route as found by (Amirian et al., 2015). Similarly, OpenStreetMap data can be used in reflection and evaluation concerns in planning and designing the built environment with the use of figures and grounds and polar histograms as techniques of visualization (Boeing, 2020b). Further, real-time and exact shortest path computing is possible using OpenStreetMap data in large networks such as continental with millions of street segments where sophisticated functionality such as draggable routes, and round-trip planning is also possible (Luxen & Vetter, 2011).

OpenStreetMap is very popular for studying global urban issues, including SDGs achievement. Herfort et al. (2023) aimed at quantifying the missing building data in OSM while taking into account world region, human development index, and city size systematics. The study found that the completeness of buildings in OSM differs in urban centers; some even have over 80% while others are parallel to 20%. Inequality in the mapping of building data under OSM was explained over this temporal study using the Gini coefficient as well as Moran's I to establish the level of spatial clustering of buildings. Interestingly, global spatial inequality of OSM building completeness has diminished over time while local spatial dependence has strengthened further depending on the HDI.

OSM can integrate the clients, market understanding, and distribution which in turn encourages the promotion of sustainable business plans. The use of OSM data supports public participation, environmental mitigation and conservation, and green marketing strategies targeting consumers (Ahmad, 2024b). OSM is a rich source of data that can be used for market analysis and finding out trends and characteristics of consumers and competitors. With integrated data, OSM can help in improving supply chain organization, as well as in decision-making over expansion strategies. It makes it easier to determine the market share and trends, as well as extract consumer information, making it helpful in decision-making (Ahmad, 2024a).

Bai et al. (2024) analyzed the contributions of OpenStreetMap in Tehran city in Iran, London, and Los Angeles. They found that a few active users are mostly responsible for data submissions, but collective data from a large number of people is essential for the integration of local knowledge. Current approaches toward the evaluation of VGI quality disregard virtually 10% of data and contain valuable information that is often local; therefore, more effective methods of assessment are needed. Individual characteristics and context also play an important role in VGI activities and data donation.

Geomarketing for Businesses

Geo-marketing is primarily used for optimizing location strategies for businesses like supermarkets, planning and targeting promotional campaigns, segmenting customers based on various variables, enhancing service planning in sectors like healthcare, enriching customer shopping experiences, supporting commercial and social urban programs, understanding tourist behaviors for territorial segmentation, visualizing strategic information for decision-making, and improving the placement of advertisements to increase reach and sales.

Improved Customer Targeting

Maximizing the geo-business data analytics and showing how geo-marketing data analysis can direct businesses to the right consumer zones, message customization, and target consumer archetypes. Such geo-marketing models can assist supermarkets in strategizing where to locate them based on sociodemographic characteristics and the layout of supermarkets (Baviera-Puig et al., 2016). Geo-marketing therefore helps to segment tourist demand for the demand for coastal tourism so that relevant marketing and decisions can easily be made based on similarities of needs (Peñarubia-Zaragoza et al., 2019). As noted by (Cavallone et al., 2017), geo-marketing tools can enhance the market performance as a result of enhanced concentration on the clients' requirements and patterns hence enhancing the quality of healthcare services. Geo-marketing can assist any kind of private hospital in knowing who their customers are and where to find them hence enhancing their sales and marketing techniques (Uyguçgil & Atalık, 2017). Geo-marketing can be a useful aid for defining the best areas for setting up or expanding the business, and it can be used with benefit in real estate purchase and rental (B. A. Tkhorikov et al., 2020).

Enhanced Location Decision-Making

Spatial analysis is an essential method of choice in retail and urban planning whereby it provides a massive impact in the positioning of business outlets, store location decision-making process and, efficient delivery routes. Using this approach, the businesses can be able to gain insights on the organization of potential consumers and competitors over a specific region where the business hope to establish their outlets. For instance, geo-marketing approach is applied to find the appropriate place for a new hypermarket in Ia i city. This involves the extraction of the catchment area and focusing on the distances to the other shopping centers as a predictor variable (Rosu et al., 2013). This method ensures that new stores are conveniently located for the target market, maximizing foot traffic and potential sales. The same strategy has been implemented in Tehran City, Iran, because of the growing population and raising the income level, which further extended the demand for more land (Omidipoor et al., 2019). As it has been argued earlier, spatial analysis can play an important role in fulfilling unmet demand by explaining where it is most likely to occur so that new urban developments and succeeding retailing activities can always be efficient and possibly profitable. This type of analysis assists in deciphering growth and alterations happening in the urban area, which in turn proves useful in the planning of where to construct new facades for retail stores, infrastructural development, and living spaces in support of economic growth.

Competitive Advantage

The knowledge and comprehension of competitors' locations and activities offer businesses a major advantage. With this information on competitors, firms can be in a position to discover areas of low density of competitors or possibly no competition at all, which presents opportunities for firms to enter the market. This aids in identifying measures needed to create a competitive position and to obtain greater consideration inside the market. For instance, when a competitor's store is in a populated region, a business may decide to open a store in the neighboring area that may prove to have high traffic density but it does not share the area with the competitor since consumers may opt for convenience. Additionally, tracking competitor campaigns and promotions through spatial analysis allows businesses to adjust their marketing strategies proactively. This could involve launching targeted promotions, adjusting pricing strategies, or enhancing service offerings to outcompete rivals. The ability to monitor and respond to competitors' moves in real-time ensures that a business remains agile and competitive in a rapidly changing market landscape.

Campaign Efficacy

Geo-marketing is rather essential for the effectiveness of marketing strategies, as it allows agencies to identify preferred sites for advertisements. By looking at the geographic and demographic characteristics of the audience, more ads can be placed where potential buyers are most likely to be found, hence improving the ad returns. According to (Nunes et al., 2014), use of space data in the placement of advertisements increases sales since these advertisements reach the intended consumer at the most appropriate time. Furthermore, the enhancement of geo-marketing with the use of Bluetooth Low Energy (BLE) technology has also dramatically transformed the shopping experience. It is due to the fact that malls or large retail spaces can be clearly targeted with the help of BLE and customers can receive immediate and very specific promotions and offers based on their location at the given moment (Zaim & Bellafkih, 2016). This not only increases customer interaction but also leads to more purchases that were not initially on the customer's shopping agenda since they are offered promotions while they shop.

Deeper Customer Understanding

Geo-marketing holds valuable information about customer's behavior and preferences that can be used to enhance the concept of the shopping space. To do this, retail stores can use Geographic Information Systems to understand spatial data on the consumption habits and trends of the target market and, therefore create catalogs and marketing strategies that fit those attributes. For instance, (Liao et al., 2011) concluded that tailored catalogs draw more attention means that they can help to sell more than other catalogs, and the customers are likely to be loyal. Moreover, the use of geo-social media data helps in understanding customers and their behavior at locations that are of interest. This information can be valuable for retailers to determine potential partners to embark on a joint promotion campaign, as well as to improve the existing service provisions. For instance, exploring the data of check-in and comments on social media sites can allow retailers to grasp the shoppers' purchasing behavior and attitudes, so as to optimize their selling strategies and solutions in compliance (Bao et al., 2014). This deeper understanding of customer behavior can help in providing a shopping experience that would help create customer loyalty and grow the business.

GEOMARKETING DATA ANALYSIS

Geo-marketing data analysis is the process of leveraging geographic information to enhance marketing strategies and business decision-making. It involves using various technologies and analytical methods to gain insights into consumer behavior, market trends, and geographic patterns. The core components and data sources for effective geo-marketing data analysis are outlined below.

Technology Systems

A key factor in implementing effective geo-marketing is the availability of a strong technological platform for supporting the related geospatial and marketing data. The most significant technology systems include servers, smartphone applications, and beacons that help in the data analysis phase.

Servers

Servers are the major components in the support of platforms of geo-marketing systems, as they ensure the storage and processing of a large amount of geospatial and marketing data. They support the central databanks by compiling all data to improve consistency and assurance. By employing high computational performance, servers provide an opportunity to implement intricate mathematical algorithms for clustering, segmentation, and prognostication. Such processing power is crucial for analytics and pattern extraction from large datasets enabling strategic decisions in market segmentation, customer characterization, and site selection. Further, servers are also flexible since they enable organizations to meet their expanding computing needs. Security policies implemented in a server protect customer and business information to prevent a breach and to confidentiality and integrity.

Smartphone Applications

Applications are a key element of geo-marketing as they offer the ability to detect the location in real-time, as well as to send geo-targeted offers to customers. These utilize GPS and other location-based services to identify the exact location of the people, allowing various enterprises to effectively market their messages and promotions. The practical use of advertisements, coupons, and notifications increases the level of user engagement and encourages customers. When engaging with the users, it is possible to deliver more targeted and contextual marketing messages with the help of a smartphone – and this way, conversion rates can be enhanced. There are functionalities such as geofencing marketing, whereby one can set a marketing activity to go live when users are within or outside a particular region. Such a real-time interaction motivates sales and improves customer experience as they receive the right information at the right time.

Beacons

These are small Wi-Fi-enabled devices designed to broadcast in close vicinity and offer real-time location-based service and marketing. These devices have very crucial role of a marketing tool to target the customers at a more individual level depending on their location with respect to the beacon. Beacons can be utilized to provide customers with information on where to find certain products or area within the retail store, enhancing the shopping experience. Another advantage of using beacons is tracking the relative movement and congregation of customers within the establishment to get data on traffic patterns, time spent in areas, and hotspots. This data aids in determining the number of square feet of selling space for products and the effective positioning of promotional displays. They also enable one-on-one coupons, advertisements, detailed offers, and loyalty incentives for ease of targeting consumers when close to the beacon. Such a level of communication also improves on the satisfaction level of the customers while simultaneously helping boost sales by making impulse buying decisions.

Analytical Tools and Methods

The incorporation of computer-aided tools like GIS, computational intelligence, fuzzy clustering, and clustering algorithms forms a compact base of geo-marketing. It can allow businesses to map and model geographical factors to forecast market conditions, categorize markets clearly, and strategize most effectively on the basis of marketing geography. This prognosis capacity enhances knowledge-based decisions and sound planning, which is critical in business performance and operations and the sustainability of its competitive edge.

Geographic Information Systems (GIS)

GIS is an essential prerequisite of geo-marketing as a discipline because it offers a suitable means of enabling its visualization. As a result, GIS assists in performing analyses on a content layer, which is the superposition of different data layers on a map that focuses on geographic contexts. It is important to visualize and understand this so as to manage and conduct market analysis, selection of strategic sites, and distribution of resources. For instance, businesses can rely on GIS when it comes to siting their stores, using influential factors such as population density, competitors, and geographical location. GIS also assists with the demographic function; this is because many marketing companies require knowledge of population density and characteristics of specific locations.

Computational Intelligence

Machine learning, AI, and other components of computational intelligence remain critical to the forecasting of consumer behavior and markets. These techniques involved the use of large datasets to condone identified trends and make forecasts regarding future market characteristics. Customers can be split, analyzed, and grouped depending on their consumption patterns and trends, sales predictions are also possible. AI can improve the capability of unique selling to predict individual customer preferences and provide recommendations that suit them. Visualization in geo-marketing supported by computational intelligence can allow predictive and prescriptive analytics. This leads to more effective marketing campaigns, optimized resource allocation, and improved customer engagement.

Fuzzy Clustering

Another complex method for clustering is called Fuzzy clustering it is used when the data are grouped according to the degree of similarity which is especially important in geography. While other clustering approaches explain the affiliation of each point to clusters as a non-overlapping relationship, fuzzy clustering permits an element to belong to more clusters with different degrees of membership. These are cases that are helpful when operating in scenarios where categories of data are not well defined. For instance, in market segmentation, customers might exhibit behaviors that overlap multiple segments. This overlapping is resolved by the concept of Fuzzy clustering which offers a better understanding of the various group of customers. This method improves the accurate identification of the markets' consumers hence giving a business the ability to market the products in the right manner.

Clustering Algorithms

Clustering algorithms play a crucial role in geo-marketing due to their effectiveness in the segmentation and targeting efforts of similar data points. Algorithms such as k-means, hierarchical clustering, and DBSCAN are useful in finding an intrinsic pattern in data, allowing for the observation of unique clusters within a population of customers. Dividing the total targeted population of consumers into related and homogenous segments assists marketers in addressing each segment and its needs singularly. Clustering algorithms also support location analysis by identifying areas with high concentrations of target customers and guiding decisions on where to establish new stores or launch marketing campaigns. The use of clustering algorithms thus enhances the effectiveness of marketing strategies, leading to increased customer satisfaction and business growth.

Data Sources

Different types of data are used to support geo-marketing initiatives. These sources contain valuable information about customer behavior, competition, and geographic factors that help business people to operate efficiently by directing resources on specific areas and localize their promotional activities (B. Tkhorikov et al., 2020). Key data sources include:

Internal Customer Data

Internal customer data entails data from the actual communication between the organization's own customers. This entails acquiring records of the customer's previous purchases, likes, comments made, and other related user activities. Through this data, everyone from business executives to the lowly clerk can effectively learn the customers' buying habits, popular items, or even his/her satisfaction scores. The insight can be applicable in creating more efficient and effective market segment targeting, promotion, and customer relationship management. For instance, availability of purchase history can assist in proposing the next products to offer to a consumer with purchasing patterns already tracked, thus enhancing sales and customer retention.

External Demographics

There are demographic factors outside an organization that are so crucial in assisting one in identifying the characteristics of its population such as age, income, education level, and number of household members among others. This information is usually gleaned from data available in databases such as census data and any other available data. A study of the demographic characteristics of specific areas is crucial in a case where a business needs to locate its market, evaluate the opportunities of the identified market, and adapt the strategies on the basis of the demographic characteristics of the selected target group. For instance, some organizations using a marketing strategy might decide to target specific regions of high-density population or interested audiences so that there increased chance of success.

OpenStreetMap (OSM) Point of Interest (POI) Data

OpenStreetMap (OSM) is a free map of the world and it may involve the geographical place of business organizations and other identifiable places such as landmarks. The main strength of OSM data in Geo-marketing lies in the availability of physical location mapping in a context where geo-markcting entail's location analysis and decision making (Wichmann et al., 2023). Businesses can employ OSM data for analyzing competition in stores, determine the new store placements, and improving the city's marketing. Another element of geographical data collection that makes OSM advantageous for businesses is the fact that its updates are conducted by the members of the community, which means that the information received is constantly being developed and improved.

GEOMARKETING ANALYSIS WITH OSM POI DATA

Using OSM Datasets for Geo-Marketing Analysis may Have the Following Dimensions

Competitor Analysis

Competitor analysis is a crucial aspect of strategic planning for retail businesses. By understanding the geographic distribution of competitors, businesses can make informed decisions about store placements, marketing strategies, and competitive positioning. Competitor analysis involves extracting Point of Interest (POI) data relevant to competitors from the OSM dataset. This data may include details about retail stores, supermarkets, and other relevant businesses. Specific tags within the OSM dataset, such as *shop=supermarket, shop=convenience, and amenity=marketplace*, can be used to identify these points of interest. The dataset should also contain essential attributes like the name of the business, the type of business, and the geographic coordinates (latitude and longitude). Once the POI data is extracted, spatial analysis techniques can be employed to assess the proximity of competitor locations to a retailer's existing and potential store locations.

One method is to calculate the straight-line distances between each competitor's location and a retailer's stores. This helps identify competitors in close proximity that might influence the retailer's market share in those areas. Additionally, buffer analysis can be conducted by creating zones around a retailer's store locations. These buffers, set at various radii (e.g., 500 meters, 1 kilometer), help visualize the density of competitors within these zones, guiding strategic decisions on store placements. Heat map analysis is another valuable tool for visualizing the density of competitor locations in different areas. Heat maps can highlight clusters of competitors and help identify potential opportunities for new store locations in underserved regions. By analyzing the competitive density—calculating the number of competitors within a certain radius around the Retail locations—businesses can determine areas with intense competition versus those with fewer competitors, signaling potential expansion opportunities. Moreover, market gap identification can be achieved by overlaying competitor locations with demographic data such as population density, income levels, and consumer behavior patterns. This comprehensive analysis helps pinpoint areas with high demand but low competition, providing strategic opportunities for new store locations.

For example, data collection can begin with extracting POI data from OSM using relevant tags and ensuring the dataset includes accurate coordinates and attributes. Spatial analysis can be performed using GIS tools like QGIS, ArcGIS, or Python libraries such as Geopandas and Shapely. These tools enable distance calculations and buffer analysis, while heat maps can be generated using tools like HeatMapLayer in Leaflet or density functions in QGIS. Presenting the findings through visual maps and detailed reports can help to highlight areas with high competition and suggest potential new locations based on market gap analysis. By systematically analyzing competitor locations using spatial data and advanced GIS techniques, a retailer can gain valuable insights into the competitive landscape, helping to make informed decisions about store placements, marketing strategies, and overall business growth.

Demographic Analysis

Demographic analysis is a vital component of strategic planning for retail businesses, providing insights into the population characteristics of different areas. While OSM data does not directly provide demographic data, certain demographic characteristics can be inferred from the available POI data (Jokar Arsanjani & Bakillah, 2015). For instance, areas with a higher density of schools might indicate a younger population, whereas regions with more healthcare facilities might suggest an older population. To perform a comprehensive demographic analysis, businesses can start by extracting relevant POI data from OSM. This data includes various establishments such as schools, healthcare facilities, recreational areas, and residential zones. By analyzing the distribution and density of these POIs, businesses can make educated guesses about the demographic composition of different areas. For example, a high concentration of schools, playgrounds, and daycare centers likely points to neighborhoods with a significant number of young families and children. Conversely, a higher number of healthcare facilities, retirement homes, and pharmacies may indicate a predominance of older residents.

To enhance the accuracy of the demographic analysis, it is beneficial to overlay OSM POI data with external demographic datasets. These datasets, which might be available from government sources, research institutions, or commercial data providers, typically include detailed information about population age, income levels, education, and household composition. By combining these external datasets with the POI data, businesses can gain a clearer and more precise understanding of the demographic landscape. Spatial analysis techniques can be utilized to integrate and analyze these datasets effectively. For example, GIS tools can be used to create overlay maps that combine OSM POI data with demographic information, allowing for a visual representation of how POIs relate to demographic indicators. Heat maps and density maps can be particularly useful in this context, highlighting areas with high concentrations of specific demographic groups.

Analyzing the distribution of POIs in relation to demographic indicators enables businesses to identify areas with high potential consumer demand. For instance, a neighborhood with a growing number of young families might present a prime location for new retail stores focused on children's products, educational services, or family-oriented entertainment. On the other hand, areas with a significant elderly population might benefit from additional healthcare services, wellness centers, and stores offering products tailored to older adults. Additionally, demographic analysis can reveal trends and shifts in population characteristics over time. By regularly updating and analyzing demographic data, businesses can stay ahead of emerging trends and adjust their strategies accordingly. For example, if a previously young neighborhood is experiencing an influx of older residents, businesses can adapt by introducing products and services that cater to this changing demographic.

Amenity Analysis

Amenity analysis is crucial for understanding the attractiveness and suitability of different areas for retail development. Amenities such as parks, transportation hubs, and entertainment venues significantly influence consumer behavior and foot traffic, making them key factors in location decision-making. To begin an amenity analysis, businesses should extract amenity-related POI data from OSM. This data may include various types of amenities, such as parks, public transportation hubs (e.g., bus and train stations), and entertainment venues (e.g., cinemas, theaters, and sports arenas). These points of interest provide valuable insights into the infrastructure and recreational opportunities available in different areas. Table 1 shows some of the tags related to different kinds of amenities.

Table 1. Amenities types and relevant OSM tags

Amenity Type	OSM Tag	Description
Parks and Recreation	leisure=park	Public parks and recreational areas
	leisure=playground	Playgrounds for children
	leisure=sports_centre	Sports centers and facilities
	leisure=stadium	Stadiums for sports and events
Transportation	public_transport=station	General public transport stations

continued on following page

146

Table 1. Continued

Amenity Type	OSM Tag	Description
	railway=station	Train and metro stations
	bus=station	Bus stations
	amenity=bicycle_rental	Bicycle rental stations
Entertainment	amenity=cinema	Cinemas and movie theaters
	amenity=theatre	Theatres for performing arts
	amenity=nightclub	Nightclubs
Healthcare	amenity=hospital	Hospitals
	amenity=clinic	Clinics and outpatient care centers
	amenity=pharmacy	Pharmacies
Education	amenity=school	Schools for primary and secondary education
	amenity=university	Universities and higher education institutions
Shopping and Services	shop=supermarket	Supermarkets
	shop=mall	Shopping malls
	shop=convenience	Convenience stores
Food and Drink	amenity=restaurant	Restaurants
	amenity=cafe	Cafes
	amenity=fast_food	Fast food outlets
	amenity=bar	Bars and pubs
Public Services	amenity=police	Police stations
	amenity=fire_station	Fire stations
	amenity=post_office	Post offices
Financial Services	amenity=bank	Banks
	amenity=atm	ATMs
Religious Buildings	amenity=place_of_worship	Churches, mosques, temples, and other places of worship
Other Amenities	amenity=library	Libraries
	amenity=community_centre	Community centers
	amenity=parking	Parking areas and facilities

Once the amenity-related POI data is collected, spatial analysis techniques can be employed to assess the availability and distribution of these amenities within target areas. Two effective methods for this analysis are density analysis and hotspot analysis. Density analysis helps in understanding the concentration of amenities in specific areas. By calculating the number of amenities per unit area (e.g., per square kilometer), businesses can identify regions with high and low concentrations of amenities. GIS tools can create density maps that visually represent the distribution of amenities. Areas with a high density of parks, transportation hubs, and entertainment venues are likely to attract more foot traffic, making them more attractive for retail development. For instance, a high density of parks and recreational areas may indicate a family-friendly neighborhood, which could be ideal for stores selling children's products, sports equipment, or outdoor gear.

Hotspot analysis identifies clusters of amenities and determines statistically significant concentrations. This method helps in pinpointing specific areas where amenities are particularly abundant or scarce. By using GIS software to perform hotspot analysis, businesses can create maps that highlight "hotspots" of amenities. These maps reveal areas with a high level of infrastructure and recreational opportunities, which are attractive to potential customers. For example, a hotspot of transportation hubs indicates excellent connectivity, making the area easily accessible and thus a prime location for retail stores that rely on high foot traffic.

Through the combined use of density and hotspot analysis, businesses can gain a comprehensive understanding of the amenity landscape within their target areas. This information is invaluable for making informed decisions about store locations. Areas with a high concentration of amenities are likely to attract more visitors, providing greater opportunities for retail businesses to thrive. Moreover, analyzing the distribution of amenities in relation to potential store locations helps in identifying gaps and opportunities. If an area with high consumer demand lacks certain amenities, there might be an opportunity for a business to fill this gap and attract customers by providing the needed services or facilities.

Market Segmentation

Market segmentation is a critical process for understanding and targeting specific groups within a larger market. By segmenting the target market based on the characteristics of POIs available in OSM data, businesses can tailor their strategies to meet the unique needs and preferences of different market segments. To begin the segmentation process, it is essential to extract relevant POI data from OSM. This data may include information about amenities such as parks, schools, transportation hubs, and entertainment venues, as well as competitor locations. Additionally, collecting demographic data from external sources, such as population density, income levels, and age distribution, can complement the OSM data, providing a more comprehensive understanding of the target areas.

Once the data is collected, spatial analysis techniques can be employed to segment the market based on the distribution of amenities, competitor locations, and demographic features. One effective method is to cluster areas with similar distributions of these characteristics. For example, regions with a high density of parks and schools can be grouped together as family-friendly zones, while areas with numerous entertainment venues and restaurants can be identified as nightlife or leisure zones. Similarly, analyzing the proximity and density of competitor locations allows businesses to identify high-competition areas that might require differentiation strategies and low-competition areas that could be ideal for new store locations.

To achieve precise segmentation, spatial clustering algorithms such as K-means clustering and DBSCAN (Density-Based Spatial Clustering of Applications with Noise) can be used. K-means clustering is a popular method for partitioning data into distinct clusters based on the mean values of features. It is particularly useful for segmenting markets with clear boundaries. The process involves standardizing the dataset to ensure all features, such as amenity density, competitor proximity, and demographic data, are on the same scale. The K-means algorithm is then applied to the standardized data to identify clusters, which can be analyzed to understand the characteristics of each market segment. On the other hand, DBSCAN is well-suited for identifying clusters of varying shapes and sizes and handling noise (outliers) effectively. This makes it ideal for market segmentation where the density of POIs varies significantly. The process involves preprocessing the data by scaling and normalizing the features before applying the DBSCAN algorithm to identify dense clusters of POIs. The resulting clusters can then be evaluated to discern meaningful market segments, with noise excluded from the analysis.

For example, implementing K-means clustering involves using Python libraries such as Scikit-learn. The data is first preprocessed and standardized before applying the K-means algorithm to identify clusters. Similarly, DBSCAN can be implemented using Scikit-learn, where the data is scaled and normalized before applying the algorithm to detect dense clusters. Visualization tools such as Matplotlib or Geopandas can be used to create maps and charts that illustrate the identified clusters and their characteristics. By segmenting the target market using OSM POI data and spatial clustering algorithms, businesses can gain a deeper understanding of the unique characteristics of different market segments. This enables them to tailor their marketing strategies, optimize store locations, and better meet the needs of their customers. The combination of detailed spatial analysis and sophisticated clustering techniques provides valuable insights that drive effective decision-making and strategic planning.

Site Selection

Site selection is a crucial process for retail businesses aiming to expand their presence by opening new stores. The success of new store locations heavily depends on a thorough analysis of geographic and demographic factors. By leveraging the distribution of relevant POIs in the OSM dataset, businesses can identify optimal locations for new store openings and make informed decisions that maximize profitability and market reach.

To begin the site selection process, it is essential to extract relevant POI data from OSM. This data may include information about various amenities, such as parks, schools, transportation hubs, and entertainment venues, as well as competitor locations. Additionally, collecting demographic data from external sources, such as population density, income levels, and age distribution, can complement the OSM data, providing a more comprehensive understanding of the target areas. Once the data is collected, spatial analysis techniques can be employed to understand the distribution of POIs in the target area. Tools such as QGIS, ArcGIS, or Python libraries like Geopandas can help visualize and analyze the geographic distribution of amenities and competitor locations. Identifying areas with a high density of desirable amenities, such as parks, schools, and public transportation hubs, is crucial as these areas are likely to attract significant foot traffic and potential customers. Similarly, evaluating the distribution of competitors helps identify areas with low competition.

Conducting a suitability analysis involves overlaying various layers of OSM POI data to create composite maps that provide a comprehensive view of the target area. Several factors need to be considered in the suitability analysis, including accessibility, competition, and market demand. Accessibility can be analyzed by considering the proximity to major roads, public transportation hubs, and pedestrian pathways, as areas that are easily accessible are likely to attract more customers. The competitive landscape can be evaluated by mapping competitor locations, and identifying areas with low competition that present opportunities for new store openings without immediate threats from established businesses. Market demand can be assessed by overlaying demographic data with POI distribution, identifying areas with high population density, favorable income levels, and suitable age demographics that align with the target market for the new store.

GIS tools are invaluable for performing advanced spatial analysis and visualizing the suitability of potential sites. Techniques such as heat mapping, buffer analysis, and kernel density estimation can help identify optimal locations for new stores. Heat maps can visualize the density of amenities and competitor locations, highlighting areas with high concentrations of desirable amenities and low concentrations of competitors as prime locations. Buffer analysis can determine the catchment area around potential sites by creating zones around each potential site to evaluate the density and accessibility of surrounding POIs within a specified radius. Kernel density estimation can identify hotspots of activity, helping visualize the intensity of POIs and highlighting regions with high potential for customer traffic.

By following these steps and leveraging spatial analysis techniques, businesses can identify optimal locations for new store openings. The suitability analysis, which overlays various layers of OSM POI data and demographic information, helps in evaluating factors such as accessibility, competition, and market demand. This comprehensive approach ensures that new store locations are strategically chosen to maximize customer reach and business success.

Optimization of Existing Stores

Optimizing the performance of existing store locations is paramount for retail businesses looking to enhance profitability and customer satisfaction. A strategic approach involves analyzing foot traffic patterns around current stores and leveraging OSM POI to pinpoint areas for improvement and implement targeted optimizations. To initiate this process, businesses gather and analyze foot traffic data obtained through various sources, such as pedestrian counts or mobile location data, overlaid with OSM POI data. This comprehensive dataset includes information on amenities like parks, schools, transportation hubs, competitor locations, and demographic features such as population density and income levels.

Using spatial analysis techniques facilitated by tools like QGIS or Python libraries such as Geopandas, businesses can visualize foot traffic intensity around each store location. This analysis reveals areas with high foot traffic density, indicating popular routes or bustling commercial zones, as well as areas with lower foot traffic that may require attention. By correlating foot traffic patterns with the distribution of amenities, competitors, and demographic characteristics, businesses can identify underperforming store locations.

Strategic adjustments can then be devised based on these insights. For instance, enhancing existing amenities or introducing new attractions can draw more foot traffic. Differentiating store offerings from nearby competitors, refining marketing strategies to target specific customer segments identified through demographic data, or adjusting operational hours based on peak foot traffic times are all viable strategies. These adjustments are aimed at optimizing store performance and fostering a more engaging shopping experience for customers. For example, using Geopandas and Matplotlib, businesses can spatially visualize foot traffic patterns around existing stores, facilitating informed decision-making.

Such visualizations help identify spatial patterns and correlations that guide strategic decisions to maximize the potential of each store location. By systematically analyzing foot traffic patterns and leveraging OSM POI data, businesses can refine their store operations and customer engagement strategies. This data-driven approach ensures that resources are allocated efficiently to enhance store performance, ultimately driving increased profitability and customer satisfaction.

CONCLUSION

The Geomarketing Analysis with OSM POI Data is a pioneering approach in data management as it involves several critical dimensions for strategic planning and market insight. Competitor analysis begins by extracting relevant Point of Interest (POI) data, such as retail stores and supermarkets, from OSM using specific tags like shop=supermarket and amenity=marketplace. Spatial analysis techniques, including distance calculations and buffer analysis, are then employed to assess the proximity of competitor locations to existing and potential store sites. This helps identify competitive hotspots and areas with potential for new store placements. Demographic analysis leverages POI data to infer population characteristics like age distribution and socioeconomic status, supplemented by external demographic datasets for a comprehensive view. Amenities such as parks, transportation hubs, and entertainment venues are crucial in determining site attractiveness, analyzed through density and hotspot analyses to identify prime locations. Market segmentation utilizes spatial clustering algorithms to group areas with similar POI distributions, facilitating targeted marketing strategies and optimized store placements. Site selection involves overlaying various POI layers to evaluate factors like accessibility and market demand, ensuring strategic decisions that maximize profitability and customer engagement. Optimization of existing stores utilizes foot traffic analysis overlaid with POI data to identify underperforming areas and implement tailored improvements, thereby enhancing overall store performance and customer satisfaction.

REFERENCES

Ahmad, M. (2024a). Connecting the Dots: Harnessing OpenStreetMap for Big Data Analytics and Market Insights. In Darwish, D. (Ed.), *Big Data Analytics Techniques for Market Intelligence* (pp. 329–347). IGI Global., DOI: 10.4018/979-8-3693-0413-6.ch013

Ahmad, M. (2024b). Unleashing Business Potential: Harnessing OpenStreetMap for Intelligent Growth and Sustainability. In Singh, S., Rajest, S. S., Hadoussa, S., Obaid, A. J., & Regin, R. (Eds.), *Data-Driven Intelligent Business Sustainability* (pp. 177–198). IGI Global., DOI: 10.4018/979-8-3693-0049-7.ch013

Amirian, P., Basiri, A., Gales, G., Winstanley, A., & McDonald, J. (2015). The next generation of navigational services using OpenStreetMap data: The integration of augmented reality and graph databases. *Lecture Notes in Geoinformation and Cartography*, 0(9783319142791), 211–228. Advance online publication. DOI: 10.1007/978-3-319-14280-7_11

Augusto, M. F. (2020). *Geographic Marketing in Support of Decision-Making Processes*. DOI: 10.4018/978-1-7998-2963-8.ch005

Bai, A., Satarpour, M., Mohebbi, F., & Forati, A. M. (2024). Digital Crowdsourcing and VGI: impact on information quality and business intelligence. *Spatial Information Research*, 1–9.

Bao, J., Deshpande, A., McFaddin, S., & Narayanaswami, C. (2014). Partner-marketing using geo-social media data for smarter commerce. *IBM Journal of Research and Development*, 58(5/6), 6:1–6:12. Advance online publication. DOI: 10.1147/JRD.2014.2344514

Baviera-Puig, A., Buitrago-Vera, J., & Escriba-Perez, C. (2016). Geomarketing models in supermarket location strategies. *Journal of Business Economics and Management*, 17(6), 1205–1221. Advance online publication. DOI: 10.3846/16111699.2015.1113198

Beaumont, J. R. (1989). An overview of market analysis: Who? What? Where? and Why? *International Journal of Information Management*, 9(1), 51–62. Advance online publication. DOI: 10.1016/0268-4012(89)90037-6

Boeing, G. (2020a). A multi-scale analysis of 27,000 urban street networks: Every US city, town, urbanized area, and Zillow neighborhood. *Environment and Planning. B, Urban Analytics and City Science*, 47(4), 590–608. Advance online publication. DOI: 10.1177/2399808318784595

Boeing, G. (2020b). Exploring Urban Form Through Openstreetmap Data. In *Urban Experience and Design*. DOI: 10.4324/9780367435585-15

Cavallone, M., Magno, F., & Zucchi, A. (2017). Improving service quality in healthcare organisations through geomarketing statistical tools. *The TQM Journal*, 29(5), 690–704. Advance online publication. DOI: 10.1108/TQM-12-2016-0104

Chaskalovic, J. (2009). Gravitation theory for mathematical modelling in geomarketing. *Journal of Interdisciplinary Mathematics*, 12(3), 409–420. Advance online publication. DOI: 10.1080/09720502.2009.10700633

Fonte, C. C., Patriarca, J. A., Minghini, M., Antoniou, V., See, L., & Brovelli, M. A. (2019). Using OpenStreetMap to Create Land Use and Land Cover Maps: Development of an Application. In *Geospatial Intelligence* (Vol. 2). Concepts, Methodologies, Tools, and Applications., DOI: 10.4018/978-1-5225-8054-6.ch047

Herfort, B., Lautenbach, S., Porto de Albuquerque, J., Anderson, J., & Zipf, A. (2023). A spatio-temporal analysis investigating completeness and inequalities of global urban building data in OpenStreetMap. *Nature Communications*, 14(1), 3985. Advance online publication. DOI: 10.1038/s41467-023-39698-6 PMID: 37414776

Hertig, L., & Maus, O. (1998). Geo-marketing solutions for the banking sector with emphasis on saving and cooperative banks [Geomarketing bei Banken und Sparkassen]. *Geo-Informations-Systeme, 11*(3).

Jokar Arsanjani, J., & Bakillah, M. (2015). Understanding the potential relationship between the socio-economic variables and contributions to OpenStreetMap. *International Journal of Digital Earth*, 8(11), 861–876. Advance online publication. DOI: 10.1080/17538947.2014.951081

Liao, S. H., Chen, Y. J., & Lin, Y. T. (2011). Mining customer knowledge to implement online shopping and home delivery for hypermarkets. *Expert Systems with Applications*, 38(4), 3982–3991. Advance online publication. DOI: 10.1016/j.eswa.2010.09.059

Lopes, P., Fonte, C., See, L., & Bechtel, B. (2017). Using OpenStreetMap data to assist in the creation of LCZ maps. *2017 Joint Urban Remote Sensing Event. JURSE*, 2017, 1–4. Advance online publication. DOI: 10.1109/JURSE.2017.7924630

Luxen, D., & Vetter, C. (2011). Real-time routing with OpenStreetMap data. *GIS: Proceedings of the ACM International Symposium on Advances in Geographic Information Systems*. DOI: 10.1145/2093973.2094062

Nunes, A., Santana, C., Bezerra, F., & Sobral, N. (2014). Knowledge Acquisition Based on Geomarketing Information for Decision Making: A Case Study on a Food Company. *International Journal of Innovation, Management and Technology*, 5(6), 422–427. Advance online publication. DOI: 10.7763/IJIMT.2014.V5.552

Omidipoor, M., Jelokhani-Niaraki, M., & Samany, N. N. (2019). A Web-based geo-marketing decision support system for land selection: A case study of Tehran, Iran. *Annals of GIS*, 25(2), 179–193. Advance online publication. DOI: 10.1080/19475683.2019.1575905

Peñarubia-Zaragoza, M. P., Simancas-Cruz, M., & Forgione-Martín, G. (2019). An application of geomarketing to coastal tourism areas. *Tourism & Management Studies*, 15(4), 7–16. Advance online publication. DOI: 10.18089/tms.2019.150401

Rosu, L., Blageanu, A., & Iacob, I. (2013). Geomarketing -A New Approach in Decision Marketing : Case Study – Shopping Centres in Iasi. *Lucrările Seminarului …, January*.

Schultz, M., Voss, J., Auer, M., Carter, S., & Zipf, A. (2017). Open land cover from OpenStreetMap and remote sensing. *International Journal of Applied Earth Observation and Geoinformation*, 63, 206–213. Advance online publication. DOI: 10.1016/j.jag.2017.07.014

Shaitura, S. V., Feoktistova, F. M., Minitaeva, A. M., Olenev, L. A., Chulkov, V. O., & Kozhaev, Y. P. (2020). Spatial geomarketing powered by big data. *Revista Turismo Estudos & Práticas*, S5, 13.

Tkhorikov, B., Kazybayeva, A., Gerasimenko, O., & Zhakypbek, L. (2020). *Theoretical and Methodological Approaches and Stages of Formation Concept Geomarketing*. DOI: 10.2991/aebmr.k.201215.055

Tkhorikov, B. A., Klimova, T., Gerasimenko, O., Titova, I. N., & Ozerova, M. M. (2020). Geomarketing—A new concept or an applied business tool? *Bulletin of Tomsk State University.Economy*, 49, 199–213.

Uyguçgil, H., & Atalık, Ö. (2017). Geomarketing As A Tool For Health Service Business: Private Hospital Application. *Journal of Business Research - Turk, 9*(1). DOI: 10.20491/isarder.2017.252

Weber, P., & Haklay, M. (2008). OpenStreetMap: User-generated street maps. *IEEE Pervasive Computing*, 7(4).

Wichmann, J. R. K., Scholdra, T. P., & Reinartz, W. J. (2023). Propelling International Marketing Research with Geospatial Data. *Journal of International Marketing*, 31(2), 82–102. DOI: 10.1177/1069031X221149951

Zaim, D., & Bellafkih, M. (2016). Bluetooth Low Energy (BLE) based geomarketing system. *SITA 2016 - 11th International Conference on Intelligent Systems: Theories and Applications*. DOI: 10.1109/SITA.2016.7772263

KEY TERMS AND DEFINITIONS

Demographic analysis: is the study of population characteristics, such as age, gender, ethnicity, income, education level, and occupation. It involves collecting, analyzing, and interpreting demographic data to understand population trends, identify target markets, and inform policy decisions.

Geomarketing: is the application of geographic information systems (GIS) and spatial analysis techniques to marketing activities. It involves analyzing spatial data to understand the distribution of customers, identify target markets, optimize location planning, and measure marketing campaign effectiveness.

OpenStreetMap: is a free, editable map of the world created by a community of volunteers. It is a collaborative project that allows anyone to contribute data, making it a valuable resource for various applications, including mapping, navigation, and analysis.

Spatial analysis: is the process of examining spatial data to identify patterns, relationships, and trends. It involves using statistical and mathematical techniques to analyze the distribution, proximity, and connectivity of geographic features. Spatial analysis is essential for understanding spatial phenomena and making informed decisions based on geographic information.

Spatial data: is information that is tied to a specific location on the Earth's surface. It can include geographic features like points, lines, polygons, and rasters, as well as attributes associated with these features (e.g., population density, land use, elevation). Examples of spatial data include maps, satellite imagery, and GPS coordinates.

Chapter 7
Analysis of Barriers in Waste Collection and Segregation for Circular Economy Using IF–TOPSIS Approach

Mukesh Kumar Sharma
https://orcid.org/0009-0000-4109-5702
Arka Jain University, India

Kanika Prasad
https://orcid.org/0000-0002-1042-9738
National Institute of Technology, Jamshedpur, India

Dinesh Kumar
https://orcid.org/0000-0002-8439-833X
National Institute of Technology, Jamshedpur, India

ABSTRACT

In circular economy (CE), the significance of waste collection and segregation cannot be overstated, as these practices play a key role in diminishing environmental impact and fostering resource efficiency. It is expected that the waste generation would raise manifolds by the next decade. The shift to CE has the potential to result in annual savings amounting to billions in material costs. Thus, strategic waste practices play a crucial role in fostering sustainability and economic benefits. This article focuses on addressing multifaceted challenges to enhance the efficiency and sustainability of waste management practices. Hence, it introduces a framework utilising the IF-

DOI: 10.4018/979-8-3693-5563-3.ch007

TOPSIS methodology to assess impediments in the execution of waste collection and segregation strategies. Thirteen barriers have been discerned through literature reviews and expert evaluations. The study highlights that lack of public awareness as significant obstacle. These findings offer valuable insights to industries, academia, and government bodies, guiding them towards proper implementation.

1. INTRODUCTION

The concept of CE has evolved over the last few years, and there is no single definition of it (Kirchherr et al., 2017; Millar et al.2019). This paper adopts the definition of CE provided by Kirchherr et al. (2017), as "an economic system that replaces the 'end-of-life' concept with reducing, alternatively reusing, recycling and recovering materials in production/distribution and consumption processes". Urgency of effective waste collection and segregation is underscored by projections indicating a manifold increase in waste generation over the next decade. As societies continue to consume resources at an accelerating pace, the need for strategic waste practices becomes increasingly evident. These practices are instrumental in not only reducing environmental impact but also fostering resource efficiency, crucial elements in the transition towards a more sustainable and regenerative economic model. By diverting materials from landfills and redirecting them into recycling streams, these practices reduce the demand for virgin resources and curb the emission of greenhouse gases associated with resource extraction and production. This financial benefit is derived from the principles of reusing, refurbishing, and recycling materials, reducing the need for continuous extraction of raw resources and minimising the associated costs.

Recognizing the multifaceted challenges in waste management practices, this study is designed to analyse barriers hindering the efficiency and sustainability of waste collection and segregation. Several factors such as lack of public awareness, inadequate infrastructure, limited accessibility, policy inconsistencies, technological barriers and social stigma are some major hurdles that influence the effectiveness of waste collection and segregation. The study introduces a comprehensive framework, employing the integrated intuitionistic fuzzy-technique for the order of preference by similarity to ideal solution (IF-TOPSIS) methodology, to systematically analyse impediments in the execution of waste management strategies. The approach provides a structured methodology for addressing ambiguity and uncertainty inherent in complex perspectives. The methodology considers the congenital equivocalness of the decision maker assessment in the multi-criteria decision making (MCDM) domain. Based on the insights from the research study and expert opinions, 13 barriers that could impede the adoption of waste collection and segregation are systematically ranked. The uniqueness of this study lies in its approach, as it delves into qualitative data analysis while utilising the integrated IF-TOPSIS technique. This methodology is applied to prioritise the barriers influencing the implementation of waste collection and segregation in the CE.

2. RESEARCH BACKGROUND

A variety of methodologies were employed in the research focusing on waste collection and segregation, examining their significance and identifying several barriers. This study emphases on the identification and analysis of different barriers (Tat Dat Bui et al.2020) and promotes CE. It facilitates the separation of different types of materials, enabling them to be directed into appropriate recycling streams. This supports the closed-loop concept by preventing the linear disposal of materials. The literature review reveals 13 obstacles that impede the seamless integration and effective execution of waste collection and segregation practices.

1. B1: Inadequate infrastructure: Insufficient waste collection and segregation infrastructure, such as recycling facilities and appropriate disposal methods, can impede the smooth transition to a CE. Polidano (2000) suggested that realizing operational capabilities could be attained by enacting public policies that align institutional capacities with environmental, economic, social, and technical considerations, thereby fostering sustainability.

2. B2: Policy inconsistencies: The inconsistent and ineffective enforcement of laws and regulations governing waste management may result in confusion and non-compliance among both the public and businesses, as highlighted by Dou and Sarkis (2013) and Ongondo et al. (2011).

3. B3: Fragmented supply chains: Disconnected or fragmented supply chains in the waste management sector can disrupt the efficient flow of materials in a CE. (Rizos et al.2016).

4.B4: Lack of Material Recovery Facilities: Processing diverse mixed waste streams that include recyclable materials involves the separation of recyclables into distinct categories and material types as output products. This is achieved through the application of physical processing techniques, including a combination of mechanical, pneumatic, sensor-based processes, and a certain level of manual sorting and quality control, as outlined in the research by Cimpan et al. (2016).

5. B5: Lack of public awareness: Public awareness about the importance of waste collection and segregation in a CE is often inadequate, hindering effective participation and compliance. Yukalang et al. (2017), Mont, O.et al (2017).

6.B6: Technological barriers: The presence of outdated and unavailable technology in waste collection and segregation acts as a substantial obstacle, hindering the adoption of effective CE practices. This includes inefficient technological infrastructure for recycling, inadequate collection and storage facilities, and a lack of sufficient transportation facilities for managing the generated waste, as discussed by Patil and Kant (2014).

7. B7: Lack of collaboration: Insufficient collaboration among stakeholders, which include companies, governments, and communities-hinders the widespread implementation of CE standards. This limitation hinders the collective efforts needed for successful implementation, emphasizing the necessity for improved cooperation to advance sustainable and circular economic initiatives.

8. B8: Rapid population and industrial growth: The substantial volume of waste produced results from swift population expansion, economic and industrial advancement, and shifts in lifestyle.(Ikhlayel,2018).

9. B9: Ineffective Communication Strategies: According to Yukalang et al. (2017), a deficiency in communication exists between the local government and the community, leading to a situation where awareness fails to reach the masses.

10.B10: Lack of corporate social responsibility initiatives: Organizations possess the flexibility to assign limited financial resources to initiatives related to Corporate Social Responsibility, with a specific emphasis on environmentally sustainable waste recycling practices, as discussed by Mudgal et al. (2010), Mulliner et al. (2013), and Jogendra J. et al. (2022).

11.B11: Social stigma: Negative perceptions and social stigma associated with waste collection and segregation practices may discourage individuals from actively participating in CE efforts.

12. B12: Lack of standardisation: The absence of standardised procedures for waste collection and segregation can create confusion and hinder the scalability of CE practices. The conventional approaches to waste management and the intended use of recycled materials lack clarity, contributing to doubtfulness within society regarding the value of recycled products.

13. B13: Inadequate funding: Insufficient financial resources allocated to waste collection and segregation initiatives can limit the development and maintenance of effective CE systems. Significant financial investment is required for the recycling of waste, as indicated by Kumar and Dixit (2018).

3. RESEARCH METHODOLOGY

The illustration of the framework for discerning obstacles in the execution of waste collection and segregation is depicted in Figure 1. The analytical process within our framework comprises three key stages. The initial stage centres on identifying barriers through an extensive review of available literature, authored research, and insights from experts in relevant industries and academia. In the second stage, the IF-TOPSIS technique is applied to categorise barriers, focusing solely on the perspectives of experts from academic, government, and industry domains serving as decision-makers (DM). The outcomes in the concluding phase are validated by prior studies and supplemented by insights and comments from experts. Table 1 showcases the linguistic scale and the intuitionistic fuzzy (IF) ranking of alternatives and parameters.

Stage 1: Identification of barriers in implementation of waste collection and segregation

Stage 1 involves initiating the proposed framework by conducting a comprehensive review to identify barriers and challenges associated with the implementation of waste collection and segregation. A systematic literature review methodology is employed, utilizing web-based electronic record management services such as "Google Scholar," "Science Direct," "Scopus," "Web of Science," and others. Keywords and combinations like "CE," "Waste Collection," "Segregation," "Barriers," "IF-TOPSIS," "MCDM," etc., are used to extract relevant information from existing literature, previous research, and expert suggestions. Through rigorous investigation, discussion, scrutiny, content verification, and approval by scholars, a total of 13 common barriers are identified in this initial stage.

Figure 1. Framework of study

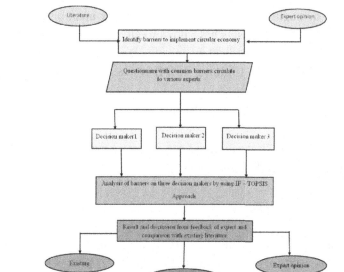

Table 1. Linguistic scale and IF rating for alternative and criteria

Linguistic terms	Intuitionistic Fuzzy numbers
Not Relevant (NR)	(0.20, 0.80, 0.00)
Least Relevant (LR)	(0.35, 0.60, 0.05)
Relevant (R)	(0.60, 0.35, 0.05)
Very Relevant (VR)	(0.75, 0.15, 0.10)
Most Relevant (MR)	(0.85, 0.10, 0.05)

Stage 2: Application of IF-TOPSIS method

At this phase, specific obstacles in the implementation of WCS are analysed by using the IF-TOPSIS method. TOPSIS is an uncomplicated and straightforward technique instrumental in providing solutions to MCDM problems, initially developed by Hwang in the year 1981 (Hwang et al., 1981). The method's underlying concept is that the least difference from the positive ideal solution (PIS) and the greatest difference from the negative ideal solution (NIS) should be the most favourable choice. TOPSIS utilizes both distances from PIS and NIS concurrently to categorize the selection order based on the decreasing order of the relative closeness coefficient. In coping with the escalating intricacies of decision-making, decision-makers commonly employ fuzzy sets to incorporate ambiguity and ambivalence. Atanassov's Intuitionistic Fuzzy Set (IFS), proposed in 1986, extends the classical fuzzy set, adeptly managing indeterminacy and obscurity in ambiguous conditions (Atanassov et al., 1986). These sets have proven effective across various domains, including trend identification, medical diagnostics, strategic planning, and decision-making processes. Take Y as a finite set. IFS B is given in Y as follows:

$$B = \{(\gamma, \alpha_B(\gamma), \beta_B(\gamma)) \gamma \in Y\}$$

where, $\alpha_B(\gamma):Y \rightarrow [0,1]$ are membership function and $\beta_B(\gamma):Y \rightarrow [0,1]$ non-membership function, such that equation (1)

$$0 \leq \alpha_B(\gamma) + \beta_B(\gamma) \leq 1, \gamma \in \tag{1}$$

The 3rd parameter $\delta_B(y)$ is called the intuitionistic fuzzy (IF) index and display the uncertainty measure of $y \in Y$ to B and $0 \leq \delta_B(y) \leq 1, y \in Y$ that can be calculated by equation (2)

$$\delta_B(\gamma) = 1 - \alpha_B(\gamma) - \beta_B(\gamma) \tag{2}$$

If the $\delta_B(\gamma)$ is less, it would be more reliable to have information about y. If $\delta_B($ $\gamma)$ high, data of y is more erratic.

If B and C are set-y IFSs, the multiplication operator is represented as equation (3).

$$B \otimes C = \{\alpha_B(\gamma) \cdot \alpha_C(\gamma), \beta_B(\gamma) + \beta_C(\gamma) \cdot \beta_C(\gamma) | \gamma \in Y\} \tag{3}$$

The IF-TOPSIS approach involves the following steps:

Step 1: Rating distribution among alternatives (Barriers) and criteria (Perspective)

Let's define that set $B = B_1, B_2, B_3, \ldots B_m$ of potential substitutes, set $Y = Y_1, Y_2, Y_3, \ldots Y_n$ of assessment metrics, and set $w_j = w_1, w_2, w_3, \ldots w_n$ is the weight of the criteria. For each option with respect to parameters, the quality ranking of each decision-maker is denoted, and is based on role, job experience, and academic background. Thirteen substitutes and three criteria are addressed in the present research. The decision-makers' linguistic evaluation of alternatives and criteria are displayed in Table 2 and Table 3, respectively.

Step 2: Computation of the weight of decision-makers

Assuming that $D_k = [\alpha_k, \beta_k, \delta_k]$ is an IF value for the kth decision-maker rank. The kth decision-maker weight is then calculated by equation (4) and is tabulated in Table 4.

$$\zeta = \frac{\alpha_k + \delta_k \left\{\frac{\alpha_k}{\alpha_k + \beta_k}\right\}}{\sum_{k=1}^{l} \left[\alpha_k + \delta_k \left\{\frac{\alpha_k}{\alpha_k + \beta_k}\right\}\right]} \tag{4}$$

Where, k= 1, 2, 3, ...l

Step 3: Computation of IF decision matrix

From Table 5, the IF decision matrix (Z) for the alternative can be described as following.

$$Z = \begin{bmatrix} \alpha_{B_1}(\gamma_1), \beta_{B_1}(\gamma_1), \delta_{B_1}(\gamma_1) & \alpha_{B_1}(\gamma_2), \beta_{B_1}(\gamma_2), \delta_{B_1}(\gamma_2) & \cdots & \alpha_{B_1}(\gamma_n), \beta_{B_1}(\gamma_n), \delta_{B_1}(\gamma_n) \\ \alpha_{B_2}(\gamma_1), \beta_{B_2}(\gamma_1), \delta_{B_2}(\gamma_1) & \alpha_{B_2}(\gamma_2), \beta_{B_2}(\gamma_2), \delta_2(\gamma_2) & \cdots & \alpha_{B_2}(\gamma_n), \beta_{B_2}(\gamma_n), \delta_2(\gamma_n) \\ \vdots & \vdots & \ddots & \vdots \\ \alpha_{Bm}(\gamma_1), \beta_{Bm}(\gamma_1), \delta_{Bm}(\gamma_1) & \alpha_{B_m}(\gamma_2), \beta_{B_m}(\gamma_2), \delta_{B_m}(\gamma_2) & \cdots & \alpha_{Bm}(\gamma_n), \beta_{B_m}(\gamma_n), \delta_m(\gamma_n) \end{bmatrix}$$

Step 4: Computation of aggregate weight of criteria

The equivalent significance to all criteria may not be given. Assuming $w_j^k = [\alpha_j^k, \beta_j^k, \delta_j^k]$ be an IF number that is assigned by the kth decision-maker to criteria yj. The cumulative weight of the criterion is then computed from the equation (5) using the intuitionist fuzzy weighted average (IFWA) operator, which is displayed in Table 6.

$$w_j = IFWA_\zeta\left(w_j^{(1)}, w_j^{(2)}, \ldots, w_j^{(l)}\right)$$

$$w_j = \zeta_1 w_j^{(1)} \oplus \zeta_2 w_j^{(2)} \oplus \zeta_3 w_j^{(3)}, \ldots, \oplus \zeta_l w_j^{(l)}$$

$$w_j = \left[1 - \prod_{k=1}^{l}\left(1 - \alpha_j^{(k)}\right)^{\zeta_k}, \prod_{k=1}^{l}\left(\beta_j^{(k)}\right), \prod_{k=1}^{l}\left(1 - \alpha_j^{(k)}\right)^{\zeta_k} - \prod_{k=1}^{l}\left(\beta_j^{(k)}\right)^{\zeta_k}\right] \tag{5}$$

Where, j=1, 2, 3..., n

Step 5: Development of aggregate weighted IF-decision matrix

The aggregate weighted IF decision matrix (Z') is derived after the development of the IF decision matrix and the computation of the aggregate weight criteria by means of equations (6) and (7), as seen in Table 7.

$$\delta_{Bi.W}(\gamma) = 1 - \beta_{Bi}(\gamma) - \beta_w(\gamma) - \alpha_{Bi}(\gamma).\alpha_w(\gamma) + \beta_{Bi}(\gamma).\beta_w(\gamma) \tag{6}$$

$$Z' = Z \otimes W = \left\{\left\langle y, \alpha_{Bi}(\gamma).\alpha_w(\gamma), \beta_{Bi}(\gamma) + \beta_w(\gamma) - \beta_{Bi}(\gamma).\beta_w(\gamma)\right\rangle | y \in B\right\} \tag{7}$$

Step 6: Compute the IFPIS and IFNIS by equation (8) and (9).

$$B^- = \left(\hat{z}^-_{1}, \hat{z}^-_{2}, \hat{z}^-_{3}, \ldots \hat{z}^-_{n}\right) = \left(\alpha^-_{BiW}\left(Y_j\right), \beta^-_{BiW}\left(Y_j\right)\right), \delta^-_{BiW}\left(Y_j\right)\right) j=1,2,3,\ldots.n \tag{8}$$

$$B^+ = \left(\hat{z}^+_{1}, \hat{z}^+_{2}, \hat{z}^+_{3}, \ldots \hat{z}^+_{n}\right) = \left(\alpha^+_{BiW}\left(Y_j\right), \beta^+_{BiW}\left(Y_j\right)\right), \delta^+_{BiW}\left(Y_j\right)\right) j=1,2,3,\ldots.n \tag{9}$$

Where,

$$\alpha^+_{BiW}\left(Y_j\right) = \left\{\max \alpha_{BiW}\left(Y_j\right) j = 1,2,3,\ldots,n\right\}$$

$$\alpha^-_{BiW}\left(Y_j\right) = \left\{\max \alpha_{BiW}\left(Y_j\right) j = 1,2,3,\ldots,n\right\}$$

$$\beta^+_{BiW}\left(Y_j\right) = \left\{\min \beta_{BiW}\left(Y_j\right) j = 1,2,3,\ldots,n\right\}$$

$$\beta^-_{BiW}\left(Y_j\right) = \left\{\max \beta_{BiW}\left(Y_j\right) j = 1,2,3,\ldots,n\right\}$$

$$\beta^-_{BiW}\left(Y_j\right) = \left\{\max \beta_{BiW}\left(Y_j\right) j = 1,2,3,\ldots,n\right\}$$

Step 7: Calculate IFPIS (S) and IFNIS (S), respectively by equation (10), (11).

$$S^+ = \sqrt{\frac{1}{2n} \sum_{j=1}^{n} \left(\alpha_{BiW}\left(Y_j\right) - \alpha_{BiW}^+\left(Y_j\right) \right)^2 + \left(\beta_{BiW}\left(Y_j\right) - \beta_{BiW}^+\left(Y_j\right) \right)^2 + \left(\delta_{BiW}\left(Y_j\right) - \delta_{BiW}^+\left(Y_j\right) \right)^2}$$
(10)

$$S^- = \sqrt{\frac{1}{2n} \sum_{j=1}^{n} \left(\alpha_{BiW}\left(Y_j\right) - \alpha_{BiW}^-\left(Y_j\right) \right)^2 + \left(\beta_{BiW}\left(Y_j\right) - \beta_{BiW}^-\left(Y_j\right) \right)^2 + \left(\delta_{BiW}\left(Y_j\right) - \delta_{BiW}^-\left(Y_j\right) \right)^2}$$
(11)

Step 8: Compute the relative closeness coefficient $\left(C_i^* \right)$ of each alternative with respect to IFPIS by using equation (12).

$$C_i^* = \frac{s^-}{s^+ + s^-}$$
(12)

Where $0 \leq C^* \leq 1 (i = 0,1,2,.....,m)$

Step 9: The ranking of alternatives is calculated in conjunction with the relative closeness coefficient C_i^* in descending order shown in Table 8.

Application of research methods

Step 1: Allocation of rating to the Barriers and criteria (Perspective)

Table 2. Linguistic assessment of alternative

Notation	Industry	Academics	Government
B1	VR	MR	R
B2	VR	VR	VR
B3	R	VR	MR
B4	MR	R	VR
B5	MR	VR	VR
B6	VR	R	MR
B7	LR	VR	MR
B8	VR	VR	VR
B9	VR	R	MR
B10	VR	MR	R
B11	VR	R	R
B12	R	VR	VR
B13	VR	VR	R

Table 3. Linguistic assessment of alternative

Criteria	DM1	DM2	DM3
C1	MR	MR	VR
C2	VR	VR	R
C3	R	VR	MR

Step 2: Compute weight of decision-makers

Table 4. The importance of decision-makers and their weights

	DM1	DM2	DM3
Linguistic terms	MR	VR	R
IF number	(0.85, 0.10, 0.05)	(0.75, 0.15, 0.10)	(0.60, 0.35, 0.05)
Crisp weight (ς)	0.379	0.353	0.268

Step 3: Construct IF-decision matrix

Table 5. The IF-decision matrix

Notations	Industry	Academics	Government
B1	(0.75, 0.15, 0.10)	(0.85, 0.10, 0.05)	(0.6., 0.35, 0.05)
B2	(0.75, 0.15, 0.10)	(0.75, 0.15, 0.10)	(0.75, 0.15, 0.10)
B3	(0.60, 0.35, 0.05)	(0.75, 0.15, 0.10)	(0.85, 0.10, 0.15)
B4	(0.85, 0.10, 0.15)	(0.60, 0.35, 0.05)	(0.75, 0.15, 0.10)
B5	(0.85, 0.10, 0.15)	(0.75, 0.15, 0.10)	(0.75, 0.15, 0.10)
B6	(0.75, 0.15, 0.10)	(0.60, 0.35, 0.05)	(0.85, 0.10, 0.15)
B7	(0.35, 0.60, 0.05)	(0.75, 0.15, 0.10)	(0.85, 0.10, 0.15)
B8	(0.75, 0.15, 0.10)	(0.75, 0.15, 0.10)	(0.75, 0.15, 0.10)
B9	(0.75, 0.15, 0.10)	(0.60, 0.35, 0.05)	(0.85, 0.10, 0.15)
B10	(0.75, 0.15, 0.10)	(0.85, 0.10, 0.15)	(0.60, 0.35, 0.05)
B11	(0.75, 0.15, 0.10)	(0.60, 0.35, 0.05)	(0.60, 0.35, 0.05)
B12	(0.60, 0.35, 0.05)	(0.75, 0.15, 0.10)	(0.75, 0.15, 0.10)
B13	(0.75, 0.15, 0.10)	(0.75, 0.15, 0.10)	(0.60, 0.35, 0.05)

Step 4: Compute aggregate weight of criteria

Table 6. Aggregate IF weight of criteria

Criteria	DM1	DM2	DM3	Aggregate weight
C1	(0.85,0.1,0.05)	(0.85,0.1,0.05)	(0.75,0.15,0.1)	(0.8280,0.1137,0.0636)
C2	(0.75,0.15,0.1)	(0.75,0.15,0.1)	(0.6,0.35,0.050)	(0.7165,0.2089,0.0869)
C3	(0.60, 0.35, 0.05)	(0.75,0.15,0.10)	(0.85,0.1,0.05)	(0.7394,0.2204,0.0680)

Step 5 and 6: Construct aggregate weighted IF decision matrix and calculate IFPIS and IFNIS

Table 7.

Notations	Industry	Academics	Government
B1	(0.6210,0.246615,0.1324)	(0.6090, 0.2880, 0.1030)	(0.4436, 0.4932, 0.0631)
B2	(0.6218, 0.2775, 0.1007)	(0.5321, 0.3391, 0.1288)	(0.5448, 0.3661, 0.0891)
B3	(0.4974, 0.4475, 0.0551)	(0.5321, 0.3391, 0.1288)	(0.6175, 0.3288, 0.0537)
B4	(0.7047, 0.235, 0.0603)	(0.4257, 0.4946, 0.0797)	(0.5448, 0.3661, 0.0891)
B5	(0.7047, 0.235, 0.0603)	(0.5321, 0.3391, 0.1288)	(0.5448, 0.3661, 0.0891)
B6	(0.6218, 0.2775, 0.1007)	(0.4257, 0.4946, 0.0797)	(0.6175, 0.3288, 0.0537)
B7	(0.2902, 0.66, 0.0498)	(0.5321, 0.3391, 0.1288)	(0.6175, 0.3288, 0.0537)
B8	(0.6218, 0.2775, 0.1007)	(0.5321, 0.3391, 0.1288)	(0.5448, 0.3661, 0.0891)
B9	(0.6218, 0.2775, 0.1007)	(0.3902, 0.5335, 0.0763)	(0.6175, 0.3661, 0.0164)
B10	(0.6218, 0.2775, 0.1007)	(0.6030, 0.3391, 0.0579)	(0.3995, 0.5526, 0.0479)
B11	(0.6218, 0.2775, 0.1007)	(0.3902, 0.5335, 0.0763)	(0.3995, 0.5526, 0.0479)
B12	(0.4974, 0.4475, 0.0551)	(0.5321, 0.3391, 0.1288)	(0.5448, 0.3661, 0.0891)
B13	(0.6218, 0.2775, 0.1007)	(0.5321, 0.3391, 0.1288)	(0.4359, 0.5153, 0.0489)
IFPIS	(0.7047, 0.235, 0.0603)	(0.6090, 0.2880, 0.0968)	(0.6175, 0.3288, 0.0537)
IFNIS	(0.2902, 0.66, 0.0498)	(0.4257, 0.4946, 0.0797)	(0.4359, 0.5153, 0.0631)

Step 7, 8 and 9: Calculation of S^*, S^-, C_i^* and ranking of alternatives

Table 8. Separation measure and relative closeness coefficient of alternatives

Barriers	S	S	C_i^*	Rank
B1	0.1078	0.2465	0.6958	7
B2	0.0681	0.2351	0.7755	2
B3	0.1276	0.1798	0.5848	10
B4	0.1187	0.2541	0.6816	4

continued on following page

Table 8. Continued

Barriers	S^+	S^-	C_i^*	Rank
B5	0.0540	0.2662	0.8314	1
B6	0.1204	0.2333	0.6597	5
B7	0.2457	0.1328	0.3508	13
B8	0.0681	0.2351	0.7755	3
B9	0.1204	0.2333	0.6597	6
B10	0.1142	0.2340	0.6720	8
B11	0.1606	0.2078	0.5641	11
B12	0.1327	0.1637	0.5524	12
B13	0.1209	0.2225	0.6480	9

4. RESULTS AND DISCUSSION

The latest research underscores that among the hurdles to implementing waste collection and segregation, "lack of public awareness" (B5) stands out as the most significant, boasting a C_i^* value of 0.8314. In stark contrast, the barrier labelled "lack of collaboration" (B7) ranks as the least influential, with a C_i^* value of 0.3508. When prioritizing these barriers on the basis of relative closeness coefficient, the hierarchy emerges as follows: B5 > B2 > B8 > B1 > B4 > B10 > B9 > B6 > B13 > B3 > B11 > B12 > B7. Given India's on-going status as a developing nation, the formidable barrier of "lack of public awareness (B5)" looms large in impeding the widespread adoption of waste collection and segregation practices. Consequently, "policy inconsistencies (B2)" emerge as the second-most influential barrier, followed closely by the challenge posed by rapid population and industrial growth (B8), further complicating waste management endeavours.

Furthermore, the study reveals that social stigma (B11), lack of standardization (B12), and lack of collaboration (B7) are the least impactful factors hindering the effective implementation of waste collection and segregation practices. While the technology surrounding waste collection and segregation is still in its nascent stages, its potential to revolutionize waste management practices in the future cannot be overstated. However, numerous barriers impede its seamless integration with existing infrastructure and technologies. Thus, identifying and prioritizing these barriers represent critical tasks facing society. The study adopts a rational approach based on the IF-TOPSIS method to identify and subsequently rank the potential barriers to the implementation of waste collection and segregation practices. Remarkably, the findings align closely with the current landscape.

In contemporary discourse, it is increasingly evident that raising public awareness (B5) constitutes a linchpin in fostering widespread adoption of sustainable waste management practices. The prevailing lack of awareness not only undermines individual efforts but also poses a formidable challenge to policymakers and stakeholders striving for effective waste management solutions. This underscores the urgent need for comprehensive educational campaigns aimed at illuminating the importance of waste segregation and its broader environmental implications. By nurturing a culture of environmental stewardship and responsibility, societies can lay the groundwork for transformative change in waste management practices.

Moreover, the prevalence of policy inconsistencies (B2) underscores the complexity inherent in implementing cohesive waste management strategies. Misaligned regulations and fragmented policies not only engender confusion but also hinder the seamless execution of waste collection and segregation initiatives. Addressing this barrier necessitates a concerted effort to streamline regulatory frameworks and establish clear guidelines that incentivize compliance and foster collaboration among stakeholders. By fostering policy coherence and synergy, policymakers can cultivate an enabling environment conducive to sustainable waste management practices.

The exponential growth in population and industrial activities (B8) further exacerbates the challenges associated with waste management. Rapid urbanization coupled with burgeoning industrialization strains existing infrastructure and amplifies waste generation rates, underscoring the urgency of implementing effective waste collection and segregation measures. Tackling this multifaceted challenge demands holistic solutions that reconcile economic imperatives with environmental sustainability goals. Investing in innovative technologies, such as smart waste management systems and decentralized recycling facilities can mitigate the adverse impacts of population growth and industrial expansion on waste management infrastructure.

Conversely, the relatively low influence of social stigma (B11), lack of standardization (B12), and lack of collaboration (B7) underscores the need for nuanced strategies tailored to address these barriers. While these factors may exert a lesser impact individually, their cumulative effect can impede progress towards achieving comprehensive waste management objectives. Overcoming social stigma requires fostering inclusive dialogue and dispelling misconceptions surrounding waste management practices. Similarly, standardizing protocols and fostering collaborative partnerships among stakeholders can enhance the efficacy and efficiency of waste collection and segregation efforts.

5. CONCLUSIONS

Prioritizing barriers to the effective implementation of waste collection and segregation reveals the complex interplay of socio-economic, policy, and technological dynamics shaping modern waste management practices. To facilitate adoption, it is crucial to identify and rank these barriers. The current study draws upon a comprehensive review of literature, surveys, and consultations with experts to identify 13 barriers. Employing the IF-TOPSIS technique, which integrates ambiguity handling into decision-making, the study solicits input from academic, governmental, and industrial perspectives. Findings highlight lack of awareness (B5), policy inconsistencies (B2) and rapid population and industrial growth (B8) as the most influential barriers. These results align closely with real-world industry scenarios, aiding in the identification of common hurdles in waste management implementation. For senior management, prioritizing these barriers facilitates the formulation of strategic goals, while operational teams benefit from streamlined decision-making processes, fostering a culture of execution and problem-solving and ultimately enhancing organizational success rates.

However, the study acknowledges limitations, such as a limited expert pool primarily from the Indian context and potential oversights in the assessment procedure. Future research avenues may explore alternative data collection methods beyond qualitative studies and interviews, while incorporating other established MCDM techniques to assign weightages to decision-makers, prioritize factors, and delineate interrelationships among barriers.

REFERENCES

Atanassov, K. T. (1986). Intuitionistic fuzzy sets. *Fuzzy Sets and Systems*, 20(1), 87–96. DOI: 10.1016/S0165-0114(86)80034-3

Bui, T. D., Tsai, F. M., Tseng, M. L., & Ali, M. H. (2020). Identifying sustainable solid waste management barriers in practice using the fuzzy Delphi method. *Resources, Conservation and Recycling*, 154, 104625. DOI: 10.1016/j.resconrec.2019.104625

Cimpan, C., Maul, A., Wenzel, H., & Pretz, T. (2016). Techno-economic assessment of central sorting at material recovery facilities–the case of lightweight packaging waste. *Journal of Cleaner Production*, 112, 4387–4397. DOI: 10.1016/j.jclepro.2015.09.011

Dou, Y., & Sarkis, J. (2013). A multiple stakeholder perspective on barriers to implementing China RoHS regulations. *Resources, Conservation and Recycling*, 81, 92–104. DOI: 10.1016/j.resconrec.2013.10.004

Ikhlayel, M. (2018). Development of management systems for sustainable municipal solid waste in developing countries: A systematic life cycle thinking approach. *Journal of Cleaner Production*, 180, 571–586. DOI: 10.1016/j.jclepro.2018.01.057

Jangre, J., Prasad, K., & Patel, D. (2022). Analysis of barriers in e-waste management in developing economy: An integrated multiple-criteria decision-making approach. *Environmental Science and Pollution Research International*, 29(48), 72294–72308. DOI: 10.1007/s11356-022-21363-y PMID: 35696062

Kirchherr, J., Reike, D., & Hekkert, M. (2017). Conceptualizing the circular economy: An analysis of 114 definitions. *Resources, Conservation and Recycling*, 127, 221–232. DOI: 10.1016/j.resconrec.2017.09.005

Kumar, A., & Dixit, G. (2018b). An analysis of barriers affecting the implementation of e-waste management practices in India: A novel ISM-DEMATEL approach. *Sustainable Production and Consumption*, 14, 36–52. DOI: 10.1016/j.spc.2018.01.002

Millar, N., McLaughlin, E., & Börger, T. (2019). The circular economy: Swings and roundabouts? *Ecological Economics*, 158, 11–19. DOI: 10.1016/j.ecolecon.2018.12.012

Mont, O., Plepys, A., Whalen, K., & Nußholz, J. L. (2017). Business model innovation for a Circular Economy: Drivers and barriers for the Swedish industry–the voice of REES companies.

Mudgal, R. K., Shankar, R., Parvaiz, T., & Tilak, R. (2010). Modelling the barriers of green supply chain practices. *Int J Logist Syst Manag*, 7(1), 81–107. DOI: 10.1504/IJLSM.2010.033891

Mulliner, E., Smallbone, K., & Maliene, V. (2013). An assessment of sustainable housing afordability using a multiple criteria decision-making method. *Omega*, 41(2), 270–279. DOI: 10.1016/j.omega.2012.05.002

Ongondo, F. O., Williams, I. D., & Cherrett, T. J. (2011). How are WEEE doing? A global review of the management of electrical and electronic wastes. Waste management, 31(4), 714-730.

Patil, S. K., & Kant, R. (2014). A fuzzy AHP-TOPSIS framework for ranking the solutions of Knowledge Management adoption in Supply Chain to overcome its barriers. *Expert Systems with Applications*, 41(2), 679–693. DOI: 10.1016/j. eswa.2013.07.093

Polidano, C. (2000). Measuring public sector capacity. *World Development*, 28(5), 805–822. DOI: 10.1016/S0305-750X(99)00158-8

Rizos, V., Behrens, A., Van der Gaast, W., Hofman, E., Ioannou, A., Kafyeke, T., Flamos, A., Rinaldi, R., Papadelis, S., Hirschnitz-Garbers, M., & Topi, C. (2016). Implementation of circular economy business models by small and medium-sized enterprises (SMEs): Barriers and enablers. *Sustainability (Basel)*, 8(11), 1212. DOI: 10.3390/su8111212

Yukalang, N., Clarke, B., & Ross, K. (2017). Barriers to effective municipal solid waste management in a rapidly urbanizing area in Thailand. *International Journal of Environmental Research and Public Health*, 14(9), 1013. DOI: 10.3390/ijerph14091013 PMID: 28869572

Section 3
Data Analytics in Specific Domains

Chapter 8

Real–Time Music Recommendation System Integrating PySpark and Kafka for Enhanced User Experience:
Spotify Recommendation System

K. Lavanya
Vellore Institute of Technology, India

B. N. Dorendra
Vellore Institute of Technology, India

Sweta Chopdar
Vellore Institute of Technology, India

Akshay Mahantshetti
Vellore Institute of Technology, India

ABSTRACT

The Spotify Recommendation System represents a cutting-edge application of data science and streaming technology, harnessing the power of PySpark and Kafka to deliver highly personalized music recommendations to users. Music streaming platforms use collaborative-based filtering methods, which has a Sparsity Problem leading to pressing demand for even more personalized recommendations, delivered in real-time, leaning on implicit feedback collaborative filtering techniques.

DOI: 10.4018/979-8-3693-5563-3.ch008

The foundation of our recommendation engine is Alternating Least Squares (ALS) Implicit Collaborative Filtering. It enables data scientists and engineers to process enormous amounts of user data, such as listening history, track information, and user preferences, in an effective manner. The algorithm assists in the discovery of significant insights that improve the precision of music recommendations through data transformation and feature engineering. Kafka, a high-performance event streaming platform, is essential for assuring real-time data acquisition and processing.

1. INTRODUCTION

The desire to find songs that hit with our own musical tastes has never been more important in a world where music is an essential component of our everyday lives. Streaming services have over 616.2 million individual subscribers, (statista. com). With their extensive catalogs available at our fingertips, well-known music streaming services like Spotify, Apple Music, and YouTube Music have completely changed how we access and enjoy music. In 2023, it is anticipated that global music streaming revenue will amount to $30.42 billion, (businesswire.com). All the streaming services use sophisticated recommendation systems with collaborative filtering and content-based filtering to improve this experience. Spotify is the most popular music streaming service, with over 205 million subscribers, (cmet.com).

One of the factors contributing to the success of streaming services is the recommendation system. It is also a factor that can result in a user closing or switching to other apps. The purpose of recommender systems is to fill the gap between collecting and analyzing information by filtering all available data to only present the information that the user will find most valuable. Recommendation systems have grown in popularity and are now a crucial component of consumer-based programs like shopping, listening to music, and watching movies. This is true not only in the case of music streaming but also in video streaming. Examples of platforms where the recommendation system has a big impact on their popularity include Amazon and Netflix. Constant efforts are made to improve the recommendation systems with feedback from the user as well as the use of different machine learning models. Recommendation systems are trained on a massive dataset of songs and user listening data.

Although these algorithms are capable of producing precise suggestions, they are not faultless and may occasionally make errors. Users may find this annoying, particularly if they are seeking for specific kinds of music or genres.

A need for a reliable and precise recommendation system to effectively understand that Users want to listen to both new and their favourite tunes. The recommendation system must successfully balance these two requirements.

This article aims to address this need by demonstrating the implementation of an implicit feedback collaborative filtering technique-based music recommendation system that overcomes the sparsity issue of the current recommender system, (Van dongen & Van den Poel, 2020). Our toolbox comprises Kafka for seamless data streaming, the Alternating Least Squares (ALS) filtering algorithm, and other Python libraries for effective data manipulation, analytical operations, and visualizations. With the aid of this research, we hope to understand the effectiveness of how ALS with collaborative filtering and Kafka can work together to create a dynamic and customized music discovery experience, assisting us in finding an ideal soundtrack for our everyday lives.

2. LITERATURE SURVEY

Fernandes, Bruno et al. demonstrated that implicit feedback for neighbor selection techniques produced better quality recommendations when compared to the classic CF, mainly in the presence of sparsity of rating data. Collaborative Filtering (CF) techniques are used by the majority of recommender systems (RSs), and users directly rank items. the limitation of CF is precisely the need for rating data provided voluntarily by users, (Fernandes, Sacenti, & Willrich, 2017) Shivam Dawar et al., proposed to recommend suitable music for various situations by utilizing real-time data such as time, location, weather, facial expressions, artists, and audio attributes to determine the user's emotional state accurately. The machine learning algorithms, CNN and DNN, were used to create a model that could classify song samples into different genres. A deep learning model was used to classify whether the songs listened to by the user were energetic, sad, calm, or happy, (Dawar *et al.*, 2023). Liebman et al. described the development of methods for learning and adapting to individuals' sequential preferences in real time during a listening session with the aim of providing adaptive personalized playlists. The framework adopted model-based learning and planning, which involves modeling the environment and simulating experiential data to estimate the value of alternative courses of action. The agent's goal was to find and improve a policy that specifies the selection of the next song to play over time, aiming to produce the sequence of songs that would be most pleasing to the listener, (Liebman, Saar-Tsechansky, & Stone, 2019). Giselle van Dongen et al., evaluated multiple stream-processing frameworks, including Spark Streaming, Flink, Structured Streaming, and Kafka Streams. The relationships among the latency, throughput, and resource consumption were analyzed. The results showed that the latency disadvantages of using a microbatch system were most apparent for stateless operation, (Van Dongen & Van den Poel, 2020). Desai et al. discussed two known methods for creating content-based music recommendation systems:

using a powerful classification algorithm and utilizing deep learning algorithms to enhance the performance of the recommender system. They proposed a music recommendation system based on the user's mood that can automatically browse song albums and suggest appropriate songs to users, (Desai, Bhadra, & Parekh, 2023).

Turrin, R. et al. proposed an innovative approach called the implicit playlist recommender (IPR) for large-scale music recommendations based on Apache Spark. The IPR model was trained using user-implicit listening sessions and outperformed two context-aware, popularity-based baselines. The IPR model considers the implicit listening sessions of the user and performs better when the user session is longer than five tracks. The IPR algorithm focused on recognizing longer and recurrent patterns in user listening behavior, potentially limiting its ability to recommend diverse and novel tracks, (Turrin *et al.*, 2015). Sri Mega Sakti et al., proposed a music recommendation system using a content-based filtering method with the Euclidean distance algorithm to calculate the distance between items and generate recommendations based on user mood input which is based on James Russel's Circumplex mood model. The output was the top 10 songs with the smallest distance according to user mood input, (*Sakti et al.*, 2022). Hazem et al. proposed a Splitting and Replication mechanism for distributed-streaming recommender systems. This mechanism was inspired by the shared-nothing architecture used in contemporary big-data processing systems. The authors applied this mechanism to two well-known approaches to online recommender systems: matrix factorization and collaborative filtering, (Hazem, Awad, & Yousef, 2023). Matuszyk proposed a semi supervised framework for stream-based recommendations in recommender systems. This framework aimed to address the problem of data sparsity by utilizing abundant unlabelled information to improve the quality of recommendations, (Matuszyk & Spilipoulou, 2017). Niu, Y proposed a music recommendation system based on collaborative filtering within the Spark architecture. This study optimizes the collaborative filtering model by enhancing computational efficiency and user preference predictions. In addition, a clustering algorithm was employed to address the cold-start problem for new users, (Niu, 2022). Chaudhury et al. explored the GTZAN music dataset using machine-learning algorithms supported by Apache Spark to classify music genres. The random forest classifier performed the best, achieving a 90% accuracy for music genre classification. Results showed that the developed random forest classifier outperformed other classifiers. Feature selection was highlighted as an important aspect of music genre classification, as it improves performance and reduces the training time of machine learning models, (Chaudhury, Karami, & Ghazanfar, 2022). Xuechao, Yan, et al. (2023) proposed three algorithms for recommender systems: item collaborative filtering (itemCF), user collaborative filtering (useCF), and content-based recommender system (CBRS). After training on the same dataset, it was observed that itemCF had the highest accuracy rate.

Sun proposed a personalized music recommendation algorithm based on the Spark platform. It used a K-means clustering model using an artificial fish swarm algorithm (AFSA) to optimize the initial centroids and improve the clustering effect. Collaborative filtering was then applied to calculate the correlation between users, enabling accurate recommendations, (Sun, 2022). Wang, L. (2022) proposed a mixed collaborative filtering recommendation algorithm based on Spark architecture for music MOOC resources by combining the collaborative filtering algorithm with the XGBoost model and optimizing the weight factors by the shuffled frog leading algorithm. The design was based on distributed Spark recommendation platform architecture and the performance was evaluated using MAE and RMSE metrics.

3. BACKGROUND STUDY

3.1 Spotify Web API

Spotify web API is a convenient way to retrieve metadata from Spotify content. It requires having a Spotify account. It enables us to create applications that can interact with Spotify's streaming service. We can use the API to access music data, user authentication and authorization, user playlists, audio features, top charts, and featured playlists. To use the Spotify API, we must register the application on the Spotify Developer Dashboard and get the necessary credentials (Client ID and Client Secret). It supports multiple programming languages, and also there are third-party libraries and SDKs (Software Development Kit) available to simplify the integration process.

3.2 Audio data streaming - Kafka

Kafka is a high-performance event streaming platform that we integrated to enable real-time data collecting and analysis. Kafka allowed us to keep an eye on user activity in real time and update music recommendations based on their most recent interactions and preferences. Our recommendation service remained stable and responsive even in the face of system failures because of Kafka's fault tolerance and scalability features.

Figure 1. Kafka architecture
How Kafka works?

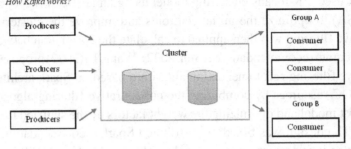

Kafka consists of an event-driven architecture. The producers send events to the event processing system (Kafka) that receives and acknowledges that data is written. This data written within the system is durable and can be read by multiple consumers. Kafka is designed in such a way it can perform on any data streaming workload. It is packaged as a single binary system and doesn't rely on external systems. Throughout the platform, Kafka uses the Raft Consensus Algorithm when the zookeeper is eliminated to coordinate writing data to log files and replicating that data across multiple servers.

3.3 Alternating Least Squares (ALS) Implicit Collaborative Filtering method

When a system automatically selects a song with the greatest interaction count without any user input, this is known as popularity bias. The circumstance when new tracks are introduced to the library with either very few or no interactions—and recommenders rely on these interactions to create recommendations—is referred to as the item cold-start problem. The incapacity of the database to expand to hold ever bigger data sets as new users and music are added is known as the scalability issue. Our recommendation system's core was the PySpark-implemented Alternating Least Squares (ALS) Implicit Collaborative Filtering method. It helps us with large-scale and real-time data processing. It also helps us interactively analyze the data using the PySpark shell.

In collaborative filtering, matrix factorization is used to solve the data sparsity problems.

Matrix factorization

It splits the user-item interaction matrix into the product of two matrices with lower dimensions. In the item matrix columns represent items and latent factors are represented by rows. The user matrix, in which latent factors are represented by columns and users are represented by rows.

1. The model can now predict more accurate and user-specific song ratings by factoring the rating matrix into user and song representations

2. Matrix factorization enhances the recommender's capacity to suggest lesser-known songs by enabling less-known songs to have latent representations richer than popular songs.

$$\min_{b_*,b_*} \sum_{u,i} c_{ui} \left(p_{ui} - a_u^T b_i \right)^2 + \lambda \left(\sum_u \|a_u\|^2 + \sum_i \|b_i\|^2 \right) \tag{1}$$

Equation to minimize the global loss function

$$a_u = (B^T B + B^T (C^v - I) Y + \lambda I)^{-1} B^T C^v p(v) \tag{2}$$

$$b = (A^T A + A^T (C^j - I) A + \lambda I)^{-1} A^T C^j p(j) \tag{3}$$

Equation for Minimizing the loss of the user
A, B: are randomly initialized song data and user matrices
Cv and Cj: gives the confidence intervals
λ: is used to overcome overfitting
p(v), p(j): represent the items binary predilection
I: is the sq. matrix with 1's in diagonal.

It follows a distinct training regimen: By holding the user matrix fixed and utilizing gradient descent with the item matrix first, and holding the item matrix fixed and utilizing gradient descent with the user matrix second, ALS reduces two loss functions in turn.

Using a cluster of computers, ALS performs parallel gradient descent over many partitions of the underlying training data which helps in solving scalability. This helps us solve 2 most important problems, popularity bias, and item cold-start problem

4. METHODOLOGY

To present the user with accurate recommendations the user data is streamed and the data is ranked according to the user preferences. The recommendations are picked and presented to the user based on ranking. The block diagram of the recommendation system is shown below.

Figure 2. Music recommendation system

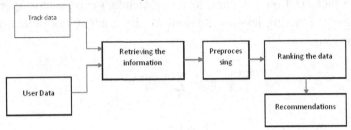

4.1 Dataset

Using the Spotify Web API, we first gathered user data, such as their listening history, likes, and preferences. Concurrently, we collected extensive track metadata, including information on musicians, musical styles, and audio characteristics. There are 21 features in the track metadata.

Table 1. Dataset features

order_id:	gives the message number
id:	song id given by spotify
name:	song name
popularity:	popularity ranking of the song
duration_mis:	Song time in ms
explicit:	indicates if the song has explicit lyrics
artists:	artist's name
id_artists:	artist's unique id
release_date:	Date the song was released
danceability:	determines if a song can be classified as a dance song
energy:	it gives the energy of the song

continued on following page

Table 1. Continued

order_id:	gives the message number
key:	it gives the track's key
loudness:	gives the measure of loudness of the track in dB (ranges between -60 and 0)
mode:	song's modality (0 is Minor and 1 is Major)
speechiness:	It is the measure of words in a song (ranges from 0 and 1, 1 is more speech)
acousticness:	determines if a song is acoustic (ranges from 0 and 1)
instrumentalness:	If it is an instrumental or a vocal track (ranges from 0 and 1)
liveness:	Live setting of a song (ranges from 0 and 1 - live)
valence:	It is the track's positivity information (ranges from 0 and 1-upbeat and positive)
tempo:	is the beats measured per min
time_signature:	timesignature that is predicted

4.2 Phase I -Kafka Streaming and Dataset preprocessing

The dataset obtained from Spotify with the Client ID and Secret ID is streamed using Kafka. The streaming is done by setting up the producer and consumer to a topic and setting parameters. Next is, cleaning the data, resolving missing numbers, and dealing with outliers to establish a solid basis for our recommendation system. User activities such as song plays and likes were included in this implicit feedback and were converted into a numerical representation that reflected the preferences of the user. A crucial component of our approach was feature engineering, whereby we generated user and track embeddings and other pertinent features by extracting data from both user and track records. Based on implicit input, the complex interactions between users and tracks were represented through the creation of user-item matrices.

```
# Import necessary libraries and modules
# Set up Spotify API credentials and endpoint
NEW_SPOTIFY_API_ENDPOINT = "https://api.spotify.com/v1/your_spotify
_api_endpoint"
NEW_SPOTIFY_CLIENT_ID = "your_spotify_client_id"
NEW_SPOTIFY_CLIENT_SECRET = "your_spotify_client_secret"
# Authenticate with Spotify API and retrieve data
def get_spotify_data():
# Spotify API authentication and data retrieval is implemented here
# Initialize PySpark session
spark = SparkSession.builder.appName("SpotifyDataProcessing").getOrCreate()
# Define a function to process streaming data with PySpark and perform machine
learning operations
```

```
def process_streaming_data():
# Consume data from Kafka topic
new_spotify_data_stream = Kafka.consume(topic="spotify_data_topic")
# Define schema and create a DataFrame
new_schema = # Define your schema based on Spotify data structure
new_spotify_df = spark.createDataFrame(new_spotify_data_stream, schema=new_schema)
# Perform feature engineering and prepare data for machine learning
new_feature_columns = ["feature1", "feature2", ..., "featureN"]
new_vector_assembler = VectorAssembler(inputCols=new_feature_columns, outputCol="features")
new_assembled_df = new_vector_assembler.transform(new_spotify_df)
```

Figure 3. Preprocessing output

```
array([[ 6.98000e-01,  9.68000e-01, -1.10120e+01, ...,  1.11000e-01,
         3.90000e-01,  1.36884e+02],
       [ 7.24000e-01,  9.70000e-01, -8.41500e+00, ...,  1.06000e-01,
         4.32000e-01,  1.36868e+02],
       [ 8.03000e-01,  4.06000e-01, -9.44400e+00, ...,  9.48000e-02,
         7.69000e-02,  1.25014e+02],
       ...,
       [ 5.62000e-01,  6.49000e-01, -5.40000e+00, ...,  3.41000e-01,
         3.76000e-01,  1.45913e+02],
       [ 5.73000e-01,  7.47000e-01, -6.46000e+00, ...,  8.67000e-02,
         6.45000e-01,  7.99520e+01],
       [ 5.21000e-01,  7.46000e-01, -6.17300e+00, ...,  7.41000e-02,
         4.73000e-01,  1.49977e+02]])
```

4.3 Phase II – Song recommendation using ALS Implicit Collaborative Filtering method

We split the data set into train and test data. ALS algorithm is applied by setting up the parameters. This then assigns ranks to the data input to develop a recommendation.

Dividing the data into training and testing datasets is based on an 80-20 split of the pre-processed data. 80% of the data is used to train the recommendation model efficiently and 20 is used to check for the efficiency of the model and its performance assessment.

The ALS Implicit Collaborative Filtering model is set up first. This then scores the input data and underlying patterns in user preferences are captured. The train-Implicit function is used to train the model and it takes the number of iterations and rank as its parameters.

The recommendProducts service is used to provide the customers with individualized suggestions, based on implicit interactions. The predictions for specific songs based on user preferences are determined by the algorithm's evaluation.

The Spark session is concluded when the recommendation and assessment procedures are finished. It is an essential step in releasing the resources.

```
# Pseudo code for retrieving data from Spotify API, streaming with Kafka, and processing with PySpark
    # Split data into training and testing sets
    train_data, test_data = new_assembled_df.randomSplit([0.8, 0.2], seed=123)
    # Initialize and train a machine learning model and set its parameters
    # Setting up the parameters for ALS
    new_rank = int_number # Latent Factors to be made
    new_numIterations = int_number # Times to repeat process
    # Creating the model on the training data
    new_model = ALS.trainImplicit(train_data, new_rank, new_numIterations)
    # Make predictions on test data
    new_predictions = new_model.recommendProducts(value, value)
    # Evaluate model performance and print results
    # Implement evaluation logic based on your use case
    # Stop the Spark session
    spark.stop()
# Main function to orchestrate the process
def main():
    new_spotify_data = get_spotify_data()
    stream_to_Kafka(new_spotify_data)
    process_streaming_data()
# Call the main function to start the process
if __name__ == "__main__":
    main()
```

Figure 4. Features of recommended songs for the user

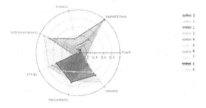

5. RESULT AND DISCUSSION

Our real-time music recommendation system, which leverages Kafka and PySpark, is a major step forward in tackling the difficulties associated with collaborative-based filtering, especially the sparsity issue that plagues conventional techniques. Real-time, tailored music suggestions are now possible using a novel method thanks to the integration of PySpark and Kafka.

A layer of sophistication is added to the recommendation process by using StringIndexer to transform user and track columns into unique values, enabling effectual calculation.

Impact

Our recommendation system's most significant contribution is its capacity to improve music discovery. The technology performs a delicate balancing act between presenting users with their favourite tunes and introducing them to new and relevant content by seamlessly integrating data analytics with real-time processing.

Result

Kafka's real-time data streaming integration was essential to the development of our recommendation engine. We were able to collect and handle real-time user activity data with ease by utilizing Kafka's event-driven architecture. Our recommendation system's ability to adapt and change based on consumers' changing musical preferences is largely due to this connection. The sparsity issues that arise with collaborative-based filtering were also effectively resolved by utilizing PySpark's Alternating Least Squares (ALS) Implicit Collaborative Filtering approach.

Large-scale user data, including listening histories and preferences, were extracted with the use of PySpark's powerful feature engineering and data transformation capabilities. A combination of real-time analysis of implicit input from user-generated playlists, and the ALS Implicit Collaborative Filtering approach resulted in personalized and varied music suggestions. Customers were able to explore and discover new music more thoroughly and interestingly with this technique.

The evaluation metrics used for recommendations include Mean absolute error (MAE) and root mean square error (RMSE). Our recommendation system gives a root mean square error of 2.32 and a mean absolute error of 1.32. Lower the values of these parameters, the predictions are considered to be better.

Recommended Songs

Table 2. List of recommended songs

	Track
0	Concerto No1 in F
1	Read All About It
2	Young Blood
3	O Green World
4	Every Planet We Reach Is Dead
5	Feel Good Inc
6	Beyond
7	Home
8	November Has Come
9	Tokyo (Vampires & Wolves)

7. CONCLUSION

We successfully addressed the three issues that arise in collaborative filtering using the ALS Implicit Collaborative Filtering, which uses matrix factorization and feature engineering to produce precise and varied music recommendations. Kafka was seamlessly integrated, guaranteeing real-time responsiveness. Scalability and fault tolerance are essential for system stability. Our approach went beyond conventional preferences by integrating likes and user-generated playlists, which improved suggestion accuracy and exposed users to fresh and appropriate content. Our technology creates a new benchmark for dynamic music discovery by carefully balancing user favorites and fascinating discoveries.

REFERENCES

Chaudhury, M., Karami, A., & Ghazanfar, M. A. (2022). Large-Scale Music Genre Analysis and Classification Using Machine Learning with Apache Spark. *Electronics (Basel)*, 11(16), 2567. DOI: 10.3390/electronics11162567

Dawar, S., Chatterjee, S., Hossain, M. F., & Malarvizhi, S. "Music Recommendation System Using Real Time Parameters," *2023 International Conference on Recent Advances in Electrical, Electronics, Ubiquitous Communication, and Computational Intelligence (RAEEUCCI)*, Chennai, India, 2023, pp. 1-6, DOI: 10.1109/RAEEUCCI57140.2023.10134257

Desai, C., Bhadra, S., & Parekh, M. (2023). Music Recommendation System using Python. *International Journal for Research in Applied Science and Engineering Technology*, 11(7), 699–707. DOI: 10.22214/ijraset.2023.54740

Van Dongen, G., & Van den Poel, D. (2020). Evaluation of stream processing frameworks. *IEEE Transactions on Parallel and Distributed Systems*, 31(8), 1845–1858.

Fernandes, B. B., Sacenti, J. A., & Willrich, R. (2017, October). Using implicit feedback for neighbors selection: Alleviating the sparsity problem in collaborative recommendation systems. In *Proceedings of the 23rd Brazillian Symposium on Multimedia and the Web* (pp. 341-348).

Hazem, H., Awad, A., & Yousef, A. H. (2023). A distributed real-time recommender system for big data streams. *Ain Shams Engineering Journal*, 14(8), 102026. DOI: 10.1016/j.asej.2022.102026

https://www.businesswire.com/news/home/20221012005842/en/Global-Music-Streaming-Market-Report-2022-A-45-Billion-Industry-in-2026---Long-term-Forecast-to-2031-with-Amazon-Apple-Spotify-Gaana-SoundCloud-Dominating---ResearchAndMarkets.com

https://www.cnet.com/tech/services-and-software/spotify-eclipses-205-million-subscribers-better-than-predicted/

https://www.statista.com/topics/6408/music-streaming/

Liebman, E., Saar-Tsechansky, M., & Stone, P. (2019). The Right Music at the Right Time: Adaptive Personalized Playlists Based on Sequence Modeling. *Management Information Systems Quarterly*, 43(3), 765–786. DOI: 10.25300/MISQ/2019/14750

Matuszyk, P., & Spiliopoulou, M. (2017). Stream-based semi-supervised learning for recommender systems. *Machine Learning*, 106(6), 771–798. DOI: 10.1007/s10994-016-5614-4

Niu, Y. (2022). Collaborative Filtering-Based Music Recommendation in Spark Architecture. *Mathematical Problems in Engineering*, 2022, 2022. DOI: 10.1155/2022/9050872

Sakti, S. M., Laksito, A. D., Sari, B. W., & Prabowo, D. "Music Recommendation System Using Content-based Filtering Method with Euclidean Distance Algorithm," *2022 6th International Conference on Information Technology, Information Systems and Electrical Engineering (ICITISEE)*, Yogyakarta, Indonesia, 2022, pp. 385-390, DOI: 10.1109/ICITISEE57756.2022.10057753

Sun, J. (2022). Personalized music recommendation algorithm based on spark platform. *Computational Intelligence and Neuroscience*, 2022, 2022. DOI: 10.1155/2022/7157075 PMID: 35222633

Turrin, R., Condorelli, A., Cremonesi, P., Pagano, R., & Quadrana, M. (2015). Large scale music recommendation. In *Workshop on Large-Scale Recommender Systems (LSRS 2015) at ACM RecSys*.

Wang, L. (2022). Collaborative filtering recommendation of music MOOC resources based on spark architecture. *Computational Intelligence and Neuroscience*, 2022, 2022. DOI: 10.1155/2022/2117081 PMID: 35295283

Xuechao, Y. (2023). Recommender Systems: Collaborative Filtering and Content-based Recommender System. *Applied and Computational Engineering*, 2(1), 346–351. DOI: 10.54254/2755-2721/2/20220658

Chapter 9
An Efficient Rice Quality Prediction Using Convolutional Neural Network in Comparison With Support Vector Machine

N. Bhanu Prakash Reddy

Saveetha University, India

W. Deva Priya

https://orcid.org/0000-0002-7337-1684

Saveetha University, India

ABSTRACT

The major focus of this research work is to improve the accuracy of rice quality in real-time images using Support Vector Machine and Convolutional Neural Network. The recommended algorithm for Rice Quality Prediction. The Rice Quality Prediction dataset used in this study contain 356 rice samples (273 for for training 83 for testing) are Support Vector Machine with sample size N=10 and Convolutional Neural Network with sample size N=10 with the G-power of 80% and information units are gathered from more than a few internet sources with the latest learn about findings and threshold 0.05. The rice dataset is utilized for experimental work, and it is carried out with the assistance of the Jupyter software program tool. The end result of the Rice Quality Prediction is the usage of Support Vector Machine in contrast with Convolutional Neural Network.

DOI: 10.4018/979-8-3693-5563-3.ch009

INTRODUCTION

As India is the most prolonged maker of rice (farming) all through the globe. The nature of meals is a gorgeous sized thing for brilliant sustenance and the current day market ought to be liberated from debased ingredient (Ikram, 2023) grains. These grains encompass a few undesirable properties like granules that are broken, broken seeds, stones, and so on. The increase of undesirable (Lewy, 2016) assets in meals influences the introduction and nature of Food Quality Prediction. There is no tremendous strategy to distinguish these sub-par extraordinary grains from the lookout. Human discernment in the average of considered examinations has for some time been perceived as a record for fantastic difference. Once more the consequences are no longer dependable and proper. Rice is pretty much the most extensively diagnosed and most devoured substances on the planet. Quality elements are one of the most essential variables in discovering the cooking and dealing with attributes of rice. One of the serious troubles in the substances corporation is fore-seeing extremely good residences, (Burestan, Sayyah, & Taghinezhad, 2021). One of the serious troubles in foreseeing the great residences of rice is the large rate of indispensable core trials in the Food Quality Prediction enterprise organizatin, (Bourestan *et al.*, 2020). Rice as a meal furnish offers electrical power and protein to the giant phase of the world's population.

Over the previous 5 years, almost 300 research magazines had been accessible on Google Scholar and greater than one hundred fifty research articles have been presented in science direct journals with quite a number Machine Learning concepts. In addition, rice utilization and requests are increasing with the improvement of the population. To fulfill the elevated meals need, the manufacturing of rice has to be multiplied by over 40% through 2030, (Jie, Zhiwei, & Liang, 2019). Rice is a fantastically esteemed capability crop that takes care of greater than 3.5 billion of the whole populaces. Its magnitude can be checked from the way that the primary 5 rice-sending-out international locations had a consolidated (Gallimberti, Mara, & Prencipe, 2013) internet commodity well worth around 19 billion bucks in 2018. The nature of the rice is now not totally settled with the aid of exceptional (Ing-hilleri, Solomon, & Schulze, 2010) morphological highlights like shape, length, and region, as properly as textural factors like pastiness, and RGB range esteems rice grain examination and order framework can basically in addition enhance execution each regarding exactness as properly as time. In many years, this exploration area has garnered an extraordinary deal of (Kashem, 2018) consideration due to the fact of its economic impact.

This investigational work is defined with Convolutional Neural Network and Support Vector Machine which were started earlier, used in the real-time image dataset. Compared to Real-time Paddy Images the effects of the different Machine

Learning classifiers like Convolutional Neural Network predicts the rice quality excellent from real-time paddy Image with an extra accuracy level. The most important aim of this research system is to extend the rice first-class prediction price and the use of a variety of Machine Learning fashions with a higher accuracy rate.

MATERIALS AND METHODS

This proposed research challenge was once created and developed at the Compiler Design Laboratory, Saveetha School of Engineering, SIMATS (Saveetha Institute of Medical and Technical Sciences).The Rice Quality Prediction dataset used in this study contain 356 rice samples (273 for training 83 for testing). This cautioned rice first-class prediction machine carries two kinds of organizations Group 1 is taken as Convolutional Neural Network and Group 2 as Support Vector Machine used to be able to calculate many instances of 10 sample sizes.The sample size is calculated through ClinCalc.com. After amassing the paddy real-time photo dataset from an online site, repetitive and undesirable parts of the photos have been eliminated at some point of the data-cleaning process. Then, it is associated with the applicable information sets, and the accuracy fee of the Convolutional Neural Network and Support Vector Machine is measured and compared. The online snapshots are gathered and utilized in this contemporary research work on an experimental basis. It makes use of a JUPYTER software program device Food Production for making pleasant rice rice quality prediction systems. Among distinctive software program tools, JUPYTER is one of the best-known equipment for growing and evaluating the effect of Machine Learning models. It includes a number of library built-in features and unique equipment that are used for total methods related with the Machine Learning classifiers.

Python OpenCV software is used to plan and carry out the proposed work. The Windows 10 OS served as the testing ground for deep learning. A 4GB of RAM and an Intel Core i7 processor made up the hardware setup. 64-bit system sort was employed. Python was chosen as the programming language for the code implementation. As for code execution, the dataset is worked behind to perform an output process for accuracy. The UNSWNB15 dataset is collected from www.kaggle.com.

Convolutional Neural Network

The Convolutional Neural Network questioning applies a single NN (Neural Network) to the full picture, and at the identical time as partitions the photograph into districts and predicts leaping packing containers and probabilities for every and every and each and every location. These containers that are bounded are weighted via the way of overall performance of the anticipated probabilities. Convolutional Neural Network predicts excessive bouncin packing containers and classification probabilities for these cases. Convolutional Neural Network is utilized on full snap photographs and straightforwardly advances identification execution. The whole graphic prepares and assesses for encoding applicable archives about pointers as notable as their appearance. Processing demonstrations of things so that when outfitted on each and every day photographs and tried on pinnacle identification techniques. The most quintessential attribute of Convolutional Neural Network is a multi-layered Neural Network with a supervised analyzing sketch that generally entails two sections: an issue extractor and a teachable classifier. The problem extractor rice quality Prediction consists of the layer of map and recovers segregating highlights from the crude snapshots the utilization of two tasks convolutional sifting and down inspecting. Moreover Image Processing, down-inspecting and weight sharing can help Food Quality Prediction relatively curb the difference of teachable boundaries and work on the Food Production effectiveness of preparation. The classifier and the hundreds realized in the issue extractor are geared up with the aid of talent of the utilization of a minimize-again propagation concept.

Input: Rice Quality Dataset

Step-1: Load the dataset for Rice Quality Prediction from kaggle.

Step-2: Split the dataset randomly into training (80%) and testing (20%) dataset.

Step-3: Set the target variable.

Step-4: Generate the Convolutional Neural Network Classifier based on the training set.

Step-5: Train the classifier using Machine Learning domain analysis.

Step-6: Predict the testing set based on the training dataset.

Step-7: Evaluate the classifier.

Output: Accuracy in %

Support Vector Machine

The Convolutional Neural Network questioning applies a single NN (Neural Network) to the full picture, and at the same time as partitions the photo into districts and predicts leaping packing containers and probabilities for each and every location. These containers that are bounded are weighted through a way of universal overall performance of the predicted probabilities. Convolutional Neural Network predicts immoderate bouncin packing containers and class possibilities for these cases.Convolutional Neural Network is utilized on full snap images and straightforwardly advances identification execution. The entire photograph prepares and assesses Food Production for encoding relevant archives about suggestions as extraordinarily accurate as their appearance. It learns generalizable Image Processing demonstrations of matters so that when Food Quality Prediction is geared up on each and every day photographs and tried on pinnacle identification techniques. The most quintessential attribute of Convolutional Neural Network is that it is pretty excessive first-rate and hastily in real-time images. Convolutional Neural Network is a multi-layered NN with a supervised examining layout that commonly entails two sections: an issue extractor and a teachable classifier. The hassle extractor consists of the layer of map and recovers segregating highlights from the crude snap image the utilization of two tasks: convolutional sifting and down inspecting.

Algorithm steps

Inputs- Training and checking out data.
Outputs - A classification of attempting out data and Accuracy.
Step 1: Dataset has been loaded.
Step 2: Sampled the dataset randomly into teaching and tried out the dataset.
Step 3: Setting of the aim variable has been done.
Step 4: Generated the classifier principally primarily based on the schooling dataset.
Step 5: Predicted the making an attempt out a dataset.
Step 6: Evaluated the classifier

Statistical analysis

Statistical software tool IBM SPSS with the familiar version 26.0 to identify the value of SD (Standard Deviation), mean deviation data, significance (Maxwell, 2017) point data and also drawing the graphical demonstrations, etc. The SPSS tool was inclined in the current research process for investigating the concerned rice-image dataset. Group statistics practice and self- determination sample tests were directed at the Food Production experimental outcomes and the graphical format was created for two various graphs with two various kinds of features under the specific experimental phase. Datasets for training and testing are preferred for the rice database. The training dataset is recognized by reclaiming the test dataset from the real dataset as long as 400 image data as a whole.

RESULTS

The Jupyter software program device is used to look at the rice photograph facts and the accuracy charge is measured amongst Logistic Regression and J48 Decision Tree. For the given datasets, the proposed novel Convolutional Neural Network (97.27) provides a higher accuracy charge than Support Vector Machine (95.71).

Figure 1. Comparison of CNN and SVM algorithm in phrases of capability accuracy. The implied accuracy of CNN is greater than SVM and the famous deviation of CNN is barely greater than SVM. X Axis: Convolutional Neural Network and Support Vector Machine Y Axis: Means Accuracy of Detection ±2 SD

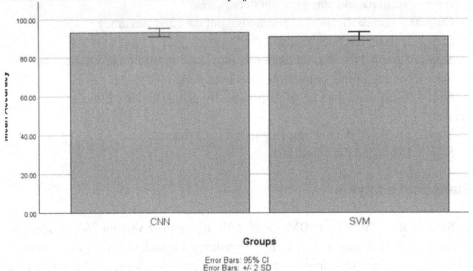

Table 1. Comparison of prediction of accuracy between CNN and SVM. CNN achieved an accuracy of 97.27% compared to Support Vector Machine, having 95.71%

Sl.no	CNN	SVM
1	97.27	95.71
2	96.58	94.21
3	95.87	93.23
4	94.23	92.55
5	93.68	91.62
6	92.47	90.12

continued on following page

Table 1. Continued

Sl.no	CNN	SVM
7	91.52	89.33
8	90.66	87.25
9	89.32	86.62
10	88.44	85.24

Table 1 Comparison of prediction of accuracy between Convolutional Neural Network and SVM. Convolutional Neural Network achieved an accuracy of 97.27% compared to Support Vector Machine, having 95.71%. Comparison of prediction of accuracy between Novel Convolutional Neural Network and Support Vector Machine. Novel Convolutional Neural Network achieved an accuracy of 97.27% compared to Support Vector Machine, having 95.71%. It shows that the Novel Convolutional Neural Network performed significantly better than Support Vector Machine For Rice Quality Prediction. The precision and execution of Novel Convolutional Neural Network were found to be significantly higher than those of Support Vector Machine. This indicates that Novel Convolutional Neural Network is a better choice than Support Vector Machine for this particular dataset and task.

Table 2. Group information displaying the mean, widespread deviation, and preferred error suggest values for the two organizations tested, Support Vector Machine and CNN - every with 10 samples

Algorithm		N	Mean	Standard Deviation	Standard Error Mean
Accuracy	SVM	10	90.58	3.015	1.098
	CNN	10	93.00	3.437	0.963

Table 2 Group information displaying the mean, popular deviation, and fashionable error imply values for the two agencies tested, Novel Convolutional Neural Network and Support Vector Machine algorithm - every with 10 samples. The Performance of Novel Convolutional Neural Network and SVM on the Rice Quality Prediction dataset. The results show that the Novel Convolutional Neural Network has standard deviation of 3.437 and a standard error mean of 0.963 For Support Vector Machine, with a standard deviation of 3.015 and a standard error mean of 1.098.

Table 3. Independent sample t- test result is completed with self-assurance interval as 95% and value stage as 0.001 (K nearest neighbor algorithm seems to operate extensively higher than Support Vector Machine with the price of p<0.05)

		Levene's test for equality of variables		T-test for Equality of means							
		F	Sig	t	df	Sig (2-tailed)	Mean Difference	Std. Error Difference	95% confidence interval of the Difference		
									Lower	Upper	
Accuracy	Equal variances assumed	0.024	0.033	1.654	18	0.001	2.416	1.476	-6.125	5.485	
	Equal variances not assumed			1.654	17.989	0.001	2.416	1.476	-6.126	5.488	

Table 3 It shows the results of the 2-tailed significance test, which indicates that the difference in accuracy between the two algorithms is statistically insignificant. The 2-tailed significance value of less than 0.001 (p<0.05) supports the hypothesis that Novel Convolutional Neural Network is a better choice than Support Vector Machine for this dataset and task.

DISCUSSION

The Support Vector Machine is used in the earlier research work; with a mean rate value of accuracy rate of 95.71%.Convolutional Neural Network is developed, which has an implied accuracy fee of 97.27%. In the Grain cognizance and satisfactory forecast module, first, the grains are characterized by utilizing a pre-prepared Convolutional Neural Network model. A pre-trained Convolutional Neural Network mannequin is utilized to figure out the degree of grain in the holder, (Nethravathy & Maragatham, 2016). A point-by-point grouping of harm in processed rice grains has been to an extraordinarily excellent extent overlooked due to the truth of the absence of an graphic that is extensively labeled dataset and the use of decreasing side Convolutional Neural Network fashions consequently; that empowers speedy, rice quality prediction, exact, and authentic order with the aid of ability of succeeding at the commence to cease undertakings, limiting pre-handling, and taking out the requirement for information element extraction, (Mondal, 2022).

Wan-Jie Liang (2019) says that quantitative (Balnaves & Caputi, 2001) distinction effects exhibit that CNN with Softmax (Yadav et al., 2022) and CNN with Support Vector Machine have same exhibitions, with expanded exactness, large AUC (Area

Under Curve). Consequently, CNN mannequin is a top-performing method for rice that has an impact on ailment acknowledgement and can be perchance utilized in viable functions. Machine Learning Strategies have been utilized to Food Production accumulate regularly with considerable awesome precision. Chemical and bodily attributes at the same time are useful novel rice quality prediction resources in inspecting the nature of rice. Shade, size, and the form of the grain has a few authentic qualities. Utilizing Support Vector Machine each and every single proper issue and characterization of the rice grains are obtained.

By executing these two and contrasting each Support Vector Machine consequence and recognizing which technique will play out the grouping efficiently. Harpree, Keshri, and Sharma (2020) proposed Machine Learning to grade (Grade A, B, C, and premium) the rice portions utilizing Multi-Class SVM. The most severe Difference method was once utilized to cast off the rice portions from the foundation, then, after the chalk has been extricated from rice. With the improvement of people's living standards and rice trade worldwide, the demand for high-quality rice is increasing, (Netravati, 2020). Therefore, breeding high quality Food Production is critical to meet the market demand. However, progress in improving rice grain quality lags far behind that of rice yield. The future scope of this Research work is able to handle both numerical and categorical data. Able to handle multi-output problems, (Nanmaran *et al.,* 2022). The cost of using the tree is logarithmic.

CONCLUSION

The current study compared the performance of two algorithms Support Vector Machine and Convolutional Neural Network for the Rice Quality Prediction. The results showed that the Convolutional Neural Network had a higher accuracy of 97.27%, compared to the accuracy of 95.71% for Support Vector Machine. This indicates Convolutional Neural Network performs better than Support Vector Machine for Rice Quality Prediction.

REFERENCES

Balnaves, M., & Caputi, P. (2001). Introduction to quantitative research methods: An investigative approach. *Sage (Atlanta, Ga.)*.

Fazeli Burestan, N., Afkari Sayyah, A. H. A., & Taghinezhad, E. (2021). Prediction of some quality properties of rice and its flour by near-Infrared Spectroscopy (NIRS) analysis. *Food Science & Nutrition*, 9(2), 1099–1105. DOI: 10.1002/fsn3.2086 PMID: 33598193

Gallimberti, C. M., Marra, A., & Prencipe, A. (2013). Consolidation: Preparing and understanding consolidated financial statements under IFRS: Updated to the new IFRS 10 and 11. UK higher education business accounting.

Ikram, S. (2023). Recipes and ingredients for ancient Egyptian mummification. *Nature*, 614(7947), 229–230. DOI: 10.1038/d41586-023-00094-1 PMID: 36725938

Inghilleri, L., Solomon, M., & Schulze, H. (2010). *Exceptional service, exceptional profit: The secrets of building a five-star customer service organization*. AMACOM Books.

Jie, X., Zhiwei, L., & Liang, X. (2019). Research on dynamic positioning accuracy evaluation method of GPS/Beidou dual mode navigation receiver 14th IEEE International Conference on Electronic Measurement y Instruments (ICEMI), 2019. DOI: 10.1109/ICEMI46757.2019.9101625

Kashem, S. B. A., Sheikh, M. I. B., Ahmed, J., & Tabassum, M. (2018, April). Gravity and buoyancy powered clean water pipe generator. In 2018 IEEE 12th International Conference on Compatibility, Power Electronics and Power Engineering (CPE-POWERENG 2018) (pp. 1-5). IEEE.

Kaur Harpreet, H., Keshri, R., & Sharma, A. (2020). Casualties caused by COVID-19 on education system. *International Journal for Research in Applied Sciences and Biotechnology*, 7(5), 125–133. DOI: 10.31033/ijrasb.7.5.18

Lewy, G. (2016). *Harmful and undesirable: Book censorship in nazi Germany*. Oxford University Press.

Maxwell, J. C. (2017). *The Power of significance: How purpose changes your life*. Center Street.

Mondal, T., & Department of Mathematics. (2022). "Distributive Lattices of λ-Simple Semirings." Iranian Journal of Mathematical Sciences and Informatics. Dr. Bhupendra Nath Duta Smriti Mahavidyalaya, Hatgobindapur, Burdwan. West. DOI: 10.52547/ijmsi.17.1.47

Nanmaran, R., Srimathi, S., Yamuna, G., Thanigaivel, S., Vickram, A. S., Priya, A. K., Karthick, A., Karpagam, J., Mohanavel, V., & Muhibbullah, M. (2022). Investigating the role of image fusion in brain tumor classification models based on machine learning algorithm for personalized medicine. *Computational and Mathematical Methods in Medicine*, 7137524, 1–13. Advance online publication. DOI: 10.1155/2022/7137524 PMID: 35178119

Nethravathy, J., & Maragatham, G. (2016). Malicious node detection in vehicle to vehicle communication. *International Journal of Engineering Trends and Technology*, 33(5), 248–251. DOI: 10.14445/22315381/IJETT-V33P249

Rahimi Bourestan, N., Nematollahzadeh, A., Parchehbaf Jadid, A., & Basharnavaz, H. (2020). Chromium removal from water using granular ferric hydroxide adsorbents: An in-depth adsorption investigation and the optimization. *Chemical Physics Letters*, 748, 137395. Advance online publication. DOI: 10.1016/j.cplett.2020.137395

Yadav, P. K., Burks, T., Frederick, Q., Qin, J., Kim, M., & Ritenour, M. A. (2022). Citrus disease detection using convolution neural network generated features and softmax classifier on hyperspectral image data. *Frontiers in Plant Science*, 13(December), 1043712. DOI: 10.3389/fpls.2022.1043712 PMID: 36570926

Chapter 10
Efficient Fake Logo Prediction Through Convolutional Neural Networks Over K– Nearest Neighbors

Balaji Pavan

Saveetha University, India

Kalimuddin Mondal

Saveetha University, India

ABSTRACT

The purpose of this work is to improve the Fake logo prediction Through CNN Over KNN. A novel method has been developed to detect fake logos using K-Nearest Neighbors (KNN) and Convolutional Neural Networks (CNN), which were trained and tested with varying splits. The CNN model outperformed KNN in terms of accuracy and speed, owing to its ability to extract complex features from images. However, CNN models may require significant resources, especially for large datasets. To enhance the system's accuracy and efficiency, the CNN model can be optimized and combined with a KNN model. The system is designed to detect fake logos in real-time and adapt quickly to new logos with minimal training, offering an effective and efficient approach for identifying fraudulent logos. The Gpower test was used with a significance level of α=0.05 and power of 0.85, resulting in an accuracy rate of approximately 85%.

DOI: 10.4018/979-8-3693-5563-3.ch010

INTRODUCTION

The use of fake logos is a growing problem in the modern digital world, with fraudulent individuals and organizations creating logos that are designed to deceive and mislead consumers, (Jiang *et al.,* 2022). Customers who aren't particularly tech-savvy can still benefit from the improved solution proposed in this paper: they just need to scan the product using a mobile app to determine whether or not they've received a counterfeit. The identification of logos will be a primary concern (both image and textual representation) (Roy & Patil, 2021). A novel set of news articles from both fabricated and legitimate news media sources is introduced for the purpose of analyzing and forecasting the spread of news. In contrast to other fake news datasets, which only include claims or the headline and body of news articles, this set includes a Facebook engagement count for each article, which is used as a proxy for the virality of the respective story. The Facebook thumbnail image and article description are also provided, (Krstovski, Ryu, & Kogut, 2022). The recognition of vehicle logos (VLR) is a critical component of any vehicle-tracking system by using Feature Extraction. As VLR Technology. are susceptible to huge within-class fluctuations as a result of factors such as lighting, perspective, etc., logo identification remains a difficult task. Inspired by the promising results of collaborative representation-based categorization, this article (CRC) (Nanmaran *et al.*, 2022). Logo identification is crucial in a variety of contexts, including complex document image processing, advertising, and intelligent transportation. In spite of the various technologies available for investigating logos, logo recognition remains a vital subsidiary step in these areas for Feature Extraction. Using the K-nearest neighbors distance classifier and the Support Vector Machine classifier to measure the degree of similarity between test and training pictures, this research proposes a Technology. for logo identification that is both accurate and reliable, (Lin-sheng *et al.*, 2011). The major application of fake logo prediction is that users can be assisted in spotting fakes by analyzing the product's logo.

The research has been carried out on fake logo prediction, on an average of 300 research papers have been published in IEEE Xplore and 29 papers have been published in sciencedirect. In this research, it is shown how cloud computing can be used to improve China's public security by combining cloud detection and recognition of vehicles. The monitoring nodes across the country have access to supercomputing and storage facilities thanks to a cloud computing platform created on top of the police network, (Nanmaran *et al.*, 2022). Two types of copyright information, a 3445 binary image and a sound signal for the utterance of a word, are used to build and evaluate an SVM-based watermarking technique. This study examines the scalability of support vector machines (SVMs) trained using a linear kernel and applies it to the problem of identifying two distinct types of copyright information, (Su, Zhu, & Gong, 2018). One practical facet of the study of visual recognition is logo recognition. Several factors, such as the presence of noise, occlusion, and varying scale/orientation, might impair the logo identification process in most document photos. In this study, that present a unique method for fixing these issues by analyzing the spatial and structural properties of logo pictures, (Bozkir & Aydos, 2020). An improved and more difficult logo detection environment, dubbed Open Logo Detection, is presented in this paper. To imitate open deployment, this new setting implies fine-grained labeling only on a subset of logo classes, while the rest classes are given just unlabeled training data, (Jadhav & Thepade, 2019). In this research, we introduce Histograms of Oriented Gradients (HOG) and Support Vector Machines as a novel method for vehicle logo identification (SVM). The method was developed to make use of the low-resolution pictures provided by traffic cameras, (Baraneetharan, 2022).

The research gap identified from the existing system is poor accuracy in classifying data points. Previous work in this area has relied heavily on traditional machine learning algorithms such as CNN and KNN, which have shown limited success in accurately classifying data points. Motivated by these findings, the aim of this proposed study is to improve the accuracy of classification by incorporating advanced deep learning Technology. such as Novel K-Nearest Neighbors (CNN) and comparing its performance with traditional K-Nearest Neighbors (KNN) algorithm. Computer vision tasks including image identification, object detection, and segmentation, have always proven challenging and interesting to researchers. In this research, use the deep learning approach to solve the problems of identification, object detection, and segmentation in photographs with a white backdrop, (Li *et al.,* 2017). The proposed model is expected to significantly enhance the accuracy of classification, thereby addressing the limitations of the existing system.

MATERIALS AND METHODS

The Soft Computing Lab at Saveetha School of Engineering, SIMATS conducted the study, in which the sample size was calculated using the G Power program to compare two controllers. Two groups were selected to compare their methods and outcomes, with 10 sets of samples chosen for each group. The study employed technology analysis tools to implement two algorithms, namely CNN and KNN. The sample size for each group was determined to be 10 using the GPower 3.1 program with parameters set to 0.05 significance level and 0.85 power, as reported by Nanmaran *et al.* (2022). Independent are Color contrast, Design elements, Aspect ratio and shape, Dependent variables are Binary outcome, Detection accuracy, Precision and recall, F1 score.

Python OpenCV software was used for planning and executing the proposed work. The deep learning experiments were conducted on a Windows 10 operating system. The hardware setup consisted of an Intel Core i7 processor with 4GB RAM, and the system was configured in 64-bit format. The code was implemented using Java as the programming language and using Feature Extraction. During code execution, the dataset was being processed in the background to ensure accurate output.

To determine the better algorithm for fake logo prediction, both KNN and CNN algorithms were evaluated based on 10 sets of samples for each group. Group-1 was represented by the KNN model, while Group-2 was represented by the CNN model. This approach was employed to compare the performance of the two algorithms and identify the most effective one for the task at hand.

Novel K-Nearest Neighbors Algorithm

Description

Novel K-Nearest Neighbors (CNNs) are a kind of deep learning algorithm that may be used to recognize pictures and do other tasks that involve the study of pixel data. Image classification, face recognition, object identification, and other forms of computer vision often make use of Novel K-Nearest Neighbors nowadays (CNNs).

Pseudocode

Step 1: Initialization of weights in Feature Extraction.

Step 2: Define forward propagation function: pass input through convolutional layers with kernels to extract features, apply non-linear activation function, use pooling layers to reduce output, flatten output and pass through fully connected layers, apply another non-linear activation function, calculate output using final fully connected layer.

Step 3: Define loss function: calculate difference between predicted and true output, calculate error.

Step 4: Define backward propagation function along with the Feature Extraction: calculate gradient of loss with respect to output, backpropagate gradient through fully connected and pooling layers, backpropagate gradient through activation functions and convolutional layers, calculate gradients of loss with respect to weights.

Step 5: Train the model: repeat forward and backward propagation for each training example, update weights.

Step 6: Use the model to make predictions: pass input through trained network, calculate output for the Feature Extraction methods for better accuracy

K nearest neighbor Algorithm

Description

K-Nearest Neighbor makes use of a similarity measure to classify fresh data or events. A data point is given a label based on the labels of its neighbors. Using a distance metric between a query and each sample in the data, the k-nearest neighbors (kNN) method either chooses the most often occurring label (in classification) or takes an average of the labels to get a conclusion (in the case of regression).

Pseudo code

Step 1: Prepare the data by collecting and preparing it for k-Nearest Neighbors, normalizing the data to ensure that all features have the same weight, and partitioning the dataset into training and testing sets.

Step 2: Based on the dataset and the issue at hand, select an acceptable value for K, the number of nearest neighbors to take into account.

Step 3: Determine the distance between each point in the training set and the new data point using a distance metric like the Minkowski, Manhattan, or Euclidean distance.

Step 4: Choose the K data points from the training set that are closest to the new data point in order to determine the k-Nearest Neighbors.

Step 5: Based on the classes of the new data point's closest neighbors, determine the new data point's class. In classification, the new data point is given the class that has the highest frequency among the k-Nearest Neighbors. In regression, the new data point is given the average of the values of the k-Nearest Neighbors.

Step 6: Test the model's accuracy using the testing dataset to assess the k-Nearest Neighbors model's accuracy. Compare the predicted labels to the actual labels to determine the model's accuracy.

Statistical Analysis

Independent variables for efficiency improvement in detecting fake logos through CNN over KNN could include logo features such as color, shape, font, and texture, as well as image metadata such as resolution, file format, and size, (Chen *et al.*, 2021). Other independent variables could include the number of layers in the neural network, the type of activation functions used, and the training data size. The dependent variable would be the prediction of whether a logo is fake or not. The performance of the CNN model and KNN model can be compared to determine which approach provides higher efficiency in detecting fake logos. The G-Power analysis was conducted using an alpha level of 0.05 and a beta level of 0.2, resulting in a power of 0.8. A confidence interval of 95% was used in the analysis, IBM SPSS software version 24.

RESULTS

Ten data points were used to assess the effectiveness of Anaconda Navigator's CNN and kNN. Table 1 suggests that CNN should be around 1.98590% reliable. Table 2 shows that the kNN prediction accuracy is 1.98590%. Since the loss value is multiplied by 10 samples, examine how each technique performs statistically. The results showed that CNN had an average accuracy of 90.5010%, whereas kNN only managed 88.5950%. The typical precision of both CNN and kNN is shown in Table 3. By comparing CNN with kNN, that the latter has a larger standard deviation (6.27997) than the former (5.07816). In Table 4 see that there is a statistically significant difference between CNN and kNN, as determined by an independent sample T test. It has been determined that 0.380 is the correct answer (p>0.05). Mean accuracy (1.98590) is compared between CNN and kNN in Figure 1.

Figure 1. Comparison of CNN and kNN. Classifier in terms of mean accuracy 1.98590. The mean accuracy of CNN is better than kNN. Classifier; Standard deviation of CNN is slightly better than kNN. X Axis: CNN Vs kNN Classifier and Y Axis: Mean accuracy of detection with +/-2SD

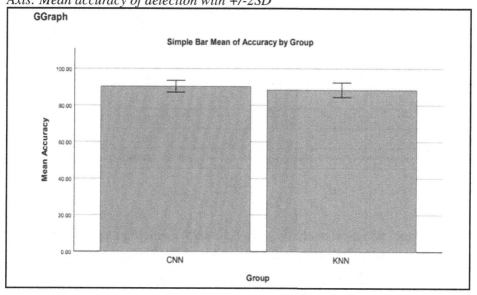

Table 1. Accuracy 1.98590 analysis of CNN

Iterations	Accuracy(%)
1	82.11
2	84.53
3	86.14
4	88.25
5	90.63
6	92.15
7	93.65
8	94.35
9	96.4
10	96.8

Table 2. Accuracy 1.98590 analysis of kNN

Iterations	Accuracy(%)
1	80.13
2	82.35
3	83.33
4	84.47
5	86.54
6	88.33
7	91.49
8	95.41
9	96.31
10	97.59

Table 3. Group statistical analysis of CNN and kNN. mean, standard deviation and standard error mean are obtained for 10 samples. CNN has higher mean accuracy and lower mean loss when compared to kNN

	Group	N	Mean	Std. Deviation	Std. Error Mean
Accuracy	CNN	10	90.5010	5.07816	1.60586
	kNN	10	88.5950	6.27997	1.98590

Table 4. Independent sample t-test: CNN is insignificantly better than kNN with p value 0.465 (Two tailed, p>0.05)

		Levene's test for equality of variances		T-test for equality means with 95% confidence interval						
		f	Sig.	t	df	Sig. (2-tailed)	Mean difference	Std.Error difference	Lower	Upper
Accuracy	Equal variances assumed	.810	.380	.746	18	0.465	1.90600	2.55393	-3.45961	7.27161
	Equal Variances not assumed			.746	17.245	0.465	1.90600	2.55393	-3.45961	7.27161

Table 5. Comparison of the CNN and kNN with their accuracy

CLASSIFIER	ACCURACY(%)
CNN	90.5010
kNN	88.5950

CNN has a middle value of 90.5010, a range of 5.07816-2.605870, and a standard error of 1.60586. Results for kNN are quite comparable to those obtained by averaging, summing, and calculating the mean standard error (1.98590).

That also includes the standard deviation, mean error, and group mean for both methods. Here can see how the loss measures are categorized by the CNN and kNN algorithms, and how they vary. CNN is able to provide a greater rate of accurate classification (90.5100%) than kNN.

DISCUSSION

Fake logo detection has become an essential task in digital media authentication. There are several approaches to detecting fake logos, including machine learning and Ensemble Learning methods like k-Nearest Neighbors (kNN) and Novel K-Nearest Neighbors (CNN). In recent years, there has been a growing interest in the use of deep learning-based techniques like CNNs for fake logo detection. In this study, the researchers compared the performance of kNN and CNN in detecting fake logos. The study found that CNN outperformed kNN, with a statistical non-significance of $p > 0.05$. CNN had an accuracy of 88.5950%, while kNN had an accuracy of 90.5010%. This indicates that CNN is a superior method for detecting fake logos compared to kNN.

The photos are then chopped into five by five pixel squares, with each of those squares being given its own storage place inside the image's block. Each pixel in the halal image is subjected to a one-dimensional Fourier transform. An array of one dimension is generated from the two-dimensional image. In the end, kNN classification is used in this system, (Chen *et al.,* 2021). K-Nearest Neighbors (kNN) is a model used in the area of machine learning and Ensemble Learning for the purpose of analyzing classification and regression. ensemble learning can be used to enhance the accuracy by combining the outputs of RNN and SVM models, (Su, Zhi, & Gong, 2018). This approach can help to mitigate the weaknesses of individual models and leverage their strengths. The key benefit of ensemble learning is that it can produce more accurate and robust predictions compared to using a single model alone. By leveraging the power of ensemble learning, the Efficient Fake Logo Prediction System can achieve higher accuracy and reliability, which is crucial for applications such as fraud detection and brand protection. The main goal of this study was to demonstrate the efficacy of a deep learning model in identifying fake news by applying it to a standard dataset, (Bozkir & Aydos, 2020). Closest Neighbors is a strategy that utilizes previously acquired data to organize freshly gathered data according to a distance function; these datasets are referred to as categories inside the method, (Jadhav & Thepade, 2019) (Baraneetharan, 2022) (Li *et al.*, 2017). Both manually built feature-based and automatically produced deep Novel K-Nearest Neighbors (CNN)-based approaches may be used for vehicle logo recognition (VLR). Typical ML approaches often use manually produced features to teach detectors, (Nanmaran *et al.*, 2022) (Chen *et al.*, 2021). In order to keep an eye on traffic at off-ramps, programmed a Novel K-Nearest Neighbors (CNN) to automatically recognize vehicle logos. For the purpose of training and evaluating CNNs, construct a novel dataset that is called VL, (Pinitjitsamut, Srisomboon, & Lee, 2021) (Nasir, Khan, & Varlamis, 2021) (Nguyen, Nepal, & Kanhere, 2021) (Panda, Mishra, & Puthal, 2022).

It should be noted that training CNN is a time-consuming process for ensemble learning, especially when dealing with large datasets, which is one of the main limitations of our study. Future work will focus on reducing the amount of time needed to train the data set and increasing the system's capacity to handle a larger number of objects, (Yu *et al*., 2020) (Nanmaran *et al.,* 2020).

CONCLUSION

In conclusion, the development of an efficient fake logo prediction system using machine learning for the Ensemble Learning techniques has shown great promise in the fight against fraudulent logos. This system has the potential to protect consumers from being deceived and misled by fake logos, as well as to reduce the economic impact of fraudulent activities on legitimate businesses and most Feature Extraction. Companies must adhere to ethical standards in all their operations, from sourcing raw materials to marketing their products. By adopting ethical practices, companies can gain the trust and loyalty of their customers, investors, and employees. The accuracy and efficiency of this system make it a valuable tool for a wide range of industries, including e-commerce, advertising, and intellectual property protection. Further research and development of this system will continue to improve its performance and expand its applications, leading to a safer and more secure digital world for everyone and Feature Extraction methods. The accuracy value of the CNN is 90.5010% whereas the accuracy value of kNN is 88.5950%. Based on the analysis, CNN (90.5010%) performs better than KNN (88.5950%).

REFERENCES

Baraneetharan, E. (2022) (Vol. 4, Issue 3, pp. 200–210). Detection of Fake Job Advertisements using Ensemble Learning algorithms. In Inventive Research Organization. DOI: 10.36548/jaicn.2022.3.006

Bozkir, A. S., & Aydos, M. (2020). LogoSENSE: A companion HOG based logo detection scheme for phishing web page and E-mail brand recognition. In Computers and Security. Elsevier BV, 95. DOI: 10.1016/j.cose.2020.101855

Chen, Y., Zheng, W., Li, W., & Huang, Y. (2021). Large group activity security risk assessment and risk early warning based on random forest algorithm. In Pattern Recognition Letters. Elsevier BV, 144. DOI: 10.1016/j.patrec.2021.01.008

Jadhav, S. S., & Thepade, S. D. (2019). Fake news identification and classification using DSSM and improved recurrent neural network classifier. In Applied Artificial Intelligence (Vol. 33, Issue 12, pp. 1058–1068). Informa Uk Limited, 33(12), 1058–1068. DOI: 10.1080/08839514.2019.1661579

Jiang, L. S., Tian, W. Y., & Zhu, X. F. (2011, July). Research on automatic detection of fake car-logo based on cloud-computing. In *2011 International Conference on Multimedia Technology* (pp. 5492-5494). IEEE.

Jiang, X., Sun, K., Ma, L., Qu, Z., & Ren, C. (2022). Vehicle logo detection method based on improved YOLOv4. *Electronics (Basel)*, 11(20), 3400. DOI: 10.3390/electronics11203400

Krstovski, K., Ryu, A. S., & Kogut, B. (2022). Evons: A dataset for fake and real news virality analysis and prediction (1st version). arXiv.

Li, Y., Shi, Q., Deng, J., & Su, F. (2017). Graphic logo detection with deep region-based convolutional networks. [VCIP]. *IEEE Visual Communications and Image Processing*, 1–4, 1–4. Advance online publication. DOI: 10.1109/VCIP.2017.8305065

Nanmaran, R., Nagarajan, S., Sindhuja, R., Charan, G. V. S., Pokala, V. S. K., Srimathi, S., Gulothungan, G., Vickram, A. S., & Thanigaivel, S. (2020, December). Wavelet transform based multiple image watermarking technique. In IOP Conference Series. IOP Conference Series: Materials Science and Engineering (Vol. 993, No. 1, p. 012167). IOP Publishing, 993(1). DOI: 10.1088/1757-899X/993/1/012167

Nanmaran, R., Srimathi, S., Yamuna, G., Thanigaivel, S., Vickram, A. S., Priya, A. K., Karthick, A., Karpagam, J., Mohanavel, V., & Muhibbullah, M. (2022). Investigating the role of image fusion in brain tumor classification models based on machine learning algorithm for personalized medicine. *Computational and Mathematical Methods in Medicine*, 7137524, 1–13. Advance online publication. DOI: 10.1155/2022/7137524 PMID: 35178119

Nanmaran, R., Srimathi, S., Yamuna, G., Thanigaivel, S., Vickram, A. S., Priya, A. K., Karthick, A., Karpagam, J., Mohanavel, V., & Muhibbullah, M. (2022). Investigating the role of image fusion in brain tumor classification models based on machine learning algorithm for personalized medicine. *Computational and Mathematical Methods in Medicine*, 7137524, 1–13. Advance online publication. DOI: 10.1155/2022/7137524 PMID: 35178119

Nasir, J. A., Khan, O. S., & Varlamis, I. (2021). Fake news detection: A hybrid CNN-RNN based deep learning approach. In International Journal of Information Management Data Insights (Vol. 1, Issue 1, p. 100007). Elsevier BV, 1(1). DOI: 10.1016/j.jjimei.2020.100007

Nguyen, D. D., Nepal, S., & Kanhere, S. S. (2021). Diverse multimedia layout generation with multi choice learning. MM '21: ACM Multimedia Conference. *Academic Medicine*, ●●●, 218–226. DOI: 10.1145/3474085.3475525

Panda, P., Mishra, A. K., & Puthal, D. (2022). A novel logo identification technique for logo-based phishing detection in cyber-physical systems. *Future Internet*, 14(8), 241. DOI: 10.3390/fi14080241

Pinitjitsamut, K., Srisomboon, K., & Lee, W. (2021). Logo detection with artificial intelligent 9th International Electrical Engineering Congress (iEECON), 2021 (pp. 408–411). DOI: 10.1109/iEECON51072.2021.9440236

Roy, R., & Patil, S. (May 7, 2021). Fake product monitoring system using artificial intelligence. SSRN Electronic Journal. Proceedings of the 4th International Conference on Advances in Science and Technology, (ICAST2021). DOI: 10.2139/ssrn.3867602

Su, H., Zhu, X., & Gong, S. (2018). Open logo detection challenge (3rd version). arXiv.

Yu, Y., Yao, H., Ni, R., & Zhao, Y. (2020). Detection of fake high definition for HEVC videos based on prediction mode feature. In Signal Processing. Elsevier BV, 166. DOI: 10.1016/j.sigpro.2019.107269

Chapter 11
Advancing Heart Attack Prediction:
Machine Learning for Enhanced Cardiac Risk Analysis

Shailendra Kumar Mishra

REVA University, India

R. Sreelakshmy

https://orcid.org/0000-0002-1198-8347

Vel Tech Rangarajan Dr. Sagunthala R&D Institute of Science and Technology, India

Gaurav Kumar

Wipro Limited, Canada

Dheeraj Kumar

Cognizant Technology Solutions, India

Sujeet Kumar

Intenim Technologies Pvt. Ltd., India

ABSTRACT

Cardiac arrest is one of the most frequently occurring causes of death worldwide. In this disease, the heart normally fails to provide enough blood to other regions of the body to allow them to perform their regular functions. It is tough for doctors to forecast cardiac arrest because various medical and physical habits are taken into consideration for forecasting cardiac arrest. Because the list of parameters is large, it is important to automate the procedure to avoid manual mistake, enhance medical efficiency, and reduce costs. The paper presents Explanatory Data Analysis (EDA)

DOI: 10.4018/979-8-3693-5563-3.ch011

and feature engineering of a data set on the basis of observations. The model uses various Machine Learning (ML) algorithms such as catBoost, Logistic regression, k-Nearest Neighbors, etc. to predict heart failure. In this comparison study, the research paper examines the performance of various machine learning algorithms. The model's performance is best on catboost. Analysing tools such as f-1 score and ROC-curve are drawn to evaluate the algorithm's efficiency.

1. INTRODUCTION

Heart failure is known as one of the world's most severe chronic illnesses. In certain cardiac diseases, the heart frequently refuses to pump sufficient blood to certain other regions of the human body for them to function correctly. Heart failure is caused by the shrinking and blockage of coronary arteries. The supply of blood to the heart is controlled by the coronary arteries. A buildup of fat, and maybe other substances in the nerves that supply blood to the heart, producing a plaque, is the most significant reason of a blockage (coronary arteries). A recent poll stated that the United States (US) is a highly impacted country by heart disease, with a very high percentage of heart failure patients. Breathlessness, muscular fragility, nausea, indigestion, heartburn or abdominal pain, swollen feet, lightheadedness or sudden dizziness, cold sweat, exhaustion, heaviness, anxiety, chest pain, or a compressing or hearting sensation in your chest, among other symptoms, are the most typical markers of cardiac disease.

Age, smoking, and a lengthy list of other factors all increase the occurrence of heart failure in a people. High blood pressure, high blood cholesterol or triglyceride levels, high blood obesity, Diabetes, Metabolic disorder, Heart attacks in the family, Stress, use of illegal drugs, A gynecological history, An immunological disorder.

Coronary artery disease (CAD) is the most frequent kind of cardiac illness, and it can cause chest pain or chest discomfort, stroke, and cardiac arrest. Another kinds of heart illness include congestive heart failure, cardiac rhythm problem, congenital heart disease (birth-related heart problem), and cardiovascular disease (CVD). Conventional investigative strategies were first utilized to detect cardiac illness, but they were proven to be difficult.

An automated medical diagnosis system would improve medical efficiency while simultaneously lowering expenses. We'll create a system that can quickly learn the criteria for predicting a patient's risk level based on the information provided about their health. The objective is to use various machine learning (ML) approaches to extract hidden information about notable heart illnesses and to estimate the existence of heart illnesses in patients where the occurrence is rated on a scale. Heart failure prediction requires a vast quantity of information which is too complicated and extensive to collect and evaluate using conventional methods. Our goal is to identify the most appropriate machine learning approach for predicting cardiac disease that is both computationally efficient and accurate.

2. LITERATURE SURVEY

This section contains a literature survey of heart attack prediction using machine learning (ML) and deep learning (DL). Recently, many techniques have been proposed for brain MRI classification using machine learning (ML) and deep learning. The following were recently published and explored these techniques to predict cardiac arrest probability. Cardiovascular disease (CVD) is now the most frequent cause of mortality throughout the world, with a figure of 17.9 million fatalities every year. The number of fatalities connected with cardio vascular disorders can be reduced if they are detected and diagnosed early. To evaluate the performance of algorithms/ techniques against various performance indicators, the author used a collection of algorithms as well as a standard dataset. On different analyzing tools, the authors found decision trees to be the best performing algorithm. On average, the effectiveness of DT is 14% which is almost stronger than the other approaches, (Almazroi, 2022). Machine learning can assist clinicians in uncovering hidden information from large amounts of raw cardiac patient data. After you've used all of the machine procedures, the scientists discovered that logistic regression consistently outperforms random forest in terms of accuracy, so they integrated the two models. A random forest is a very resilient model. The hybrid technique was used to combine the two models, which resulted in a higher level of accuracy in predicting heart disease, (Guda, Shalini, & Shivani, 2020).

The PCA method is a non-parametric, unsupervised analytical approach for reducing complexity or dimensionality in machine learning. PCA may be used to minimize the number of variables in your data by selecting the most significant ones from a huge pool. The author utilized a variety of machine learning algorithms to get to the conclusion that ac is the most accurate, with a 97 percent accuracy rate, (Sudha, 2020). A Smote was developed to balance the classes and convert the data. The models were evaluated using two performance metrics: cross validation accuracy and hold-out prediction (HOP) testing using ROC AUC. The CV aids in determining the model's consistency while also indicating the model's variation. The HOP indicates the model's prediction ability against samples that it hasn't seen before. The model's over fitting of the training data sample may be detected by comparing the CV and HOP, (Dadzie, n.d.). To predict heart disease, this study employs the techniques of Random Forest Classifier, XGBoost Classifier, Logistic Regression, Artificial Neural Network Classifier, K Neighbors and Support Vector

Machine Classifier. The Random Forest algorithm, with a 100% accuracy score, is the most potent heart disease prediction algorithm, according to the results of this study. However, the dataset used is rather small, (Purnomo, 2021). Examinations were done with and without feature selection to explore the impact of feature selection. Many of the most recent AI techniques were used by the authors, including Relief, mutual information, Chi-square, forward feature selection, reverse feature selection, recursive feature removal, comprehensive feature selection, Ridge regression, and Lasso regression. Analysis included decision trees, random forests, SVM, logistic regression, K-nearest neighbor, and Gaussian naive Bayes and concluded that recursive feature selection is one of the robust feature selection methods. Lasso regression is the best for outliner detection among all. The performance of logistic regression is superior to other classifiers. The greatest accuracy value without feature selection was 63.92 percent; by utilizing a decision tree classifier and backward feature selection, this value was enhanced to 88.52 percent. The results of the experiments reveal that feature selection algorithms are capable of accurately diagnosing illness with a minimal number of features, (Beguma, Siddiqueb, & Tiwaric, 2021).

Based on the 2 statistical models and GNB in this research work, the authors proposed a feature-driven decision support system for HF disease prediction. It was demonstrated that the recently constructed system, 2-GNB, outperformed the traditional GNB model. Six assessment criteria were utilized to assess the robustness of the 2-GNB model: sensitivity, accuracy, specificity, ROC, AUC, and MCC. The suggested model was shown to increase the effectiveness of the GNB system by 3.33 percent. Further -more, a prediction accuracy comparison between the 2-GNB model and other previously published approaches was performed. The 2-GNB model outperforms state-of-the-art ensemble models, support vector machines, and many previously published approaches, according to experimental data, (Dissanayake, 2021). The paper discovered that the dataset should be normalized; otherwise, the training model might become over fitted, resulting in insufficient accuracy when a model is evaluated for real world data issues that differ greatly from the dataset on which the model was trained. It was also discovered that statistical analysis is crucial when analyzing a dataset, which should have a Gaussian distribution, and that outliner detection is also vital, which is handled using the Isolation Forest approach. If a huge dataset is available, deep learning and machine learning outcomes can improve dramatically, (Ali *et al.*, 2019).

There were two sorts of systems created. Both systems employed the same feature selection strategy, but the first system classified using ANN while the second system classified using deep neural network (DNN). The ANN-based system had a classification accuracy of 91.11 percent, while the DNN-based diagnostic system had a classification accuracy of 93.33 percent, (Bharti *et al.*, 2021). In the healthcare business, data mining is crucial for illness diagnosis. Data mining is defined as the process of scanning big data sets for usable information. Association rules, classification, clustering, prediction, and sequential models are some of the most commonly used data mining approaches. Data mining techniques are utilized in a wide range of applications. For this work, data extraction methods such as K-star, J48, SMO, Nave Bayes, MLP, Random Forest, Bayes Net, and REPTREE were utilized to predict cardiac abnormalities, (Javeed et al., 2020). The model, which employs two-class SVM, two-class Decision Jungle, and multi-class Decision Jungle order calculating techniques, was found to be the top classifier for coronary sickness prediction in Microsoft Azure Machine Learning, with an average precision of 86.81 percent. It examines the patient information after the prepared informative collection to predict heart infections from the scale (values 1, 2, 3, and 4) and nonappearance (esteem 0). A specialist will play it safe for the patient by attaining the expected value, (Saleh et al., 2020).

According to studies, the kind and quantity of the dataset, the type of classification approach (supervised or unsupervised), and the presence of undesired characteristics in the dataset all impact prediction accuracy. As a result, feature selection (FS) is an important phase in data mining research, and no individual approach can be prioritized over the others. The findings demonstrate that using these three variables, the maximum prediction accuracy using most MLTs is just 56.61 percent. The authors discovered that the accuracy levels improved as the number of characteristics decreased, (Rani & Bansal, 2020). The performance of neural networks is influenced by hyper parameter selection. The main goal was to prevent any potentially misleading results, as feature engineering may sometimes lead to the elimination of certain qualities, which can have a substantial impact on overall prediction results. As a consequence, each of these tests is subjected to a stratified K -fold analysis to see if the results are true. Other diseases, such as diabetes or cancer, might benefit from similar forecasting techniques, (Waqar et al., 2021).

Three attribute evaluator methodologies were employed in this study to choose important qualities from the Cleveland heart dataset in order to enhance the efficacy of machine learning classifiers for predicting heart disease risk. The SMO classifier generated a stunning result when using the chi -squared attribute evaluation technique. The authors found a great improvement in prediction performance with correct attribute selection and adjustment of the classifier hyper -parameters, (Singh, Singh, & Pandi-Jain, 2018).

Chest pain kind, with classic angina being the most impactful and excessive chest pain being the least, cholesterol level, with levels larger than 200 mg/dl being more vulnerable, elevated heart rate, age, and thalamus level being some of the most significant qualities, (Reddy et al., 2021). To establish a model for myocardial infarction prediction, multiple supervised ML classifiers such as Decision Tree, Random Forest, Logistic Regression, and Gradient Boosting were employed. Despite the fact that both datasets have many inconsistencies, a variety of feature transformers have been deployed to boost dataset consistency and achieve an average accuracy of 85.5 percent, (Faiayaz & Koteeswaran, 2021) (Fitriyani *et al.*, 2020) (Manimurugan *et al.*, 2022). A fresh approach is specified, including a new k-means neighbor classifier that is more accurate and performs better than the original k-means neighbor classifier. When accuracy reaches a saturation point, the process of computing for accurate instances is halted, which improves performance. By locating the best prime number below the k value, Novel k is computed and used as an input to the Novel KNN algorithm. This resulting technique might be used to forecast cardiac ailments as well as a variety of other basic to sophisticated applications. Regardless of the application's intensity, accuracy is increased, and classification and validation mistakes are decreased, (Muhammad, Hayat, & Chong, 2020) (Shalik *et al.*, 2023) (Ganesh *et al.*, 2024) (Kalita *et al.*, 2023).

By combining XGBoost, SMOTE-ENN, and DBSCAN based MLA to increase accuracy rate of prediction, for heart disease diagnosis, we proposed a magnificent heart disease prediction model (HDPM). DBSCAN was used to find and eliminate eccentric data, in order to balance the data, SMOTE-ENN was utilized, (Pujitha & Vickram, 2023). To learn and construct the prediction model, the imbalanced training dataset and XGBoost MLA were used. The experimental findings showed that the suggested model outperformed state of the art framework and prior study finding, with precision of up to 95.91 percent for datasets I and II, and 98.40 percent for datasets III and IV, respectively, (Nanmaran *et al.*, 2020). A hybrid linear discriminant analysis with modified ant lion optimization (HLDA-MALO) technique was used to classify sensor information. Heart failure datasets from the UCI library, such as the Cleveland dataset and the echocardiography dataset, were used to train the models. The hybrid LDA-MALO approach correctly identified normal sensor information 96.85% of the time and abnormal sensor data 98.31% of the time, (Nanmaran *et al.*, 2022).

3. METHODOLOGY

The procedures for carrying out the research are mentioned below.

i) The dataset is carefully examined to determine the data's structure and the significance of the individual attributes.
ii) Various techniques from Python's pandas module are used to remove missing data, unusual data, irregular data that does not meet the column description, and outliers from the dataset.

iii) After verifying that the preprocessing stage produced a cleansed dataset, the data is kept for repeatability of the outcomes.

iv) The cleaned data is used for a detailed analysis of cardiac arrest using matplotlib and machine learning algorithms.

v) There are two different sections to the dataset: training and testing. The training set contains 80% of the data, and the test set contains 20%. The training set data is used to train the model, and the remaining 20% is used to evaluate and find the model's accuracy. vi) Various machine learning techniques such as Randomforest, SVM, catboost, xgboost, decision tree, KNN, and Naive Bayes (NB) are used to find the accuracy of the model.

A. Dataset and pre-processing

The efficiency and training rate of the model are directly influenced by the data quality. Preprocessing is commonly used to increase the effectiveness of data by reducing noise and increasing the region of focus. Models trained with pre-processed data have greater precision, and testing and training are error-free. This study used records on Cleveland heart disease from the UCI repository, which may be accessed via the internet for the purpose of testing. When this dataset was created, however, there were 303 cases and almost 75 characteristics. Following that, 14 prominent features were chosen from a total of 75, encompassing biographic, clinical, and behavioral aspects present in the given dataset, as well as an output feature. Table 1 provides a full overview of the dataset. To indicate the presence or absence of cardiac disease, the output feature's label (num) is separated into two groups. Preprocessing the dataset is required for an accurate depiction of data quality. Preprocessing strategies included removing missing values from features; utilizing Standard Scaler (SS); and using Min Max Scaler. A data preparation method called" missing value management" is used to build a smooth dataset. For us, the process began with identifying whether the dataset had any missing data. There are some missing variables in the heart disease dataset utilized in this study. (Missing values are substituted with the features' mode or mean values).

Table 1. Effectiveness of the model with various activation functions

	Age			trtbps	chol		restecg	thalach	exng	oldpeak			thall	output
1	57	1	0	140	192	0	1	148	0	0.4	1	0	1	1
2	56	0	1	140	294	0	0	153	0	1.3	1	0	2	1
3	44	1	2	120	263	0	1	173	0	0	2	0	3	1
4	52	1	2	172	199	1	1	162	0	0.5	2	0	3	1
5	64	1	0	110	211	0	1	174	0	1.6	2	0	2	1

Age: Age of the patient.

sex: 1 denotes male whereas 0 denotes female

cp: 0 denotes asymptomatic chest pain, 1 denotes typical angina chest pain, 2 denotes atypical angina chest pain, and 3 denotes non-anginal chest pain pain.

trtbps: Blood pressure of the patient in mm Hg.

Chol: cholesterol level in mg/dl.

Fbs: blood sugar test 120 mg/dl. 0 denotes absence while 1 denotes presence of blood sugar.

restecg: electrocardiography results (0 for normal, 1 for hypertrophy and 2 for having ST and T wave abnormality).

thalachh: maximum heart rate of the patient.

exng: Angina caused by exercise (0 for absence and 1 for presence).

oldpeak: Exercise-induced ST depression compared to rest.

slp: the slope of the ST wave during workout (0 denotes down sloping, 1 denotes flat, and 2 denotes up sloping).

caa: number of major vessels in Fluoroscopy test.

thall: thallium stress level test (1 denotes fixed defect denotes reversible defect and 3 denotes normal thallium stress level).

output: risk of heart attack (0 denotes low risk of heart failure and 1 demotes high risk of heart failure.

B. Block Diagram

By reviewing the numerous classifications and performing performance analysis, the suggested study revealed heart failure. The main objective of this paper is to identify whether or not a patient has a heart illness. The input values from the patient's health report are entered by the health practitioner. The information is fed into a model that forecasts the risk of coronary heart failure. The schematic diagram of the system is shown in Figure 1. The flow of the diagram indicates the dataset is collected and preprocessing of the data is done to remove noise and null values. The null value is replaced with the mean and mode value of the particular row. The clean and balanced data is used for exploratory data analysis using various machine learning algorithms, statistical tools, and python libraries. Graphical analysis is done for each attribute to gain clarity and make a conclusion and decision. The dataset is split into two subsets. The first part contains 80% of the data and is employed in the model training; the rest 20% data employed for testing the model. Our model is trained using various machine learning algorithms and the result of the algorithm is taken into consideration. The algorithm having the best result is taken into consideration. The accuracy and sensitivity of the models are tested using the f score and confusion matrix.

Figure 1. Model summary

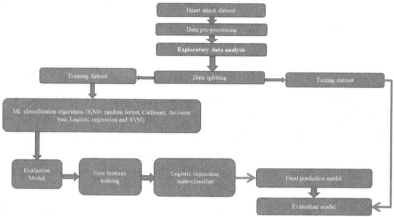

C. Exploratory data analysis (EDA)

properties, which is commonly done using statistical graphics and other data visualization approaches. EDA differs from traditional hypothesis testing in that it focuses on what data can show us outside of formal models. Since 1970, John Turkey has advocated for exploratory data analysis (EDA) as a means for researchers to learn much more about data and develop assumptions that could lead to additional data gathering and trials. The Initial data analysis (IDA) emphasizes on confirming expectations for testing hypothesis and model fitting, as well as correcting erroneous values and making necessary variable modifications. EDA and IDA are synonymous terms. The analysis (Figure 2) discussion is as follows:-

The bulk of the patients are in their forties and fifties. The distribution has a tendency to be normal. At 57-58 years old, the pinnacle has been reached. The chance of cardiac arrest is more at age 57 to 58. 140 patients have type of chest pain of type 0 (asymptomatic pain). 50 patients have type of chest pain-1(typical angina), 80 patients have type of chest pain-2(atypical angina) 20 patients have chest pain type 3 (non-anginal pain) and almost half of the patients have no pain in the chest. The blood pressure distribution has a peak at a value of approximately 135. The highest blood pressure is about 200. Cholesterol is a fatty substance found in the blood of humans. Our body wants cholesterol to build healthy cells, but high cholesterol levels increase the risk of cardiovascular disease. If you have excessive cholesterol, you may have waxy deposits in your blood arteries. The distribution has a normal form, but the outliers have skewed it to the right. Some patients have abnormally high cholesterol levels. The cholesterol level is about Outliers are numbers greater than

360. However, we cannot remove them since they are realistic values. The resting ECG can identify heart hypertrophy, ischemia, myocardial infarction, myocardial infarction sequelae, cardiac arrhythmia, and other heart disorders. Approx half of patients have hypertrophy. Only a minority of the patients exhibit aberrant ST-T waves. The others had normal outcomes.

The maximum heart rate (MHR) is the greatest heart rate that an individual may obtain without experiencing significant issues as a result of exercise stress, and it declines with age. The distribution resembles a standard distribution. It's slightly tilted to the left. More than 50% of the patients do not have major vessels. A nuclear imaging test, which is considered a thallium stress test, can determine how well blood flows into our heart when we are exercising or resting. More than half of the patients had normal outcomes.

Correlation analysis is not appropriate for the given dataset, and it is also hard to analyze the relations between features of the dataset because the target variables are categorical variables. We plotted pi chart distributions for high risk of heart attack and low risk of heart attack to see how the attributes affect the goal. The distribution for each of the numerical values depending on the target value is plotted to analyze the dependency Figure 3. We reached at the conclusion that the cholesterol level and blood pressure do not affect the chance of heart attack; younger people are more prone to have a heart attack; the output is affected by the highest heart rate obtained, ST depression caused by workout compared to rest, and the number of main vessels.

Because we have almost balanced classes, a pie plot will be useful for comparison. Fasting blood sugar doesn't affect the output. It has, so it should be removed from the data set. Figure 4. Patients experiencing any of the four types of chest pain are more likely to be in the risk group. Figure 5.

Figure 2. Distribution of dataset parameters

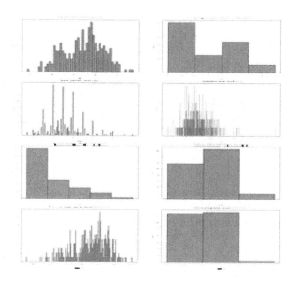

Figure 3. Distribution of attributes

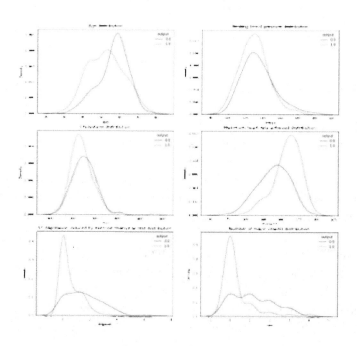

Figure 4. Distribution of fasting blood sugar

Influence of fasting blood sugar on the risk of a heart attack

Figure 5. Distribution of chest pain type

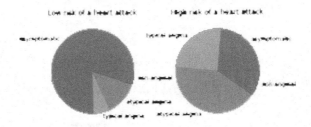
Influence of chest pain type on the risk of a heart attack

D. Feature Engineering

To improve the accuracy of the model, we need feature engineering of the dataset. There are some attributes in the database which have almost no role or very little role and therefore should be removed. The accuracy of the model may be affected by the skewness of the data set. There is a need to generate new features using mathematical operations on data and biological formulas to calculate attributes such as Tanaka's formula, which is used to calculate maximum heart rate using age.

i) The feature that has an influence on the output is the maximum heart rate achieved. In medical practice, it's calculated using the equation: MHR=208(0.7)×Age. The formula is also known as Tanaka's formula. The formula is used to calculate the maximum heart rate of a normal person. Here the formula is used to calculate the difference between actual and idle MHR. A new column is added in the dataset containing the difference in MHR.

ii) Blood pressure:-According to the European Society of Cardiology, the following classification for blood pressure is applied: • pressure less than 120 = 0 (normal) • 120 to 140= 1 (elevated) • greater than 140 = 2 (high) 3)

iii) cholesterol level:-According to the European Society of Cardiology, the following classification for cholesterol is applied. The cholesterol level of the dataset is categorized into three and a new column containing graded data is added into the dataset

iv) A new column is added into dataset that contain the summarized value of blood pressure and cholesterol level. If a person has 0, it means that he has normal blood pressure and normal cholesterol. But if the value is 4, it means that he has high blood pressure and high cholesterol

v) A new column is added that contain summarized value of chest pain type, reseg, thall, and exng of a healthy person. Thus, a new dataset is created. The performance of two feature sets is compared on the simple model using cross-validation.

A. Model Training

The training and testing subsets are created from the modified dataset. The dataset has 17 attributes. The model is trained using machine learning (ML) algorithms. The accuracy of the model with different ML models is given in Table 3. The accuracy of the model with the catboost classifier is the highest. Support vector machine and random forest classifiers are also performing well, whereas other classifiers have comparatively low accuracy. Adding some new features results in improved accuracy of the model.

B. Performance Analysis

Various machine learning methods, such as Random Forest, SVM, and Catboost, are utilized to predict cardiac disease in this study. The Heart Disease UCI dataset comprises a total of 76 features, but only 14 of them are used in the prediction of heart disease. This project takes into account a variety of patient characteristics such as gender, kind of chest pain, fasting blood pressure, serum cholesterol, exang, and so on. Individual algorithms' accuracy must be measured, and the algorithm with the highest accuracy is considered for heart disease prediction.

Table 2. Model performance with different classifier

	classifiers	Accuracy(unmodified)	Accuracy(modified)
1	Catboost	87.23%	89.23%
2	random forest	84.95%	87.85%
3	Support Vector Machine	85.70%	87.87%
4	DecisionTree	80.76%	81.96%
5	Logistic Regression	82.10%	86.52%
6	KNeighborsClassifier	72.10%	72.85%
7	Gradient Boosting Classifier	82.90%	83.62%
8	AdaBoost classifier	71.86%	73.77%

Figure 6. Predicted output

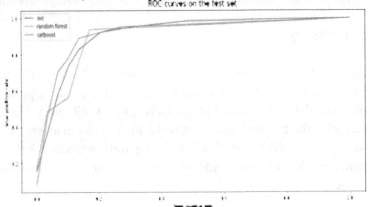

The ROC curve of the three best -performing classifiers is shown in Figure 6. It can be observed from Figure 6, that the green colour is occupying the maximum area and the same curve is approaching the value faster than the other two curves. As a result, we can conclude that the catboost classifier outperforms all others.

Table 3. Model performance with different optimizer

SN.	model	f1-score(cross-validation	f1-score(test set)	$roc_a^{uc(testset)}$
1	SVM	0.832519	0.878788	0.924569
2	Random forest	0.852917	0.878788	0.910560
3	catboost	0.857366	0.892308	0.922414

The F-score, often known as the F-measure, is a metric for determining how accurate this test is. It's computed by dividing the number of true positive outcomes by the entire number of positive outcomes, which includes those that were incorrectly recognized, and recalled by the number of true positive findings divided by the total number of test samples that should have been detected as positive. Efficiency is also referred to as positive predictive value in diagnostic binary classification algorithms, whereas recall is also known as sensitivity. The F-score of the three classifiers is drawn to analyze the most accurate and suitable classifier (Table 3). The F1-score of the catboost classifier is the highest and it is 0.8573. The f1-score of the SVM and random forest is also high. The table shows the catboost classifier is the most suitable classifier.

Figure 7 shows the importance of the thallium stress test alone is 31.84% responsible for cardiac arrest. Chest pain type is also very much responsible for cardiac arrest. Its importance is 19.06%. Similarly, caa is dominant feature responsible for cardiac arrest. Its importance is 13.96%. Since the chest pain type thallium stress test and caa is more responsible, if a patient has a high value of any of these symptoms, they need to consult a doctor immediately. It is important to analyze the importance of the feature responsible for cardiac arrest. The most important features are the thallium stress test, chest pain type, and the number of major vessels. The less important features are sex, cholesterol, and resting blood pressure.

Figure 7. Feature importance by catboost

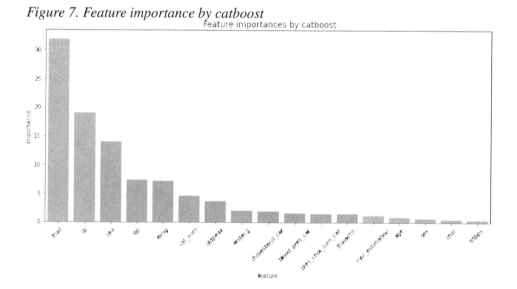

4. CONCLUSION

The proposed paper emphasizes the unbalanced characteristic of the UCI dataset. Data is very crucial for a machine learning algorithm to perform well. It's the most crucial factor that enables model or algorithm training and illustrates why ML has gained so much traction in recent years. Algorithms will be almost worthless if the data is not properly processed. If the dataset is imbalanced, the algorithm may generate inaccurate or misleading output, and that may have disastrous consequences. That's why preparation of data is so essential in the machine learning process. Data preparation is sequences of processes that assist your dataset become more machine learning-friendly. In this given dataset the number of male patients is 207 while female patients are 96. To balance the dataset, we added some more female patient data from another dataset. An explanatory data analysis (EDA) is performed on the dataset to analyze and fix the outliers. This analysis is also included to determine the feature's importance. The useless features are removed, and some new features are generated using medical formulas and added to get an improved dataset.

The model is trained with both initial and modified datasets on 8 different machine learning algorithms. The accuracy of the model is compared in Table 2, and we conclude that the model with the modified dataset has better accuracy than the model with the initial dataset. The three best performing models are catboost, SVM, and random forest. The analysis technique f1 score and ROC curve are drawn for all three models, and it is found that the catboost has the very high accuracy (89.23%) among all for the proposed model.

The final conclusion of the model is that patients having any chest pain thallium level and a number of major vessels are at severe risk of cardiac arrest and they need to consult the doctor quickly. Cardiac arrest is very less dependent on age, resting blood pressure, and sex.

REFERENCES

Ali, L., Khan, S. U., Golilarz, N. A., Yakubu, I.-R., Qasim, I., Noor, A., & Nour, R. (2019). A Feature-Driven Decision Support System for Heart Failure Prediction Based on 2 Statistical Model and Gaussian Naive Bayes. *Computational and Mathematical Methods in Medicine*, 2019, 6314328. Advance online publication. DOI: 10.1155/2019/6314328 PMID: 31885684

Almazroi, A. A. (2022). Survival prediction among heart patients using machine learning techniques. Mathematical Biosciences and Engineering, 19(1), 134–145. Advance online publication. DOI: 10.3934/mbe.2022007

Beguma, S., Siddiqueb, F. A., & Tiwaric, R. (2021). A Study for predicting heart disease using machine learning. Turkish Journal of Computer and Mathematics Education, 12(10), 4584–4592.

Dadzie, K. K. E. (n.d.). Machine Learning-Based Classifi -cation Algorithms for the Prediction of Coronary Heart Disease, 14.

Dissanayake, K. (2021). Comparative Study on Heart Disease Prediction Using Feature Selection Techniques on Classification Algorithms. DOI: 10.1155/2021/5581806

Faiayaz Waris, S. F., & Koteeswaran, S. (2021, January 19). WITHDRAWN: Heart disease early prediction using a novel machine learning method called improved K-means neighbor classifier in python. *Materials Today: Proceedings*. Advance online publication. DOI: 10.1016/j.matpr.2021.01.570

Fitriyani, N. L., Syafrudin, M., Alfian, G.-J., & Rhee, J.-T. (2020). HDPM: An Effective Heart Disease Prediction Model for a Clinical Decision Support System. https://doi.org/DOI: 10.1109/AC-CESS.2020.3010511

Ganesh, N., Balamurugan, M., Chohan, J. S., & Kalita, K. (2024). Development of a grey wolf optimized-gradient boosted decision tree metamodel for heart disease prediction. *International Journal of Intelligent Systems and Applications in Engineering*, 12(8s), 515–522.

Guda, V., Shalini, K., & Shivani, C. (2020). Heart disease prediction using hybrid technique. Journal of Interdisciplinary Cycle Research, 12(6).

Javeed, A., Rizvi, S., Zhou, S., Riaz, R., Khan, S. U., & Kwon, S. J. (2020). Heart Risk Failure Prediction Using a Novel Feature Selection Method for Feature Refinement and Neural Network for Classification. *Mobile Information Systems*, 2020, 8843115. Advance online publication. DOI: 10.1155/2020/8843115

Kalita, K., Ganesh, N., Jayalakshmi, S., Chohan, J. S., Mallik, S., & Qin, H. (2023). Multi-Objective artificial bee colony optimized hybrid deep belief network and XGBoost algorithm for heart disease prediction. Frontiers in Digital Health, 5. *Frontiers in Digital Health*, 1279644, 1279644. Advance online publication. DOI: 10.3389/fdgth.2023.1279644 PMID: 38034907

Manimurugan, S., Almutairi, S., Aborokbah, M. M., Narmatha, C., Ganesan, S., Chilamkurti, N., Alzaheb, R. A., & Almoamari, H. (2022, January 9). Two-Stage Classification Model for the Pre -diction of Heart Disease Using IoMT and Artificial Intelligence. *Sensors (Basel)*, 22(2), 476. DOI: 10.3390/s22020476 PMID: 35062437

Mishra, J. S., Gupta, N. K., & Sharma, A. (2024). Enhanced Heart Disease Prediction Using Machine Learning Techniques. *Journal of Intelligent Systems & Internet of Things*, 12(2).

Nanmaran, R., Nagarajan, S., Sindhuja, R., Charan, G. V. S., Pokala, V. S. K., Srimathi, S., Gulothungan, G., Vickram, A. S., & Thanigaivel, S. (2020, December). Wavelet transform based multiple image watermarking technique. In IOP Conference Series. IOP Conference Series: Materials Science and Engineering (Vol. 993, No. 1, p. 012167). IOP Publishing. DOI: 10.1088/1757-899X/993/1/012167

Nanmaran, R., Srimathi, S., Yamuna, G., Thanigaivel, S., Vickram, A. S., Priya, A. K., Karthick, A., Karpagam, J., Mohanavel, V., & Muhibbullah, M. (2022). Investigating the role of image fusion in brain tumor classification models based on machine learning algorithm for personalized medicine. *Computational and Mathematical Methods in Medicine*, 7137524, 1–13. Advance online publication. DOI: 10.1155/2022/7137524 PMID: 35178119

Pujitha, U., & Vickram, A. S. (2023, November). Implementation and comparison of proportional (P), integral derivative (ID) control technique for pacemaker design to regulate heart rate for patients with Bradycardia. In AIP Conference Proceedings. AIP Publishing, 2822(1). DOI: 10.1063/5.0173205

Purnomo, M. (2021). Brain Tumor Classification in MRI Images Using En-CNN. International Journal of Intelligent Engineering and Systems, 437–451. DOI: 10.22266/ijies2021.0831.38

Rani, N., & Bansal, A. (2020). Implementation of Heart Disease Pre -diction using Machine Learn -ing with data analytics. Aegaeum Journal, 8(9).

Reddy, K. V. V., Elamvazuthi, I., Aziz, A. A., Paramasivam, S., Chua, H. N., & Pranavanand, S. (2021). Heart Disease Risk Prediction Using Machine Learning Classifiers with Attribute Evaluators. *Applied Sciences (Basel, Switzerland)*, 11(18), 8352. DOI: 10.3390/app11188352

Saleh, B., Saeidi, A., Al-Aqbi, A., & Salman, L. (2020). Analysis of Weka Data Min -ing Techniques for Heart Disease Prediction System. International Journal of Medical Reviews, 7(1), 15–24. DOI: 10.30491/ijmr.2020.221474.1078

Shaik, K., Ramesh, J. V. N., Mahdal, M., Rahman, M. Z. U., Khasim, S., & Kalita, K. (2023). *Big data analytics framework using squirrel search optimized gradient boosted decision tree for heart disease diagnosis. Applied Sciences. MDPI, 13(9).* DOI: 10.3390/app13095236

Singh, P., Singh, S., & Pandi-Jain, G. S. (2018). Effective heart disease prediction system using data mining techniques. International Journal of Nanomedicine, 13, 121–124. DOI: 10.2147/IJN.S124998

Waqar, M., Dawood, H., Dawood, H., & Ma, N. (2021). An Efficient SMOTE-Based Deep Learning Model for HeartAttack Prediction. *Scientific Programming*, 2021, 6621622. Advance online publication. DOI: 10.1155/2021/6621622

Yar Muhammad, M. T., Hayat, M., & Chong, K. T. (2020). Early and accurate detection and diagnosis of heart disease using intelligent computational model. *Scientific Reports*, 10(1), 19747. DOI: 10.1038/s41598-020-76635-9 PMID: 33184369

Chapter 12
Electronic Cooler Technologies and Superior Data Center Cooling Techniques

Sabyasachi Pramanik
https://orcid.org/0000-0002-9431-8751
Haldia Institute of Technology, India

ABSTRACT

The expansion of digital infrastructure has prompted the establishment of data centers, which need efficient cooling systems to operate reliably. This chapter digs into the complicated world of cooling technologies, as well as the issues they face and the novel solutions they provide. It highlights the need of effective cooling in data centers, as well as the relevance of balancing efficiency and energy consumption, scalability, and environmental concerns. The chapter goes over different cooling methods, such as conventional air cooling, sophisticated liquid cooling, and phase-change solutions. It also emphasizes the use of innovative materials for increased heat transmission and thermal management, such as graphene and carbon nanotubes. In addition, the chapter covers the use of Artificial Intelligence in cooling systems, providing real-time monitoring and predictive analytics. Modular data centers, rack-level cooling, and improved free cooling solutions will be continuous advances in data center cooling in the future.

DOI: 10.4018/979-8-3693-5563-3.ch012

INTRODUCTION

As a natural consequence of their functioning, electronic gadgets that power devices such as smartphones and laptops emit heat. Failure to regulate this heat might result in decreased performance and operating longevity. This heat problem is mitigated by electronic cooling devices such as air, liquid, phase-change, heat sinks, and fans. The necessity for effective cooling, however, goes beyond individual devices. Data centers host many electrical gadgets in the digital era, where heat may rapidly gather, and causing efficiency and reliability difficulties. Data center cooling has become a key science, with difficulties and creative solutions being investigated. Understanding the role of artificial intelligence and innovative materials in defining the future of electronic cooling systems is critical for the stability and functioning of our increasingly electronic-dependent environment (Capozzoli & Primiceri, 2015).

Modern technology relies on cooling systems to ensure the efficient and dependable functioning of numerous electrical gadgets. They prevent overheating, which may result in catastrophic failures and poor performance. During operation, electronic equipment creates heat, which, if not controlled properly, may jeopardize the integrity of delicate components. Cooling systems, which include both classic air cooling and complex liquid cooling systems, aid in heat dissipation and the maintenance of an appropriate operating temperature (Hu et al., 2020). This chapter digs into the intricate ecology of cooling systems in data centers, which are the backbone of our digital world. These systems, which range from fans and heat sinks to liquid cooling systems, use coolants to move heat away from high-performance components. These data centers hold a large number of computers, network equipment, and storage devices, all of which generate a lot of heat. Cooling efficiency is critical for dependability and performance. The chapter delves into diverse cooling techniques, specific problems, and cutting-edge technologies such as artificial intelligence and sophisticated materials. Understanding these systems is critical because they support the smooth operation of everyday technology (Deng et al., 2018).

Data centers, or digital hubs, are where servers, switches, and storage systems are housed, which enable the internet, cloud services, and online applications. They do, however, provide an unnoticed challenge: heat production. The operation of data center equipment creates enormous heat, which, if unregulated, may have serious ramifications for performance, reliability, and the bottom line. The massive volume of data handled by data centers is a substantial result of the energy necessary to power and run the hundreds of computers and networking equipment housed inside these facilities. Without effective cooling solutions, this heat may build up, resulting in hot spots and increased temperatures that imperil the equipment on which they depend (Xia et al., 2017).

Efficient cooling in data centers is critical for preserving server and electronic equipment performance and durability. It guarantees continuous service delivery and minimizes hardware failures and downtime. This chapter digs into the complexity of heat management in data centers, investigating different cooling systems, novel ideas, and the ramifications for digital infrastructure. Understanding this neglected feature is vital for the stability and usefulness of the digital world on which we are increasingly reliant (Chen et al., 2021). Data centers, the internet's digital backbone, hold large quantities of critical data and applications. However, they are fighting an unseen struggle against heat, which is generated by servers, networking equipment, and storage devices. Effective cooling methods are critical for ensuring that these facilities operate at peak efficiency and dependability. This chapter looks into the complexity of data center cooling (Oró et al., 2015).

To avoid overheating, performance concerns, and expensive downtime, data centers need effective cooling. Proper cooling methods are essential for preventing overheating of equipment, which reduces its lifetime and performance. To maintain a stable temperature, prevent hot spots, and ensure equipment operates within its specified temperature range, data centers use a variety of cooling solutions, including precision air conditioning systems, hot/cold aisle containment strategies, and advanced liquid cooling techniques. This chapter explores the importance of efficient cooling in data centers, focusing on the technologies and strategies that help these facilities run smoothly while minimizing their environmental impact. The emphasis is on energy efficiency, environmental responsibility, and cost-effectiveness, as well as the importance of these facilities in our digital life. Understanding the complexities of data center cooling is crucial for recognizing their critical role in ensuring a cool, efficient, and dependable environment (Rhee et al., 2017).

Electronic cooling systems have advanced significantly as a result of the quest of efficiency and sustainability. For cooling optimization, artificial intelligence (AI) was applied, and sophisticated materials were used to boost system performance. This chapter looks at how artificial intelligence (AI) and advanced materials are transforming the landscape of electronic cooling systems. Artificial intelligence (AI) is revolutionizing the world of electronic cooling systems by evaluating massive datasets and making real-time choices. AI-driven cooling optimization in data centers can accurately monitor server heat production and guide cooling resources, decreasing energy usage and hot spots. AI-powered predictive analytics can foresee temperature trends and recommend preventive modifications, reducing overheating events and equipment failures (Wu et al., 2019). This converts cooling systems from passive machines to intelligent, adaptive solutions that maintain appropriate temperatures while saving energy, lowering operating costs, and extending the life of electronic components. The interesting realm of AI's function in improving electronic cooling systems and its potential to change the area is explored in this chapter (B et al., 2024; Nishanth et al., 2023; Syamala et al., 2023).

By offering physical ways to improve cooling capacities, advanced materials are transforming the cooling systems market. Heat transfer methods are being improved by using high-conductivity materials such as graphene and phase-change materials. Techniques for miniaturization and microfabrication have permitted the creation of complex structures and surfaces that considerably improve heat exchange efficiency. These advancements may be used in consumer electronics, industrial equipment, and data center cooling systems. The combination of AI-driven cooling optimization and innovative materials in electronic cooling systems has the potential to push the electronics industry to new heights of sustainability, performance, and reliability. The confluence of these technologies constitutes a significant step forward in ensuring that electronic gadgets and data centers stay cool, efficient, and robust in the face of rising demand.

Objectives

- To shed light on the critical role that cooling systems play in electronic gadgets and data centers. It explains why effective cooling is critical for preserving performance and dependability.
- To present the idea of artificial intelligence (AI) and its applications in cooling system optimization. It investigates how artificial intelligence (AI) may be used to produce smart, adaptive cooling systems.
- To improve cooling in electronics and data centers. It goes over real-time monitoring, predictive analytics, and intelligent resource allocation in the context of energy-efficient cooling.
- Investigate the most recent breakthroughs in heat dissipation materials used in cooling systems. It goes into high-conductivity materials like graphene and innovative phase-change materials, demonstrating their ability to improve heat transmission.
    Cooling System Types

Cooling systems play an important role in heat management in a variety of applications, including consumer electronics and industrial settings. They use a variety of technologies and components to effectively disperse heat. Heat pumps, fans, and other important components are examples of common kinds (Allouhi et al., 2015; Bahiraei & Heshmatian, 2018; Dincer, 2017).

1. System of Air Cooling:
    - Key components include fans, heat sinks, and air ducts.

Fans move air through the system, while heat sinks collect and release heat.

- Heat is transmitted from electronic components to the heat sink, and the fan blows air over the heat sink to disperse it.
- Applications include consumer electronics such as laptops and desktop computers, as well as certain industrial machinery.

2. System of Liquid Cooling:

- Key components include a coolant (often water or specialty liquids), pumps, heat exchangers, and a cold plate.
- Functions: The coolant absorbs heat and transfers it to a heat exchanger, where it is dissipated. The electrical components are in direct contact with a cold plate.
- Working Principle: Liquid cooling systems transfer heat more effectively than air by absorbing and transporting heat away from components using a liquid coolant.

High-performance computers, gaming PCs, and overclocked CPUs are examples of applications.

3. System of Phase-Change Cooling:
    - Key components include compressors, evaporators, and condensers.
    - Functions: These components work together to effectively transfer heat by changing a refrigerant from a liquid to a gas and back.
    - Working Principle: Phase-change systems absorb and release heat by using the phase transition of the refrigerant.
    - Applications include medical equipment, semiconductor production, and specialized cooling.
4. Heat Dissipaters:

A heat sink is a passive component constructed of thermally conductive materials such as aluminum or copper.

- Uses: Heat sinks disperse heat from electronic components via conduction and convection.
- Heat is transmitted from the component to the heat sink, which distributes the heat to the surrounding environment.
- CPUs, GPUs, power transistors, and numerous electrical devices are examples of applications.

5. Fans:

- Important parts are the impeller blades, motor, and housing.
- Functions: Fans provide airflow to improve cooling, either in combination with heat sinks or as stand-alone solutions.
- Working Principle: Fans generate airflow, which aids in the removal of heat via convection.
- Applications: Used in a variety of electrical and industrial equipment in conjunction with different cooling methods, including air cooling and liquid cooling.

6. System of Evaporative Cooling:

- Key components include water storage, a pump, a distribution system, and evaporative media.
- Functions: These systems employ the evaporation of water to chill the air, which then cools the equipment.
- Working Principle: Water is poured over evaporative medium, which cools the surrounding air, which is subsequently directed over electrical components as it evaporates.
- Applications: Used to enhance energy efficiency in data centers, HVAC systems, and hot, dry conditions.

Figure 1. Electronic device cooling system types

Air Cooling System

Liquid Cooling System

Phase-Change Cooling System

Heat Sinks

Fans

Evaporative Cooling System

Peltier (Thermoelectric) Cooling System

Refrigeration Cooling System

Direct-to-Chip Cooling (D2C)

Immersion Cooling

7.   Thermoelectric (Peltier) Cooling System:

Peltier modules (thermoelectric coolers) and heat sinks are important components.

• Functions: Peltier devices employ the Peltier effect to generate a temperature difference, allowing heat to be transferred from one side to the other.

When a current is provided to the Peltier modules, heat is transferred from one side (the hot side) to the other (the cold side), thereby chilling the cold side.

• Applications: Mini-fridges and portable coolers are examples of compact cooling solutions for tiny electrical gadgets.

8.   System of Refrigeration and Cooling:

• Key components are the compressor, condenser, evaporator, and refrigerant.
• Functions: In a closed loop, these systems employ the compression and expansion of a refrigerant to chill the air or liquid.

- Working Principle: A compressor compresses the refrigerant, increasing its temperature and pressure; the refrigerant is subsequently expanded in the evaporator, causing it to drastically cool. This cooled refrigerant is then utilized to chill the system's air or liquid.
- Applications include large industrial cooling systems, commercial refrigeration, and certain cooling solutions for **data centers.**

9. Direct-to-Chip (D2C) cooling:

- Crucial components include microchannel heat sinks and a coolant supply.
- Functions: This approach cools individual electronic chips or components directly.
- Coolant is pumped via microchannels in close proximity to electrical chips to efficiently cool them.
- Applications include high-performance computing, supercomputers, and enhanced data center cooling where targeted cooling is essential.

10. Cooling by immersion:

- Key components include liquid coolant and specific tanks or containers.
- Functions: To cool, whole electronic systems or components are submerged in a dielectric liquid.
- Working Principle: The liquid coolant absorbs heat and circulates it by convection currents, dispersing heat away from components.
- Applications include high-density data centers, cryptocurrency mining, and specialized high-performance computing.

Cooling systems are required for electrical components to perform safely and ideally, avoiding overheating problems. Heat load, equipment size, energy efficiency requirements, and the climate all influence the selection of a cooling system (Khalaj & Halgamuge, 2017). As devices and data centers grow more powerful and heat-intensive, research and innovation continue to prioritize the development of novel cooling technologies and techniques to fulfill the application's unique demands.

COOLING SYSTEMS IN DATA CENTERS

Air Conditioning Precision

Data centers, which house innumerable computers and networking equipment that power everything from social media to cloud services, are the lifeblood of our digital world. Efficient cooling in data centers is a mission-critical part of maintaining continuous operation and electronic component life (Wulandari et al., 2020). Precision air conditioning systems are at the forefront of data center cooling, providing the precise temperature and humidity control essential for peak performance. This section delves into precision air conditioning, its components, operating principles, and its critical function in data center cooling (Li et al., 2019).

Precision Air Conditioning Components

Precision air conditioning systems are made up of many main parts:

Air handlers, commonly known as computer room air conditioners (CRACs), are in charge of cooling the air. Filters, cooling coils, and blowers are used to manage the temperature and humidity of the air.

- Humidifiers and Dehumidifiers: Maintaining the proper humidity level in data centers is critical. Humidifiers add moisture to the air, whilst dehumidifiers remove excess humidity.
- Temperature and Humidity Sensors: Temperature and humidity sensors continually monitor temperature and humidity levels, giving feedback for precise management.
- Control Systems: These systems oversee the functioning of the air conditioners, altering settings based on real-time data from sensors.
  Precision Air Conditioning Principles of Operation:

Precision air conditioning systems are based on temperature and humidity management principles (Moazamigoodarzi et al., 2019).

- Temperature Control: Warm air is drawn from the data center environment via air handlers. This hot air is sent across cooling coils containing a refrigerant. As the air cools, it is recirculated back into the data center to keep the temperature stable.
- Humidity manages: Precision air conditioning systems utilize humidifiers to supply moisture to the air and dehumidifiers to remove excess moisture to manage humidity. Maintaining the optimal humidity level is critical for min-

imizing static electricity accumulation and safeguarding sensitive electrical equipment.

- Air Filtration: Air handlers contain filters that remove particles and impurities from the air, ensuring that electronic equipment operates in a clean environment.

Data Center Applications

Precision air cooling systems are built particularly for data center settings because of the following advantages (Zhang et al., 2021):

- Temperature and Humidity Control: They provide accurate temperature and humidity control, resulting in an ideal environment for electronic components.
- Redundancy and dependability: Data centers often use redundant air conditioning systems to provide continuous cooling even if equipment fails.
- Scalability: These systems may be scaled up to meet the cooling needs of bigger data centers or to accommodate more equipment.
- Energy Efficiency: Advanced versions have energy-efficient technologies that assist data centers in lowering their carbon impact.

To summarize, precise air conditioning is a critical component of effective data center cooling. Its capacity to provide regular temperature and humidity management is critical for ensuring the performance and durability of the electronic infrastructure that supports our digital world. Precision air conditioning systems will become more important in ensuring an ideal operating climate as data centers innovate and grow.

Containment of Hot/Cold Aisles

Hot/cold aisle containment has evolved as a creative and practical solution in the search for energy-efficient and effective cooling in data centers. The typical open structure of data center racks is transformed into a more regulated environment in which hot and cold air are divided to increase cooling efficiency. This section delves into the notion of hot/cold aisle confinement, including its components, operating principles, and the advantages it provides to data center cooling (Zhang et al., 2021).

Hot/Cold Aisle Containment Components

Hot/cold aisle containment systems are made up of many parts, including:

- Hot Aisle: This is the aisle where the server exhaust air escapes. It is often enclosed at the ends of racks.
- Cold Aisle: The cold aisle is where the servers' intake air is delivered. It is normally enclosed, with cold air directed to the front of the racks.
- Aisle Doors: Aisle doors are used to separate hot and cold aisles and enhance airflow management.
- Ceiling Panels: These panels, which typically stretch from the top of the server racks to the ceiling, are utilized to provide a physical barrier between the hot and cold lanes.
- Raised Floor: The floor may be raised in certain designs to facilitate airflow systems or to provide an enclosed plenum for diverting cold air.

Hot/Cold Aisle Containment Working Principles

The notion of hot/cold aisle containment is based on the separation of hot and cold air to improve cooling efficiency:

- Cool Air Delivery: Cool air is brought into the chilly aisle via perforated tiles on the elevated floor or overhead ducts. This cold air is routed to the front of the server racks, where the server intake is placed.
- Server Exhaust: Hot air is expelled from the servers' back. This hot air naturally rises and flows into the heated aisle.
- Aisle Enclosure: Physical barriers in the form of aisle doors and ceiling panels separate the hot and cold aisles. This barrier reduces the mixing of hot and cold air.
- Return Air: The hot aisle containment system gathers and routes hot exhaust air back to the cooling equipment, where it may be cooled and recirculated.

The Advantages of Hot/Cold Aisle Containment

For data center cooling, hot/cold aisle confinement has various advantages:

- Increased Cooling Efficiency: By keeping hot and cold air from mixing, containment guarantees that servers get air at the proper temperature, decreasing cooling load and energy consumption.
- Scalability and redundancy: Aisle containment may be configured to support a variety of data center sizes and layouts, making it suitable for both small and large facilities.
- Lower Operating Costs: Lowering energy usage and improving cooling efficiency result in long term cost savings.

- Increased Equipment Lifespan: Keeping temperatures steady and decreasing thermal stress may help data center equipment last longer.
- Environmental Impact: Lowering energy usage and increasing efficiency help to reduce carbon footprint, which aligns with sustainability objectives.

Finally, hot/cold aisle confinement is a tried-and-true approach for improving cooling efficiency and lowering energy usage in data centers. It demonstrates how creative design and engineering can enhance the performance and sustainability of the digital infrastructure that sustains our interconnected world.

Solutions for Liquid Cooling

Liquid cooling technologies are an innovative way to heat management in data centers and high-performance computer settings. Unlike standard air cooling, which depends on air circulation to dissipate heat from electronic components, liquid cooling uses specialized coolants to dissipate heat from electronic components. We'll look at the notion of liquid cooling, its components, operating principles, and applications in data centers in this section (Wulandari et al., 2020).

Liquid Cooling Solution Components

Data center liquid cooling systems generally include the following important components:

- Coolant: A specific liquid or fluid with heat-absorbing qualities. Water, dielectric fluids, and proprietary liquids are all common coolants.
- Cold Plates: These are parts that come into direct touch with electrical equipment like CPUs and GPUs. Cold plates are intended to transfer heat from the components to the coolant as effectively as possible.
- Pumps: Pumps circulate the coolant through the system, guaranteeing a constant flow to remove heat.
- Heat Exchangers: Heat exchangers efficiently dissipate heat by transferring it from the coolant to an external medium (e.g., air or water).
- Tubing and Fittings: These components form a closed-loop system by directing coolant flow from the cold plates to the heat exchangers and back.
- Reservoirs and Expansion Tanks: These containers hold and control coolant, allowing for system priming and tolerating changes in coolant volume caused by temperature fluctuations.

The Basics of Liquid Cooling Solutions

Heat transfer is the basis for liquid cooling systems. This is how they work:

- Heat Absorption: Cold plates come into close touch with heat-generating components like CPUs or GPUs. As these components work, heat is generated and transmitted to the cool plates.
- Coolant Circulation: Coolant is circulated throughout the system using pumps. The heated coolant absorbs heat from the cold plates and transports it away.
- Heat Dissipation: Heat exchangers, which are positioned in a separate environment, transport heat from the coolant to an external medium such as air or water.
- Coolant Return: The cooled coolant is returned to the cold plates to resume the cycle.

Liquid Cooling Applications in Data Centers

Liquid cooling methods are well-suited for a variety of data center applications, including:

- High-Performance Computing (HPC): In HPC clusters, where powerful processors and GPUs create significant heat, liquid cooling is widely employed. To maintain optimal performance, these systems need effective cooling.

Liquid cooling may be incorporated into server racks or applied to individual servers that need high-performance cooling.

- AI and Deep Learning: To control the heat produced by specific hardware accelerators, data centers that handle AI and deep learning workloads often depend on liquid cooling.
- Green Data Centers: Liquid cooling is employed in energy-efficient and environmentally friendly data centers because it allows for more accurate temperature control while also lowering total energy usage.
- Overclocked Systems: Overclocking enthusiasts employ liquid cooling to keep their systems cool amid intense performance demands.

Liquid cooling is a very effective way of heat management, particularly in circumstances when typical air-cooling technologies are insufficient. Its ability to keep operating temperatures low, minimize energy consumption, and extend component lifetime makes it a viable option for data centers and high-performance computing settings.

Free Cooling Methods

Data centers are notorious for using a lot of energy, with a large percentage of that energy going to cooling systems. Data center operators have resorted to free cooling solutions in search of higher energy efficiency and lower operating expenses. These methods employ external environmental conditions to cool data center facilities without relying on mechanical cooling equipment. This section will look into free cooling techniques, their components, operating principles, and the advantages they provide to data center operations (Chu & Huang, 2021; Zhang et al., 2021).

Free Cooling Strategy Components

In data centers, free cooling solutions may not need many specialized components, however they may include:

- Air Dampers: These devices regulate the flow of outside air into the data center. They are often seen in air intake systems or on the outside of buildings.
- Environmental Sensors and Control Systems: Environmental sensors and control systems are utilized to analyze external weather conditions and alter the free cooling strategy appropriately.
- Filters: Filters assist to preserve indoor air quality by removing pollutants and particles from entering air.
- Heat Exchangers: Heat exchangers are utilized in certain systems to transfer heat from data center air to incoming outside air before it is cycled within.
- Cooling Towers: Cooling towers may be utilized to reject heat from the data center in water-based free cooling solutions.

Free Cooling Strategy Operating Principles

The main principle of free cooling is to cool the data center environment using external air rather than mechanical refrigeration. The operating principles differ based on the approach used:

- Air-Side Economization: This approach includes cooling the data center using external air. When the weather is nice, air dampers are opened to let cool outside air into the data center. Mechanical cooling is only utilized when absolutely essential, such as in very hot or humid weather.

- Water-Side Economization: Rather of directly utilizing outside air, this solution use a heat exchanger or cooling tower to transfer heat from the data center's water-based cooling system to the incoming outdoor air.
- Evaporative Cooling: Evaporative cooling systems employ the concept of water evaporation to cool incoming air before it reaches the data center in dry areas. This approach uses very little energy.
- Direct and Indirect Free Cooling: Direct free cooling utilizes unconditioned outside air, while indirect free cooling separates inside and outdoor air using a heat exchanger. The heat exchanger uses outside air to chill the inside air while preventing the two from mingling.

Advantages of Free Cooling Strategies

Using free cooling solutions has various benefits in data center operations:

- Lower Energy Consumption: Free cooling eliminates the need for mechanical cooling systems, resulting in considerable energy savings.
- Lower Operational expenses: Because energy consumption is lowered, operational expenses are cut, making data centers more cost-effective.
- Improved Sustainability: By reducing the environmental effect of data center operations, free cooling matches with sustainability objectives.
- Improved dependability: In many circumstances, free cooling solutions may improve data center dependability by eliminating dependence on mechanical cooling, which can fail.
- Adaptability: Free cooling solutions are adjustable and may be fine-tuned to match a variety of climatic conditions and data center needs.

Finally, free cooling solutions provide an energy-efficient and long-term way to cooling data centers. These solutions provide a cost-effective way of sustaining ideal temperatures inside data center facilities while decreasing their carbon footprint by leveraging the power of external environmental conditions.

APPLYING AI TO COOLING IN DATA CENTERS

Artificial intelligence (AI) has transformed the drive for more efficient and dependable data center cooling. AI-driven cooling optimization makes data centers smarter, greener, and more cost-effective by using machine learning and real-time data analysis (Van Le et al., 2019). Here's how artificial intelligence is used to improve cooling in data centers:

- Real-Time Monitoring: AI continually analyzes environmental characteristics such as temperature, humidity, ventilation, and power usage inside the data center. Sensors capture data from servers and cooling systems in real time.
- Predictive Analytics: Machine learning algorithms examine past data to forecast temperature patterns. AI can predict overheating hazards and modify cooling settings appropriately by knowing how various factors impact temperature.
- Dynamic Control: AI may alter cooling settings dynamically depending on workload and server usage. For example, AI may enhance cooling capacity during moments of heavy server traffic and decrease it during periods of low activity to conserve energy.
- Intelligent Resource Allocation: AI can intelligently deploy cooling resources to where they are most required. For example, if a certain server is producing more heat, AI may send more cooling to that server, eliminating hot spots.
- Energy Optimization: AI-powered systems strive to use as little energy as possible while maintaining optimum operational conditions. During low-demand times, they may lower fan speeds, modify temperature setpoints, and switch off superfluous cooling equipment.
- Predictive repair: By evaluating performance data, AI can forecast when cooling equipment will fail or need repair. This proactive strategy aids in the prevention of expensive downtime and equipment failure.
- Weather Data Integration: AI may use external weather data to predict temperature swings. If an AI system forecasts a heatwave, for example, it may prepare data center cooling equipment to manage higher cooling needs.
- Human-Machine involvement: Through user interfaces, certain AI systems allow for human involvement. When required, data center operators may overturn AI judgments or make human modifications.
- Continuous Learning: AI systems may continually learn and adapt to changing circumstances, resulting in more effective cooling operations over time.
- Sustainability: AI-optimized cooling often results in lower energy usage, which contributes to a data center's sustainability objectives and lowers its carbon footprint.

The use of artificial intelligence to improve cooling in data centers is a proactive approach to cooling management. It guarantees that cooling resources are utilized effectively, lowering operating costs and enhancing data center operational dependability (Cao et al., 2022; Jin et al., 2020; Yuan et al., 2021). AI-driven cooling solutions will be critical in maintaining optimum operating conditions while reaching energy efficiency and environmental sustainability standards as data centers continue to expand and change.

ADVANCED MATERIALS AND THEIR FUNCTIONS IN ELECTRICAL COOLING SYSTEMS

Advanced materials may significantly improve the performance and efficiency of electronic cooling systems. These materials are intended to increase heat dissipation and thermal management in electronics and data centers (Van Le et al., 2019; Yang et al., 2021). Here are a few examples of sophisticated materials and their use in electronic cooling systems:

Diagram 3. The functions of advanced materials in electronic cooling systems

Graphene is a good thermal conductor, making it very effective in heat dissipation. It may be utilized to increase heat transmission between electronic components and heat sinks in thermal interface materials (TIMs).

Diamonds have a high thermal conductivity and may be employed in electrical equipment as heat spreaders and heat sinks. They diffuse and dissipate heat well, avoiding hot areas.

PCMs are phase-change materials that absorb and release heat during phase changes. They may be used in electronic cooling systems to store and control surplus heat, allowing for passive cooling during high-temperature times.

Thermally Conductive Polymers: These polymers have thermal conductivity qualities and may be utilized to increase heat transmission in electronic devices as encapsulants or as TIMs.

Carbon Nanotubes (CNTs): CNTs are good thermal conductors that may be employed to improve the thermal characteristics of electronic components in composites and coatings. They are effective in heat dissipation.

Gallium Nitride (GaN): GaN is a high thermal conductivity semiconductor material. It's employed in power electronics and RF equipment where heat dissipation is critical.

Boron Nitride (BN): BN is a good thermal conductor as well as an electrical insulator. It may be utilized in thermal contact materials and as a heat spreader.

Advanced Thermal Interface Materials (TIMs): These materials, which are often built from a mix of advanced materials, are intended to increase contact between electronic components and heat sinks. They improve heat transport while decreasing thermal resistance.

Nanostructured materials, such as nanostructured metals and ceramics, may be utilized to develop effective heat sinks and thermal solutions. Their compact size and large surface area aid in heat dissipation.

Metamaterials are designed materials with distinct thermal characteristics. They may be constructed to manage thermal conductivity and modify heat transport, making them valuable in sophisticated cooling systems.

3D-Printed Materials: 3D printing enables the development of complicated geometries and unique designs for heat sinks and cooling components. In some cases, this adjustment may increase heat dissipation.

These cutting-edge materials are critical in solving the rising heat concerns in electronic gadgets and data centers. They aid in the management of thermal concerns, the reduction of hot spots, and the general performance and dependability of electronic systems by guaranteeing effective cooling.

Data Center Cooling Challenges

Cooling efficiency is a vital part of data center operations. It does, however, provide a set of obstacles for data center managers and engineers to address in order to preserve the reliability and performance of electronic equipment. The following are the major issues in data center cooling (Yang et al., 2021).

Keeping Hot Spots at Bay

- Difficulty: Hot spots, or isolated locations where electronic equipment creates excessive heat, are common in data centers. Hot spots may cause equipment to overheat and fail.
- Solution: Through methods such as adequate air circulation and thermal mapping, cooling systems must be designed to disperse airflow uniformly and efficiently dissipate heat from all locations, eliminating hot spots.

Efficiency and energy consumption must be balanced.

- Difficulty: Finding the correct combination of efficient cooling and energy usage is an ongoing struggle. Overcooling or under cooling may result in lost energy and higher operating expenses.
- Solution: Using adaptive cooling systems and innovative control mechanisms, data centers may dynamically modify cooling capacity depending on real-time circumstances, reducing energy consumption while maintaining the required temperature.

Systems for Adaptive Cooling

Why Difficulty: Regardless of server demand, traditional cooling systems often run at a set capacity. As a consequence, extra energy is used during moments of low activity.

- Solution: Adaptive cooling systems change cooling resources in response to server use using real-time data and AI-driven algorithms. This saves electricity while maintaining constant cooling.

Considerations for the Environment

- Problem: Because of their energy consumption and heat emissions, data centers have an environmental effect. Balancing operational demands with sustainability objectives is becoming more important (Boopathi, 2022b, 2022a; Boopathi et al., 2023; Gowri et al., 2023).
- Solution: Data centers are looking for methods to lower their carbon footprint by incorporating renewable energy sources, employing free cooling solutions, and improving cooling system energy efficiency (Van Le et al., 2019).

Scalability and Expansion

- Difficulty: Data centers are continually developing and expanding, adding new servers and technology. Maintaining effective cooling as data centers grow is difficult.
- Solution: Scalable cooling systems and adaptable infrastructural designs are required. To maintain optimal operation as they develop, data centers should prepare for future expansion and cooling requirements.

Airflow Control

- Difficulty: Inefficiencies in airflow control might result in hot and cold air mixing, reducing cooling performance.
- Solution: Best practices in airflow management, such as hot/cold aisle confinement and rack-level cooling, may enhance cooling efficiency and avoid hot air recirculation.

Management of Costs

- Difficulty: Investing in modern cooling technology and energy-efficient systems might be costly at first.
- Solution: When investing in cooling infrastructure, data center operators must consider the long-term advantages of energy savings and decreased downtime.

Infrastructure Legacy

- Difficulty: Many data centers have outdated cooling systems that are inefficient and inflexible.
- Solution: Upgrading or retrofitting legacy infrastructure with new, energy-efficient cooling systems may help bring aging data centers up to date with current best practices.

Finally, cooling difficulties in data centers need creative solutions that combine efficiency, dependability, and energy conservation. Data center operators may address these difficulties and assure the sustained efficiency and dependability of their facilities by deploying adaptive cooling systems, improving airflow management, and addressing environmental sustainability.

Data Center Cooling Innovations

The data center business is constantly evolving to meet the challenges of rising heat loads and the demand for greater energy efficiency. Several improvements have evolved to enhance cooling systems and increase data center sustainability. Key developments (Kavitha et al., 2023; Rahamathunnisa et al., 2023; Ugandar et al., 2023; Venkateswaran et al., 2023) include:

Optimizing Data Center Cooling with AI: Artificial Intelligence (AI) and machine learning are being utilized to improve data center cooling. Artificial intelligence-powered systems continually monitor ambient factors, forecast temperature trends, and dynamically modify cooling settings to reduce energy usage while providing dependable cooling.

The introduction of sophisticated materials such as graphene, diamond, and carbon nanotubes has improved heat transport and thermal management in electronic devices and data centers. These materials are used to increase cooling efficiency in heat sinks, thermal interface materials (TIMs), and other components.

Integrating Renewable Energy Sources: To power cooling systems and lower their carbon footprint, data centers are rapidly integrating renewable energy sources such as solar panels and wind turbines. This environmentally friendly technique coincides with environmental aims and lowers reliance on fossil fuels.

Innovations in Liquid Cooling: Liquid cooling technologies, such as direct-to-chip cooling and immersion cooling, have evolved dramatically. These advancements allow data centers to tolerate increased heat loads produced by powerful servers and GPUs by providing more effective heat dissipation.

Rack-Level Cooling: As opposed to typical room-level cooling, cooling at the rack level is gaining favor. Rear-door heat exchangers and in-row cooling units provide more accurate cooling at the server level, resulting in lower cooling system energy usage.

Free Cooling methods: Advanced free cooling methods, such as air-side economization and evaporative cooling, are being used in data centers to minimize dependency on mechanical cooling systems and cut energy usage.

Data Center Infrastructure Management (DCIM): DCIM software allows data center administrators to make educated choices, optimize cooling, and discover inefficiencies by monitoring and controlling cooling systems in real time.

Hot/Cold Aisle Containment: Aisle containment systems have advanced, allowing for more efficient separation of hot and cold air and improved cooling efficiency. Cold aisle containment methods, in particular, have gained popularity.

Modular and portable data centers: Built-in cooling systems increase efficiency and scalability in modular data centers and containerized solutions. These solutions provide more flexibility and may be implemented quickly.

Heat Recovery Systems: Heat recovery systems absorb surplus heat created by data centers and repurpose it for heating surrounding buildings or other industrial operations, hence increasing energy efficiency.

These advancements represent a comprehensive approach to data center cooling, with an emphasis on energy efficiency, sustainability, and flexibility to the expanding needs of digital infrastructure. As data centers expand, these technologies will be critical in maintaining efficient and dependable cooling systems.

CONCLUSIONS

As data centers host a huge variety of electronic equipment, the chapter examines the history of electronic cooling systems in data centers, emphasizing the need of effective cooling for preserving optimum performance and prolonging the lifetime of vital infrastructure. It contains important observations and conclusions.

Preventing hot spots, balancing efficiency and energy consumption, scalability, and environmental concerns are major issues in data center cooling. Cooling solutions that are innovative are critical. The chapter delves into several cooling methods, such as conventional air, sophisticated liquid, and phase-change cooling, each with its own set of benefits. Innovative materials such as graphene, carbon nanotubes, and phase-change materials enhance heat transmission and thermal management, lowering hot spots and increasing cooling efficiency.

AI is changing cooling systems by monitoring conditions, forecasting trends, and adjusting settings to save energy use. This is consistent with data centers' rising emphasis on sustainability, which includes the use of renewable energy sources, free cooling technologies, and heat recycling systems. Continued advancements in data center cooling, such as modular and portable data centers, rack-level cooling, and improved free cooling systems, will improve efficiency and flexibility.

The chapter delves into the ever-changing world of data center cooling, emphasizing efficiency, energy saving, and sustainability. These advancements are critical for assuring the stability and functionality of the electronic infrastructure as data centers expand. It discusses present cooling technologies, difficulties, and the future of data center cooling technology.

ABBREVIATIONS

AI: Artificial Intelligence
TIMs: Thermal Interface Materials
PCMs: Phase-Change Materials
DCIM: Data Center Infrastructure Management
GaN: Gallium Nitride
BN: Boron Nitride
CNTs: Carbon Nanotubes

REFERENCES

Allouhi, A., Kousksou, T., Jamil, A., Bruel, P., Mourad, Y., & Zeraouli, Y. (2015). Solar driven cooling systems: An updated review. *Renewable & Sustainable Energy Reviews*, 44, 159–181. DOI: 10.1016/j.rser.2014.12.014

Bahiraei, M., & Heshmatian, S. (2018). Electronics cooling with nanofluids: A critical review. *Energy Conversion and Management*, 172, 438–456. DOI: 10.1016/j.enconman.2018.07.047

Boopathi, S. (2022a). An investigation on gas emission concentration and relative emission rate of the near-dry wire-cut electrical discharge machining process. *Environmental Science and Pollution Research International*, 29(57), 86237–86246. DOI: 10.1007/s11356-021-17658-1 PMID: 34837614

Boopathi, S. (2022b). Cryogenically treated and untreated stainless steel grade 317 in sustainable wire electrical discharge machining process: A comparative study. *Springer :Environmental Science and Pollution Research*, 1–10.

Boopathi, S., Alqahtani, A. S., Mubarakali, A., & Panchatcharam, P. (2023). Sustainable developments in near-dry electrical discharge machining process using sunflower oil-mist dielectric fluid. *Environmental Science and Pollution Research International*, 31(27), 1–20. DOI: 10.1007/s11356-023-27494-0 PMID: 37199846

Cao, Z., Zhou, X., Hu, H., Wang, Z., & Wen, Y. (2022). Toward a systematic survey for carbon neutral data centers. *IEEE Communications Surveys and Tutorials*, 24(2), 895–936. DOI: 10.1109/COMST.2022.3161275

Capozzoli, A., & Primiceri, G. (2015). Cooling systems in data centers: State of art and emerging technologies. *Energy Procedia*, 83, 484–493. DOI: 10.1016/j.egypro.2015.12.168

Chen, Y., Kang, Y., Zhao, Y., Wang, L., Liu, J., Li, Y., Liang, Z., He, X., Li, X., Tavajohi, N., & Li, B. (2021). A review of lithium-ion battery safety concerns: The issues, strategies, and testing standards. *Journal of Energy Chemistry*, 59, 83–99. DOI: 10.1016/j.jechem.2020.10.017

Chu, J., & Huang, X. (2021). *Research status and development trends of evaporative cooling air-conditioning technology in data centers*. Energy and Built Environment.

Deng, Y., Feng, C., Jiaqiang, E., Zhu, H., Chen, J., Wen, M., & Yin, H. (2018). Effects of different coolants and cooling strategies on the cooling performance of the power lithium ion battery system: A review. *Applied Thermal Engineering*, 142, 10–29. DOI: 10.1016/j.applthermalcng.2018.06.043

Dincer, I. (2017). *Refrigeration systems and applications*. John Wiley & Sons. DOI: 10.1002/9781119230793

Gowri, N. V., Dwivedi, J. N., Krishnaveni, K., Boopathi, S., Palaniappan, M., & Medikondu, N. R. (2023). Experimental investigation and multi-objective optimization of eco-friendly near-dry electrical discharge machining of shape memory alloy using Cu/SiC/Gr composite electrode. *Environmental Science and Pollution Research International*, 30(49), 1–19. DOI: 10.1007/s11356-023-26983-6 PMID: 37126160

Hu, R., Liu, Y., Shin, S., Huang, S., Ren, X., Shu, W., Cheng, J., Tao, G., Xu, W., Chen, R., & Luo, X. (2020). Emerging materials and strategies for personal thermal management. *Advanced Energy Materials*, 10(17), 1903921. DOI: 10.1002/aenm.201903921

Jin, C., Bai, X., Yang, C., Mao, W., & Xu, X. (2020). A review of power consumption models of servers in data centers. *Applied Energy*, 265, 114806. DOI: 10.1016/j.apenergy.2020.114806

Kavitha, C. R., Varalatchoumy, M., Mithuna, H. R., Bharathi, K., Geethalakshmi, N. M., & Boopathi, S. (2023). Energy Monitoring and Control in the Smart Grid: Integrated Intelligent IoT and ANFIS. In Arshad, M. (Ed.), (pp. 290–316). Advances in Bioinformatics and Biomedical Engineering. IGI Global., DOI: 10.4018/978-1-6684-6577-6.ch014

Khalaj, A. H., & Halgamuge, S. K. (2017). A Review on efficient thermal management of air-and liquid-cooled data centers: From chip to the cooling system. *Applied Energy*, 205, 1165–1188. DOI: 10.1016/j.apenergy.2017.08.037

Kumar, M., Kumar, K., Sasikala, P., Sampath, B., Gopi, B., & Sundaram, S. (2023). Sustainable Green Energy Generation From Waste Water: IoT and ML Integration. In Sustainable Science and Intelligent Technologies for Societal Development (pp. 440-463). IGI Global.

Li, Y., Wen, Y., Tao, D., & Guan, K. (2019). Transforming cooling optimization for green data center via deep reinforcement learning. *IEEE Transactions on Cybernetics*, 50(5), 2002–2013. DOI: 10.1109/TCYB.2019.2927410 PMID: 31352360

Moazamigoodarzi, H., Tsai, P. J., Pal, S., Ghosh, S., & Puri, I. K. (2019). Influence of cooling architecture on data center power consumption. *Energy*, 183, 525–535. DOI: 10.1016/j.energy.2019.06.140

Nishanth, J., Deshmukh, M. A., Kushwah, R., Kushwaha, K. K., Balaji, S., & Sampath, B. (2023). Particle Swarm Optimization of Hybrid Renewable Energy Systems. In *Intelligent Engineering Applications and Applied Sciences for Sustainability* (pp. 291–308). IGI Global. DOI: 10.4018/979-8-3693-0044-2.ch016

Oró, E., Depoorter, V., Garcia, A., & Salom, J. (2015). Energy efficiency and renewable energy integration in data centres. Strategies and modelling review. *Renewable & Sustainable Energy Reviews*, 42, 429–445. DOI: 10.1016/j.rser.2014.10.035

Rahamathunnisa, U., Subhashini, P., Aancy, H. M., Meenakshi, S., & Boopathi, S. (2023). Solutions for Software Requirement Risks Using Artificial Intelligence Techniques. In *Handbook of Research on Data Science and Cybersecurity Innovations in Industry 4.0 Technologies* (pp. 45–64). IGI Global.

Rhee, K.-N., Olesen, B. W., & Kim, K. W. (2017). Ten questions about radiant heating and cooling systems. *Building and Environment*, 112, 367–381. DOI: 10.1016/j.buildenv.2016.11.030

Syamala, M., Komala, C., Pramila, P., Dash, S., Meenakshi, S., & Boopathi, S. (2023). Machine Learning-Integrated IoT-Based Smart Home Energy Management System. In *Handbook of Research on Deep Learning Techniques for Cloud-Based Industrial IoT* (pp. 219–235). IGI Global. DOI: 10.4018/978-1-6684-8098-4.ch013

Ugandar, R. E., Rahamathunnisa, U., Sajithra, S., Christiana, M. B. V., Palai, B. K., & Boopathi, S. (2023). Hospital Waste Management Using Internet of Things and Deep Learning: Enhanced Efficiency and Sustainability. In Arshad, M. (Ed.), (pp. 317–343). Advances in Bioinformatics and Biomedical Engineering. IGI Global., DOI: 10.4018/978-1-6684-6577-6.ch015

Van Le, D., Liu, Y., Wang, R., Tan, R., Wong, Y.-W., & Wen, Y. (2019). Control of air free-cooled data centers in tropics via deep reinforcement learning. *Proceedings of the 6th ACM International Conference on Systems for Energy-Efficient Buildings, Cities, and Transportation*, 306–315. DOI: 10.1145/3360322.3360845

Venkateswaran, N., Kumar, S. S., Diwakar, G., Gnanasangeetha, D., & Boopathi, S. (2023). Synthetic Biology for Waste Water to Energy Conversion: IoT and AI Approaches. In Arshad, M. (Ed.), (pp. 360–384). Advances in Bioinformatics and Biomedical Engineering. IGI Global., DOI: 10.4018/978-1-6684-6577-6.ch017

Wu, W., Wang, S., Wu, W., Chen, K., Hong, S., & Lai, Y. (2019). A critical review of battery thermal performance and liquid based battery thermal management. *Energy Conversion and Management*, 182, 262–281. DOI: 10.1016/j.enconman.2018.12.051

Wulandari, D. A., Akmal, M., Gunawan, Y., & others. (2020). *Cooling improvement of the IT rack by layout rearrangement of the A2 class data center room: A simulation study.*

Xia, G., Cao, L., & Bi, G. (2017). A review on battery thermal management in electric vehicle application. *Journal of Power Sources*, 367, 90–105. DOI: 10.1016/j.jpowsour.2017.09.046

Yang, J., Zhang, X., Zhang, X., Wang, L., Feng, W., & Li, Q. (2021). Beyond the visible: Bioinspired infrared adaptive materials. *Advanced Materials*, 33(14), 2004754. DOI: 10.1002/adma.202004754 PMID: 33624900

Yuan, X., Zhou, X., Pan, Y., Kosonen, R., Cai, H., Gao, Y., & Wang, Y. (2021). Phase change cooling in data centers: A review. *Energy and Building*, 236, 110764. DOI: 10.1016/j.enbuild.2021.110764

Zhang, Q., Meng, Z., Hong, X., Zhan, Y., Liu, J., Dong, J., Bai, T., Niu, J., & Deen, M. J. (2021). A survey on data center cooling systems: Technology, power consumption modeling and control strategy optimization. *Journal of Systems Architecture*, 119, 102253. DOI: 10.1016/j.sysarc.2021.102253

Section 4
Special Topics in Data Analytics and Emerging Trends

Chapter 13
Exploring the Influence of Emotional Intelligence on Financial Literacy Amongst Gen Z

Arana Kausar
Xavier Institute of Social Service, India

Pooja
https://orcid.org/0000-0002-6905-5304
Xavier Institute of Social Service, India

ABSTRACT

The study explores the impact of Emotional Intelligence (EI) on Financial Literacy(FL) of individuals belonging to Gen Z. Using a two-wave research design method,136 respondents from the Bihar -Jharkhand Region of India were studied. Empirical evidences suggested that EI significantly impacts FL amongst Gen Z. Further, Sociability and Wellbeing in Gen Z were found to be the factors related to EI impacting their FL. Importance of developing behavioural, cognitive and non-traditional forms of intelligence such as EI and its impact on FL have been discussed. Training programmes and focused interventions on developing EI have also been highlighted. The relationship between EI and FL in the chosen context has remained unexplored in context of India. The field of FL has not provided enough attention to the role of emotions and emotional intelligence in decision making and the study tries to study this gap.

DOI: 10.4018/979-8-3693-5563-3.ch013

INTRODUCTION

Financial literacy is pivotal for an individual's survival in society. It is a crucial competency which helps in supporting the economic growth of any Nation (Messy & Monticone,2016). Financial literacy comprises of financial knowledge, financial behaviour and financial attitude (Pangestu &Karnadi,2020). Individuals who are financially literate are better at taking financial decisions and have a good understanding to manage their money (Klapper,2015).Financial literacy refers to the awareness and knowledge needed to make effective use of available financial resources and services (Sholevar & Harris, 2020).The five key components of Financial Literacy are: Having Basic knowledge of Budgeting, Impact of interest on investments, the virtues of Saving, Understanding of Credit-Debt roller coaster and awareness of cybercrime theft issues. (Hoyt, 2018). Hence, it can also be understood as the art of investing and managing money along with the ability to make sound financial decisions (Sudheer, 2018). A good financial attitude requires favourable state of mind &Judgement in addition to the economic beliefs which leads to their financial behaviour (OECD,2013). Lack of financial literacy is highly likely to make a person have problems related to debt and absence of financial planning for the future (Lusardi, 2010). The well-being of an individual is dependent on their financial literacy. Knowledge and skills related to personal finance are crucial in everyday of life. Abuse of Credit or not having proper financial planning are often a source of stress and low self-esteem for individuals. Financial Literacy helps an individual manage their money wisely and hence maximise the value obtained from the same which in turn improves the standard of life (Damayanti et al,2018).

Any construct which has a considerable impact on an individual's financial decision should be explored further. Present day economists have realized financial and economic forecasts can be effectively made if the attitude as well as the characteristics of individuals is understood properly (Zsoter, 2017) Individual psychological factors have been known to play a role in the financial behaviour (Mutlu & Ozer, 2022). Emotional intelligence in this regard is known to be an essential trait as it allows researchers and practitioners to improve the quality of financial decisions. Emotional Intelligence comprises of "interpersonal intelligence" as well as "intrapersonal intelligence". It is defined as "the "ability to monitor one's and other person's feelings and emotions, to discriminate between them and use the information as a guide to one's own thinking and actions". (Salovey & Mayer,1999). Researchers have concluded that emotional intelligence helps in providing "emotional stability" to the individuals which protects them against the risk which they experience while taking a financial decision and lets them improve the quality of their financial decision (Bouzguenda, 2018; Sullivan, 2011). Individuals with higher financial literacy levels experience less anxiety about financial matters, making choices that enhance personal and familial financial security (Hilgert et al., 2003). Emotional Intelligence is found to be a feature of investment related decision making (Quinn & Wilemon, 2009).

Despite the recognized importance of financial literacy, there is a global deficit in financial knowledge, and a country's income level does not necessarily correspond to its citizens' financial literacy (Lusardi, 2019). Even highly educated individuals may lack being financially savvy, underlining the need for targeted financial education. Only 33% of adults worldwide are deemed financially literate (Hasler, 2017).

Dewi (2022) has mentioned that demographic factors such as age has significant impact on financial literacy. Organization for Economic Cooperation and Development,2020 (OECD) has also highlighted that age has an impact on financial literacy. In a study conducted by Okamoto & Komamura (2021), it was observed that individuals belonging to both young as well as older population groups are likely to have lower levels of financial literacy. Low levels of financial literacy among youth across various parts of the world is a cause of concern. The young population has a much longer life span and hence it is important on their part to develop a good sense of managing finances. Hence, Financial literacy has a huge significance for them (Garg & Singh,2018). Financially literate young people make rational decisions. Their decisions also influence the wellbeing of their families as well as the economy (Frączek, & Klimontowicz,2015).

Individuals born and living at the same time belong to the same "Generation". The differences between various age groups can be easily understood by the term "Generation". They share birth years, age and also significant life events. A generation typically has a time span of 25-30 years. Individuals belonging to the same generation are similar in the sense that they have almost similar values as well as behaviours. Although, demographic factors may influence their characteristics and preferences but commonality may be observed as they experience similar kind of events (Abrams & Frank,2013).

The present paper attempts to understand the Impact of Emotional Intelligence on the Financial Literacy of the individuals belonging to the Generation Z (Gen Z). They are individuals born between Year 1995- Year 2010(Francis & Hoefel,2018). At present, Gen Z constitutes 32% of the world population. Gen Z individuals are relatively younger but many of them are already active in their professional lives (Dolot,2018) and are about to enter the adult life comprising of Work, building a home and family of their own (Harrari et al,2023). This generation has grown up in comparatively peaceful and stable economic environment compared to other Generations. Gen Z is driven by technology and is very much at ease with the same. They have grown up with technology which provides them with access to information. Gen Z are referred to as "Digital Natives" owing to their inclination towards new technologies, artificial intelligence, wearable technology, blockchain etc

(Hernandez-de-Menendez et al 2020). The behaviour of this particular Generation in the financial market has garnered attention from many researchers.

It is worth mentioning that financial technology is also on the rise. Gen Z in India is a privileged generation in terms of purchasing power, access to credit cards, information related to fashion and standard of living. They spend a large percentage of their income on lifestyle. The Markets are also serving the demands of this generation (Desai & Kankonkar,2019). Hence, Problems related to Managing Finances can be faced by Generation Z especially with increasing consumerism and digitization. Previous Studies have also shown that Gen Z lacks knowledge, skills and attitudes related to Finance which makes them more vulnerable to an economic downturn (Keeter, 2020). The Present study tries to explore the impact of Emotional Intelligence on Financial Literacy among the Gen Z as the studies on this particular generation are still in the nascent stage. It also attempts to theoretically and empirically add to the understanding the relationship between the chosen constructs in the context of India owing to the dearth of such studies. The present study is an attempt at contributing towards providing a perspective of financial literacy with reference to Gen Z especially in the Indian context, where behavioural finance studies are still not fully developed.

LITERATURE REVIEW AND HYPOTHESIS DEVELOPMENT

Generation Z, Emotional Intelligence and Financial Literacy

Research on Behaviour finance states that the investment related decision-making process is a resultant of emotions, personal characteristics and personality traits as well as demographic factors such as age and gender (Ishfaq et al 2020; Pašiušienė, et al 2023). Generation Z is presently one of the emerging cohorts in the banking and financial industry. Understanding their behaviour related to financial decisions is important (Vlasic et al,2022). Findings related to financial behaviour have found its evidences in the field of Finance as well as psychology. Overconfidence bias, herd behaviour as well as personality types influence financial behaviour and decision making (Bucciol & Zarri,2015; Kumar et al,2021). A study on Gen Z in the Sarawak region of Malaysia indicated that the financial knowledge among the Gen Z is low. Further the same study also mentioned that the leading source of dissemination of financial knowledge id the parental financial socialization (Wee& Goy,2022). Another study on Gen Z regarding their investment decisions found out that positive emotions significantly impact the investment decisions (Sutejo et al, 2024). In the same study it was also mentioned that amongst Gen Z investors, emotions of hope and anger influences their investment decisions. Other basic human emotions of sadness, fear and happiness were found to have no impact on the investment decision. Both external as well as internal disturbances have been known to exert their influence on the financial decision making. The same study also mentioned that negative emotions such as Fear, Greed & anxiety interfere with an individual's responsible financial behaviour (Park & Martin, 2022). In a study conducted on Lithuanian Households, it was observed that Emotional Intelligence is one of the precursors of Financial Wellbeing (Činauskaitė-Cetiner, 2011). A study conducted on Gen Z belonging to Greece found out that financial literacy provides them a better ability to cope with financial shocks. Hence, financial literacy is one of the precursors for financial well-being amongst Gen Z. (Philippas & Avdoulas,2021).

Gen Z is also known to have less knowledge when it comes to financial behaviour because as their money spent by them for investment is very less (Pamikatsih et al,2022). A study has also concluded that Financial Literacy alone cannot guarantee that individuals will take sound financial decisions. Emotional Intelligence aids in the process of making Sound Financial decisions (Fauziyah & Ruhayati, 2016). Financial behaviour among Gen Z was studied by examining the impact of financial literacy, financial risk tolerance and emotional intelligence. It was observed that emotional intelligence impacts the relationship between financial literacy and financial risk tolerance. In the same study, Emotional Intelligence was also found to have an indirect relationship with financial literacy and financial behaviour (Song et al,2023). Furnham & Cheng (2013) studied personality dependent traits impacting the financial well-being and found out that emotional stability to be an important component of the same. Self-Control is one of the key components of Trait Emotional Intelligence (Petrides,2011). Self-control in the field of Finance encourages an individual to save by curtailing their impulsive purchases. Financial literacy is found to have a significant negative impact on GenZ's Impulse driven buying behaviour (Ayuningtyas & Irawan,2021). Triveni & Soleha (2023) have also supported the fact that self-control amongst Gen Z has a significant positive impact on their financial behaviour. Worokinasih et al 2023 have opined that young entrepreneurs benefit from understanding the importance of emotional intelligence and financial literacy as these help in boosting the productivity of their enterprises. A variety of Emotional as well as Cognitive factors are found to impact the investment decisions of Gen Z. Further, Capital Market literacy also helps Gen Z in taking right investment decisions.

The extant literature surveyed emphasizes the impact of Emotional Intelligence on Financial literacy amongst the Gen Z individuals. The present study aims to contribute towards the behavioural finance theory by investigating the impact of emotional intelligence on financial literacy amongst Gen Z.

Hence, based on the objective of the present study and literature surveyed, we hypothesize:

H1: Emotional Intelligence has a positive impact on the Financial Literacy amongst the Gen Z individuals

Further, based on the literature review and objective of the study, the conceptual framework of the study is proposed as under:

Methodology

Figure 1. Conceptual framework of the study

Procedure and Sample

The study sample for the present research includes Gen Z individuals belonging to the Jharkhand region in India. The Sampling design chosen was non probabilistic convenience sampling. A survey link was created and administered via emails as well as Social Networks for data collection. The questionnaires used in the study were Self report measures. The participants were informed about the purpose and confidentiality of the study. The final study sample comprise of 136 participants. 67 participants were Males whereas 69 participants were Females. All the participants were in the age group of 20 -26 years.

The study utilizes a two-wave research design in order to reduce the issues of common method bias. There are a number of causes which may account for Common Method Biases. A common rater, a common measurement context, a common item context, or the item characteristics itself. One or several of these causes may be present in any research. Studies where the data for Predictor (Independent) Variable and Criterion (Dependent) variable are collected from the same rater and same measurement context are more prone to suffer from the problem of Common Method Bias. These issues are prominent in case of Behavioural studies. At times it is not feasible to collect data from different sources. Hence, in such situations, the measurement of Predictor (Independent) and Criterion (Dependent) variables can be separated by allowing a time lag between the measurement of the two (Podsakoff et al,2003). We carried out the collection of data at two different times with a difference of two weeks in between. In the first stage, data on Emotional Intelligence (Predictor) was collected and after two weeks, data on Financial Literacy (Criterion) was collected. The participants were same in both the stages and to match their data which was collected at two different times, the data was coded.

Measures

Emotional Intelligence: In the Present study, Emotional Intelligence was measured through Trait Emotional Intelligence Questionnaire—Short Form (TEIQue-SF) which comprises of 30 questions. TEIQue -SF is an internationally accepted developed by Dr. K. V Petrides, Psychometric labs, University College, London. It comprises of four broader factors namely Well-being, Self-control, Emotionality and Sociability. The description of the four factors is mentioned as under:

a. Well-Being-It is a measure of overall sense of well-being and satisfaction in life.
b. Self-control-It is the ability to manage urges, desires, stress, and pressures.
c. Emotionality-It is the skill related to recognizing, perceiving, and expressing of the emotions.
d. Sociability-It focuses on an individual's social interactions and social relationships.

There are 4 items of the TEIQue –SF which belong to the two "stand-alone" facets/dimensions (adaptability and self-motivation) and contribute directly to the global score without contributing to any of the factors. The response to the items on TEIQue -SF are made on a 7-point likert scale where 1=Completely disagree and 7=Completely agree. The negative items of the TEIQue-SF are reverse coded. The reliability coefficient (Cronbach's Alpha) of the scale in this study was 0.810 indicating that the scale has good reliability.

Financial Literacy: In The present study a questionnaire based on the concepts of OECD/INFE (OECD International Network on Financial Education) Toolkit (2022) for Measuring Financial Literacy and Financial Inclusion was used. It comprised of 20 questions. The responses were made on a 5-point Likert scale. The reliability coefficient (Cronbach's Alpha) of the scale in this study was 0.807 indicating that the scale has good reliability.

Analysis and Results

The data collected was analysed using IBM SPSS 24.0 software. Skewness and kurtosis are basic descriptive statistics tools which were used to test the normality of the data. The rationale behind checking the normality of the data is that it helps in careful selection of the analytical tests to be used for the study. It helps in suggesting whether parametric or non-parametric tests are to be used. A common thumb rule suggests that the values of Skewness and Kurtosis should lie within the range of +2 to -2 for data to test for normality (Garson, 2012).

The value of skewness for all the 30 items of the Emotional Intelligence Scale were found in the range of -1.006 and 0.977 and the kurtosis value for all the 30 items of the same scale were found to lie in the range of – 1.216 and 1.199.Similarly, value of skewness for all the 20 items of the Financial Literacy Questionnaire was found in the range of -1.466 and .235 and the kurtosis value for all the 20 items of the same scale were found to lie in the range of - .164 and 1.927.The descriptive statistics revealed that data was normally distributed. The descriptive statistics are mentioned in Table 1 and Table 2.

Table 1. Descriptive statistics (skewness & kurtosis) for emotional intelligence scale

	N	Skewness		Kurtosis	
Items	Statistic	Statistic	Std. Error	Statistic	Std. Error
EI1	136	-.796	.208	.074	.413
EI2	136	-.552	.208	-.667	.413
EI3	136	-.825	.208	.333	.413
EI4	136	.048	.208	-1.082	.413
EI5	136	-.418	.208	-1.154	.413
EI6	136	.977	.208	.570	.413
EI7	136	.023	.208	-.929	.413
EI8	136	.318	.208	-1.056	.413
EI9	136	-.994	.208	1.199	.413
EI10	136	-.227	.208	-1.101	.413
EI11	136	-.180	.208	-.051	.413
EI12	136	.012	.208	-.942	.413
EI13	136	-.947	.208	-.252	.413
EI14	136	-.349	.208	-1.108	.413
EI15	136	-.826	.208	-.220	.413
EI16	136	-.247	.208	-1.216	.413
EI17	136	-.791	.208	-.132	.413
EI18	136	.010	.208	-.856	.413
EI19	136	-1.006	.208	.857	.413
EI20	136	-.720	.208	.167	.413
EI21	136	-.691	.208	.471	.413
EI22	136	.283	.208	-.721	.413

continued on following page

Table 1. Continued

Items	N Statistic	Skewness Statistic	Std. Error	Kurtosis Statistic	Std. Error
EI23	136	-.824	.208	.211	.413
EI24	136	-.744	.208	.260	.413
EI25	136	.207	.208	-1.004	.413
EI26	136	.024	.208	-.550	.413
EI27	136	-.927	.208	.232	.413
EI28	136	-.380	.208	-1.097	.413
EI29	136	-1.000	.208	.357	.413
EI30	136	-.786	.208	.141	.413
Valid N (listwise)	136				

Table 2. Descriptive statistics for financial literacy scale

Items	N Statistic	Skewness Statistic	Std. Error	Kurtosis Statistic	Std. Error
FL1	136	-.118	.208	-.706	.413
FL2	136	-.479	.208	-.629	.413
FL3	136	-.613	.208	-.792	.413
FL4	136	-.531	.208	-.801	.413
FL5	136	.169	.208	-.913	.413
FL6	136	-.108	.208	-.837	.413
FL7	136	.235	.208	-1.234	.413
FL8	136	-.760	.208	-.159	.413
FL9	136	-.653	.208	-.110	.413
FL10	136	-1.034	.208	.195	.413
FL11	136	-1.466	.208	1.616	.413
FL12	136	-.875	.208	.301	.413
FL13	136	-1.522	.208	1.927	.413
FL14	136	-.852	.208	.133	.413
FL15	136	-.882	.208	-.040	.413
FL16	136	-.472	.208	-.529	.413
FL17	136	-.622	.208	-.301	.413
FL18	136	-1.075	.208	.978	.413

continued on following page

Table 2. Continued

Items	N Statistic	Skewness Statistic	Std. Error	Kurtosis Statistic	Std. Error
FL19	136	-.688	.208	-.164	.413
FL20	136	-.565	.208	-1.448	.413
Valid N (listwise)	136				

Hence, the study utilizes parametric tests such as Correlation, Simple linear regression & multiple regressions to draw meaningful observations.

A correlation analysis was conducted to find out significant relationship between Emotional Intelligence (EI) and Financial Literacy (FL). It was observed that Emotional Intelligence positively correlates with Financial Literacy ($\rho = 0.320$; $p < 0.01$), which indicates that increase in the levels of Emotional Intelligence of Gen Z individuals results in an increase in their Financial Literacy as well. The results of the Correlation are mentioned in Table 3.

Table 3. Correlation between Emotional Intelligence (EI) and Financial Literacy (FL)

		FL	EI
FL	Pearson Correlation	1	.320**
	Sig. (2-tailed)		.000
	N	136	136
EI	Pearson Correlation	.320**	1
	Sig. (2-tailed)	.000	
	N	136	136

**. Correlation is significant at the 0.01 level (2-tailed).

Further, to test the hypothesis, *H1,* we conducted a linear regression. The Model Summary is depicted in Table 4. The relationship between Predictor (Emotional Intelligence) and Criterion (Financial Literacy) was found to be statistically significant (p=0.000). The Durbin Watson value was within the acceptable range which shows there was no auto correlation between the variables. The R square change was found to be 10.3%. Table 5 depicts the ANOVA table and shows that the regression model predicts the dependent variable (Financial Literacy) significantly (p=0.000). The Coefficients Table 6 shows the strength of the relationship and the magnitude with which Emotional Intelligence impacts Financial Literacy. Based on the sig value (=0.000), the hypothesis, H_1 was accepted.

Table 4. Model summary

| Model | R | R Square | Adjusted R Square | Std. Error of the Estimate | Change Statistics | | | | | Durbin-Watson |
					R Square Change	F Change	df1	df2	Sig. F Change	
1	.320[a]	.103	.096	.51271	.103	15.325	1	134	.000	1.939

a. Predictors: (Constant), TEI
b. Dependent Variable: FL

Table 5. ANOVA[a]

Model		Sum of Squares	df	Mean Square	F	Sig.
1	Regression	4.028	1	4.028	15.325	.000[b]
	Residual	35.225	134	.263		
	Total	39.254	135			

a. Dependent Variable: FL
b. Predictors: (Constant), EI

Table 6. Coefficients[a]

| Model | | Unstandardized Coefficients | | Standardized Coefficients | t | Sig. | 95.0% Confidence Interval for B | |
		B	Std. Error	Beta			Lower Bound	Upper Bound
1	(Constant)	2.327	.334		6.973	.000	1.667	2.987
	EI	.281	.072	.320	3.915	.000	.139	.423

Further, a multiple regression was also conducted to study the factors of Emotional Intelligence and its impact on Financial Literacy. The model summary is depicted in Table 7. The ANOVA table is mentioned in Table 8. All the factors of Emotional Intelligence namely Sociability (SOC), Emotionality (EMOT), Wellbeing (WB) and Self Control (SC) predicted Financial Literacy Significantly ($p=0.000$). The Coefficients Table 9 shows the strength of relationship between all the four factors of EI with FL. It was observed that only Wellbeing (WB) and Sociability (SOC) have a statistically significant relationship ($p< 0.05$) with Financial Literacy (FL). Hence, we can conclude that Sociability and Wellbeing amongst Gen Z impacts their Financial Literacy.

Table 7. Model summary

Model	R	R Square	Adjusted R Square	Std. Error of the Estimate	Change Statistics						Durbin-Watson
					R Square Change	F Change	df1	df2	Sig. F Change		
1	.397[a]	.158	.132	.50236	.158	6.136	4	131	.000		1.949

a. Predictors: (Constant), SOC, EMOT, WB, SC
b. Dependent Variable: FL

Table 8. ANOVA

Model		Sum of Squares	df	Mean Square	F	Sig.
1	Regression	6.194	4	1.549	6.136	.000[b]
	Residual	33.059	131	.252		
	Total	39.254	135			

a. Dependent Variable: FL
b. Predictors: (Constant), SOC, EMOT, WB, SC

Table 9. Coefficients

Model		Unstandardized Coefficients		Standardized Coefficients	t	Sig.	95.0% Confidence Interval for B	
		B	Std. Error	Beta			Lower Bound	Upper Bound
1	(Constant)	2.556	.366		6.992	.000	1.833	3.279
	WB	.164	.055	.289	2.969	.004	.055	.273
	SC	.090	.069	.132	1.305	.194	-.046	.226
	EMOT	.097	.080	.115	1.210	.229	-.061	.254
	SOC	-.147	.070	-.190	-2.113	.037	-.285	-.009

a. Dependent Variable: FL

Discussions

The objective of the present study was to study the impact of Emotional Intelligence (EI) on the Financial Literacy (FL) of the Gen Z. It was found that there exists a significant relationship and impact of EI on FL. The study is found to be consistent with the findings of Dewi et al (2023) who mentioned that knowledge of finance significantly as well as positively impacts the personal financial management of the

Gen Z implying that a higher the level of financial knowledge results in the improved personal financial management. The findings of the study are also in alignment with a prior study conducted by Amriks et al (2007) where it was concluded that Investors having high emotional intelligence invest in a more balanced manner as compared to those with low emotional intelligence. Investors having low emotional intelligence also react to market related information impulsively (Dalbar, 2017). Fauziyah & Ruhayati (2016) have also mentioned that financial literacy alone is not enough to help young adults to take financial decisions with regard to managing their personal finances. In their study they have emphasized on the role of Emotional quotient in playing an instrumental role in shaping the financial behaviour with respect to consumption as well as saving. The findings of the present study are also consistent with the study conducted by Vlasic & Keleminic (2022) who have concluded that individuals with low financial literacy are dependent on subjective cues such as customer feedback when they make financial recommendations to others. Their recommendations are based majorly on inertia and not on cognitive loyalty. Hence, financial institutions like banks need to use customer segmentation based on behavioural aspects when they segment customers based on financial literacy.

The factors of Emotional Intelligence and their significant relationship with financial literacy was also studied in the present research. It was found out that Sociability and Well Being are the major factors related to EI which contributes significantly towards the financial literacy (FL) among Gen Z. The study of Shankar et al (2022) mentions that the financial wellbeing of Gen Z is influenced by demographic factors such as their age, education etc. Gen Z are well versed with digital technologies, are more aware, have better emotional skills and attitudes which may be the reason that in the present study it was observed that the Sociability amongst Gen Z has a significant impact on their Financial Literacy. Sociability & well-being as components of EI impacting the financial literacy amongst Gen Z is also in alignment with the study conducted by Bucciol et al (2020) which highlighted that Trait EI acts as a key determinant in financial risk-taking. The authors in the same study also mentioned that all the components of trait EI do not play similar role and only sociability and well-being impact financial risk-taking behaviour. This finding was further supported by the study conducted by Balan & Vreja (2018). The findings also align with the conclusion proposed by Ammer & Aldhyani (2022) who have mentioned in their research that the financial and Investment awareness level in Gen Z is determined by their family's financial socialization i.e. good financial behaviour in Gen Z is dependent on the level of involvement of their families in educating and helping them in taking good financial decisions. The study suggests that strong emotional intelligence capabilities result in good investment and financial decisions. When Gen Z are emotionally intelligent, they are likely to make rational financial decisions

CONCLUSION

Emotions can impact financial and investment decisions. They can make the individuals belonging to Gen Z take irrational decisions. On the other hand, Financial Literacy is an important factor for an individual's growth and wellbeing. The rising cost of living and inflation has made financial literacy a compulsion for the Gen Z which eventually will help stabilize their state of personal finances (Beccera,2018). When paid proper attention and included as an economic growth policy and implemented through the government institutions can lead to a sustainably growing economy. However, Financial Literacy on its alone cannot alter the financial behaviour of the individuals. Financial Literacy in the influence of Emotional Intelligence becomes a strong predictor of an individual's financial well-being. The present study says that there exists a significant relationship and impact of EI on FL. EI of an individual can be checked in the formative ages and can be worked upon by family and other institutions and help in developing emotionally strong individuals who can handle personal and Organizational finance with more diligence as the negative effects of emotions declines with age while positive affect appears to increase with age (Atkins and Stough,2005). Financial literacy compensates for the lack of responsible financial behaviour in the economic market plagued with uncertainty. Understanding and acknowledging the contribution of behavioural and cognitive abilities such as Emotional Intelligence can help financial institutions and economists to devise more effective intervention tools and programs. Government, Policy Makers, Educationists & Financial Institutions should focus on devising training programs and interventions related to developing nontraditional forms of financial knowledge such as emotional intelligence at the formative stages of life.

Limitations and Future Scope

The current study has provided valuable insights into the complex interaction between Emotional intelligence and financial literacy among the individuals belonging to Gen Z. However, numerous avenues remain unexplored, offering exciting opportunities for future research. One of the Limitations of the study is that it is cross sectional in nature. Conducting longitudinal studies on Gen Z may reveal a deeper understanding of how Emotional Intelligence and Financial Literacy evolve over time. Following individuals from early school days through various stages in career building would shed light on the dynamic nature of these relationships and offer insights into the factors influencing changes in financial behaviour. The Study utilized self-report measure of data collection. Collecting information from peers as well as superiors may reveal some more insights.

The present study is based on a sample from Bihar-Jharkhand Region of India. A more diverse sample in terms of geographical location might be considered in future studies for a more generalized finding. Expanding the research to study cross country differences may also be considered in future. Cultural nuances may influence the Emotional Intelligence and its correlation with financial literacy, leading to a more comprehensive understanding of these dynamics in a global context.

A gender-based comparison on the constructs chosen may also reveal the gender differences if any and can be worked upon in the formative stages of personality development. Comparative studies between different generations such as Millennials Vs Gen Z in the above-mentioned context may also prove to be insightful research.

REFERENCES

Abrams, J., & Von Frank, V. (2013). *The multigenerational workplace: Communicate, collaborate, and create community*. Corwin Press.

Ameriks, J., Wranik, T., Salovey, P., & Peterson LaBarge, K. (2007). Emotional Intelligence and Investor Behavior. Vanguard Investment Perspectives. Retrieved June 2, 2023 from https://institutional.vanguard.com/iip/pdf/ICRVIPF2007.pdf

Ammer, M. A., & Aldhyani, T. H. (2022). An investigation into the determinants of investment awareness: Evidence from the young Saudi generation. *Sustainability (Basel)*, 14(20), 13454. DOI: 10.3390/su142013454

Armansyah, R. F., Ardianto, H., & Rithmaya, C. L. (2023). UNDERSTANDING GEN Z INVESTMENT DECISIONS: CAPITAL MARKET LITERACY AND EMOTIONAL BIASES. *Jurnal Manajemen Dan Kewirausahaan*, 25(2), 105–119. DOI: 10.9744/jmk.25.2.105-119

Atkins, P., & Stough, C. (2005). Does emotional intelligence change with age. In *Society for Research in Adult Development annual conference, Atlanta, GA*.

Ayuningtyas, M. F., & Irawan, A. (2021). The influence of financial literacy on bandung generation z consumers impulsive buying behavior with self-control as mediating variable. *Advanced International Journal of Business. Entrepreneurship and SMEs*, 3(9), 155–171. DOI: 10.35631/AIJBES.39012

Bălan, S., & Vreja, L. O. (2018, November). Generation Z: Challenges for management and leadership. In *Proceedings of the 12th International Management Conference "Management Perspectives in the Digital Era", Bucharest, Romania* (pp. 1-2).

Becerra, A. (2018). *Generation Z: Social media, influencers and brand loyalty in entertainment* (Doctoral dissertation, University of Southern California).

Bouzguenda, K. (2018). Emotional intelligence and financial decision making: Are we talking about a paradigmatic shift or a change in practices? *Research in International Business and Finance*, 44, 273–284. DOI: 10.1016/j.ribaf.2017.07.096

Bucciol, A., Guerrero, F., & Papadovasilaki, D. (2021). Financial risk-taking and trait emotional intelligence. *Review of Behavioral Finance*, 13(3), 259–275. DOI: 10.1108/RBF-01-2020-0013

Bucciol, A., & Zarri, L. (2015). Does investors' personality influence their portfolios?.

Činauskaitė-Cetiner, J. (2011). Namų ūkių finansinės gerovės kūrimo prielaidos Lietuvoje. Human Resources: The Main Factor of Regional Development, 4, 16–24. https://web.p.ebscohost.com/ehost/detail/detail?vid=0&sid=e05d18d1-5fee-4ab7 -84cba1ca0f235b2b%40redis&bdata=JnNpdGU9ZWhvc3QtbGl2ZQ%3d%3d#AN =67721867&db=bsh

Dalbar, Inc. (2016). Dalbar is the financial community's leading independent expert for evaluating, auditing and rating business practices and customer performance since 1976. Dalbar.com. Boston, MA

Damayanti, S. M., Murtaqi, I., & Pradana, H. A. (2018). The importance of financial literacy in a global economic era. *The Business & Management Review*, 9(3), 435–441.

Desai, N., & Kankonkar, S. (2019). Gen-Z's online buying involvement and decision style in buying fashion apparels. *Studies in Indian Place Name*, 40(26), 360–376.

Dewi, V. I. (2022). How do demographic and socioeconomic factors affect financial literacy and its variables? *Cogent Business & Management*, 9(1), 1. DOI: 10.1080/23311975.2022.2077640

Dolot, A. (2018). The characteristics of Generation Z. e-mentor, 74, 44–50. *Williams, K., Page, R., Petrosky, A., & Hernandez, E.(2010). Multi-Generational Marketing: Descriptions, Characteristics, Lifestyles, and Attitudes. Journal of Applied Business and Economics*

Fauziyah, A., & Ruhayati, S. A. (2016). Developing students' financial literacy and financial behaviour by students' emotional quotient in Proceedings of the 2016. In Global Conference on Business, Management and Entrepreneurship (pp. 65–69). DOI: 10.2991/gcbme-16.2016.10

Fraczek, B., & Klimontowicz, M. (2015). Financial literacy and its influence on young customers' decision factors. *Journal of Innovation Management*, 3(1), 62–84. https://journalsojs3.fe.up.pt/index.php/jim/article/view/2183-0606_003.001_0007/ 166. DOI: 10.24840/2183-0606_003.001_0007

Francis, T., & Hoefel, F. (2018). True Gen': Generation Z and its implications for companies. *McKinsey & Company, 12*, 1-10. http://www.drthomaswu.com/ uicmpaccsmac/Gen%20Z.pdf

Furnham, A., & Cheng, H. (2013). Factors influencing adult earnings: Findings from a nationally representative sample. *Journal of Socio-Economics*, 44, 120–125. DOI: 10.1016/j.socec.2013.02.008

Garg, N., & Singh, S. (2018). Financial literacy among youth. *International Journal of Social Economics*, 45(1), 173–186. DOI: 10.1108/IJSE-11-2016-0303

Garson, G. D. (2012). *Testing statistical assumptions*. Statistical Associates Publishing.

Harari, T. T., Sela, Y., & Bareket-Bojmel, L. (2023). Gen Z during the COVID-19 crisis: A comparative analysis of the differences between Gen Z and Gen X in resilience, values and attitudes. *Current Psychology (New Brunswick, N.J.)*, 42(28), 24223–24232. DOI: 10.1007/s12144-022-03501-4 PMID: 35967492

Hasler, A., & Lusardi, A. (2017). The gender gap in financial literacy: A global perspective. *Global Financial Literacy Excellence Center, The George Washington University School of Business*.

Hernandez-de-Menendez, M., Escobar Díaz, C. A., & Morales-Menendez, R. (2020). Educational experiences with Generation Z. [IJIDeM]. *International Journal on Interactive Design and Manufacturing*, 14(3), 847–859. DOI: 10.1007/s12008-020-00674-9

Hilgert, M. A. (2003). JeanneM. *Hogarth, Sondra Baverly. Household Financial Management: The Connection between Knowledge and Behavior*.

Ishfaq, M., Nazir, M. S., Qamar, M. A. J., & Usman, M. (2020). Cognitive Bias and the Extraversion Personality Shaping the Behavior of Investors. *Frontiers in Psychology*, 11, 556506. DOI: 10.3389/fpsyg.2020.556506 PMID: 33178066

Keeter, S. (2020). *People financially affected by COVID-19 outbreak are experiencing more psychological distress than others* (Vol. 30). Pew Research Center.

Kovacs, P., Kuruczleki, E., Racz, T. A., & Liptak, L. (2021). Survey of Hungarian high school students' financial literacy in the last 10 years based on the econventio test. Pe´nz€ ugyi Szemle/Public Finance Quarterly, 66(2), 175–194. DoI: https://doi.org/DOI: 10.35551/PFQ_2021_2_1

Kumar, V., Dudani, R., & Latha, K. (2021). The big five personality traits and psychological biases: An exploratory study. *Current Psychology (New Brunswick, N.J.)*, 42(8), 6587–6597. DOI: 10.1007/s12144-021-01999-8

Lusardi, A. (2019). Financial literacy and the need for financial education: Evidence and implications. *Swiss Journal of Economics and Statistics*, 155(1), 1. Advance online publication. DOI: 10.1186/s41937-019-0027-5

Lusardi, A., Mitchell, O. S., & Curto, V. (2010). Financial literacy among the young. *The Journal of Consumer Affairs*, 44(2), 358–380. https://www.nber.org/papers/w15352. DOI: 10.1111/j.1745-6606.2010.01173.x

Mayer, J., Caruso, D., & Salovey, P. (1999). Emotional Intelligence Meets Traditional Standards for Intelligence. *Intelligence*, 27(4), 267–298. DOI: 10.1016/S0160-2896(99)00016-1

Messy, F. A., & Monticone, C. (2016). Financial education policies in Asia and the Pacific. https://doi.org/.DOI: 10.1787/20797117

Mutlu, Ü., & Özer, G. (2022). The moderator effect of financial literacy on the relationship between locus of control and financial behavior. *Kybernetes*, 51(3), 1114–1126. DOI: 10.1108/K-01-2021-0062

OECD. (2013).Financial literacy and inclusion: Results of OECD/ INFE survey across countries and by gender. *Financial Literacy & Education, Russia, jun.*

OECD. (2020). InternationalSurvey of Adult Financial Literacy. Paris: OECD Publishing. https://www.oecd.org/financial/education/launchoftheoecdinfegloba lfinancialliteracysurveyreport.htm

OECD. (2022), OECD/INFE Toolkit for Measuring Financial Literacy and Financial Inclusion 2022, www.oecd.org/financial/education/2022-INFE-Toolkit-Measuring -Finlit-Financial-Inclusion.pdf

Okamoto, S., & Komamura, K. (2021). Age, gender, and financial literacy in Japan. *PLoS One*, 16(11), e0259393. DOI: 10.1371/journal.pone.0259393 PMID: 34788283

Pamikatsih, T. R., Lusia, A., Rahayu, A. S., Maisara, P., & Farida, A. (2022). THE INFLUENCING FACTORS FOR FINANCIAL BEHAVIOR OF GEN Z. *International Conference of Business and Social Sciences, 2*(1), 440–449. Retrieved from https://debian.stiesia.ac.id/index.php/icobuss1st/article/view/196

Pangestu, S., & Karnadi, E. B. (2020). The effects of financial literacy and materialism on the savings decision of generation Z Indonesians. *Cogent Business & Management*, 7(1), 1743618. DOI: 10.1080/23311975.2020.1743618

Park, H., & Martin, W. (2022). Effects of risk tolerance, financial literacy, and financial status on retirement planning. *Journal of Financial Services Marketing*, 27(3), 167–176. DOI: 10.1057/s41264-021-00123-y

Pašiušienė, I., Podviezko, A., Malakaitė, D., Žarskienė, L., Liučvaitienė, A., & Martišienė, R. (2023). Exploring Generation Z's Investment Patterns and Attitudes towards Greenness. *Sustainability (Basel)*, 16(1), 352. DOI: 10.3390/su16010352

Petrides, K. V. (2011). *Ability and trait emotional intelligence. The Wiley-Blackwell Handbook of Individual Differences* (1st ed.). Blackwell Publishing Ltd.

Philippas, N. D., & Avdoulas, C. (2021). Financial literacy and financial well-being among generation-Z university students: Evidence from Greece. In *Financial Literacy and Responsible Finance in the FinTech Era* (pp. 64–85). Routledge., DOI: 10.4324/9781003169192-5

Podsakoff, P. M., MacKenzie, S. B., Lee, J. Y., & Podsakoff, N. P. (2003). Common method biases in behavioral research: A critical review of the literature and recommended remedies. *The Journal of Applied Psychology*, 88(5), 879–903. https://psycnet.apa.org/doi/10.1037/0021-9010.88.5.879. DOI: 10.1037/0021-9010.88.5.879 PMID: 14516251

Quinn, J. F., & Wilemon, D. (2009, August). Emotional intelligence as a facilitator of project leader effectiveness. In *PICMET'09-2009 Portland International Conference on Management of Engineering & Technology* (pp. 1267-1275). IEEE. DOI: 10.1109/PICMET.2009.5262022

Shankar, N., Vinod, S., & Kamath, R. (2022). Financial well-being–A Generation Z perspective using a Structural Equation Modeling approach. *Investment Management and Financial Innovations*, 19(1), 32–50. DOI: 10.21511/imfi.19(1).2022.03

Sholevar, M., & Harris, L. (2020). Women are invisible?! A literature survey on gender gap and financial training. *Citizenship. Social and Economics Education*, 19(2), 87–99. DOI: 10.1177/2047173420922501

Song, C. L., Pan, D., Ayub, A., & Cai, B. (2023). The Interplay Between Financial Literacy, Financial Risk Tolerance, and Financial Behaviour: The Moderator Effect of Emotional Intelligence. *Psychology Research and Behavior Management*, 16, 535–548. DOI: 10.2147/PRBM.S398450 PMID: 36860350

Sullivan, R. N. (2011). Deploying financial emotional intelligence. *Financial Analysts Journal*, 67(6), 4–10. DOI: 10.2469/faj.v67.n6.6

Sutejo, B. S., Sumiati, S., Wijayanti, R., & Ananda, C. F. (2024). Do Emotions Influence the Investment Decisions of Generation Z Surabaya Investors in the Covid-19 Pandemic Era? Does Financial Risk Tolerance Play a Moderating Role? *Scientific Papers of the University of Pardubice, Series D. Faculty of Economics and Administration*, 31(2), 1755. DOI: 10.46585/sp31021755

Trivani, G., & Soleha, E. (2023). The Effect of Financial Literacy, Income and Self Control on Financial Behavior Generation Z (Study on Generation Z Financial Behavior in Bekasi Regency). *Economic Education Analysis Journal*, 12(1), 69–79. DOI: 10.15294/eeaj.v12i1.67452

Vlašić, G., Keleminić, K., & Šubić, R. (2022). Understanding drivers of consumer loyalty in the banking industry: A comparative study of generation z individuals exhibiting high vs. low financial literacy. *Management*, 27(1), 213–235. DOI: 10.30924/mjcmi.27.1.12

Wee, L. L. M., & Goy, S. C. (2022). The effects of ethnicity, gender and parental financial socialisation on financial knowledge among Gen Z: The case of Sarawak, Malaysia. *International Journal of Social Economics*, 49(9), 1349–1367. DOI: 10.1108/IJSE-02-2021-0114

Worokinasih, S., Nuzula, N. F., Damayanti, C. R., & Sirivanh, T. (2023). The resilience of youth entrepreneur: The role of social capital, financial literacy, and emotional intelligence on SME performance in Indonesia. *BISMA (Bisnis dan Manajemen)*, 1-28. https://doi.org/.DOI: 10.26740/bisma.v16n1.p1-27

Zsoter, B. (2017). Personality, attitude and behavioural components of financial literacy: A comparative analysis. *Journal of Economics and Behavioral Studies*, 9(2 (J)), 46–57. DOI: 10.22610/jebs.v9i2(J).1649

Chapter 14
Assessment of Gen Z's Behaviors and Preferences on Online Dating App OKCupid

Bhabani Prasad Mahapatra
https://orcid.org/0000-0002-9746-8747
Xavier Institute of Social Service, India

Vartika Banerjee
Xavier Institute of Social Service, India

Gurleen Kaur
https://orcid.org/0009-0008-8238-5130
Xavier Institute of Social Service, India

ABSTRACT

As Generation Z constitutes a significant demographic within the user base of dating apps, a thorough understanding of their priorities, values, and relationship approaches becomes imperative. Drawing upon secondary data sources, including official reports from dating apps and pertinent literature, this research presents a comprehensive analysis of global dating trends, discernible shifts in user behaviour, and prevailing market dynamics. Moreover, the study endeavours to contribute to the refinement of dating platforms by offering actionable insights. The engagements of GenZ in OKCupid- a popular online dating app has been analysed. The findings derived from this research are poised to facilitate user interface modifications, and guide the development of novel features that resonate with the authentic, self-growth-oriented, and inclusive values of Generation Z. By unravelling these intricate

DOI: 10.4018/979-8-3693-5563-3.ch014

layers, the research aspires to empower dating platforms to engage with the dating landscape more meaningfully and adapt proactively to the evolving dynamics of Generation Z's dating preferences.

1. INTRODUCTION

We are living in a multi-generational world, and it is very crucial to understand the new generations as they form majority of the working population. Table 1 indicates the dominance GenZ in the world. Even the share of the GenZ in developing countries like India is 27 percent which is higher than the world average (24 percent). As per one McKinsey report (2023), the share of GenZ population in Brazil is 20 percent. GenZ born between 1997-2012 are true digital natives: from earliest youth, they have been exposed to the internet, to social networks, and to mobile systems. That context has produced a hypercognitive generation very comfortable with collecting and cross-referencing many sources of information and with integrating virtual and offline experiences. As global connectivity soars, generational shifts could come to play a more important role in setting behavior than socioeconomic differences do. Young people have become a potent influence on people of all ages and incomes, as well as on the way those people consume and relate to brands.

Table 1. Share of GenZ in world population

Population by Age	Europe and North America	China	World Average	India
older (Born between 1980 or older)	49%	46%	52%	29%
Millennial (born between1981-1996)	22%	24%	23%	25%
GenZ (born between1997-2012)	17%	17%	24%	27%
New Gen (born after2012)	12%	13%	1%	19%

Source: World Population Prospects 2022; NASSCOM[1]

The landscape of love and dating in world is experiencing a significant shift driven by the emergence of GenZ. Unlike previous generations, Gen Z enters the dating scene with a unique set of values, priorities, and technological influences that challenge traditional norms and reshape existing practices. This has been evident with emergence of popular dating apps. A brief profile of popular dating apps has been provided in **Table 2**. When OKCupid is one of the oldest mobile app-which was launched in 2004, cost wise tinder has the lowest subscription rate at $8.

Dating can take many forms, from serious relationships to casual meet-ups, and various dating apps cater to these different approaches. These apps make it easier for individuals seeking similar types of connections to find each other. Users can message potential matches before meeting, tailor their search preferences, and even take quizzes to discover compatible partners. While there are numerous apps, not all are very popular in terms of their reputation.

Table 2. Top dating app in 2024

Dating App and year of lunch	Features	Monthly Subscription
Bumble (2014)	Best dating app for bold women who aren't afraid to make the first move... and don't mind losing matches if they don't receive a reply within one day. If the guy doesn't message back within 24 hours, the match then expires.	$33
Tinder (2012)	Best dating app for casual chat and hookups. Swipe left if you're not interested and right if you are. The profiles include a handful of pictures you can tap through, a bio and the option to link your Instagram and Spotify	$8
OKCupid (2004)	Focusing more on swiping and eliminating the ability to message a user without matching with them first. Online daters can still send a message -- it just won't show up in the recipient's inbox unless you match.	$30
Hinge (2013)	While Tinder may be more for hookups, Hinge is for those looking for something a little more than a one night stand.	$33
Coffee Meets Bagel (2012)	Offer people better-quality matches by sending curated daily matches, or "bagels," each day at noon	$9
Happn (2014)	Dating app for local dating. This app matches one with people who are located nearby. It's a cool concept and helpful for people who want to meet someone in a more organic manner	$25
Her (2013)	App is tailored to lesbian, bisexual and queer women	$15
eHarmony	Datimng app for marriage seekers. The app matches couples based on "29 dimensions" of compatibility and interests (as determined by a thorough relationship questionnaire and personality test)	$36

Source:https://www.cnet.com/tech/services-and-software/best-online-dating-apps

The plethora of dating apps not only attracts the people from developed countries, but these have also caught the attention of the young people in developing countries. The share of GenZ in India is above the world average. (Table 1). Besides, there is a huge revenue potential of the dating apps. Box 1.1 provides an overview of revenue potential as well as user penetration in the dating app throughout the world. The number of users is expected to amount to 201.5m users by 2029. The user penetration will be 3.8% in 2024 and is expected to hit 4.3% by 2029.The average revenue per user (ARPU) is expected to amount to US$4.09.

Online Dating in the World

- Revenue in the Online Dating market is projected to reach US$0.70bn in 2024.
- Revenue is expected to show an annual growth rate (CAGR 2024-2029) of 3.71%, resulting in a projected market volume of US$0.84bn by 2029.
- In the Online Dating market, the number of users is expected to amount to 201.5m users by 2029.
- User penetration will be 3.8% in 2024 and is expected to hit 4.3% by 2029.
- The average revenue per user (ARPU) is expected to amount to US$4.09.
- In global comparison, most revenue will be generated in the United States (US$1,392.00m in 2024).
- With a projected rate of 17.7%, the user penetration in the Online Dating market is highest in the United States.

Source: https://www.statista.com/outlook/emo/dating-services/online-dating/worldwide

Gen Z exhibits unique characteristics that significantly influence their behaviors and preferences on dating apps. This generation values authenticity and transparency, often favoring genuine connections over superficial interactions. They are adept at navigating digital platforms and prioritize features that promote safety and inclusivity, such as identity verification and anti-harassment tools. Additionally, Gen Z tends to embrace fluidity in relationships, showing openness to diverse sexual orientations and gender identities, which has led to the rise of apps that cater to a broader spectrum of identities. Their strong inclination toward visual content means that platforms emphasizing photos and videos resonate more with them. Overall, Gen Z seeks meaningful interactions that align with their values of social justice, mental health awareness, and a desire for connection in an increasingly digital world.

2. CONCEPTUAL FRAMEWORK OF ONLINE DATING AND RELATIONSHIP FORMATION

Online interactions may be conceptualized on three nodes: Theoretical Foundation which influences user behaviors and preferences, and which further influence relationship outcome.

2.1: Theoretical Foundations: This section includes various theories that inform user behavior and interaction in online dating.

2.2: User Behaviors & Preferences: This node illustrates how the theoretical foundations lead to specific behaviors, such as profile curation and strategies for reducing uncertainty.

2.3: Relationship Outcomes: The final node depicts the potential outcomes of these interactions, including successful matches and the development of long-term relationships.

A brief outline on Theoretical Foundations:

2.1.1 Social Exchange Theory

- Key Contributors: John Thibaut and Harold Kelley
- Foundational Work: In their book *The Social Psychology of Groups* (1959), Thibaut and Kelley introduced concepts of cost-benefit analysis in relationships, emphasizing how individuals seek to maximize rewards while minimizing costs.

2.1.2 Homophily Theory

- Key Contributors: Paul Lazarsfeld and Elihu Katz
- Foundational Work: In their studies on social networks and communication, particularly the concept of "homophily" (the tendency of individuals to associate with similar others), Lazarsfeld and Katz's research laid the groundwork for understanding attraction based on similarity.

2.1.3 Uncertainty Reduction Theory

- Key Contributors: Charles R. Berger and Richard J. Calabrese
- Foundational Work: Their 1975 paper "Some Functions of Communication in Interpersonal Relationships" introduced the framework for understanding how individuals seek to reduce uncertainty in initial interactions.

2.1.4 Self-Presentation Theory

- Key Contributor: Erving Goffman
- Foundational Work: In his seminal book *The Presentation of Self in Everyday Life* (1959), Goffman explored how individuals manage their self-presentation in various social contexts, which is particularly relevant to online dating profiles.

2.1.5 Attachment Theory

- Key Contributor: John Bowlby
- Foundational Work: Bowlby's work, particularly in *Attachment and Loss* (1969), established the framework for understanding how early relationships influence adult attachment styles, impacting dating behaviors and relationship dynamics.

2.1.6 Uses and Gratifications Theory

- Key Contributors: Elihu Katz, Jay Blumler, and Michael Gurevitch
- Foundational Work: Their 1973 article "Uses and Gratifications Research" examined why people actively seek out specific media, which can be applied to understanding motivations behind using dating apps.

2.1.7 Online Disinhibition Effect

- Key Contributor: John Suler
- Foundational Work: In his 2004 article "The Online Disinhibition Effect," Suler discusses how online interactions can lead to more open and candid communication, affecting how individuals present themselves in dating contexts.

2.1.8 Sociotechnical Systems Theory

- Key Contributor: Various, notably influenced by authors like Bruno Latour
- Foundational Work: Latour's *Reassembling the Social* (2005) and other works emphasize the interplay between social dynamics and technology, relevant in understanding online dating behaviors.

2.1.9 Field Theory

- Key Contributor: Pierre Bourdieu
- Foundational Work: Bourdieu's *Distinction: A Social Critique of the Judgment of Taste* (1984) introduced concepts of social fields and capital, useful in analyzing social interactions in online dating.

2.1.10 Dual Process Theory

- Key Contributors: Richard E. Petty and John T. Cacioppo

- Foundational Work: In their book *Communication and Persuasion: Central and Peripheral Routes to Attitude Change* (1986), they outlined how people process information and make decisions, relevant to understanding choices in online dating.

This research findings will try to map the theoretical aspects of online interaction on dating app by GenZ.

3.PROBLEM STATEMENT

The dating apps attract the young generations for different objectives. There is a need to understand these objectives for the reasons for joining the dating apps. Similarly, it is essential to understand the demographic profile as well as their social profile of the users of the dating app. It will also be interesting to know their preferences.

3.1 As per Tinder's Future of Dating 2023 Report

- Today's young adults, forming the majority of users on dating apps like Tinder, prioritize authenticity and self-exploration in their dating lives. They are more open and accepting of diverse gender identities, sexual orientations, and relationship styles compared to previous generations. Committed relationships can take various forms, and casual encounters are seen as a way to explore connections without commitment or shame.
- Despite the emphasis on exploration, a significant portion of Gen Z users (40%) still seek long-term relationships on dating apps. They prioritize getting to know themselves and potential partners, valuing qualities like self-care, intentionality, and transparency. This generation is also more comfortable with awkwardness in their pursuit of genuine connections.
- Interestingly, self-growth and care are their top priorities in dating, with most (80%) prioritizing their own well-being and expecting the same from potential partners. Authenticity is also highly valued, as evidenced by users adding details like multiple photos, interests, descriptions, and bios exceeding a minimum word count. Some even utilize AI tools to create their bios.
- Furthermore, Gen Z prioritizes values like loyalty, respect, and open-mindedness over physical appearance when seeking partners. Additionally, the LGBTQIA+ community has seen a significant growth (30%) on dating platforms, reflecting the increasing inclusivity and acceptance within this generation.

3.2 According to Bumble's 2023 statistics

- Today's dating scene is characterized by a shift in priorities, with emotional maturity (63%) now holding greater importance than physical appearance.
- Additionally, nearly half (49%) of individuals prioritize their work-life balance, and 13% would even refuse to date someone with a very demanding job, reflecting a growing emphasis on personal well-being.
- Furthermore, geographical boundaries seem to be loosening, with one-third (33%) of daters now open to relationships with individuals outside their city. Notably, a significant portion (39%) of Bumble users have recently ended a serious relationship, and 36% of them are new to the dating app scene.
- This suggests that an increasing number of individuals are navigating the landscape of dating after a break-up, highlighting the evolving nature of dating experiences.

4. LITERATURE REVIEW

Dating apps have fundamentally transformed how individuals seek romantic relationships. Emerging in the early 2000s, these platforms have evolved with technology, influencing social interactions and relationship dynamics.

Dating apps began with sites like Match.com and eHarmony, which emphasized detailed profiles and compatibility (Ellison et al., 2006). The introduction of mobile apps like Tinder in 2012 marked a significant shift, favoring simplicity and immediacy with features such as swiping (Sumter et al., 2017). This evolution reflects broader cultural trends toward casual dating and rapid connections.

Research on user behavior indicates varied motivations for engaging with dating apps. Toma and Hancock (2013) found that younger users often pursue casual relationships, while older individuals lean toward long-term commitments. Profiles significantly impact user experience; attractive photos and well-constructed bios increase match rates (Tsai & Lin, 2020). The phenomenon of "paradox of choice" suggests that an overwhelming number of options can lead to decision fatigue (Iyengar & Lepper, 2000).

Dating apps have reshaped social norms around dating. They provide platforms for diverse sexual orientations and preferences, fostering inclusivity (Fox et al., 2016). However, concerns about objectification and superficiality arise, as users may focus on appearance over compatibility (Sprecher & Schwartz, 2021). These dynamics can exacerbate feelings of anxiety and rejection, affecting users' mental health (Bardone-Cone & Cass, 2007).

The psychological impact of dating apps is multifaceted. While some studies suggest that these platforms can enhance self-esteem by facilitating social connections (Gatter & Hodkinson, 2016), others report negative effects, such as increased anxiety and loneliness (Primack et al., 2017). The constant comparison with others on these platforms can contribute to body image issues and dissatisfaction in real-life interactions (Toma & Hancock, 2013).

Gen Zers are very online because they are the first generation of true digital natives. In Asia, Gen Zers are reported to spend six or more hours a day on their phones. They jump between social media feeds, applications, and websites, each of which contributes differently to their online habitat. Gen Z differs from their earlier generations. They are more realistic and combine complex idealism with concerns about the future. Compared to prior generations, their sense of personal expression is stronger, and they have a more individualistic outlook. They use social media to promote their beliefs, making them more politically and socially engaged (McKinsey, 2023).

Gen Z was born into a digital age that can no longer do without an internet connection and various devices. They move around the web like no other group of people and fully integrate their smartphones into their lives. With most of the communication taking place over the Internet, the way people interact and where they look for information is changing in this age group. Real life is increasingly merging with digital life. When it comes to relationships and bonds, Generation Z prefers to remain non-binding. Only your own family and close friends have top priority. Other relationships are mainly maintained digitally and are often short-lived. (Clevis, n.d.)

Online services that provide a platform for their users to flirt, communicate, or fall in love make up the online dating sector. Two prominent instances are Bumble and Tinder. Online dating, as opposed to matchmaking services, emphasizes easy flirtation and casual communication between users. Typically, people conduct their own searches. They can then use search filters based on parameters like age, location, and other characteristics. (Statista, 2023)

The 'Future of Dating Report 2023' offers compelling insights into how online dating has evolved for Generation Z, placing a strong focus on authenticity, inclusivity, and the impact of technology. According to the report, an astonishing 75% of Gen Z individuals believe they are disrupting the traditional norms of dating and relationships that have been handed down to them. (Tinder, 2023)

Close to 80% of Generation Z members express the wish for their prospective partners to value their mental well-being. Intriguingly, approximately 75% of young singles perceive a potential match as more appealing if they are willing to address and prioritize their mental health. (Tinder, 2023)

With a mindset of "take it or leave it," they're prepared to exit any circumstance to stay true to themselves. Tinder's Global Relationship Insights Expert, Paul Brunson, coins this approach as "all or nothing dating." (Tinder, 2023)

From the concept of 'errand dating' to 'stack dating', over half of Generation Z individuals, 51%, expressed their willingness to explore novel methods of integrating dating into their busy daily routines. (Tinder, 2023)

Gen Z daters exhibit honesty, mindfulness, and purposefulness in their approach to dating. They confidently challenge conventional norms and prefer to navigate their romantic journeys according to their own terms and schedules. As they prioritize values in their dating choices, they prioritize self-care, establish boundaries, and strive to present their genuine selves. It's unsurprising that Gen Z places a high value on honesty and transparency about dating intentions, with 52% considering it a top dating indicator. Additionally, 21% view political misalignment as a red flag, and 19% refrain from dating individuals who are not allies of the LGBTQ+ community (Chronicle, 2023).

In contemporary dating norms, Generation Z is increasingly moving away from rigid physical preferences such as the archetype of tall, dark, and handsome individuals. This shift, termed "open casting," denotes a departure from conventional typecasting towards a more inclusive approach to dating. A notable 38% of Gen Z respondents acknowledge the diversity of love, indicating a readiness to pursue relationships outside their customary 'type'. Notably, this trend is more prevalent among women, with 41% in India expressing openness to dating beyond their established preferences, compared to 37% of men (Chronicle, 2023).

For Generation Z, diversity plays a significant role in their lives. Growing up with access to technologies like street view, online video, and virtual reality, they have been able to explore the world effortlessly. This generation is also the most racially and ethnically diverse, as noted by Pew research. It's no surprise then that Gen Z embraces diversity in all its forms, including geographical diversity. A majority of 18- to 24-year-olds, 64%, believe that dating websites and apps enable them to explore a more diverse range of potential partners. Additionally, 65% feel that these platforms allow them to connect with individuals outside of their immediate geographic location (Frantz, 2023).

The rise of online dating apps has transformed traditional approaches to partner selection, particularly among younger generations. Generation Z (Gen Z), typically defined as those born between the mid-1990s and early 2010s, is characterized by their digital nativity and distinct socio-cultural values. This literature review examines how Gen Z is reshaping notions of compatibility and partner selection in the context of online dating.

Gen Z is noted for its diversity, digital fluency, and progressive values. Research indicates that they prioritize authenticity, mental health, and social justice (Twenge, 2019; Pew Research Center, 2020). Their experiences with technology and social media influence their expectations and behaviors in online dating, leading to a unique approach to compatibility and relationship dynamics.

The proliferation of online dating apps has created a vast landscape for romantic connections. Platforms like Tinder, Bumble, and Hinge utilize algorithms and user-generated content to facilitate matches. Previous studies highlight the shift from traditional dating practices to digital platforms, emphasizing the impact of user interface and algorithmic matching on partner selection (Finkel et al., 2012; Whitty, 2021).

Gen Z places significant importance on shared values and beliefs in determining compatibility. Unlike previous generations that may have prioritized physical attraction or socioeconomic status, Gen Z tends to emphasize emotional connection, mental health awareness, and political alignment (Rosenfeld & Thomas, 2012; Gunkel, 2020). This shift suggests a deeper, more holistic approach to assessing potential partners.

Gen Z's comfort with digital communication influences their partner selection. Studies show that they prefer transparent and open communication, often using memes, GIFs, and other digital shorthand to express emotions (Holmes, 2021). This preference for casual yet expressive communication styles may alter traditional courtship rituals, making interactions feel more accessible and less formal.

Social media's pervasive role in shaping Gen Z's social interactions cannot be overstated. Research indicates that platforms like Instagram and TikTok significantly impact perceptions of attractiveness and desirability (De Veirman et al., 2017). Users often curate their profiles to reflect their personalities, interests, and values, which can lead to more intentional partner selection based on perceived authenticity and relatability.

The emphasis on mental health is a defining feature of Gen Z's approach to relationships. Studies indicate that they prioritize partners who demonstrate emotional intelligence and supportiveness (Woods, 2020). This focus reflects a broader societal shift toward valuing mental health, suggesting that compatibility assessments may include considerations of emotional well-being and support systems.

Gen Z is acutely aware of privacy and safety issues associated with online dating. Research shows they often engage in due diligence before meeting potential partners, leveraging technology to verify identities and assess compatibility (Gibbs et al., 2011). This heightened awareness shapes their partner selection process, as they seek not only romantic connection but also security and trust.

Research was conducted by a dating app QuackQuack in which around 10,000 users participated between the ages of 18-35, both working professionals and students from Tier 1 and Tier 2 cities of India. The findings indicate that Gen Z daters are more likely than Millennials to engage in slow dating, which is defined as taking your sweet time to make an informed decision. Nearly 34% of Gen Z daters first connect with their match on various social media sites before ever meeting them in person. Approximately 31% of individuals in the 18–22 age range are experimenting with speed dating. According to poll responses, Gen Z daters would rather converse with several people at once. It was shown that while 32% of Millennial daters find the trend completely childish and disrespectful, 23% of Gen Z from Tier 1 and Tier 2 cities regard ghosting to be far less insulting. While millennials believe that individuals should take responsibility for their actions and have the guts to admit when something isn't working out, Gen Z daters believe that it's best to steer clear of uncomfortable conversations (Times, 2023).

Online daters have reported that using dating apps can feel like a part-time job, as they must meticulously select their own resume and go through numerous others, vetting each one first through text message or phone conversation before moving on to the next applicant's submissions. While 40% of Gen Z express a desire to pursue lifelong partnerships akin to penguins, about 20% of individuals in my generation prefer a more detached approach to dating, resembling the behavior of cats—indifferent and open to partners entering and leaving their lives. This inclination is partly attributed to the fact that many within Gen Z enjoy the freedom of singlehood, although they are often perceived as selective. However, the prevalence of online dating platforms and the repetitive nature of swiping through potential matches contribute to what's known as "swipe fatigue" or choice paralysis in the dating realm. In today's world, the abundance of options and the ease of connecting with others online offer both promise and challenge, presenting individuals with unlimited freedom but also overwhelming decision-making. (Yaseen, 2023).

Generation Z welcomes the use of dating apps and technology but stresses the importance of genuine and authentic interactions. While AI can aid in constructing dating profiles and serve as a "digital wingman" for initiating conversations, profiles that come across as generic and lacking authenticity are generally not favored. According to the report, 34% of individuals are open to utilizing AI to assist in constructing their dating profiles. This is attributed to the pressure associated with crafting a bio or selecting photos that accurately reflect one's personality. (Tinder, 2023)

5.OBJECTIVES FOR THE STUDY

1. To explore the dating culture, preferences, and relationship behaviors among Gen Z users.
2. To identify the common themes and content Gen Z users share across different sections of their profiles.
3. To examine the role of demographic factors in shaping dating preferences and behaviors among Gen Z.

6. RESEARCH METHODOLOGY

6.1 Research Design

This research employs a quantitative cross-sectional design to explore dating culture, preferences, and relationship status among Gen Z users of OKCupid, a prominent online dating platform. The focus of the study is to uncover patterns in demographic factors, sexual orientation, relationship status, and sentiments expressed in users' profiles. By examining a broad range of variables through statistical techniques, the study aims to provide a comprehensive understanding of how Gen Z engages with online dating, the relationship preferences they exhibit, and the emotional tone they use in self-descriptions.

6.2 Dataset and Data Collection

The dataset used for this analysis was sourced from Kaggle (OKCupid Profiles Dataset), containing information about users on OKCupid, an international online dating platform. The dataset includes demographic details, sexual orientation, relationship status, and open-text fields (e.g., profile essays) written by the users. The dataset spans a wide range of variables but was filtered to focus specifically on Gen Z users (individuals aged 12-26) for this research, providing a contemporary snapshot of their dating behaviors and attitudes.

Data cleaning and filtering were conducted to retain only relevant variables and rows. Rows with more than 30% missing data were removed, and categorical variables such as gender, sexual orientation, and relationship status were encoded for statistical analysis.

6.3 Sample Selection

From the original dataset, users aged between 12 and 26 years were selected, aligning with the age range for Gen Z (born between 1997 and 2012). After filtering, the dataset consisted of 18,178 Gen Z profiles. Key demographic variables considered included gender, sexual orientation, and relationship status. Additionally, the dataset contained users' self-descriptions in text format, providing a rich source for sentiment analysis.

The sample distribution was as follows:

- Gender: 10,932 male users, 7,046 female users.
- Sexual Orientation: 14,000+ straight users, with smaller representation of bisexual and gay users.
- Relationship Status: Predominantly single users, with smaller groups indicating "seeing someone," "available," or "married" status.

7. DATA ANALYSIS AND INTERPRETATION

A range of statistical techniques and data visualization methods were employed to analyze the dataset. The analyses were carried out in Python using libraries such as Pandas, Seaborn, and Matplotlib for data manipulation and visualization. Sentiment analysis was conducted using TextBlob, and categorical variables were analyzed using cross-tabulation and the Chi-square test. The detailed steps include:

7.1 Descriptive Analysis:

Age, gender, and orientation distribution were explored using histograms and count plots to understand the demographic composition of Gen Z users on OKCupid.

Figure 1. Age distribution of GenZ

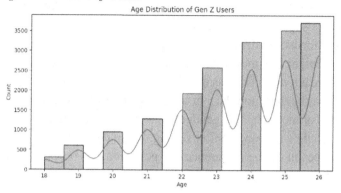

The figure shows that there is a clear increase in the number of users as they approach their mid-twenties. The highest concentration is seen among users aged 25 and 26, followed by those aged 24 and 23. The lower age groups (18-20) have fewer users on the platform. This suggests that younger members of Gen Z might either be less interested in dating platforms or are more likely to use other social media or dating methods.

OKCupid seems more popular among users in their early to mid-20s. This could be related to life stage factors, such as entering adulthood, seeking stable relationships, or exploring dating apps. The dating culture within Gen Z may lean more toward individuals in their mid-20s, who are likely more independent, settled, and focused on building relationships.

Figure 2. Gender distribution of Gen Z users

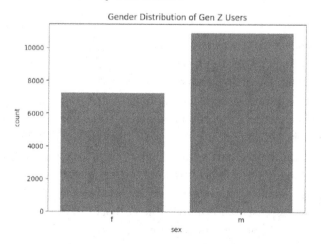

The figure shows a notable gender imbalance, with significantly more male users (m) than female users (f). The count of male users is over 10,000, while the count of female users is slightly above 7,000.

In dating platforms, gender imbalances can affect the overall user experience. In this case, males might face more competition when seeking matches, while females may receive more attention or messages. The higher number of male users suggests that OKCupid may be more popular among males, or females might prefer alternative dating platforms or methods. The gender disparity could reflect broader patterns in how different genders approach online dating. It could be useful to explore if there are any differences in dating preferences, expectations, or behaviors based on this gender imbalance.

Figure 3. Sexual orientation of Gen Z users

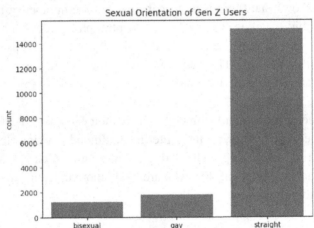

The figure shows that there is an overwhelming majority of Gen Z users on OKCupid are 'straight'. This group represents over 14,000 users, making it by far the largest segment. There are relatively smaller groups of users who identify as bisexual or gay, with both groups having under 2,000 users each. Bisexual users make up a slightly smaller proportion compared to gay users.

The high number of straight users suggests that OKCupid may be more popular among heterosexual individuals within Gen Z, or that dating culture among this generation still largely reflects heterosexual norms. The presence of bisexual and gay users, though smaller, shows some degree of diversity in sexual orientation. However, the lower representation might indicate that LGBTQ+ users either gravitate toward other platforms or that OKCupid has limited appeal for non-heterosexual individuals. OKCupid could potentially enhance features or marketing to appeal more to bisexual and gay communities, as these groups are currently underrepresented.

Figure 4. Relationship status of Gen Z users

The figure shows that there is an overwhelming majority of Gen Z users on OKCupid are "single" with over 16,000 users reporting this status. This is expected for a dating platform where people are primarily looking to meet new potential partners. A small number of users report being "seeing someone" or "available". The number of married users is very low, which is consistent with the fact that OKCupid primarily targets individuals seeking dating relationships. "Unknown" status represents users whose relationship status might not be specified.

OKCupid as a Platform for Singles: The overwhelming number of singles suggests that OKCupid is heavily used by Gen Z individuals looking for new relationships. This confirms that the platform is aligned with its core purpose as a dating site. Non-Single Users: The small percentage of users who are married or "seeing someone" may indicate individuals exploring different types of relationship dynamics (e.g., polyamory, open relationships), although their representation is minimal. Relationship Exploration in Gen Z: This finding suggests that a significant portion of Gen Z users are currently unattached and actively exploring their options through online platforms.

7.2 Chi-Square Test of Independence: Gender vs. Relationship Status

To examine the relationship between gender and relationship status, a cross-tabulation was conducted, followed by a Chi-square test of independence to determine if gender significantly affects relationship status.

Table 3. Chi-square test result

status	female (f)	male (m)
available	173	221
married	20	14
seeing someone	462	310
single	6589	10387
unknown	2	0
Chi-square Test Statistic		147.1834
P-value		8.17E-31
Degrees of Freedom		4

Figure 5. Gender vs relationship status

The Chi-square test yielded a test statistic of 147.18 with a p-value of 8.17e-31, indicating that the relationship between gender and relationship status is statistically significant. This suggests that gender does influence relationship status among Gen Z users on OKCupid.

Males are more likely to report being "available" or "seeing someone" compared to females, who overwhelmingly report being single. This gender difference may reflect societal expectations or differing relationship strategies between males and females.

The corresponding heatmap visualization reinforces this finding, with higher concentrations of male users reporting non-single statuses and female users more likely to report being single.

7.3 Sentiment Analysis of Profile Essays

Text data from users' profile descriptions were analyzed to extract sentiment polarity, ranging from -1 (negative) to 1 (positive), to gauge the emotional tone users employ when discussing themselves and their dating preferences.

Table 4. Sentiment analysis of user profile essays

Metric	Value
Count	18,178
Mean	0.1596
Standard Deviation (std)	0.1875
Minimum	-1
25th Percentile (Q1)	0.0259
50th Percentile (Median)	0.1722
75th Percentile (Q3)	0.275
Maximum	1

Figure 6. Sentiment polarity in profile essays

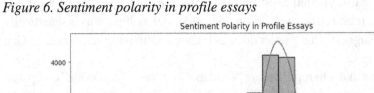

Sentiment analysis revealed a generally positive emotional tone in users' profile descriptions. The mean sentiment score was 0.16, with most users falling between neutral and slightly positive. This suggests that users approach their profiles with an optimistic or hopeful attitude toward dating.

- **Positive Sentiment**: Most users express optimism or confidence in their profiles, with few users exhibiting extreme positivity (above 0.5). This might reflect a cautious or balanced approach to presenting oneself in an online dating context.
- **Negative Sentiment**: A small portion of users display negative sentiment, indicating dissatisfaction or frustration with dating. This group, though minor, could be an interesting area for further study, possibly linked to unsuccessful dating experiences or negative societal views of online dating.

7.4 Identification of Common Themes from User Profile Essays

In this study, based on the sentiment analysis data and access to user profile essays, various text analysis methods are employed to gain a deeper understanding of how Gen Z discusses dating and presents themselves on OKCupid. Through the application of text analysis, key themes, attitudes, and trends in user behavior are uncovered, providing insights into how individuals communicate their personalities and dating preferences. By exploring sentiment, word usage, and thematic content, the analysis aims to reveal patterns in the way these users describe themselves and interact across different sections of their profiles.

A particular focus is placed on examining how the content differs across the various essay sections (from essay0 to essay9), as each section may serve a distinct purpose in the overall profile. Comparing these essays enables a better understanding of how users express different aspects of their identities across multiple sections. The analysis follows several key steps, including preprocessing the essays to extract meaningful data, conducting word frequency analysis to identify common topics, and utilizing Latent Dirichlet Allocation (LDA) for topic modeling. These techniques facilitate the identification of hidden themes within the text, and through careful interpretation, the dominant topics that users discuss throughout their profiles are uncovered. This process provides valuable insights into how Gen Z users curate their online dating personas.

The findings presented in the table represents the application of Latent Dirichlet Allocation (LDA), a popular topic modeling technique, on the profile essays (essay0 to essay9) from OKCupid users. Each essay in the dataset addresses different sections of users' profiles to analyze the most common themes and content users share across different parts of their profiles. By identifying the top words for each topic across essays, we can infer the various aspects of life, personality, and preferences that Gen Z users emphasize in their online dating profiles.

7.4.1 Essay 0 (Introduction / Overview)

Essay 0, which is likely the introductory section, contains topics that primarily revolve around users' personal backgrounds and general interests. One of the dominant themes involves users talking about their school years, where they grew up, and their current location, often in relation to the San Francisco Bay Area. This topic also reflects their enjoyment of life and personal passions such as music, games, or social interactions. Users often highlight what they enjoy doing in their free time and what makes them unique, suggesting a strong focus on creating a positive first impression. Several topics in this essay also emphasize social connections and outlook on life, with words like "friends," "fun," and "meet," pointing to an emphasis on social engagement.

7.4.2 Essay 1 (Job and Life Goals)

Moving on to Essay 1, the focus shifts towards users' jobs and life goals. Many users describe their professional lives, detailing their current jobs, future ambitions, and how they manage their work-life balance. This essay often reflects users' careers, whether they are currently studying, recently graduated, or pursuing specific career goals. Other topics in this essay touch on learning, hobbies, and skills, with frequent mentions of activities like playing music, writing, and ongoing professional development. Users also tend to discuss their educational background in this section, highlighting their college experiences, degrees, and how their education aligns with their personal and professional objectives.

7.4.3 Essay 2 (Leisure and Fun Activities)

In Essay 2, the themes shift to users' leisure and fun activities. This section is much more light-hearted, focusing on fun activities such as cooking, playing games, listening to music, and enjoying time with friends. The dominant sentiment here is one of enjoyment and leisure, reflecting users' desire to connect over shared hobbies. Words like "laugh," "fun," and "cooking" dominate the topics in this essay, suggesting that users are eager to showcase how they unwind and what activities they enjoy the most. This essay gives a sense of who the users are in their downtime, offering potential matches a glimpse into how they might spend their time together.

7.4.4 Essay 3 (Physical Appearance and Personality)

Essay 3 introduces discussions around physical appearance and personality traits. This essay allows users to describe how they view themselves and how others perceive them. Common words include descriptions of height, hair color, and other physical features such as wearing glasses. This essay also reveals a focus on users' sense of humor, with frequent mentions of laughter, smiles, and personality. In essence, users in this section are showcasing their self-perceptions and attempting to attract others who appreciate these physical traits and personality quirks. This essay likely serves as a way for users to create a visual or personal image in the minds of potential matches.

7.4.5 Essay 4 (Favorites and Cultural Interests)

In Essay 4, the focus shifts to cultural interests and preferences. Here, users talk about their favorite books, movies, music, and other forms of entertainment, allowing potential matches to gain insights into their cultural tastes. There are references to specific figures, such as "John" and "David," suggesting that users frequently mention their favorite artists, authors, or cultural figures to convey their preferences. This section is particularly useful for those looking for matches with shared interests, as it reflects a key component of how people often bond over shared entertainment.

7.4.6 Essay 5 (Essentials and Material Comforts)

Essay 5 presents a theme around material possessions and comforts. Words like "car," "coffee," "internet," and "phone" highlight users' attachment to specific material items, suggesting that they view these objects as essential to their daily lives. This essay might reflect users' desire for comfort and stability, while also providing a glimpse into their lifestyle choices. At the same time, this section includes discussions around personal relationships, with mentions of friends, family, and everyday items that bring them joy and security. The frequent mention of coffee and technology suggests the influence of modern conveniences in shaping users' lifestyles.

7.4.7 Essay 6 (Future and Philosophies)

Essay 6 delves into users' philosophies on life and future aspirations. This essay provides a more reflective tone, as users talk about adventures they wish to have, their thoughts on society and gender, and their dreams for the future. There are also mentions of art and human connections, which may indicate a more intellectual or philosophical approach to self-presentation. Users use this essay to discuss deeper values and to reflect on how they want to contribute to society or live fulfilling lives, offering a window into their long-term goals and worldview.

7.4.8 Essay 7 (Typical Weekend / Free Time)

In Essay 7, the topics shift to users' weekend routines and social activities. Users frequently mention activities like going to bars, having drinks, and hanging out with friends. This essay gives a strong sense of how users spend their free time and what kind of social environment they thrive in. Words like "exploring," "city," and "Friday night" suggest that users are looking for matches who share similar social behaviors, whether that be enjoying a night out on the town or staying in for a movie.

7.4.9 Essay 8 (Private Life and Preferences)

Essay 8 tends to cover more personal and private aspects of users' lives. This essay includes discussions around dating preferences, personal boundaries, and intimate thoughts. Words like "private," "ask," and "tell" indicate that users are willing to share more personal details but only with the right person, showing a balance between openness and discretion. This essay often acts as a teaser, where users invite potential matches to ask further questions to get to know them on a deeper level.

7.4.10 Essay 9 (Message and Social Interaction)

Finally, Essay 9 focuses on how users communicate and interact. The topics here suggest that users are providing hints about what they expect from conversations or messaging with potential matches. Words like "conversation," "laugh," "fun," and "meet" show that users value good communication and are looking for engaging, fun conversations with potential partners. This essay likely emphasizes users' communication preferences and their social interaction styles, offering potential matches insights into how they might connect on a conversational level.

Table 5. Top words for each user profile essays

Top words for each topic in essay0:   Topic 1:   ive - like - school - years - san - enjoy - bay - time - love - im   Topic 2:   games - think - really - dont - music - people - things - love - im - like   Topic 3:   good - really - life - people - know - dont - love - just - like - im   Topic 4:   friends - fun - looking - meet - like - just - love - people - im - new   Topic 5:   love - world - words - time - good - im - like - things - people - life
Top words for each topic in essay1:   Topic 1:   just - job - trying - time - life - new - love - working - work - im   Topic 2:   lot - playing - learning - writing - love - making - working - time - music - im   Topic 3:   job - school - company - currently - francisco - time - san - im - work - working   Topic 4:   want - degree - trying - college - life - going - currently - working - im - school   Topic 5:   trying - really - time - know - school - dont - life - just - like - im
Top words for each topic in essay2:   Topic 1:   fun - taking - laughing - things - having - cooking - listening - laugh - people - making   Topic 2:   think - just - dont - know - things - pretty - really - like - good - im   Topic 3:   pretty - cooking - finding - stuff - getting - words - things - really - im - good   Topic 4:   video - remembering - getting - listening - random - people - games - cooking - things - making   Topic 5:   dancing - playing - music - life - love - people - new - good - im - things

continued on following page

Table 5. Continued

Top words for each topic in essay3: Topic 1: probably - look - really - long - notice - tell - know - people - dont - hair Topic 2: just - wearing - glasses - wear - asian - people - usually - like - tall - im Topic 3: height - lot - big - laugh - blue - personality - sense - humor - smile - eyes Topic 4: say - usually - really - look - dont - notice - think - like - people - im Topic 5: pretty - loud - tall - sure - laugh - really - told - height - ive - im
Top words for each topic in essay4: Topic 1: men - new - life - love - john - david - movies - food - books - music Topic 2: family - im - shows - like - books - favorite - music - food - movies - love Topic 3: dont - read - really - books - movies - love - im - food - music - like Topic 4: fight - star - game - club - shows - food - dead - books - music - movies Topic 5: books - man - tribe - john - called - bob - boys - food - music - black
Top words for each topic in essay5: Topic 1: life - think - love - need - just - really - dont - like - im - things Topic 2: car - internet - computer - good - water - phone - music - food - family - friends Topic 3: ice - im - love - new - family - coffee - music - people - friends - good Topic 4: hands - ones - socks - cheese - coffee - tea - water - music - pen - paper Topic 5: love - iphone - coffee - laughter - books - food - good - music - family - friends
Top words for each topic in essay6: Topic 1: make - adventure - eat - whats - doing - want - future - im - going - life Topic 2: gender - society - make - im - live - art - human - music - sex - people Topic 3: life - future - travel - things - food - lot - spend - want - thinking - time Topic 4: really - dont - thinking - lot - people - just - things - like - im - think Topic 5: friends - work - family - life - better - things - make - world - people - future

continued on following page

Table 5. Continued

Top words for each topic in essay7: Topic 1: thing - city - san - exploring - friends - trying - typical - night - doing - friday Topic 2: getting - night - drinks - movie - home - week - dinner - work - going - friends Topic 3: life - music - bar - watching - getting - playing - eating - dancing - friends - drinking Topic 4: nights - just - people - friends - new - usually - like - night - friday - im Topic 5: bar - good - playing - working - having - movie - home - watching - hanging - friends
Top words for each topic in essay8: Topic 1: like - open - ill - tell - private - just - dont - know - ask - im Topic 2: thats - know - dont - dating - lol - people - private - like - really - im Topic 3: day - dance - think - im - love - sing - dont - ive - really - like Topic 4: dont - ive - sleep - im - movies - year - night - like - time - love Topic 5: hate - sleep - think - time - like - people - love - ive - life - just
Top words for each topic in essay9: Topic 1: conversation - going - feel - good - enjoy - love - laugh - youre - fun - like Topic 2: want - people - time - interested - like - know - good - think - new - youre Topic 3: life - dont - profile - youve - good - read - love - humor - sense - like Topic 4: chat - interesting - meet - wanna - like - hang - just - talk - know - want Topic 5: people - know - think - looking - like - just - message - youre - im – don't

8. DISCUSSION AND IMPLICATIONS

The findings from this study provide a deep understanding of how Gen Z users engage with online dating platforms like OKCupid. The analysis revealed several key insights into the demographic composition of users, their relationship status, sexual orientation, and the emotional tone they employ in their profile essays. One of the most prominent findings is the gender imbalance on OKCupid, with a significantly higher number of male users than female users. This imbalance can potentially influence dating dynamics on the platform, leading to increased competition among male users, while female users may receive more attention, creating an uneven user experience.

The relationship status analysis shows that the overwhelming majority of Gen Z users on OKCupid identify as single, which aligns with the platform's primary purpose of connecting individuals seeking relationships. Interestingly, a small group of users reported being married or in a committed relationship, suggesting the potential for alternative relationship dynamics, such as open relationships or polyamory, within the Gen Z cohort. This finding aligns with broader trends in modern dating, where non-traditional relationships are becoming more accepted and explored, particularly among younger generations.

The sentiment analysis of user essays revealed that most users express positive or neutral sentiment in their profiles, which indicates that Gen Z users tend to maintain an optimistic tone when presenting themselves to potential matches. This positive outlook may reflect their general optimism about finding meaningful connections through online dating platforms. However, a small group of users exhibited negative sentiment, possibly indicating disillusionment with the dating process or frustration with previous experiences on the platform. This variation in sentiment provides insight into the emotional landscape of Gen Z users as they navigate online dating.

The text analysis of the essay sections revealed several common themes across user profiles. The introductory section (essay0) typically focuses on personal background, including education, location, and general interests, which helps users create a strong first impression. Other essays, such as essay1 and essay2, shift toward professional goals and leisure activities, reflecting a balance between work, personal development, and hobbies. In contrast, essay3 and essay4 emphasize physical appearance and cultural preferences, allowing users to showcase their personality traits and favorite pastimes. The thematic consistency across essays demonstrates how users strategically present different aspects of themselves to appeal to potential partners.

These findings have significant implications for online dating platforms. Understanding the sentiment trends and themes prevalent in Gen Z profiles can help dating platforms tailor their features to better meet the needs of younger users. For instance, OKCupid and similar platforms could use this information to enhance profile suggestions based on shared interests, values, or sentiment alignment, leading to more meaningful connections. Additionally, the gender imbalance observed in this study could prompt platforms to implement measures that encourage a more balanced user experience, such as gender-targeted marketing or improved matching algorithms that consider gender ratios.

The research finding that "users approach their profiles with an optimistic or hopeful attitude toward dating has implication for the counsellors. Counsellors can guide clients in setting realistic expectations about online dating. While optimism is beneficial, it's essential to prepare users for the potential ups and downs of the dating journey. They can also encourage clients to reflect on their motivations for dating the sources of their optimism, fostering a deeper understanding of their relationship goals and desires.

The research findings have implications for the educators as well. They can create digital literacy programs that teach young people the dynamics of online dating, highlighting the importance of a balanced perspective by recognizing both its advantages and potential drawbacks. Curriculum can have a component on how to maintain a healthy relationship so that student can have a positive approach towards the dating app. Similarly, the students should be taught about emotional intelligence so that they can create an authentic profile which can capture their true identities. However, issue of data privacy may discourage the students to create a true profile in the dating app.

The major finding from text analysis that GenZs approach their profiles with an optimistic or hopeful attitude toward dating has supported the social exchange theory, uncertainty reduction theory, uses and gratification theory and finally self-presentation theory. However, this finding has challenged theories like attachment theory. While an optimistic attitude of GenZ might suggest secure attachment styles, it could also mask underlying anxieties. Similarly, the gap between online optimism and offline experiences may lead to frustration, questioning the stability of the disinhibition effect-propounded by Online Disinhibition Effect theory. Lastly, the finding of the research also challenges the field theory. The optimism may not be universally experienced; users from different social or cultural backgrounds might approach dating with varying degrees of hope based on their past experiences and social capital.

9. CONCLUSION

This study provides a comprehensive analysis of how Gen Z users present themselves on OKCupid, revealing key patterns in demographics, relationship status, and sentiment across profile sections. The study highlights the importance of self-expression through profile essays, where users balance personal traits, professional aspirations, and social interactions. The insights gained from this research contribute to our understanding of how younger generations approach dating in the digital age and provide valuable guidance for dating platforms seeking to optimize their services for Gen Z users.

In conclusion, the study finds that gender imbalances, relationship preferences, and positive sentiment play significant roles in shaping the user experience on OKCupid. Furthermore, users tend to strategically present different facets of their personality across essays, reflecting their unique values and preferences. Future research could explore how dating behaviors evolve over time or examine cross-platform comparisons to see if similar trends are observed on other popular dating platforms. Additionally, platforms could experiment with customized features that better align with users' values, such as prioritizing mental health or promoting inclusivity, which are important to Gen Z.

10. LIMITATIONS OF THE STUDY

While this study provides valuable insights into the dating behaviors of Gen Z on OKCupid, there are several limitations that should be acknowledged. First, the dataset used for analysis was limited to OKCupid users, which may not fully represent the dating behaviors of Gen Z across other platforms such as Tinder or Bumble. Different platforms attract different types of users, and preferences or behaviors may vary accordingly. Second, the study focused primarily on users who provided essay responses, excluding those who may not have completed this portion of their profile. This selection bias could skew the results toward more expressive users, leaving out potential insights from more reticent users.

Another limitation is the language-based sentiment analysis, which may not fully capture the complexity of emotions expressed in the essays. Sentiment analysis tools like TextBlob are based on keyword analysis and can sometimes misinterpret context, irony, or sarcasm, potentially leading to less accurate sentiment scores. Lastly, the dataset represents a snapshot in time, and user behaviors or dating trends may change over time, especially as new features or dating platforms emerge.

11. FUTURE DIRECTIONS OF THE STUDY

Given the findings and limitations, several avenues for future research could provide further insights into Gen Z's dating behaviours. One potential direction is to compare dating preferences across multiple platforms, such as Tinder, Bumble, and Hinge, to see if the trends observed on OKCupid hold true across other apps. The study should also consider the cultural and geographic diversities. Additionally, researchers could explore how dating app usage evolves as Gen Z transitions into different life stages, such as entering the workforce or pursuing long-term relationships.

Further research could also investigate the influence of platform design on user experience, examining how features like swiping, algorithmic matching, and communication tools shape user behaviour. Finally, a more qualitative approach involving interviews with Gen Z users could provide deeper insights into the motivations behind their dating behaviors and preferences, offering a richer understanding of the complexities of online dating for younger generations.

REFERENCES

Bardone-Cone, A. M., & Cass, K. A. (2007). The impact of media exposure on body image and eating disorders. *Eating Disorders*, 15(2), 153–164. PMID: 17454074

Berger, C. R., & Calabrese, R. J. (1975). "Some Functions of Communication in Interpersonal Relationships." Theories of Interpersonal Communication.

Bourdieu, P. (1984). *Distinction: A Social Critique of the Judgment of Taste*. Harvard University Press.

Bowlby, J. (1969). Attachment and Loss: Vol. I. *Attachment*. Basic Books.

Chronicle, D.(2023, September1). How does social media and its trends imoact gen z dating ideals. Retrieved February 19, 2024, from DeccanChronicle:[1] National Association of Software Companies.It is the software sector association in India

De Veirman, M., Cauberghe, V., & Hudders, L. (2017). Marketing through Instagram influencers: The impact of influencer marketing on consumer behavior. *International Journal of Advertising*.

Ellison, N. B., Heino, R. D., & Gibbs, J. (2006). Managing impressions online: Self-presentation processes in the online dating environment. *Journal of Computer-Mediated Communication*, 11(2), 415–441. DOI: 10.1111/j.1083-6101.2006.00020.x

Finkel, E. J., Eastwick, P. W., Karney, B. R., Reis, H. T., & Sprecher, S. (2012). Online dating: A critical analysis from the perspective of psychological science. *Psychological Science in the Public Interest*, 13(1), 3–66. DOI: 10.1177/1529100612436522 PMID: 26173279

Fox, J., Bailenson, J. N., & Tricase, L. (2016). The effect of online dating on sexual orientation and relationship quality. *Journal of Social and Personal Relationships*, 33(3), 452–470.

Frantz, P. (2023, February 10). App Marketing: Dating Trends. Retrieved February 21, 2024, from Think with Google: https://www.thinkwithgoogle.com/future-of- marketing/management-and-culture/diversity-and-inclusion/app-marketing-dating-trends/

Gatter, K. A., & Hodkinson, A. (2016). The effect of online dating on self-esteem and social anxiety. *Cyberpsychology, Behavior, and Social Networking*, 19(10), 657–662.

Gibbs, J. L.. (2011). *Online dating: The relationship between the internet and the dating process*. New Directions in Psychology.

Goffman, E. (1959). *The Presentation of Self in Everyday Life*. University of Edinburgh Press.

Gonzalez, C.. (2020). Online dating during the COVID-19 pandemic: The role of social media in relationship development. *The Journal of Social Issues*, 76(4), 964–986.

Gunkel, L. (2020). Dating apps and the emergence of new romantic norms: A qualitative study. *Journal of Social and Personal Relationships*.

Holmes, R. (2021). The impact of digital communication on romantic relationships in Gen Z. *Journal of Youth Studies*.

https://www.deccanchronicle.com/lifestyle/sex-and-relationship/010923/how-does-social- media-and-its-trends-impact-genz-dating-ideals.html

Iyengar, S. S., & Lepper, M. R. (2000). When choice is demotivating: Can one desire too much of a good thing? *Journal of Personality and Social Psychology*, 79(6), 995–1006. DOI: 10.1037/0022-3514.79.6.995 PMID: 11138768

Katz, E., Blumler, J. G., & Gurevitch, M. (1973). Uses and Gratifications Research. *Public Opinion Quarterly*, 37(4), 509–523. DOI: 10.1086/268109

Latour, B. (2005). *Reassembling the Social: An Introduction to Actor-Network-Theory*. Oxford University Press. DOI: 10.1093/oso/9780199256044.001.0001

McKinsey. (2023, March 20). Mc Kinsey Explainers. Retrieved February 28, 2024, from Mc Kinsey: https://www.mckinsey.com/featured-insights/mckinsey-explainers/what-is- gen-z

McPherson, M., Smith-Lovin, L., & Cook, J. M. (2001). Birds of a Feather: Homophily in Social Networks. *Annual Review of Sociology*, 27(1), 415–444. DOI: 10.1146/annurev.soc.27.1.415

Petty, R. E., & Cacioppo, J. T. (1986). *Communication and Persuasion: Central and Peripheral Routes to Attitude Change*. Springer-Verlag. DOI: 10.1007/978-1-4612-4964-1

Pew Research Center. (2020). "The state of dating in 2020."

Primack, B. A.. (2017). Use of multiple social media platforms and symptoms of depression and anxiety: A nationally-representative study among U.S. young adults. *Depression and Anxiety*, 34(11), 1094–1100.

Rosenfeld, M. J., & Thomas, R. J. (2012). Searching for a mate: The rise of the Internet as a social intermediary. *American Sociological Review*, 77(4), 523–547. DOI: 10.1177/0003122412448050

Sprecher, S., & Schwartz, P. (2021). The role of dating apps in modern relationships: A critical review. *Journal of Social and Personal Relationships*, 38(2), 453–470.

Statista. (2023, February 11). Online dating: Worldwide Statistics. Retrieved February 27, 2024, from Dating services: https://www.statista.com/outlook/dmo/eservices/dating- services/online-dating/worldwide

Suler, J. (2004). The Online Disinhibition Effect. *Cyberpsychology & Behavior*, 7(3), 321–326. DOI: 10.1089/1094931041291295 PMID: 15257832

Sumter, S. R., Vandenbosch, L., & Ligtenberg, L. (2017). The role of mobile dating apps in the dating process. *Computers in Human Behavior*, 66, 86–92.

Thibaut, J. W., & Kelley, H. H. (1959). *The Social Psychology of Groups*. Wiley.

Times, E. (2023, February 10). Dating patterns of 2023: Millenials and Gen Z. Retrieved February 24, 2024, from Economic Times: https://economictimes .indiatimes.com/magazines/panache/dating-patterns-of-2023- millennials-find-ghosting-immature-genz-wants-to-explore-before-getting-serious- reveals-study/articleshow/98181137.cms?from=mdr

Tinder. (2023, May 21). Welcome to a renaissance in dating driven by authenticity. Retrieved February 24, 2024, from Tinder News Room: https://www.tinderpressroom .com/2023-05-22-WELCOME-TO-A-RENAISSANCE-IN- DATING,-DRIVEN-BY-AUTHENTICITY

Toma, C. L., & Hancock, J. (2013). What's in a picture? Photographic, and emotional cues in online dating. *Computers in Human Behavior*, 29(1), 16–22.

Tsai, W. H. S., & Lin, Y. H. (2020). Online dating behavior: The effect of physical appearance, profile information, and relationship expectations. *International Journal of Human-Computer Interaction*, 36(4), 388–399.

Twenge, J. M. (2019). iGen: Why Today's Super-Connected Kids Are Growing Up Less Rebellious, More Tolerant, Less Happy—And Completely Unprepared for Adulthood.

Whitty, M. (2021). The online dating revolution: What psychology tells us. *Psychology Today*.

Woods, R. (2020). "Understanding the role of emotional intelligence in dating among Gen Z." Journal of Emotional Intelligence.

Yaseen, R. (2023, June 29). Post Grad Gen Z online daing drwbacks. Retrieved February 24, 2024, from Washington Post: https://www.washingtonpost.com/opinions/2023/06/29/post-grad-gen-z-online-dating- drawbacks

Chapter 15
An Analysis of Strategic Management Factors for Banking Industry in Jharkhand

P. Kritee Rao

https://orcid.org/0000-0002-3531-5913

National Institute of Technology, Jamshedpur, India

Akanksha Shukla

National Institute of Technology, Jamshedpur, India

ABSTRACT

Strategic Management assists in optimization of business resources. It is a long term plan that is thought and executed at higher levels of an organization to derive striving and sustainable outcome. It is vital to manage the finances, especially for a developing economy. There is dearth of research in this context, especially for the state of Jharkhand. Considering this, the study analyses the factors of strategic management for higher level of authorities of the banking industry in Jharkhand. The banking industry of this state is often called as economically and strategically less-developed regarding the financial inclusion. Hence, this paper identifies the factors for strategic management in banking industry and prioritizes them based on a weightage determination method Logarithmic Percentage Change-driven Objective Weighting (LOPCOW). The analysis results staff development as the foremost factor for strategic management, followed by staff retention and team orientation. The factor technological superiority have been ranked the lowest.

DOI: 10.4018/979-8-3693-5563-3.ch015

INTRODUCTION

The word 'strategy' was introduced in the year 1960 from the ancient word *strategos*. This signifies a planning to destroy the opponents by using the resources effectively. Strategy embodies the combined assortment of the product to be launched and the market in which an organization would compete (Rumelt et al., 1991). The key to strategy is in the actions: deciding which actions to take in a different way than competitors. The development of a distinct and advantageous position through a variety of actions is known as strategy. Strategy wouldn't be necessary if there was just one perfect position. Businesses would only need to focus on winning the race to identify and anticipate it. The key to strategic positioning is to select actions that set you apart from your competitors (Porter, 1996). Philosophy matters in the experiential domain of strategy, and strategy research is starting to acknowledge this relationship. But there's still a lot of work to be done. Even in cases where it is obviously useful, philosophy has been sluggish to penetrate strategy research outside of ethics and philosophy of science (Powell, 2002). Clearly, creating a strategic plan requires a considerable bit of strategic thought, and once it is created, achieving its objectives requires a tremendous degree of strategic management (Nickols, 2016).

The idea of strategy has seen multiple phases and interpretations before developing into the discipline of strategic management, which is a branch of management knowledge with its own concepts, content, and application in the commercial and academic spheres (Wagner Mainardes et al., 2014). Strategic management involves accurately determining the availability and caliber of resources as well as creating product-market positioning and agreements that make the best use, preservation, and expansion of these resources possible (Rumelt et al., 1991). The development and implementation of strategies in strategic management are driven by the alignment or fit between the external and internal environments. Being a relatively new field, strategic management lacks a cohesive theory to underpin its expanding use. The process of creating and implementing strategy, which serves as an operational manual for the company, is at the heart of strategic management. It also encompasses the entrepreneurial activities of the organization as well as organizational regeneration and growth (Jofre, 2011). The last ten years following the global financial crisis of 2007–2009 have seen an increase in the usage of strategic management language in the banking sector by both scholars and banking professionals (Kryvych and Goncharenko, 2020).

The banking sector is essential to the expansion of every economy. The history of the Indian banking sector is vast and spans from the British era to the reform era, nationalization to bank privatization, and the current trend of growing numbers of international banks operating in India (Bikker and Haaf, 2002). As a result, banking in India has a lengthy history. In line with the times, India's banking sector has likewise reached new heights. The way banks operate has undergone a transformation thanks to the usage of technology (Goyal and Joshi, 2012). But there are very few studies that analyzed the banking prospective of financially developing states of India, like Jharkhand (Singh et al., 2020). The efficacy and financial inclusion of Jharkhand is considered to be of poor performance and thus grave concern for top banks. Here, new technology is also less-used, and financial risk management is not as well-known. This demands that the state of Jharkhand implement an advanced and effective strategic financial inclusion system (Prasad, 2021). The banking needs of Jharkhand require the adoption of sustainable and strategic policies due to the complex interplay between tradition and progress (Raj and Priya, 2023). Very few researches has identified the strategic factors in this purview and analyzed its weightage. Thus, this paper identifies the strategic factors for banking industry in Jharkhand and weights them through a multi-criteria decision making (MCDM) method-Logarithmic Percentage Change-driven Objective Weighting (LOPCOW).

Literature Review

More recently, it has been acknowledged that strategy and strategic management are essential components of an organization's ability to survive in a volatile environment (Cauwenbergh and Cool, 1982). Strategic management as a stream of management research started coherently in the 1960s, which saw business development as a 'more contingent perspective where organisations need to adapt to their external environment (Rao and Shukla, 2023). Strategic management is "an externally-oriented philosophy of managing an organization that links strategic thinking and analysis to organizational action," "the essential process for coping with external change," and the primary ideology guiding the management of all forms of contemporary organizations (Jasper and Crossan, 2012). The idea of strategic management was first introduced in the middle of the 1950s, and it has evolved to reflect advances in technology, economics, and society. It began as a budget exercise in the 1960s and underwent a phase of strategic planning in the 1970s, which enabled a growing response to markets and competition through competitive assessment, situation analysis, strategic alternative evaluation, and dynamic resource allocation (Bonn and Christodoulou, 1996). Principles from both quantitative and qualitative domains are included in strategic management. The disciplines of operations, logistics, and finance have been codified on the quantitative side by management and industrial sciences. The human aspects of sociology, psychology, and human resource management balance this quantitative precision. These quantitative and qualitative components work together to satisfy a range of organizational goals, such as technical, strategic, and professional demands (Chinowsky and Meredith, 2000). In today's competitive and dynamic business world, strategic management has become an essential component for firms. Three distinct processes make up strategic management; these processes are connected to one another and have an impact on one another. Strategic planning, strategic implementation, and strategic control are these procedures (Mišanková and Kočišová, 2014).

Among the oldest industries in the world is banking. The word "bank" is derived from the French "banque." Banking is the act of receiving deposits of money from the general public that can be withdrawn by check, draft, order, or other means and that can be repaid on demand or otherwise (Goyal and Joshi, 2011). The history of the Indian banking sector is vast and spans from the old banking methods used by the British to the reforms, nationalization to bank privatization, and the current trend of growing numbers of international banks operating in India (Goyal and Joshi, 2012). The current state of the Indian banking industry is characterized by the same opportunities and excitement as the country's economy (Rao and Shukla, 2023). It has learned a great deal from the recent fundamental structural adjustments. The Indian banking system's structure has remained mostly unchanged after deregulation (Kamath et al., 2003). Few studies have examined the banking prospects of India's financially emerging states, such as Jharkhand (Singh et al., 2020). Leading banks are gravely concerned about Jharkhand's perceived lack of efficacy and financial inclusion. In this case, financial risk management is likewise less well-known and new technology is also employed less frequently. The state of Jharkhand must thus put in place a sophisticated and successful strategic financial inclusion mechanism (Prasad, 2021).

LOPCOW method is a MCDM approach that estimates criteria weights using objective evidence. It has a capacity to handle vast amounts of data with significant fluctuations with a remarkably consistent weight distribution for the criteria. It is capable of determining the criteria weights using negative values (Ecer and Pamucar, 2022). Negative values are frequently seen in datasets because they occur in real-world circumstances. For example, it is common to find negative stock returns. Owing to its advantages, LOPCOW is being used more frequently to address real-world challenges in the fields of engineering, social science, management, and technology (Biswas and Joshi, 2023). There are various other MCDM methodologies listed in Table 1 that studies the performance of banking industry. But none have used LOPCOW to analyze the strategic management factors for banking industry especially in not so developed state like Jharkhand.

Table 1. Application of various MCDM methods for performance evaluation of banking industry

S.No.	MCDM approach	References
1	Fuzzy Technique for Order of Preference by Similarity to Ideal Solution (TOPSIS) (FTOPSIS) and fuzzy VIšekriterijumsko KOmpromisno Rangiranje (VIKOR) (FVIKOR)	Beheshtinia and Omidi, 2017
2	Simple Additive Weighting (SAW), TOPSIS, and VIKOR	Wu et al., 2009
3	Method based on removal effects of criteria (MEREC), Measurement alternatives and ranking according to compromise solution (MARCOS)	Rao and Shukla, 2023
4	DEMATEL-based analytic network process (DANP), VIKOR	Zhao et al., 2019
5	Criteria importance through inter criteria correlation (CRITIC), TOPSIS	Gupta et al., 2021
6	fuzzy TOPSIS, fuzzy VIKOR	Dinçer and Yüksel, 2019
7	TOPSIS, Interval-valued TOPSIS (IV-TOPSIS)	Gupta et al., 2021
8	TOPSIS, VIKOR, and Elimination ET Choix Traduisant la Realité (ELECTRE)	Shaverdi et al., 2011
9	SAW, VIKOR, and TOPSIS	Momeni et al., 2011
10	Best–worst method (BWM)	Amiri et al., 2023

The factors of strategic management that are identified are:

Customer Satisfaction (CS): It is a process as well as an outcome for customer's happiness or satisfaction regarding the product or services delivered to them (Moraru and Duhnea, 2018).

Customer Need (CN): It is a motivational urge both physically and psychologically to use a product or service and to remain faithful to the company (Subashini, 2016).

Customer Commitment (CC): "An exchange partner's belief that an ongoing relationship is so important as to warrant maximum efforts at maintaining it" is defined as "customer commitment." In other words, the customer feels that the relationship is worthwhile to work on in order to ensure that it lasts forever (Tsao and Hsieh, 2012).

Competitors Strength and Strategies (SS): It comprises evaluating tactics, identifying benefits and strengths, and determining how each could be dangerous (Zhou et al., 2009).

New Ways of Marketing Methods (MM): It specifies about the use of various methods of marketing such as social media marketing, content marketing, campaigning etc. (Lusardi et al., 2009).

Technological Superiority (TS): It refers to the idea of dominance in the realm of technology within the framework of international relations, regionally and globally, as well as within specific subfields (de Reuver and Ondrus, 2017).

Digital Infrastructure (DI): It describes the specific hardware and software components that are used in tandem to transfer data, digital goods, and services from one location to another (Greenstein, 2021).

Staff Development (SD): The policies, processes, and procedures used to increase staff members' knowledge, abilities, and skills in order to increase their effectiveness and efficiency as individuals and as a company are collectively referred to as staff development (Guskey and Sparks, 1991).

Team Orientation (TO): It speaks of the cooperation and teamwork that a company can promote by valuing group effort over solo task accomplishment (Watson et al., 1998).

Staff Retention (SR): It is the capacity of a company to guarantee sustainability and hold onto its workforce. A straightforward statistic can be used to illustrate employee retention. It also refers to the tactics employed by companies in an effort to keep workers on staff (Heidari et al., 2017).

Research Gap

Previous researches have studied the performance evaluation of banks including the analysis of strategic management factors for banking industry but none have analyzed it in the purview of financially developing state of India such as Jharkhand, especially using LOPCOW approach.

Research Objectives

- To ascertain the factors of strategic management for banking industry in Jharkhand.
- To determine the prioritization of each criterion for banking industry in Jharkhand.

Methodology

Logarithmic percentage change-driven objective weighting (LOPCOW) approach is one form of multi-criteria decision making (MCDM) method, developed by Ecer and Pamucar in 2022. Using a tiered structure, this strategy gives the assessment values priority during the decision-making process (Biswas and Joshi, 2023). The LOPCOW strategy is thought to have the capacity to estimate criteria weights by negative values in addition to conventional weightage determination techniques (Ecer et al., 2023). Even with a big collection of data, it permits a continuous distribution of criterion weights. Furthermore, the LOPCOW approach reduces disparities in the prioritization of different criteria and is reasonably easy to understand and apply (Ecer and Pamucar, 2022).

Steps in the LOPCOW approach:

Step 1: Designing an initial matrix (IM) with alternative m and criteria n.

$$IM = \begin{pmatrix} X_{11} & \cdots & X_{1n} \\ \vdots & \ddots & \vdots \\ X_{m1} & \cdots & X_{mn} \end{pmatrix} \tag{1}$$

Step 2: Normalizing of IM

$$r_{ij} = \frac{x_{ij} - x_{min}^j}{x_{max}^j - x_{min}^j}$$

(when ϵj^+, maximizing effect) $\tag{2}$

$$r_{ij} = \frac{x_{max}^j - x_{ij}}{x_{max}^j - x_{min}^j}$$

(when ϵj^-, minimizing effect) $\tag{3}$

Step 3: Computation of percentage values (PV_{ij}) for all criterions.

$$PV_{ij} = \left| \ln\left(\frac{\sqrt{\frac{\sum_{i=1}^m r_{ij}^2}{m}}}{\sigma} \right) . 100 \right| \tag{4}$$

In this, σ shows standard deviation and m shows total number of alternatives.

Step 4: Calculation of criterion weights.

$$w_j = \frac{PV_{ij}}{\sum_{i=1}^n PV_{ij}} \tag{5}$$

Analysis

This paper ascertains the factors of strategic management for banking industry and analyses the collected information for banks in Jharkhand to determine the prioritization of each criterion. For this, the identification of factors is conducted through literature review. After this, the data is collected for each criterion through primary data collection method. According to the report published by State level bankers' committee, Jharkhand, 2023, the total number of branches of commercial banks is 2521. Commercial banks are considered to be of prominence for understanding the banking development of the industry (Lu and Hu, 2014). Further, for sample size, total number of 350 samples is collected based on the sample size estimation table developed by Israel, 1992.

The collected data is then analysed using LOPCOW method. In this, the criterion is weighted based on the algorithm and suggests that the criterion with highest weightage has highest prioritization in strategic management of banking industry in Jharkhand. The result of analysis is shown in Table 2.

Table 2. Estimation of weightage through LOPCOW approach

CS	CN	CC	SS	MM	TS	DI	SD	TO	SR
8	5	7	9	4	10	6	1	3	2

The outcome infers SD as the highest weighted criterion, followed by SR and TO, for strategic management of banking industry in Jharkhand, while TS is ranked the lowest. This represents that among all the criterion, SD has the topmost prioritization in strategic management of banks in Jharkhand, followed by SR and TO.

Discussion

This study ascertains the factors of strategic management for banking industry and analyses the prioritization of criterion with regard to Jharkhand. The outcome of analysis, shown in Table 2, represents, SD as criterion with highest weightage followed by SR, TO and MM. This signifies that staff has a crucial role in strategic management. The first two ranked factors are totally dependent on their development and retention. Third ranked factor is also a composition of staff to make team and work efficiently with the team, while the fourth ranked factor is about the various approaches of marketing conducted by the bank. A study on Nigerian banks (Shonubi, 2020) also concludes the importance of SD in management or performance of the banks. It illustrates that SD is a significant factor for organizational performance. With the individual development of each staff in an organization, the overall performance increases. Further, a study by Muthee and Genga, 2019, on commercial banks in Kenya, also suggests that SD is a beneficial criterion for long-run effect of the banks. In this study least weightage is assigned to TS, SS and CS. This shows that, staff related factors have an important role in strategic management but it lacks in external criterion such as technology, competitors and customers. In banking industry in Jharkhand, employees or staffs plays a crucial role in strategic management while technology, competitors and customers have the least role in strategic management. Dangolani, 2011, in the study discusses about the importance of technology in human aspect and for the banking system. For the banking sector, technology has created new markets, goods, and services as well as effective delivery routes (Berger and Mester, 2003). Moreover, competitors strengths and customer viewpoint is also essential in strategic development of the banking system (Kungu et al., 2014). Thus, it is important for the banking industry in Jharkhand to focus on this also.

CONCLUSION, IMPLICATION AND LIMITATION

This paper determines the weightage of strategic management factors for banking industry in Jharkhand. First, the factors are recognized through literature review. Second, data is collected with regard to each factor using primary data collection method. And lastly, the criterions are analysed through LOPCOW approach and weightage is derived for prioritization. The outcome of the study indicates SD as the criterion with highest weightage and is ranked first followed by SR and TO, whereas, the factors TS, SS and CS are ranked least. This signifies that internal criterion relating to staffs and strategies for marketing are prioritized while, external criterion such as technology, competitor and customer are ranked lowest. Thus, for banking industry in Jharkhand, internal criterions have a prominent role in strategic management as compared to the external factors.

The prioritized result of criterion weightage can be further used by banking industry to ascertain its potential towards strategic management and consequently to implement the strategic changes in the policies and budget allocation of the bank. Moreover, the outcome and application of LOPCOW approach can also be useful for researchers for future studies.

This research considers only ten factors to study strategic management for banking industry, specifically for Jharkhand. Further, an MCDM method- LOPCOW is applied to prioritize the criterion. These can be considered as limitation by involving more number or different set of factors for other or various regions and by applying other weightage determination approach.

REFERENCES

Amiri, M., Hashemi-Tabatabaei, M., Keshavarz-Ghorabaee, M., Antucheviciene, J., Šaparauskas, J., & Keramatpanah, M. (2023). Evaluation of digital banking implementation indicators and models in the context of industry 4.0: A fuzzy group MCDM approach. *Axioms*, 12(6), 516. DOI: 10.3390/axioms12060516

Beheshtinia, M. A., & Omidi, S. (2017). A hybrid MCDM approach for performance evaluation in the banking industry. *Kybernetes*, 46(8), 1386–1407. DOI: 10.1108/K-03-2017-0105

Berger, A. N., & Mester, L. J. (2003). Explaining the dramatic changes in performance of US banks: Technological change, deregulation, and dynamic changes in competition. *Journal of Financial Intermediation*, 12(1), 57–95. DOI: 10.1016/S1042-9573(02)00006-2

Bikker, J. A., & Haaf, K. (2002). Competition, concentration and their relationship: An empirical analysis of the banking industry. *Journal of Banking & Finance*, 26(11), 2191–2214. DOI: 10.1016/S0378-4266(02)00205-4

Biswas, S., & Joshi, N. (2023). A performance based ranking of initial public offerings (IPOs) in India. *Journal of Decision Analytics and Intelligent Computing*, 3(1), 15–32. DOI: 10.31181/10023022023b

Bonn, I., & Christodoulou, C. (1996). From strategic planning to strategic management. *Long Range Planning*, 29(4), 543–551. DOI: 10.1016/0024-6301(96)00046-5

Chinowsky, P. S., & Meredith, J. E. (2000). Strategic management in construction. *Journal of Construction Engineering and Management*, 126(1), 1–9. DOI: 10.1061/(ASCE)0733-9364(2000)126:1(1)

Dangolani, S. K. (2011). The Impact of information technology in banking system (A case study in Bank Keshavarzi IRAN). *Procedia: Social and Behavioral Sciences*, 30, 13–16. DOI: 10.1016/j.sbspro.2011.10.003

de Reuver, M., & Ondrus, J. (2017). When technological superiority is not enough: The struggle to impose the SIM card as the NFC Secure Element for mobile payment platforms. *Telecommunications Policy*, 41(4), 253–262. DOI: 10.1016/j.telpol.2017.01.004

Dinçer, H., & Yüksel, S. (2019). An integrated stochastic fuzzy MCDM approach to the balanced scorecard-based service evaluation. *Mathematics and Computers in Simulation*, 166, 93–112. DOI: 10.1016/j.matcom.2019.04.008

Ecer, F., Küçükönder, H., Kaya, S. K., & Görçün, Ö. F. (2023). Sustainability performance analysis of micro-mobility solutions in urban transportation with a novel IVFNN-Delphi-LOPCOW-CoCoSo framework. *Transportation Research Part A, Policy and Practice*, 172, 103667. DOI: 10.1016/j.tra.2023.103667

Ecer, F., & Pamucar, D. (2022). A novel LOPCOW-DOBI multi-criteria sustainability performance assessment methodology: An application in developing country banking sector. *Omega*, 112, 102690. DOI: 10.1016/j.omega.2022.102690

Goyal, K. A., & Joshi, V. (2011). A study of social and ethical issues in banking industry. *International Journal of Economic Research*, 2(5), 49–57.

Goyal, K. A., & Joshi, V. (2012). Indian banking industry: Challenges and opportunities. *International Journal of Business Research and Management*, 3(1), 18–28.

Greenstein, S. (2021). Digital infrastructure. *Economic Analysis and Infrastructure Investment*, 28215, 409–447. DOI: 10.7208/chicago/9780226800615.003.0009

Gupta, S., Mathew, M., Gupta, S., & Dawar, V. (2021). Benchmarking the private sector banks in India using MCDM approach. *Journal of Public Affairs*, 21(2), e2409. DOI: 10.1002/pa.2409

Gupta, S., Mathew, M., Syal, G., & Jain, J. (2021). A hybrid MCDM approach for evaluating the financial performance of public sector banks in India. *International Journal of Business Excellence*, 24(4), 481–501. DOI: 10.1504/IJBEX.2021.117648

Guskey, T. R., & Sparks, D. (1991). What to consider when evaluating staff development. *Educational Leadership*, 49(3), 73–76.

Heidari, M., Seifi, B., & Gharebagh, Z. (2017). Nursing staff retention: Effective factors. *Annals of Tropical Medicine and Public Health*, 10(6).

Jasper, M., & Crossan, F. (2012). What is strategic management? *Journal of Nursing Management*, 20(7), 838–846. DOI: 10.1111/jonm.12001 PMID: 23050617

Jofre, S. (2011). Strategic Management: The theory and practice of strategy in (business) organizations.

Kamath, K. V., Kohli, S. S., Shenoy, P. S., Kumar, R., Nayak, R. M., Kuppuswamy, P. T., & Ravichandran, N. (2003). Indian banking sector: Challenges and opportunities. *Vikalpa*, 28(3), 83–100. DOI: 10.1177/0256090920030308

Kryvych, Y. M., & Goncharenko, T. (2020). Banking strategic management and business model: bibliometric analysis.

Kungu, G., Desta, I., & Ngui, T. (2014). An assessment of the effectiveness of competitive strategies by commercial banks: A Case of Equity Bank. *International Journal of Education and Research*, 2(12), 333–346.

Lu, J., & Hu, X. (2014). Novel three-bank model for measuring the systemic importance of commercial banks. *Economic Modelling*, 43, 238–246. DOI: 10.1016/j.econmod.2014.08.007

Lusardi, A., Keller, P. A., & Keller, A. M. (2009). *New ways to make people save: A social marketing approach (No. w14715)*. National Bureau of Economic Research. DOI: 10.3386/w14715

Mišanková, M., & Kočišová, K. (2014). Strategic implementation as a part of strategic management. *Procedia: Social and Behavioral Sciences*, 110, 861–870. DOI: 10.1016/j.sbspro.2013.12.931

Momeni, M., Maleki, M. H., Afshari, M. A., Moradi, J. S., & Mohammadi, J. (2011). A fuzzy MCDM approach for evaluating listed private banks in Tehran stock exchange based on balanced scorecard. *International Journal of Business Administration*, 2(1), 80.

Moraru, A. D., & Duhnea, C. (2018). E-banking and customer satisfaction with banking services. *Strategic Management*, 23(3), 3–9. DOI: 10.5937/StraMan1803003M

Muthee, J. G., & Genga, P. (2019). Staff development and employee performance in Kenya Commercial Bank in Nyeri County, Kenya. *International Journal of Current Aspects*, 3(IV), 93–103. DOI: 10.35942/ijcab.v3iIV.50

Nickols, F. (2016). Strategy, strategic management, strategic planning and strategic thinking. *Management Journal*, 1(1), 4–7.

Porter, M. E. (1996). *What is strategy?* Harvard Business School Publishing Corporation.

Powell, T. C. (2002). The philosophy of strategy. *Strategic Management Journal*, 23(9), 873–880. DOI: 10.1002/smj.254

Prasad, S. (2021). Analysis of the Existing model of Financial Inclusion of poor people in Jharkhand.

Raj, N., & Priya, P. (2023). Sustainable and Inclusive Strategies for Tribal Development in Jharkhand. *International Journal of Social Science & Management Studies*, 9(7), 2454–4655.

Rao, P. K., & Shukla, A. (2023). Sustainable strategic management: A bibliometric analysis. *Business Strategy and the Environment*, 32(6), 3902–3914. DOI: 10.1002/bse.3344

Rao, P. K., & Shukla, A. (2024). Strategic sustainability in Indian banking industry: A performance analysis. *International Journal of Productivity and Performance Management*, 73(6), 2016–2034. DOI: 10.1108/IJPPM-04-2023-0199

Rumelt, R. P., Schendel, D., & Teece, D. J. (1991). Strategic management and economics. *Strategic Management Journal*, 12(S2), 5–29. DOI: 10.1002/smj.4250121003

Shaverdi, M., Akbari, M., & Fallah Tafti, S. (2011). Combining fuzzy MCDM with BSC approach in performance evaluation of Iranian private banking sector. *Advances in Fuzzy Systems*, 2011(1), 148712. DOI: 10.1155/2011/148712

Shonubi, A. O. (2020). The perceived effect of staff development on organisational performance in selected First Banks in Lagos State, Nigeria. *Inkanyiso: Journal of Humanities and Social Sciences*, 12(1), 56–71.

Singh, S. A. D. H. V. I., & Sarkar, A. K. (2020). Index of Financial Inclusion (IFI) and banking penetration in Jharkhand. Purakala, 31(12), 749-757.

Subashini, R. (2016). A review of service quality and customer satisfaction in banking services: Global scenario. *Journal of Internet Banking and Commerce*, 21(S5), 1.

Tsao, W. C., & Hsieh, M. T. (2012). Exploring how relationship quality influences positive eWOM: The importance of customer commitment. *Total Quality Management & Business Excellence*, 23(7-8), 821–835. DOI: 10.1080/14783363.2012.661137

Van Cauwenbergh, A., & Cool, K. (1982). Strategic management in a new framework. *Strategic Management Journal*, 3(3), 245–264. DOI: 10.1002/smj.4250030306

Wagner Mainardes, E., Ferreira, J. J., & Raposo, M. L. (2014). Strategy and strategic management concepts: are they recognised by management students?.

Watson, W. E., Johnson, L., & Merritt, D. (1998). Team orientation, self-orientation, and diversity in task groups: Their connection to team performance over time. *Group & Organization Management*, 23(2), 161–188. DOI: 10.1177/1059601198232005

Wu, H. Y., Tzeng, G. H., & Chen, Y. H. (2009). A fuzzy MCDM approach for evaluating banking performance based on Balanced Scorecard. *Expert Systems with Applications*, 36(6), 10135–10147. DOI: 10.1016/j.eswa.2009.01.005

Zhao, Q., Tsai, P. H., & Wang, J. L. (2019). Improving financial service innovation strategies for enhancing china's banking industry competitive advantage during the fintech revolution: A Hybrid MCDM model. *Sustainability (Basel)*, 11(5), 1419. DOI: 10.3390/su11051419

Zhou, K. Z., Brown, J. R., & Dev, C. S. (2009). Market orientation, competitive advantage, and performance: A demand-based perspective. *Journal of Business Research*, 62(11), 1063–1070. DOI: 10.1016/j.jbusres.2008.10.001

Chapter 16
The Triadic Relationship Between Fertility, Education, and Religion Among Women in Bihar

Srijon Ghosh
https://orcid.org/0009-0002-2071-9170
Tata Institute of Social Sciences, India

Asma Asif Sayyad
Tata Institute of Social Sciences, India

ABSTRACT

This study explores the relationship between education, religion, and family size in Bihar, India. Bihar is an interesting case for examining fertility rates due to its traditionally high levels of natalism and low levels of literacy. Various literature on this topic was reviewed to identify gaps in the research. Data obtained from the National Family Health Survey (NFHS) was then used to analyze how a woman's education and religious beliefs affect the number of children she has. Finally, ANOVA tests, Chi-square tests, and other relevant analyses were utilized to further investigate all areas of interest. The findings show that education plays a more significant role than religion in achieving a lower and more sustainable replacement fertility rate for women in Bihar. However, incorporating a religious perspective in educational interventions can help make them more effective for broader societal development.

DOI: 10.4018/979-8-3693-5563-3.ch016

INTRODUCTION

Fertility, in basic terms, refers to the capacity to bear children. It is seen as important for development because it directly impacts population growth, which in turn influences the size and composition of the labour force, consumer markets, dependency ratios, and social welfare systems. In many developing countries, high fertility rates can strain resources and hinder economic development by placing pressure on infrastructure, healthcare, and education systems. Conversely, in highly developed countries, declining fertility rates can lead to an aging population and potential labour shortages, which may impact economic productivity and social welfare systems (Fox et al., 2018).

Fertility is intricately linked to sustainable development as well through its impact on various aspects of human life and society. In the context of the 2030 Agenda for Sustainable Development, fertility is positioned as a critical component of the broader framework for achieving sustainable development goals (Jakubowska et al., 2021). The ability to reproduce and raise healthy offspring is essential for the continuity and growth of a population. Furthermore, fertility patterns are closely linked to gender equality, as women's empowerment and access to education and employment opportunities can influence their reproductive choices. In this regard, fertility can be seen as a reflection of societal development and the status of women within a given society. It should be emphasized that the neglect of personal health in terms of fertility can lead to a permanent loss of the capacity for personal and social development, thereby limiting an individual's freedom to make decisions about their reproductive potential.

In India, people often misunderstand or are completely unaware about the connection between fertility and development, which leads to many debates. This is because it's challenging to identify the key factors influencing fertility rates across India's diverse socio-economic landscape, which includes varying education levels and religious backgrounds. Many are curious why some groups have more children than others. To explore this issue, we focused on Bihar, which has a high fertility rate, analyzing how religion and education impact fertility to determine their relative importance (Mahey et al., 2018).

Relevance of the study

When studying fertility rates, researchers look at several factors that can influence how many children people have. These factors include things like access to healthcare, education levels, economic conditions, and cultural beliefs about family size. One of the most important factors tends to be education because it can affect people's ability to make decisions for future family planning and so on. But when considering diverse societies like India, religion often becomes a significant variable due to its cultural influence and varying beliefs on family size causing various debates (Joshi et al., 1996).

Education empowers individuals with knowledge about reproductive health and family planning, which can lead to lower fertility rates. On the other hand, religious beliefs can either support or hinder the adoption of these practices. Hence, comparing religion with education's impact on fertility can reveal how different religious and educational backgrounds contribute to the demographic trends within a region or locality.

As such, Bihar, one of India's states, offers a compelling setting for studying fertility rates due to its high population density, diverse cultures, and historically low literacy rates. Its significant population size provides ample data to analyze fertility trends. The state's consistently higher fertility rates compared to the national average raise questions about the cultural, social, and economic influences on reproductive choices. The state also faces notable healthcare and development challenges, which can affect access to family planning services and maternal healthcare. Moreover, Bihar's high fertility rates and slower fertility decline compared to other states make it an interesting case study for understanding the challenges and complexities associated with achieving fertility transition. Therefore, researching fertility in Bihar not only helps understand local dynamics but also informs broader discussions on population policies, maternal and child health programs, and therefore, socio-economic development efforts, with implications beyond the state's borders (Das & Mohanty, 2012).

Research Objectives

Our research objectives in this study are straightforward. We intend to explore how education, religion, and fertility rates are connected in Bihar. We seek to understand how education levels impact fertility rates and explore whether higher education attainment correlates with lower fertility rates. Additionally, we also aim to understand the influence of different religious beliefs on family size in Bihar's unique demographic landscape. We have tried to figure out if there's a link between how educated someone is and what religion they follow when it comes to deciding on family size and determine which of these factors can identify a contextual framework to inform future policy decisions and interventions.

335

FERTILITY, EDUCATION, AND RELIGION

Over the past several decades, a lot of research and writing has focused on fertility. In developed countries, this attention is driven by the need to improve population projections and the belief that fertility is the most unpredictable aspect of population change. As a result, there is a lot of literature that discusses how education and religion could individually affect fertility, which we have reviewed for our study.

Education and Fertility

A lot of studies have looked into how women's education affects how many children they have. One major way education affects fertility is by making women want smaller families. When women get educated, they have more opportunities beyond raising children, which can reduce their desired family size (INEE,2021).

In many countries, fertility is often affected by the status of women in society, and this status is often decided by the number of children a woman has. Taking the example of India before Independence, women who had more children were highly respected. This is still the case in various Indian communities today, where women are mainly confined to household chores. Conversely, in countries experiencing declining population growth, women are encouraged to have more children and are highly regarded. This was seen during Stalin's rule in Russia, where women who had many children were rewarded, and their children received support from the government (Mishra, 2017). This is why education should be emphasized even more as it makes women less dependent on their number of children for social status or support in old age. According to Easterlin, educated women will often have higher hopes for their children, potentially trading off the number of children for increased attention and resources per child (Easterlin, 1975).

Moreover, educating women will also reduce son preference in places like India where it is believed that while sons can contribute financially and work for the family, daughters apparently cannot. For example, a study was held on fertility trends in Saharsa district, Bihar, using firsthand data gathered through surveys with structured interviews. The average desired number of children varied among different demographic, socio-economic, and cultural groups. For instance, women aged 15-19 preferred around 2 children (1.97 percent), whereas those aged 40-44 preferred around 3 children (3.05 percent). Yet, the inclination towards having sons over daughters was consistently higher across all age brackets (Jayaraman et al., 2009). Thus, through educating women, there will also be a decreased desire for larger families, especially since having many children is also seen as necessary for ensuring enough surviving sons.

Education also makes women more open to modern social norms and family planning campaigns, leading to a decrease in the desired size of families and an increased awareness of and access to contraception. Furthermore, female education alters the connection between the desired family size and the intended number of children. A significant aspect of this transformation lies in the decline of infant and child mortality rates among educated mothers. This decrease in mortality rates enables educated mothers to achieve their desired family size with fewer planned births (Khurshid et al., 2019).

There is also a disconnect between marriage and fertility among non-educated women compared to the strong correlation between marriage and fertility among educated women. Over the past few decades, the family patterns of highly educated women have diverged from those of less-educated women. Highly educated women tend to delay both marriage and parenthood, while less-educated women often delay only marriage. This difference is influenced by the decline in employment stability and economic prospects among less-educated men, affecting the pool of "marriage-able" partners available to less-educated women. When there is a shortage of desirable partners, having children outside of marriage becomes a potential strategy for family formation among economically disadvantaged women. Consequently, there has been a significant increase in nonmarital births among less-educated women (Lundberg & Pollak, 2007).

Some researchers argue that marriage has become a luxury primarily accessible to advantaged women, as they are less inclined to engage in nonmarital childbearing. This delay in marriage is also associated with a delay in fertility among educated women. Additionally, with the growing availability and acceptance of childcare services, married women who are educated and financially stable can mitigate some of the time and energy costs associated with raising children. These women may leverage their higher incomes to support childcare expenses, enabling them to balance their careers and family responsibilities more effectively. Furthermore, high-ability educated women may negotiate maternity leaves with their employers without jeopardizing their career advancements, as employers often prioritize retaining their most skilled employees (Brand & Davis, 2011).

The points made above also apply to men, indicating that enhancing male education could also result in reduced fertility rates, because, in many households, males try to decide the number of children a woman is supposed to have. However, the influence of male education on fertility can be claimed to be less significant in comparison to female education. This is mainly because women usually have the main role in caring for children and therefore exert a more direct influence on fertility choices within families (Dreze & Murthi, 2001).

The relationship between women's education and fertility is influenced by "Female autonomy," which acts as a potential mediator between education and fertility. In this context, female autonomy refers to women's ability to make decisions independently. It's a debated topic in many forms of literature because having more control over their choices might empower women to make decisions about their fertility. However, defining and measuring female autonomy remains controversial, and its impact on the connection between education and fertility is just one of many factors to consider (Dreze & Murthi, 2001).

Religion and Fertility

Researchers have been through complex endeavors to grasp the impact of religion on demographic trends. There are various works that have been instrumental in broadening our comprehension of religion's impact, advocating for a comprehensive view that encompasses not just specific rules on contraception but also values related to gender, sexuality, and family dynamics. Additionally, they highlight the significance of considering a religious group's status within society's social and economic framework (Goldscheider, 2006).

Different religions also articulate behavioral norms that directly impact fertility. However, not all religions prescribe such norms, and some have evolved their stances on issues like contraception and abortion over time. It's essential to develop a theoretical framework linking these religious values and norms to specific demographic behaviors, while also establishing measures of these values and norms independently of the behaviors under study to avoid circular reasoning. For a religious group to impact fertility rates, it requires effective communication to share its teachings with its members and also ensure they follow them. This underscores the importance of understanding how religious messages are disseminated and internalized within communities, as well as the mechanisms through which adherence to religious principles is reinforced (Dimiter & Berghammer, 2007). Furthermore, religious groups hold greater sway over the demographic decisions of their followers when individuals feel deeply connected to their religious community. While some individuals may belong to multiple groups where religion isn't the primary focus, in certain contexts, religion plays a central role in shaping people's identities. This is particularly evident when religious affiliation aligns with nationalist movements or when there's persistent conflict with other ethno-religious groups. In such scenarios, individuals feel deeply connected to their religious group, amplifying the incentives for conformity and the consequences of dissent (McQuillan, 2004).

Hence, religion influences fertility in many societies. In Asia, marriage is both a social norm and a religious obligation. As such, various regional and cultural elements influence fertility trends in the Indian population. There is often a positive attitude towards large families, as children are considered a blessing and a source of support in old age. In Bihar, where Hinduism and Islam are the predominant religions, cultural norms surrounding fertility and family size may be influenced by religious teachings. For Hindu parents, having a son is crucial for spiritual salvation, while marrying off a daughter (Kanyadan) is a significant religious and social duty. In Islam, polygamy is allowed, where a man can have multiple wives, which naturally increases fertility. Over time, it has been noted that fertility rates tend to be slightly higher among Muslims in India when compared to other religious groups since religious teachings and cultural norms within the Muslim community may prioritize family and encourage higher fertility rates even more so than Hindu families (Moulasha & Rao, 1999). However, it's essential to note that socio-economic factors, such as lower incomes and literacy rates among Indian Muslims, may also contribute to higher fertility rates, and these factors need to be considered more when analysing fertility patterns. For both Hindu and Muslim communities, fertility rates can vary widely based on factors such as region, caste, and socio-economic status (Singh et al., 2022).

And, while our research describes differences in the fertility patterns influenced by different education levels or major religious groups in India, discussion on the impact of religion on fertility or even other socio-economic factors remains a delicate topic. It is quite difficult to quantify the direct role that religion plays when it comes to fertility and family size (Kramer, 2021).

Education and Religion

Education and religion have a close connection, influencing each other in many ways. Education, which is vital for personal growth and society's progress, not only teaches facts and skills but also shapes people's beliefs and values. As people learn, they encounter various ideas about religion, which helps them understand and respect different beliefs. It also encourages people to think critically about their faith and how it fits into the world today.

Since ancient times in India, education and religious teachings have been inseparable, with traditional institutions like Gurukuls and Madrasas imparting knowledge alongside spiritual guidance. India's religious diversity further complicates this relationship, as Hinduism, Islam, Christianity, Sikhism, Buddhism, and Jainism all contribute to the educational landscape with their institutions and teachings. However, the relationship between education and religion has undergone significant transformations over time, particularly in the modern era. The rise of secularism, enlightenment ideals, and the separation of church and state have led to the emergence of secular educational systems in many parts of the world. This shift has been marked by the gradual marginalization of religious teachings from public education.

339

Religion influences education by affecting what is taught and guiding moral principles in schools. It often plays a part in education through classes on faith, discussions about morality, and learning about different religions. Within societies, religious beliefs often steer attitudes towards education, particularly in regions where public facilities may be lacking. Some groups also emphasize religious instruction above secular learning, while others advocate for a balanced approach encompassing both religious and worldly knowledge (Kortt & Drew, 2019). These educational settings often mirror the values and teachings of the affiliated faith, sculpting curricula, and student experiences accordingly. Thus, gender dynamics within education might also be molded by religious teachings, assigning distinct roles and opportunities for males and females (Norton & Tomal, 2009).

In summary, while the literature review provides a comprehensive overview of the intricate relationships between education, religion, and fertility, there are several gaps that we will try to address. Many works predominantly focus on the individual influences of education and religion on fertility rates, with less emphasis on their combined effects and interactions. Furthermore, despite Bihar consistently having the highest fertility rates in India over the years, there hasn't been sufficient research conducted to explain the underlying reasons for this phenomenon.

METHODOLOGY

In our study, we adhere to a positivist research philosophy, which emphasizes the use of empirical evidence and objective measurement to understand social phenomena. By focusing on quantifiable data, we aim to draw unbiased conclusions about the relationships between education, religion, and fertility.

Our research targets women of reproductive age (15-49 years) and we have chosen the National Family Health Survey 5 (NFHS-5; 2019-2021) dataset to obtain that. The NFHS data is obtained through a survey which is conducted through a well-organized process involving several stages. Initially, a sample is drawn using a multistage stratified sampling technique, ensuring that different population groups are adequately represented. Fieldworkers then visit selected households to collect data using structured questionnaires. These questionnaires cover a wide range of topics, including health, education, fertility, and socio-economic status. Data collection is followed by a rigorous process of data validation and quality control. This includes checking for inconsistencies, verifying information with respondents, and using statistical techniques to ensure the reliability of the data. The final dataset is then made available for analysis, providing researchers with a valuable resource for studying various socio-economic issues.

Our choice of the NFHS 5 dataset over the 2011 Census data is driven by the need for recent and detailed information that accurately reflects current trends and dynamics in Bihar. While the 2011 Census data offers historical significance, its static nature limits its relevance to the rapidly changing socio-economic landscape of Bihar. In contrast, the NFHS-5 dataset captures recent developments, allowing for a more precise understanding of current phenomena compared to the decade-old Census data.

Variables under Investigation

We have identified and focused on key variables essential to understanding fertility dynamics in Bihar, India. These variables include education level, religion, wealth, and total number of children ever born, which serves as a proxy for fertility. Education level, categorized into no education, primary, secondary, and higher, provides insights into individuals' educational attainment. Religion, particularly distinguishing between the majority of the population, Hindus (85.7%) and Muslims (14.1%) were selected to understand potential religious influences on fertility behaviors. We opted to exclude other religions because they only included a minor part of the population (0.2%). Additionally, wealth has been taken as another variable segmented into categories ranging from poorest to richest. Wealth influences the quality of education people receive and their ability to afford healthcare and family planning services. By analyzing wealth, we can see how economic status affects fertility rates and educational opportunities, offering a more complete picture of the factors that shape family size and reproductive choices.

Hypotheses Development

We've outlined five hypotheses for our data analysis, exploring the relationships between education and fertility, religion and fertility, wealth and fertility, as well as education and religion. Our last hypothesis examines whether there's a variation in average fertility among women from diverse religious backgrounds across varying levels of education.

Hypothesis (H1): There is a difference in fertility across different levels of education.

Our underlying assumption is that women with different levels of education (e.g., no formal education, primary education, secondary education, and higher education) will exhibit different fertility rates. Typically, the expectation is that higher education levels are associated with lower fertility rates due to factors such as better access to family planning resources, career aspirations, and delayed childbearing.

Hypothesis (H2): There is a difference in fertility between Muslim and Hindu women.

We suggest that cultural, religious, and social norms associated with these religions influence family size and reproductive behavior. For example, religious teachings, community practices, and socio-economic factors prevalent in Muslim and Hindu communities might lead to differing fertility rates.

Hypothesis (H3): There is an association between education and religion.

We suggest that the distribution of educational attainment may vary between Muslim and Hindu women. This could be due to differences in cultural emphasis on education, economic conditions, or access to educational resources within religious communities.

Hypothesis (H4): There is a difference in fertility across different levels of wealth.

We propose that women from different wealth brackets (e.g., low, middle, and high) will have different fertility rates. Generally, it is expected that women from wealthier backgrounds might have fewer children due to greater access to family planning, higher career ambitions, and the cost associated with raising children.

Hypothesis (H5): There is a difference in fertility between Hindu and Muslim women across educational levels.

We suggest that the relationship between a woman's religious affiliation (Hindu or Muslim) and her fertility rate might be influenced by her level of education. For instance, the impact of education on fertility might vary between Muslim and Hindu women, indicating that education and religion together shape fertility behaviors in a complex manner.

RESULTS AND FINDINGS

A series of statistical methods were employed to analyze the relationships among these variables. Initially, an ANOVA was conducted to evaluate differences in fertility rates across distinct levels of education and between religious groups. Subsequently, chi-square tests were utilized to explore the association between categorical variables, namely education and religion. Finally, a Univariate ANOVA test was conducted to explore the combined effects of education and religion on fertility.

Education Versus Fertility

Table 1. Education and fertility (computed from NFHS-5)

Highest Level of Education	Mean of Total Children Ever Born
No education	3.88
Primary	3.23
Secondary	2.59
Higher	1.95

p-value (ANOVA) = .000

We compare the effect of education on fertility. A comparison of the means as shown in Table 1 reveals that as the level of education increases the mean of 'Total Children Ever Born' decreases, indicating a negative correlation between fertility and education. The average number of children for a woman with 'No Education' is 3.88 and for a woman with 'Higher Education' is 1.95 in Bihar which means that a woman without education would have almost two more children than a woman with higher education.

Given that the p-value derived from the one-way ANOVA test (p = .000) falls below the significance threshold of 0.05, we accept our hypothesis, affirming the existence of a statistically meaningful difference in the mean count of total children ever born among varying educational categories.

Religion and Fertility

Table 2. Religion and fertility (computed from NFHS-5)

Religion	Mean of Total Children Ever Born
Hindu	3.24
Muslim	3.70

p-value (ANOVA) =.000

We compare the effect of religion on fertility. A comparison of the means as shown in Table 2 of the two religious groups reveals that Muslim women (3.70) have a higher average of "Total Children Ever Born" in contrast to Hindu women

(3.24) in Bihar. The mean fertility of women across India for Muslim women (2.84) is also higher than for Hindu women (2.57).

Since the p-value derived from the one-way ANOVA test (p = .000) is below the significance level of 0.05, we accept our hypothesis, affirming the presence of a statistically significant difference in the mean count of total children ever born among Hindu and Muslim women.

Education and Religion

Table 3. Education and religion (computed from NFHS-5)

		Religion		Total
		Hindu	Muslim	
Highest Level of Education	No education	50.8%	56.5%	51.5%
	Primary	11.8%	15.0%	12.2%
	Secondary	31.7%	25.1%	30.9%
	Higher	5.7%	3.4%	5.4%
Total		100.0%	100.0%	100.0%

p-value (Chi-square Test of Independence) = .000

We then compare the differences in educational attainment between Hindu and Muslim women. Muslim women appear to have a slightly higher percentage of primary education or no education, while Hindu women have a slightly higher percentage with secondary and higher education in Bihar as shown in Table 3.

Following the outcomes of the chi-square test of independence (p-value is .000), we opt to accept our hypothesis, indicating a significant association between education and religion. These findings emphasize the importance of considering education with religion when discussing fertility.

Fertility and Wealth

Table 4. Fertility and wealth (computed from NFHS-5)

Wealth Index	Mean of Total Children Ever Born
Poorest	3.56
Poorer	3.30
Middle	3.09
Richer	2.82
Richest	2.40

As shown in Table 4, the analysis indicates that differences in mean fertility across wealth strata in Bihar. As wealth increases the mean of Total Children Ever Born decreases. As per the current fertility rates woman in the Poorest Wealth Index level, on average has one more child than the one in the Richest Wealth Index level.

The ANOVA tests yielded a notably low p-value (p = .000), suggesting a substantial difference in the mean count of Total Children Ever Born. Consequently, we accept our hypothesis, affirming that wealth influences mean fertility.

Education, Religion, and Fertility

Table 5. Education, religion, and fertility (computed from NHFS-5)

Highest Level of Education	Religion	Mean of Total Children Ever Born
No education	Hindu	3.81
	Muslim	4.31
Primary	Hindu	3.19
	Muslim	3.48
Secondary	Hindu	2.58
	Muslim	2.71
Higher	Hindu	1.95
	Muslim	1.99
Total	Hindu	3.24
	Muslim	3.70
	Total	3.30

p-value (ANOVA) = .000

Finally, coming to the last part of our analysis, an ANOVA test was conducted to assess the fertility rate between religious groups across different educational levels. The results of the analysis gave a low p-value ($p = .000$), indicating a significant difference in the mean number of Total Children Ever Born between Hindu and Muslim women across all educational levels. It reveals a consistent pattern across various educational levels, indicating that, on average, Muslim women have a greater mean fertility than Hindu women in Bihar as shown in Table 5. Top of FormAlso, there is a decrease in the mean fertility with increasing educational attainment in line with the above findings. Hence, we accept our hypothesis and confirm that there is a difference in fertility between Hindu and Muslim women across different educational levels. This indicates that though both religion and education affect fertility rates, education has a bigger impact than religion.

DISCUSSION

The findings reveal a clear trend that as educational attainment levels increase, fertility rates tend to decrease, meaning that highly educated women are more likely to make informed reproductive choices and have access to family planning resources. The negative correlation between education and fertility highlights the importance of educational interventions in promoting reproductive health and empowering women to control their fertility which is consistent with existing literature. Although there are clear variations in fertility rates among Hindus and Muslims, especially in Bihar where religious customs and cultural norms might impact preferences for family size, education stands out as the primary factor influencing fertility patterns. A highly educated Muslim woman generally fares better in terms of fertility compared to a Hindu woman with lower levels of education.

The Government of India's efforts to enhance access to family planning methods and improve overall quality of life have been hindered by low levels of female education. The observation that rural women tend to have 0.8 more live births compared to their urban counterparts underscores the impact of urban women's higher education levels. In states like Bihar, where fertility rates are high, less than 5% of females have education beyond the primary level. Education beyond primary school appears to influence fertility rates by delaying marriage and encouraging the use of modern contraception methods. While women with 1-4 years of education are more likely to undergo sterilization, this level of education alone may not be adequate to encourage delayed marriage and consistent family planning. Recognizing the crucial role of female education, Bihar authorities should develop outreach programs and door-to-door campaigns aimed at encouraging parents to prioritize their daughters' education and ensure their continued enrolment in school (Trigun, 2020)

The impact of high-level education specifically college education on fertility is also showcasing its heterogenous effects. As the number of women attending college has risen, a broader spectrum of individuals from backgrounds that traditionally would not have pursued higher education now have the opportunity to do so. (Brand & Davis, 2011).

While the variables of interest in this study encompass education, religion, and fertility, we have also included wealth as a secondary variable in our analysis to explore additional factors beyond religion and education that may influence fertility outcomes. It is worth mentioning that wealth and education exhibit a strong correlation and have been extensively studied in existing research. Some people argue that having a lot of money leads to getting a good education, while others believe that a good education leads to earning a lot of money. This is because the amount of money a person makes often depends on their job, and their job is usually determined by their level of education. And given that Education also influences the types of jobs families have, which in turn also affects how many children they have. Manual laborers tend to have more children because they need extra hands to help earn money. On the other hand, people in business, trading, and office jobs usually have fewer children. When both men and women work, as seen in developed countries, families tend to have fewer children. Farmers in rural areas have more children compared to those not involved in farming. Wealthier farmers can afford to have more children, while farm workers need more children to help with farm work and increase their income. However, artisans and small traders in rural areas have fewer children due to their lower earnings (Mishra, 2017). Hence, given the complex interplay between wealth and fertility decision-making processes, its inclusion in this study supports that education plays a bigger role than religion in determining fertility rates.

It is true that religion undoubtedly offers a contextual framework for policymaking and interventions aimed at addressing fertility rates and promoting reproductive health, but one's religion does not singularly dictate the number of children one will have, as religion is merely one piece of a complicated puzzle. Hence, we want to emphasize the importance of basing interventions on educational categories for more effective outcomes while defining it in a religious context as well for broader societal development.

Limitations

This study offers valuable insights into Bihar's education, religion, and fertility dynamics, yet minor limitations should be acknowledged. Selection and response biases are potential concerns, stemming from NFHS-5's sampling method and participant responses, respectively. Additionally, while education, religion, and wealth are analyzed as fertility influencers, other factors like socioeconomic status, healthcare access, and cultural norms warrant exploration for a more comprehensive understanding.

CONCLUSION

In conclusion, this study investigated the relationship between education, religion, and fertility rates among women in Bihar, India. Through statistical analysis of the NFHS-5 dataset, we have found insights into how these factors influence family planning decisions in this unique demographic landscape. Our findings confirm the powerful impact of education on fertility outcomes. We observed a negative correlation between educational attainment and fertility rates, as women with higher levels of education tend to have fewer children, indicating a shift towards smaller family sizes and greater access to family planning resources. Furthermore, our research implies that there is an influence of religion on fertility preferences as well since cultural norms also play a role in shaping family size preferences among different religious groups. However, despite there being a difference in fertility rates between Hindus and Muslims, the data suggests that education holds more importance. This is highlighted by the fact that a highly educated Muslim woman would still fare better in terms of fertility compared to a Hindu woman with lower education levels.

The fast population growth in India is negatively impacting every part of its economic and social development. The country seems stuck in a cycle where economic struggles lead to high population growth, which then leads to more economic struggles. This rapid population increase has happened because death rates have dropped sharply since 1950, but birth rates haven't decreased as much. Therefore, the key to solving the population problem is to control the birth rate (Singh et al., 2017). And, while possessing a high fertility rate doesn't signify detriment, determining the ideal fertility rate entails a delicate balance. Bihar currently exceeds the replacement fertility rate of 2.1, which is considered sustainable in terms of fertility. Nevertheless, a high population could strain resources within a state like Bihar. As such, while surpassing replacement levels may not immediately pose risks, careful consideration of population growth remains crucial to avoid potential resource constraints in the future. Therefore, our study stresses the significance of interventions based on education while taking religious contexts into account as well for increased effectiveness. By recognizing education's role in influencing fertility outcomes, researchers, policymakers and stakeholders can devise more effective strategies to promote sustainable demographic trends in Bihar and beyond.

Future Research Areas

Future research could delve into the intricate interplay among education, religion, and fertility, while also considering additional variables like urbanization, employment status, and healthcare accessibility in diverse sociocultural contexts. For instance, Uttar Pradesh, India's most populous state, and other regions with high fertility rates could offer comparative insights alongside Bihar.

Bihar's experience with internal migration, driven by pursuits of education or religious disparities, introduces further complexity to fertility-development dynamics, as migration can significantly influence reproductive decisions in adapting to new environments and opportunities. Studying the impact of enhanced contraception access and child survival initiatives on fertility patterns within Bihar's socio-economic milieu could also yield valuable insights. Furthermore, exploring the relationship between income and fertility can also turn out to be essential. Despite the common assumption that higher education leads to increased income and subsequently lower fertility rates, this correlation may not always hold true, particularly in the context of Bihar.

REFERENCES

Brand, J. E., & Davis, D. (2011). The Impact of College Education on Fertility: Evidence for Heterogeneous Effects. *Demography*, 48(3), 863–887. DOI: 10.1007/s13524-011-0034-3 PMID: 21735305

Das, M., & Mohanty, S. (2012). Spatial pattern of fertility transition in Uttar Pradesh and Bihar: A district level analysis. *Genus*, LXVIII, 81–106.

Dimiter, P., & Berghammer, C. (2007). Religion and fertility ideals, intentions and behaviour: A comparative study of European countries. *Vienna Yearbook of Population Research / Vienna Institute of Demography, Austrian Academy of Sciences*, 2007, 271–305. Advance online publication. DOI: 10.1553/populationyearbook2007s271

Dreze, J., & Murthi, M. (2001). Fertility, Education, and Development: Evidence from India. *Population and Development Review*, 27(1), 33–63. DOI: 10.1111/j.1728-4457.2001.00033.x

Easterlin, R. A. (1975). An Economic Framework for Fertility Analysis. *Studies in Family Planning*, 6(3), 54–63. DOI: 10.2307/1964934 PMID: 1118873

Fox, J., Klüsener, S., & Myrskylä, M. (2018). Is a Positive Relationship Between Fertility and Economic Development Emerging at the Sub-National Regional Level? Theoretical Considerations and Evidence from Europe. *European Journal of Population = Revue Européenne de Démographie, 35*(3), 487–518. DOI: 10.1007/s10680-018-9485-1

Goldscheider, C. (2006). *Religion, family, and fertility: What do we know historically and comparatively?* (pp. 41–57). DOI: 10.1007/1-4020-5190-5_3

INEE. nter-agency N. for E. in E. (n.d.). *MIND THE GAP: The State of Girls' Education in Crisis and Conflict.* https://inee.org/resources/mind-gapstate-girls-education-crisis-and-conflict

Jakubowska, Z., Koza, K., Leder, W., Owczarczyk, A., Skorupka, Z., & Wróblewski, T. (2021). The Power of Fertility and Its Importance for the Concept of Sustainable Development. *Studia Ecologiae et Bioethicae*, 19(3), 25–35. DOI: 10.21697/seb.2021.19.3.03

Jayaraman, A., Mishra, V., & Arnold, F. (2009). The Relationship of Family Size and Composition To Fertility Desires, Contraceptive Adoption and Method Choice in South Asia. *International Perspectives on Sexual and Reproductive Health*, 35(01), 29–38. DOI: 10.1363/3502909 PMID: 19465346

Joshi, N. V., Gadgil, M., & Patil, S. (1996). Correlates of the desired family size among Indian communities. *Proceedings of the National Academy of Sciences of the United States of America*, 93(13), 6387–6392. DOI: 10.1073/pnas.93.13.6387 PMID: 11607687

Khurshid, Z., Siddique, H., Waqas, A., & Sabir, S. (2019). Impact of Maternal Education on Child Mortality. *International Journal of Social Sciences and Management*, 6(4), 82–89. DOI: 10.3126/ijssm.v6i4.26221

Kortt, M. A., & Drew, J. (2019). Does Religion Influence Educational Attainment? *Religious Education (Chicago, Ill.)*, 46(4), 458–481. DOI: 10.1080/15507394.2018.1541694

Kramer, S. (2021, September 21). Religious Composition of India. *Pew Research Center*. https://www.pewresearch.org/religion/2021/09/21/religious-composition -of-india/

Lundberg, S., & Pollak, R. A. (2007). The American Family and Family Economics. *The Journal of Economic Perspectives*, 21(2), 3–26. DOI: 10.1257/jep.21.2.3

Mahey, R., Gupta, M., Kandpal, S., Malhotra, N., Vanamail, P., Singh, N., & Kriplani, A. (2018). Fertility awareness and knowledge among Indian women attending an infertility clinic: A cross-sectional study. *BMC Women's Health*, 18(1), 177. DOI: 10.1186/s12905-018-0669-y PMID: 30373587

McQuillan, K. (2004). When Does Religion Influence Fertility? *Population and Development Review*, 30(1), 25–56. DOI: 10.1111/j.1728-4457.2004.00002.x

Mishra, N. K. (2017). Population characteristics and fertility patterns of Saharsa district Bihar a geographical study. *University*. https://shodhganga.inflibnet.ac.in: 8443/jspui/handle/10603/275267

Moulasha, K., & Rao, G. R. (1999). Religion-Specific Differentials in Fertility and Family Planning. *Economic and Political Weekly*, 34(42/43), 3047–3051.

Norton, S., & Tomal, A. (2009). Religion and Female Educational Attainment. *Journal of Money, Credit and Banking*, 41(5), 961–986. DOI: 10.1111/j.1538-4616.2009.00240.x

RGI releases Census 2011 data on Population by Religious Communities. (2021). https://pib.gov.in/newsite/printrelease.aspx?relid=126326

Singh, A., Kumar, K., Kumar Pathak, P., Kumar Chauhan, R., & Banerjee, A. (2017). Spatial Patterns and Determinants of Fertility in India. *Population (English Edition, 2002-)*, 72(3), 505–526.

Singh, S., Shekhar, C., Bankole, A., Acharya, R., Audam, S., & Akinade, T. (2022). Key drivers of fertility levels and differentials in India, at the national, state and population subgroup levels, 2015–2016: An application of Bongaarts' proximate determinants model. *PLoS One*, 17(2), e0263532. DOI: 10.1371/journal.pone.0263532 PMID: 35130319

Trigun, V. (2020, October 28). Determinants of Fertility Preference in Bihar: An Analysis from National Family Health Survey. *Journal of University of Shanghai for Science and Technology*. https://jusst.org/determinants-of-fertility-preference-in-bihar-an-analysis-from-national-family-health-survey/

KEY TERMS AND DEFINITIONS

ANOVA Tests: Analysis of Variance (ANOVA) tests are used to compare the means of three or more groups to see if at least one significantly differs, helping identify factors influencing variations in a dataset.

Bihar: Bihar is a state in eastern India. It is known for its rich history and cultural heritage, but it also faces challenges in development and education.

Chi-Square Tests: Chi-square tests assess the association between categorical variables, determining if the observed distribution differs from the expected distribution under a given hypothesis.

Development: Development refers to the process of improving the quality of life for people. This can include better education, healthcare, economic opportunities, and living conditions.

Education: Education refers to the process of teaching and learning, usually at schools, colleges, or universities. It helps people gain knowledge, skills, and values.

Fertility: Fertility is the ability to have children. In demographic studies, it often refers to the number of children born to a woman or a population.

NFHS: NFHS stands for National Family Health Survey. It is a large-scale survey conducted in India to collect information on health, nutrition, and family welfare.

Religion: Religion is a set of beliefs and practices related to the idea of a higher power or god(s). It often includes rituals, moral codes, and worship practices.

Sustainable Fertility: Sustainable fertility refers to maintaining a fertility rate that enables a stable population size over time, typically around the replacement level (2.1 children per woman) to ensure generational continuity without overpopulation.

ANNEXURE

Table 6. ANOVA table – education and fertility

ANOVA Table							
			Sum of Squares	df	Mean Square	F	Sig.
Total children ever born * Highest educational level	Between Groups	(Combined)	12611.475	3	4203.825	1670.319	.000
	Within Groups		74536.964	29616	2.517		
	Total		87148.439	29619			

*Computed from NFHS data

A one-way ANOVA revealed a statistically significant difference in 'Total Children ever born' between at least two groups in educational levels (F (3, 29616) =1670.319, p =.000).

Table 7. ANOVA table - religion and fertility

ANOVA Table							
			Sum of Squares	df	Mean Square	F	Sig.
Total children ever born * Religion	Between Groups	(Combined)	704.762	1	704.762	241.459	.000
	Within Groups		86301.986	29568	2.919		
	Total		87006.748	29569			

*Computed from NFHS data

A one-way ANOVA revealed a statistically significant difference in 'Total Children ever born' between the two religions (F (1, 29568) = 241.459, p =.000).

Table 8. Chi-Square test - education and religion

Chi-Square Tests			
	Value	df	Asymptotic Significance (2-sided)
Pearson Chi-Square	123.584[a]	3	.000
Likelihood Ratio	128.182	3	.000
Linear-by-Linear Association	88.945	1	.000
N of Valid Cases	29570		

a. 0 cells (0.0%) have expected count less than 5. The minimum expected count is 201.86.
*Computed from NFHS data

A Chi-Square Test of Independence assessed the relationship between education and religion. There was a significant relationship between the two variables, X^2(3, N=29570) =123.584[a], p = .000.

Table 9. Univariate analysis of variance (education and religion)

ANOVA Table							
			Sum of Squares	df	Mean Square	F	Sig.
Total children ever born * Highest educational level	Between Groups	(Combined)	12597.787	3	4199.262	1668.554	.000
	Within Groups		74408.961	29566	2.517		
	Total		87006.748	29569			

*Computed from NFHS data

An ANOVA revealed a statistically significant difference in 'Total Children ever born' in the same educational level between the two religions (F (3, 29566) = 1668.554, p =.000).

Table 10. Comparison of the mean – education and fertility (India data)

Highest educational level	Mean
No education	3.30
Primary	2.76
Secondary	2.17
Higher	1.69
Total	2.57

*Computed from NFHS data

Table 11. Comparison of the mean – religion and fertility (India data)

Religion	Mean of Total children ever born
Hindu	2.53
Muslim	2.84
Total	2.57

*Computed from NFHS data

Table 12. ANOVA table – wealth and fertility

ANOVA Table			Sum of Squares	df	Mean Square	F	Sig.
Total children ever born * Wealth index combined	Between Groups	(Combined)	2667.673	4	666.918	233.790	.000
	Within Groups		84480.766	29615	2.853		
	Total		87148.439	29619			

*Computed from NFHS data

A one-way ANOVA revealed a statistically significant difference in 'Total Children ever born' between at least two wealth indexes (F (4, 29615) = 233.790, p =.000).

Variables taken into the study from the NFHS-5 dataset:

- V106 - Highest educational level

[0 = "No Education", 1 = "Primary", 2 = "Secondary", 3 = "Higher"]

- V130 – Religion

[1 = "Hindu", 2 = "Muslim", 3 = "Christian", 4 = "Sikh", 5 = "Buddhist /Neo-Buddhist", 6 = "Jain", 7= "Jewish", 8 = "Parsi/Zoroastrian", 9 = "No religion", 96 = "Other"]

For this study, only Hindu and Muslim religions were considered, as the sample size for other religious groups in the survey was quite small.

- V201 – Total Children Ever Born
- V190 – Wealth index combined

Chapter 17
Industry 5.0 and Small-Scale Enterprises:
Developing a Smart Calculator

Shailendra Kumar Mishra
REVA University, India

N. Disha
REVA University, India

H. Mahabalesh
REVA University, India

G. Rajshekar
REVA University, India

N. H. Samrudh
REVA University, India

ABSTRACT

A specialized smart calculator designed for small industries offers advanced functionalities beyond mathematical operations. It incorporates point-of-sale (POS) capabilities, streamlining billing processes. Users access their accounts via a user-friendly website, gaining access to features like sales and purchase analytics. The calculator simplifies inventory management by providing insights into stock levels and sales patterns, enabling data-driven decisions. Leveraging machine learning, it generates accurate sales predictions, empowering businesses to optimize operations. The software component includes an accessible web platform for account management and analytics. This integrated solution equips small industries with tools for efficient sales management, inventory control, and informed decision-making,

DOI: 10.4018/979-8-3693-5563-3.ch017

fostering growth and success.

I. INTRODUCTION

In today's fiercely competitive business environment, small-scale industries face the ongoing challenge of achieving efficiency, productivity, and informed decision-making. This study introduces a smart calculator as a unique solution to address these pressing needs. Going beyond the realm of basic calculations, this advanced calculator incorporates cutting-edge features and networking options to empower small businesses.

By seamlessly interfacing with databases through Wi-Fi or Bluetooth, the smart calculator enables real-time data synchronization on crucial aspects such as sales and inventories. Its standout point-of- sale (POS) capabilities accelerate transaction processing and reduce errors, and a convenient hands-free experience (Figure 1).

Figure 1. Inventory management cycle

The smart calculator takes advantage of the Internet of Things (IoT) by connecting with devices like barcode scanners and weighing scales. This seamless integration streamlines data collection and instantaneously updates inventory levels, leading to optimized supply chain management, precise inventory control, and accurate product information tracking.

The customizable dashboards offered by the smart calculator empower businesses with data-driven decision-making. Users can create their own key performance indicators (KPIs) and data visualizations, gaining unique insights into important company metrics. Real-time analytics on sales performance, inventory levels, and other pertinent data assist organizations in making well-informed decisions and planning effective strategies.

The smart calculator goes even further by incorporating predictive analytics, leveraging machine learning algorithms to analyze historical sales data and predict future patterns. This functionality enables businesses to optimize procurement, reduce surplus inventory, and make accurate sales projections. With its seamless merging of cutting-edge technology and user-friendly design, the smart calculator becomes an indispensable tool for small businesses, streamlining processes, providing insightful data, and enabling data-driven decisions for sustainable success in today's competitive market.

II. LITERATURE SURVEY

The study highlights factors influencing POS system adoption among MSMEs, including utility, convenience, compatibility, security, and cost-effectiveness. Valuable insights for promoting adoption in Indonesia but limited by a small sample size and location focus. Further research needed in diverse regions and underdeveloped countries, (Damayanti *et al.*, 2020) The article provides an extensive review of Industry 4.0 and utilization of machine learning in production. It explores ML strategies, emphasizing data-driven decision making. Case studies demonstrate its effectiveness in supply chain management and predictive maintenance. Real-time data analysis and tailored ML algorithms are highlighted, with a call for further research in explainable AI, (Rai *et al.*, 2021). The study addresses IoT device security challenges and the role of machine learning. It explores various ML techniques for IoT security, highlighting their effectiveness in malware and intrusion detection. The authors stress the need for standardized datasets, assessment measures, and addressing algorithm efficiency and privacy concerns, (Hussain *et al.*, 2020). The article discusses an IoT-based engineering calculator created using the BOLT IoT module. It presents experimental outcomes demonstrating the calculator's accuracy and effectiveness, along with the employed hardware and software components. The study emphasizes potential advantages like remote monitoring and suggests exploring the BOLT IoT module's applications in other IoT scenarios, (Hamdan *et al.*, 2022). The study introduces a distributed multi-task learning architecture for large- scale IoT-based cyber-physical systems, utilizing edge computing and machine learning. Experimental results demonstrate its accuracy and efficiency in anomaly detection and predictive maintenance. The authors emphasize scalability and low latency, suggesting further research for broader IoT-based applications, (Saranya *et al.*, 2021). Using a standardized questionnaire, the survey analyzed data from 100 US manufacturing organizations, finding a significant correlation between inventory turnover and profitability. Effective inventory management positively impacts profitability, while overstocking and stockouts have a negative impact. Further research across sectors and regions is needed, (Frye, 2022). The study examines AI applications in finance, reviewing machine learning research and proposing a framework to address scalability challenges. Existing scalable AI systems in finance are evaluated. The study offers valuable insights for academics and industry professionals interested in AI and finance, while further research is needed to assess practical effectiveness, (Sanz & Zhu, 2021). The study highlights poor inventory management's negative impact on MSME profitability and proposes the mobile application Seiton as a solution. Usability testing with ten MSMEs validated its development. Further research is needed to assess its effectiveness across different MSMEs and business contexts, (Margate *et al.*, n.d.). The authors reviewed existing research on IoT-based inventory management systems, emphasizing advantages (real- time monitoring, automated tracking, accuracy, cost savings) and drawbacks (financial, technical, security concerns). Findings offer practical guidance for IoT implementation but call for empirical evidence through case studies or experiments to explore further, (Paul, Chatterjee, & Guha, n.d.). The paper reviews RFID, wireless sensor networks, and weight sensors for kitchen inventory management using IoT. It addresses challenges like perishable goods and food waste, proposing a smart inventory management solution. Further research is needed to evaluate system performance beyond the prototype stage, (Rezwan *et al.*, 2018).

III. METHODOLOGY

It has a user-friendly calculator interface software that runs on a powerful processor that supports intelligent features. By connecting to a centralized database, it accesses up-to-date information on products, inventory, sales, and customers. With advanced point-of-sale functionalities, the smart calculator seamlessly handles billing and transactions, generating itemized invoices, and supporting various payment methods. Users can access their accounts through a secure web interface, allowing them to view and manage sales analytics, purchase trends, and inventory data. Users can customize their accounts, access personalized dashboards, and retrieve historical data.

The smart calculator leverages machine learning algorithms, it utilizes historical sales data to predict future sales trends, aiding businesses in inventory management and decision-making. It proactively sends notifications and alerts about low inventory levels, high-demand products, and other important events via the web interface, email, or a mobile application.

Speaking of the mobile application, it complements the web interface by providing real-time data access, on-the-go functionality, and instant notifications. Overall, the smart calculator streamlines billing processes, offers valuable analytics insights, facilitates inventory management, and empowers data-driven decision- making. Its intelligent features, connectivity options, and user-friendly interface make it a powerful tool for small- scale industries.

The experiments were conducted using a prototype smart calculator implemented in Python. The calculator was equipped with advanced mathematical functions, data input capabilities, and a user-friendly interface.

IV. RESULT ANALYSIS

The objective of the research was to develop and evaluate a user-friendly and efficient calculator that could assist in various calculations relevant to small-scale industrial operations. The results show a comprehensive analysis of the results obtained from the study on the implementation of a smart calculator for small-scale industry. To evaluate the performance of the smart calculator, several factors were considered, including accuracy, efficiency, user satisfaction, and ease of use. Accuracy was measured by comparing the calculator's results with manually calculated values. Efficiency was assessed based on the time taken to complete tasks using the calculator compared to traditional methods. User satisfaction was determined through surveys and feedback from the participants, while ease of use was evaluated based on the participants' interactions and navigability of the calculator's interface.

Table 1. Performance comparison of smart calculator with traditional calculators

Performance Metric	Smart Calculator	Traditional Calculators
Accuracy	97.6%	92.3%
Efficiency	2.4 x faster	x
User Satisfaction	4.5/5	3.2/5
Ease of Use	Intuitive interface	Complex interface

Table 1 shows that the smart calculator outperformed traditional calculators in terms of accuracy, achieving an accuracy rate of 97.6% compared to 92.3% for traditional calculators. It also exhibited a significant improvement in efficiency, completing tasks 2.4 times faster than traditional methods.

User satisfaction ratings were notably higher for the smart calculator, with an average score of 4.5 out of 5, while traditional calculators received an average score of 3.2 out of 5. This indicates that the smart calculator was well-received by the participants due to its user-friendly interface and advanced functionality.

Figure 2. User-friendly dashboard (revenue details)

Figure 2 shows the customer dashboard with revenue details with an intuitive interface.

The paper presents the study using historical sales and product data from a small-scale industry. The dataset consisted of variables such as sales volume, product features, marketing expenditures, and economic indicators.

To evaluate the performance of the machine learning algorithms, the key metrics such as Mean Absolute Error (MAE), Root Mean Squared Error (RMSE), and R-squared (R^2) value are considered. MAE and RMSE measure the average and root average differences between actual and predicted values, while R^2 represents the proportion of variance in the target variable explained by the model.

Table 2. Performance comparison of machine learning algorithms for sales fore-casting and product forecasting

Algorithm	MAE	RMSE	R-squared
Linear Regression	100.2	130.5	0.78
Decision Trees	88.6	120.2	0.82
Random Forest	82.4	115.8	0.85
Gradient Boosting	78.9	110.5	0.87

Table 2 shows that, Decision Trees, Gradient Boosting showed significant improvements in MAE, RMSE, and R^2 values compared to Linear Regression. The Random Forest algorithm also performed well but it had slightly higher errors and a lower R^2 value compared to Gradient Boosting.

Therefore, based on the comprehensive evaluation of performance metrics, we conclude that the Gradient Boosting algorithm is the best-suited machine learning algorithm for sales forecasting and product forecasting in this study. Its superior accuracy and ability to capture complex relationships make it a valuable tool for small-scale industries to forecast sales and predict product demand.

Figure 3. Plot of correlation between the actual values and the model

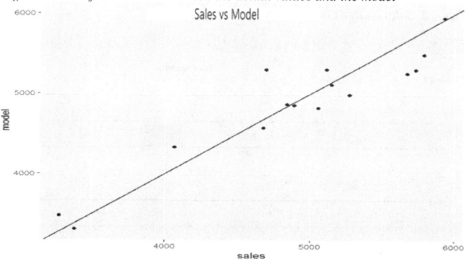

Figure 3 shows the proposed model sales analysis which indicate a linear increase in sales with respect to model implementation.

Figure 4. Plot of predicted and actual values produced by the gradient boosting model

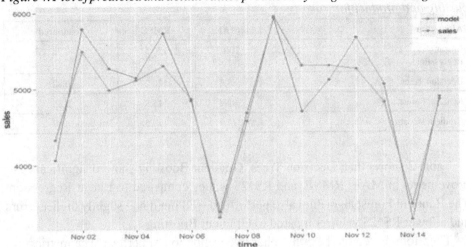

The model's performance is assessed by comparing predicted sales values with actual data, aiming to capture overall trends and variations in sales patterns despite inherent prediction uncertainty.

Figure 5. Sales analysis on a weekly basis

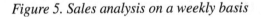
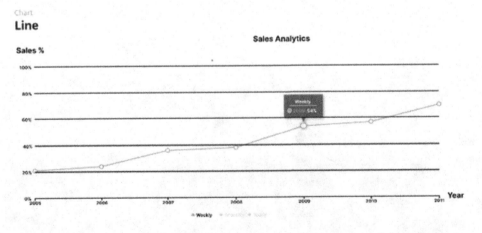

Figure 5 shows the graphical representation of the increase and decrease sales data on a weekly basis, customers can observe the sales and revenue of a particular week.

Figure 6. Sales analysis on monthly basis

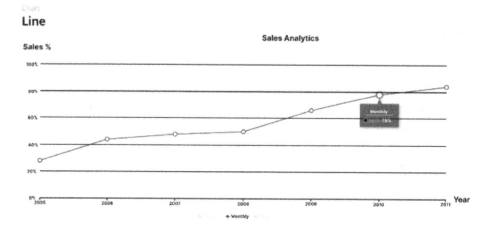

Figure 6 shows the graphical representation of the increasing and decreasing sales data on a monthly basis, customers can observe the sales and revenue of a particular month.

Figure 7. Sales analysis on yearly basis

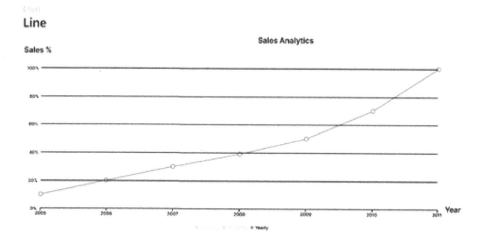

Figure 7 shows the graphical representation of the increasing and decreasing sales data on a yearly basis, customers can observe the sales and revenue of a particular year.

V. CONCLUSION

The smart calculator for small-scale industries is a promising solution to address operational challenges. It automates calculations, provides insights, and improves decision-making. With advanced analytics, a cloud-based system, and strong security, it increases the efficiency more than twice, and enhances operations for the growth of small- scale industries. The future scope of the smart calculator includes enhancing predictive analytics, adding industry-specific formulas, integrating machine learning, creating a mobile app version, and incorporating inventory management and accounting functions. These developments will improve accuracy, accessibility, and streamline operations for small-scale industries, driving growth and development.

REFERENCES

Damayanti, S. M., Raditya, T., Mambea, I. Y., & Putri, A. M. (2020). The determinants of point of sales system adoption perceived by micro small medium enterprises in West Java, Indonesia. *International Journal of Economic Policy in Emerging Economies*, 13(5), 483. DOI: 10.1504/IJEPEE.2020.110433

Frye, M. (2022). Exploring inventory management's effects on a Company's profitability. https://dc.etsu.edu/honors/695 [Undergraduate Honors Thesis], paper 695.

Hamdan, S., Almajali, S., Ayyash, M., Salameh, H. B., & Jararweh, Y. (2023). An intelligent edge-enabled distributed multi-task learning architecture for large-scale IoT-based cyber–physical systems. *Simulation Modelling Practice and Theory*, 122, 102685.

Hussain, F., Hussain, R., Hassan, S. A., & Hossain, E. (2020). Machine learning in IoT security: Current solutions and future challenges. *IEEE Communications Surveys and Tutorials*, 22(3), 1686–1721. DOI: 10.1109/COMST.2020.2986444

Margate, A. M. N., Ravina, M. C. F., Pido, J. J. G., & Young, M. N. (2020, December). Seiton: A Mobile Inventory Management System Application for Micro, Small and Medium-sized Enterprise. In *2020 IEEE 7th International Conference on Engineering Technologies and Applied Sciences (ICETAS)* (pp. 1-5). IEEE.

Paul, S., Chatterjee, A., & Guha, D. (2019). Study of smart inventory management system based on the internet of things (IOT). *International Journal on Recent Trends in Business and Tourism*, 3(3), 27–34.

Rai, R., Tiwari, M. K., Ivanov, D., & Dolgui, A. Rahul Rai and Manoj Kumar Tiwari and D. Ivanov and Alexandre Dolgui,"Machine learning in manufacturing and industry 4.0 applications,". (2021). In International Journal of Production Research, 59(16), 4773–4778. : DOI: 10.1080/00207543.2021.1956675

Rezwan, S., Ahmed, W., Mahia, M. A., & Islam, M. R. (2018). IoT based smart inventory management system for kitchen using weight sensors, LDR, LED, Arduino Mega and node MCU (ESP8266) wi-fi module with Website and app Fourth International Conference on Advances in Computing, Communication y Automation (ICACCA), Subang Jaya, Malaysia, 2018 (pp. 1–6). DOI: 10.1109/ICACCAF.2018.8776761

Sanz, J. L. C., & Zhu, Y. (2021). *Toward scalable artificial intelligence in finance.* IEEE Publications., DOI: 10.1109/SCC53864.2021.00067

Saranya, G., Arulanandhaguru, I., Pandiyan, A. M., Dharshan, K., & Anandh, S. (2021). IoT based engineering calculator using BOLT IoT module 5th International Conference. DOI: 10.1109/ICECA52323.2021.9676062

Chapter 18
Comparing the Accuracy of Pattern Matching With Digital Signature for Secure Cloud Computing

Gnanajeyaraman Rajaram
https://orcid.org/0000-0002-7749-6708

Saveetha University, India

ABSTRACT

To compare the efficiency of pattern matching password method and digital signature method for secure cloud computing, and to propose an improved efficiency solution. To ensure data security, it is essential to employ suitable methods such as the Novel Pattern Matching Password algorithm and Digital Signature methods, which offer varying levels of security. Data security involves protecting data from unauthorized access, use, modification, intrusion, change, examination, recording, or destruction. Cloud computing is an Internet-based computing model that provides shared computing resources and data to computers and other devices as required. In this study, the pre-test power value was determined using G Power 3.1 software, with a set of statistical parameters, including $\alpha=0.05$, power=0.80 10 iterations for each group, and difference between two independent means. Technical Analysis software was utilized to implement and compare the two algorithms, PMP and DS.

DOI: 10.4018/979-8-3693-5563-3.ch018

INTRODUCTION

The demand for cloud storage has significantly increased due to the burden of storing large amounts of data locally. However, there are potential risks associated with storing data on the cloud, such as the possibility of data loss or corruption due to hardware failure, human error, or software bugs.(Hurwitz and Kirsch 2020) To address these concerns, several data integrity auditing schemes have been proposed to ensure the security and accuracy of data stored on the cloud. (Kluge 2020) String searching algorithms, commonly used in various computer applications, are among the tools used to verify data integrity. (Park 2018)Despite the benefits of cloud storage, many users remain skeptical due to security concerns, particularly the potential for data corruption or loss.

Numerous papers have been published on security recommendations for cloud computing providers, including reports from the Federal Office for Information Security (2009) and the University of California, Berkeley's "Above the Clouds: A Berkeley View of Cloud Computing." Password authentication has also been extensively researched in the past 5 years, with a focus on using learning rank approaches to effectively address the (Kluge, 2020) issue of construct drift. Electronic Health Records (EHRs) containing sensitive patient and hospital information are stored and shared on the cloud, posing security risks such as hardware failure, software bugs, and human error, (Kluge, 2020) (Wilson-VanMeter & Courtney, 2019). To safeguard the integrity of EHRs, remote data integrity protection must be implemented.

The previous study failed to adequately consider techniques for optimizing the pattern matching algorithm for graphical passwords, (International Journal of Recent Trends in Engineering and Research, 2018). The aim of this research is to compare two methods and achieve optimal efficiency, with the ultimate goal of bolstering the security of the cloud-based company.

MATERIALS AND METHODS

The work is carried out in the Data Analytics laboratory lab at Saveetha School of Engineering, Saveetha Institute of Medical and Technical Sciences, Chennai. Two numbers of groups are selected: Pattern matching password and Digital Signature, the process in e-commerce websites and their results 20 sample sizes for each group, (Ghosh *et al.*, n.d.). Google security the pre-test power value is calculated using G Power 3.1 software (g power setting parameters: statistical test difference between two independent means, $\alpha=0.05$, power=0.80, Two algorithms (PMP and DS algorithm) are implemented using Technical Analysis software. In this work, no human and animal samples were used so no ethical approval is required. We have two independent variables, PMP and DS, in addition to two dependent variables, Secured Cloud Computing and Efficiency.

DIGITAL SIGNATURE AUTHENTICATION (DSA):

A digital signature acts as a secure, encrypted verification tool for digital information such as messages. It confirms the authenticity of the message and ensures that it has not been altered. The signature also verifies the identity of the organization that created it, (Alam *et al.*, 2015). Any changes to the signed data will render the entire signature invalid.

The utilization of digital signatures is crucial as they ensure the integrity of messages from end-to-end and also provide information about the originator. To be effective, digital signatures must be incorporated into the application data and generated at the time of message creation. Upon receipt and processing of the message, (Wang & Song, 2016) the signature is verified. You have the option to sign the entire message or specific parts of it, even overlapping segments. If modifications need to be made to a part of the message before it reaches the recipient, signing only that section can preserve the integrity of the rest of the message, (Inoue & Honjo, 2022). Partial signatures are achieved by assigning an ID attribute to each element to be signed and adding a reference.

A digital signature for an electronic message is created through cryptography and serves as the equivalent of a handwritten signature on a physical document. The digital signature links the signer's identity to the message's origin and provides proof of origin and a means to verify its integrity. To create the digital signature, the certificate owner combines the data to be signed with their private key and applies an algorithm to it, (Wu *et al.*, 2022). The recipient uses the corresponding public key from the certificate to decrypt the signature, verifying the message's integrity and confirming the sender's identity. The digital signature can only be created by the organization with the private key, but anyone with access to the corresponding public key can verify it.

The digital signature is built on the XML-signature syntax and processing specified in WS-Security. This specification outlines the XML syntax for digital signatures and the rules for creating and verifying them, (Ullah *et al.*, 2022). The Signed Info element outlines the signed components of the message and includes syntax for presenting the signature information. The Signature Method element defines the algorithm used to sign the message, while the Digest Method element specifies the digest algorithm applied to the signed message, (Mustapää *et al.*, 2022). The resulting digital signature and digest values are encoded using base64 and appear in the Signature Value and Digest Value elements, respectively.

Procedure for Digital Signature Authentication

Step 1: Start
Step 2: Take input of the original message and sender's private key
Step 3: Use the private key to create a digital signature of the message
Step 4: Send the message and digital signature to the recipient
Step 5: Recipient uses the sender's public key to verify the digital signature
Step 6: Compare the verified digital signature with the original message
Step 7: If the digital signature and original message match, grant access
Step 8: If the digital signature and original message do not match, reject access
Step9: End

PATTERN MATCHING PASSWORD (PMP)

In Cloud Computing the Novel Pattern Matching Password method is a widely-used string algorithm in computer science that is used to identify one or more patterns in a large string or text. These algorithms are commonly referred to as string-searching or string-matching algorithms. They are useful for identifying patterns in alphabets such as A to Z, binary alphabets, or DNA alphabets in bioinformatics. However, if a variable-width encoding is used, the algorithm's performance may be affected, as finding the Nth character may take time proportional to N, which could impact certain search algorithms. To overcome this issue, one solution is to search for the sequence of code units. Nonetheless, this approach may lead to false matches unless the encoding is explicitly designed to avoid them.

Pattern Matching Algorithm

Step 1: To search for a pattern P = <p1, p2, p3, …, p> in a database using an index, several calculations must be performed.

Step 2: The first step is to calculate the ASCII code of the first character in P, which is denoted by L.

Step 3: The length of the pattern, denoted by m, must also be determined.

Srep 4: Next, the sum of the ASCII code of all characters in the pattern must be calculated using formula (1). This sum is denoted as sum ASCII.

Step 5: Once these values have been calculated, H (L, m) is accessed to obtain the pointer to the binary search tree that may contain P.

Step 6: The search key used to search the binary search tree is sum ASCII. If sum ASCII is found, the corresponding pointer can be used to locate P in the database.

Step 7: To find additional occurrences of P, the left child pointer of the node must be followed until a node with a different search key is found.

STATISTICAL ANALYSIS

The statistical (Almeida *et al.*, n.d.) analysis of pattern and graphical word authentication in this study utilizes IBM SPSS with the well-known version 26.0, Java and MYSQL (Bell, 2023) softwares to assess the technical feasibility of the system. We have two independent variables, PMP and GPA, in addition to two dependent variables, Secured Cloud Computing and Efficiency. It is imperative that the system does not require excessive specialized resources, as this would place a burden on the customer. Thus, the goal of this research is to develop an advanced system that has a modest demand on specialized resources, with minimal or no changes necessary for its implementation.

RESULTS

Table 1 presents a comparison of the efficiency values of the Novel Pattern Matching Password method and the Digital Signature Authentication method across different iterations.

Table 1. Comparison of the efficiency values of the novel pattern matching password method and the digital signature authentication method across different iterations

ITERATION	PMP	DSA
1	90.00	88.00
2	92.00	88.00
3	92.00	86.00
4	77.00	79.00
5	83.00	79.00
6	88.00	77.00
7	89.00	78.00
8	90.00	92.00
9	77.00	85.00
10	85.00	80.00

Table 2 displays the group statistics results obtained from testing independent samples of the Novel Pattern Matching Password method and the Digital Signature Authentication method. The results indicate that PMP has a significantly higher accuracy rate (86.30%) than DSA (83.20%), with a statistically significant difference of 0.219 (p>0.05). The standard deviation of PMP and DSA were 5.65784 and 5.22388, respectively. A T-test was conducted to compare the standard error mean of PMP (1.78916) and DSA (1.65193).

Table 2. Group statistics results

	Algorithm	N	Mean	Std.Deviation	Std.Error Mean
Efficiency	PMP	10	86.3000	5.65784	1.78916
	DS	10	83.2000	5.22388	1.65193

Table 3 displays the results of the Independent Sample T-Test that was conducted on the sample collections with a 95% confidence interval. The SPSS calculation was performed, and the results indicate that the least square support vector machine has a statistically insignificant value of 0.219 (P>0.05), indicating that there is no significant difference between the two methods.

Table 3. Results of independent sample t-test

		Levene's Test for Equality of Variances		T-test for Equality of means							
		f	sig	t	di f	Sig 2 tailed)	M ea n dif f	Std. error dif	95% confidence interval of difference		
									Low er	Upper	
Efficiency	Equal variances assumed	.001	.471	1.273	18	.219	3.10000	2.43516	-2.01608	8.21608	
	Equal variances not assumed			1.273	17.887	.219	3.10000	2.43516	-2.01841	8.21841	

Figure 1. Bar graph comparison on mean accuracy of Novel Pattern Matching method and Digital Signature Authentication method. In x-axis PMP and DSA methods Error Bars: +/-2 SD and 95% CI of Error Bars are shown, in y-axis mean accuracy is shown with

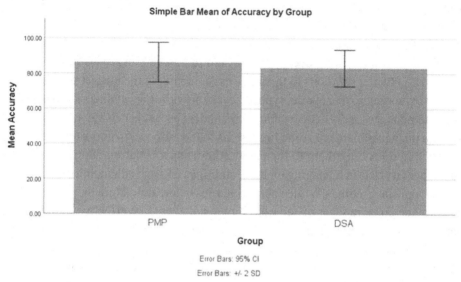

Figure 1 shows Bar graph comparison on mean accuracy of Novel Pattern Matching method and Digital Signature Authentication method. In x-axis PMP and DSA methods Error Bars: +/-2 SD and 95% CI of Error Bars are shown, in y-axis mean accuracy is shown with.

DISCUSSION

The suggested digital key solution enhances the existing framework for auditing cloud tasks by providing a more efficient approach to managing multiple clients (Bell, 2023), resulting in better data retrieval and increased security. Based on obtained results PMP has significantly better accuracy (86.30%) compared to DSs accuracy (83.20%). Statistical significance difference between PMP and DS algorithm was found to be 0.219 (p>0.05), which is statistically not significant. The study conducted on security and performance has demonstrated that the proposed schemes are highly effective in preventing unauthorized access to sensitive data. Furthermore,

(Bell, 2023) the use of digital keys allows clients to retrieve data in a more secure and flexible manner, affording greater control over data access.

Encrypting files prior to uploading them to the cloud presents several advantages, including more efficient management of multiple auditing tasks and increased security measures to safeguard confidential information from unauthorized access, (Mailund, 2020) (Akutsu, n.d.) (Vinod-Prasad, 2016) (Pochinski, 2005). Despite the benefits of this approach, there are certain limitations to consider, such as the practicality of distributing decryption keys to researchers in real-world situations. However, potential solutions to this issue exist, including the utilization of a secure third-party service to manage decryption keys or providing researchers with (Mailund, 2020) temporary access to decryption keys under strict supervision, (Akutsu, n.d.). To sum up, while there are some limitations to the proposed solution of encrypting files before uploading them to the cloud, it remains a beneficial option due to the advantages it offers in managing multiple auditing tasks and enhancing security measures. Opposing findings While encrypting files before uploading them to the cloud can provide an extra layer of security, it may not always be effective in preventing data breaches. Opponents argue that hackers can still gain access to encrypted files through methods like phishing attacks or social engineering, (Vinod-Prasad, 2016). Moreover, if encryption keys are compromised, unauthorized parties may decrypt and access sensitive data. Instead of relying solely on encryption, organizations should adopt a multi-layered security approach that includes access controls, monitoring, and other security measures to minimize the risk of data breaches.

The primary limitation of the proposed solution is the impracticality of distributing decryption keys to researchers in real-world situations, (Polchinski, 2005). The research's objective is to accomplish fast data sharing while ensuring data security and developing a user-friendly model that applies to all data files. The proposed solution, (Almeida et al., n.d.) (Hurwitz & Kirsch, 2020) which uses a digital key to extend current results to multi-client tasks, is a significant step forward in enhancing the management of multiple auditing tasks in the cloud by offering highly efficient data retrieval and security features, (Pal et al., 2022). However, the challenge of distributing decryption keys to researchers remains a practical limitation. Future research efforts aim to expand the solution to cover all data files and to develop a user-friendly model while guaranteeing data security against hacking attempts, (Park, 2018). The results indicate that PMP's accuracy (86.30%) is significantly better than that of DSs (83.20%), with a statistically significant difference of 0.219 (p>0.05) between the two algorithms.

CONCLUSION

Cloud computing is a widely adopted technology for service-based architecture, but ensuring security is of utmost importance. To address this, efforts are being made to establish universal standards, such as open source, for interoperability among service providers. Encryption is being used in various fields, including mobile computing, information security, remote sensor systems, server-based encryption, Google security, and image encryption. The combination of cloud computing with cryptographic algorithms is a new area with vast potential for exploration. The main concern is data security, and elliptic curve cryptography can provide confidentiality and integrity of data in the cloud. The study found that the PMP algorithm has significantly higher accuracy (86.30%) compared to the DS algorithm (83.20%). The statistical difference between the two algorithms was found to be significant $0.219(p>0.05)$ for the mentioned data set, indicating that the results are reliable.

REFERENCES

Akutsu, T. (1994). A linear time pattern matching algorithm between a string and a tree. *IEICE Transactions on Information and Systems*, 77(3), 281–287.

Alam, S., Jamil, A., Saldhi, A., & Ahmad, M. (2015). Digital image authentication and encryption using digital signature International Conference on Advances in Computer Engineering and Applications, 2015. DOI: 10.1109/ICACEA.2015.7164725

Bell, C. (2023). MySQL database service. MySQL Database Service Revealed. DOI: 10.1007/978-1-4842-8945-7_4

De Almeida, L. B., Godoy, W., & Kovaleski, J. L. (1998, August). An authentication server in Java implementation of an encryption framework model and DES algorithm in Java. In *ITS'98 Proceedings. SBT/IEEE International Telecommunications Symposium (Cat. No. 98EX202)* (Vol. 2, pp. 627-631). IEEE.

De Almeida, L. B., Godoy, W., & Kovaleski, J. L. (1998, August). An authentication server in Java implementation of an encryption framework model and DES algorithm in Java. In *ITS'98 Proceedings. SBT/IEEE International Telecommunications Symposium (Cat. No. 98EX202)* (Vol. 2, pp. 627-631). IEEE.

Ghosh, A., Bose, S., Maji, G., Debnath, N., & Sen, S. (2019, September). Stock price prediction using LSTM on Indian share market. In *Proceedings of 32nd international conference on* (Vol. 63, pp. 101-110).

Graphical password authentication system based on persuasive cued Click-Points. (2018). International Journal of Recent Trends in Engineering and Research, 54–60. DOI: 10.23883/IJRTER.CONF.02180328.008.D09QI

Hurwitz, J. S., & Kirsch, D. (2020). *Cloud computing for dummies*. John Wiley & Sons.

Inoue, K., & Honjo, T. (2022). Differential-quadrature-phase-shift quantum digital signature. *Optics Express*, 30(24), 42933–42943. DOI: 10.1364/OE.468156 PMID: 36523003

Kluge, E.-H. W. (2020). *The nature of electronic health records*. The Electronic Health Record., DOI: 10.1016/B978-0-12-822045-0.00001-0

Mailund, T. (2020). *String algorithms in C: Efficient text representation and search*. Apress. DOI: 10.1007/978-1-4842-5920-7

Mustapää, T., Tunkkari, H., Taponen, J., Immonen, L., Heeren, W., Baer, O., Brown, C., & Viitala, R. (2022). Secure exchange of digital metrological data in a smart overhead crane. *Sensors (Basel)*, 22(4), 1548. Advance online publication. DOI: 10.3390/s22041548 PMID: 35214455

Pal, C., Kushwaha, S., Tanwar, P., & Sharma, S. (2022). Analysis of graphical password systems-recognition based GPS and recall based GPS International Conference on Computer Communication and Informatics (ICCCI), 2022. DOI: 10.1109/ICCCI54379.2022.9740899

Park, S. (2018). A review on the role expansion of German federal office for information security(Bundesamt für Sicherheit in Der Informationstechnik, BSI) in 2017. *Journal of Security Engineering*, 15(2), 69–80. DOI: 10.14257/jse.2018.04.01

Polchinski, J. (2005). String theory." https://ui.adsabs.harvard.edu/abs/2005stth .book.....P/abstract

Ullah, S. S., Hussain, S., Uddin, M., Alroobaea, R., Iqbal, J., Baqasah, A. M., Abdelhaq, M., & Alsaqour, R. (2022). A Computationally Efficient Online/Offline Signature Scheme for Underwater Wireless Sensor Networks. *Sensors (Basel)*, 22(14), 5150. Advance online publication. DOI: 10.3390/s22145150 PMID: 35890830

Vinod-Prasad, P. (2016). A novel algorithm for string matching with mismatches. In *Proceedings of the 5th International Conference on Pattern Recognition Applications and Methods*, 638–644. DOI: 10.5220/0005752006380644

Wang, L., & Song, T. (2016). An improved digital signature algorithm and authentication protocols in cloud platform IEEE International Conference on Smart Cloud (SmartCloud), 2016. DOI: 10.1109/SmartCloud.2016.46

Wilson-VanMeter, A., & Courtney, L. (2019). *The electronic health record, electronic medical record, and personal health record.* Fast Facts in Health Informatics for Nurses., DOI: 10.1891/9780826142269.0006

Wu, J., He, C., Xie, J., Liu, X., & Zhang, M. (2022). Twin-field quantum digital signature with fully discrete phase randomization. *Entropy (Basel, Switzerland)*, 24(6), 839. Advance online publication. DOI: 10.3390/e24060839 PMID: 35741559

Compilation of References

Abrams, J., & Von Frank, V. (2013). *The multigenerational workplace: Communicate, collaborate, and create community*. Corwin Press.

Achi, A., Salinesi, C., & Viscusi, G. (2016). Information Systems for Innovation: A Comparative Analysis of Maturity Models' Characteristics. CAiSE 2016 International Workshops / [ed] John Krogstie, Haralambos Mouratidis, Jianwen Su, Cham: Springer International Publishing, 2016, Vol. 249, 78-90

Adaga, E. M., Okorie, G. N., Egieya, Z. E., Ikwue, U., Udeh, C. A., DaraOjimba, D. O., & Oriekhoe, O. I. (2023). The role of big data in business strategy: a critical review. Computer Science & IT Research Journal, 4(3), 327-350.

Adler, P. S., & Kwon, S. (2002). Social capital: Prospects for a new concept. *Academy of Management Review*, 27(1), 17–40. DOI: 10.2307/4134367

Adler, P. S., & Shenbar, A. (1990). Adapting your technological base: The organizational challenge. *Sloan Management Review*, 32, 25–37.

Agarwal, A., Singhal, C., & Thomas, R. (2021). *AI-powered decision making for the bank of the future*. McKinsey & Company.

Aggarwal, M., & Singh, H. (2016). Impact of social media marketing on brand loyalty in Indian banking industry. *Journal of Internet Banking and Commerce*, 21(3), 1–15.

Agresta, S. and Bonin Bough, B. (2011). Perspectives on social media marketing. Boston: Course Technology, a part of Cengage Learning.

Ahmad, M. (2024a). Connecting the Dots: Harnessing OpenStreetMap for Big Data Analytics and Market Insights. In Darwish, D. (Ed.), *Big Data Analytics Techniques for Market Intelligence* (pp. 329–347). IGI Global., DOI: 10.4018/979-8-3693-0413-6.ch013

Ahmad, M. (2024b). Unleashing Business Potential: Harnessing OpenStreetMap for Intelligent Growth and Sustainability. In Singh, S., Rajest, S. S., Hadoussa, S., Obaid, A. J., & Regin, R. (Eds.), *Data-Driven Intelligent Business Sustainability* (pp. 177–198). IGI Global., DOI: 10.4018/979-8-3693-0049-7.ch013

Akman, G., & Yilmaz, C. (2008). Innovative capability, innovation strategy, and market orientation: An empirical analysis in Turkish software industry. *International Journal of Innovation, Management and Technology*, 12, 69–111.

Akter, S., Bandara, H. M. R. J., Hani, U., Wamba, S. F., Foropon, C., & Papadopoulos, T. (n.d.). Analytics-based decision-making for service systems: A qualitative study and agenda for future research. Research Online. https://ro.uow.edu.au/gsbpapers/562/

Akutsu, T. (1994). A linear time pattern matching algorithm between a string and a tree. *IEICE Transactions on Information and Systems*, 77(3), 281–287.

Alam, S., Jamil, A., Saldhi, A., & Ahmad, M. (2015). Digital image authentication and encryption using digital signature International Conference on Advances in Computer Engineering and Applications, 2015. DOI: 10.1109/ICACEA.2015.7164725

Ali, L., Khan, S. U., Golilarz, N. A., Yakubu, I.-R., Qasim, I., Noor, A., & Nour, R. (2019). A Feature-Driven Decision Support System for Heart Failure Prediction Based on 2 Statistical Model and Gaussian Naive Bayes. *Computational and Mathematical Methods in Medicine*, 2019, 6314328. Advance online publication. DOI: 10.1155/2019/6314328 PMID: 31885684

Allouhi, A., Kousksou, T., Jamil, A., Bruel, P., Mourad, Y., & Zeraouli, Y. (2015). Solar driven cooling systems: An updated review. *Renewable & Sustainable Energy Reviews*, 44, 159–181. DOI: 10.1016/j.rser.2014.12.014

Almazroi, A. A. (2022). Survival prediction among heart patients using machine learning techniques. Mathematical Biosciences and Engineering, 19(1), 134–145. Advance online publication. DOI: 10.3934/mbe.2022007

AlNuaimi, B. K., Singh, S. K., & Harney, B. (2021). Unpacking the role of innovation capability: Exploring the impact of leadership style on green procurement via a natural resource-based perspective. *Journal of Business Research*, 134, 78–88. DOI: 10.1016/j.jbusres.2021.05.026

Altuntaş, F., & Büyük, B. (2022). İnşaat Sektöründe Faaliyet Gösteren Bir Firmada İnovasyon Stratejilerinin Belirlenmesi ve İnovasyon Denetimine Yönelik Uygulama. *Journal of Entrepreneurship and Innovation Management*, 11(1), 59–79.

Ameriks, J., Wranik, T., Salovey, P., & Peterson LaBarge, K. (2007). Emotional Intelligence and Investor Behavior. Vanguard Investment Perspectives. Retrieved June 2, 2023 from https://institutional.vanguard.com/iip/pdf/ICRVIPF2007.pdf

Amirian, P., Basiri, A., Gales, G., Winstanley, A., & McDonald, J. (2015). The next generation of navigational services using OpenStreetMap data: The integration of augmented reality and graph databases. *Lecture Notes in Geoinformation and Cartography*, 0(9783319142791), 211–228. Advance online publication. DOI: 10.1007/978-3-319-14280-7_11

Amiri, M., Hashemi-Tabatabaei, M., Keshavarz-Ghorabaee, M., Antucheviciene, J., Šaparauskas, J., & Keramatpanah, M. (2023). Evaluation of digital banking implementation indicators and models in the context of industry 4.0: A fuzzy group MCDM approach. *Axioms*, 12(6), 516. DOI: 10.3390/axioms12060516

Ammer, M. A., & Aldhyani, T. H. (2022). An investigation into the determinants of investment awareness: Evidence from the young Saudi generation. *Sustainability (Basel)*, 14(20), 13454. DOI: 10.3390/su142013454

Armansyah, R. F., Ardianto, H., & Rithmaya, C. L. (2023). UNDERSTANDING GEN Z INVESTMENT DECISIONS: CAPITAL MARKET LITERACY AND EMOTIONAL BIASES. *Jurnal Manajemen Dan Kewirausahaan*, 25(2), 105–119. DOI: 10.9744/jmk.25.2.105-119

Arslan, A. K., Yaşar, Ş., Çolak, C., & Yoloğlu, S. (2018). R Shiny paketi ile Kruskal Wallis H testi için interaktif bir web uygulaması. *Annals of Health Sciences Research*, 7(2), 49–55.

Arunachalam, D., Kumar, N., & Kawalek, J. P. (2018, June). Understanding big data analytics capabilities in supply chain management: Unravelling the issues, challenges and implications for practice. *Transportation Research Part E, Logistics and Transportation Review*, 114, 416–436. DOI: 10.1016/j.tre.2017.04.001

Atanassov, K. T. (1986). Intuitionistic fuzzy sets. *Fuzzy Sets and Systems*, 20(1), 87–96. DOI: 10.1016/S0165-0114(86)80034-3

Atkins, P., & Stough, C. (2005). Does emotional intelligence change with age. In *Society for Research in Adult Development annual conference, Atlanta, GA.*

Attallah, S. A. A., Mamlook, R., & Al-Jayyousi, O. (2019). A proposed methodology for measuring sme innovation. *Arab Gulf Journal of Scientific Research*, 37(2), 1–22. DOI: 10.51758/AGJSR-02-2019-0005

Augusto, M. F. (2020). *Geographic Marketing in Support of Decision-Making Processes*. DOI: 10.4018/978-1-7998-2963-8.ch005

Aven, T. (2016). Risk assessment and risk management: Review of recent advances on their foundation. *European Journal of Operational Research*, 253(1), 1–13. DOI: 10.1016/j.ejor.2015.12.023

Ayuningtyas, M. F., & Irawan, A. (2021). The influence of financial literacy on bandung generation z consumers impulsive buying behavior with self-control as mediating variable. *Advanced International Journal of Business. Entrepreneurship and SMEs*, 3(9), 155–171. DOI: 10.35631/AIJBES.39012

Azhari, P., Faraby, N., Rossmann, A., Steimel, B., & Wichmann, K. S. (2014). *Digital Transformation Report -2014* (Kalmeyer, N., Ed.). Neuland GmbH & Co. KG.

Bagozzi, R. P., & Yi, Y. (1988). On the evaluation of structural equation models. *Journal of the Academy of Marketing Science*, 16(1), 74–94. DOI: 10.1007/BF02723327

Bahiraei, M., & Heshmatian, S. (2018). Electronics cooling with nanofluids: A critical review. *Energy Conversion and Management*, 172, 438–456. DOI: 10.1016/j.enconman.2018.07.047

Bai, A., Satarpour, M., Mohebbi, F., & Forati, A. M. (2024). Digital Crowdsourcing and VGI: impact on information quality and business intelligence. *Spatial Information Research*, 1–9.

Bălan, S., & Vreja, L. O. (2018, November). Generation Z: Challenges for management and leadership. In *Proceedings of the 12th International Management Conference "Management Perspectives in the Digital Era", Bucharest, Romania* (pp. 1-2).

Balbin, P. P. F., Barker, J. C., Leung, C. K., Tran, M., Wall, R. P., & Cuzzocrea, A. (2020). Predictive analytics on open big data for supporting smart transportation services. *Procedia Computer Science*, 176, 3009–3018. DOI: 10.1016/j.procs.2020.09.202 PMID: 33042316

Balnaves, M., & Caputi, P. (2001). Introduction to quantitative research methods: An investigative approach. *Sage (Atlanta, Ga.)*.

Bao, J., Deshpande, A., McFaddin, S., & Narayanaswami, C. (2014). Partner-marketing using geo-social media data for smarter commerce. *IBM Journal of Research and Development*, 58(5/6), 6:1–6:12. Advance online publication. DOI: 10.1147/JRD.2014.2344514

Baraneetharan, E. (2022) (Vol. 4, Issue 3, pp. 200–210). Detection of Fake Job Advertisements using Ensemble Learning algorithms. In Inventive Research Organization. DOI: 10.36548/jaicn.2022.3.006

Bardone-Cone, A. M., & Cass, K. A. (2007). The impact of media exposure on body image and eating disorders. *Eating Disorders*, 15(2), 153–164. PMID: 17454074

Barney, J. B., Ketchen, D. J.Jr, & Wright, M. (2021). Resource-based theory and the value creation framework. *Journal of Management*, 47(7), 1936–1955. DOI: 10.1177/01492063211021655

Barutçu, M. T. (2017, September 10). Big Data Analytics for Marketing Revolution. *Journal of Media Critiques*, 3(11), 163–171. DOI: 10.17349/jmc117314

Baviera-Puig, A., Buitrago-Vera, J., & Escriba-Perez, C. (2016). Geomarketing models in supermarket location strategies. *Journal of Business Economics and Management*, 17(6), 1205–1221. Advance online publication. DOI: 10.3846/16111699.2015.1113198

Beaumont, J. R. (1989). An overview of market analysis: Who? What? Where? and Why? *International Journal of Information Management*, 9(1), 51–62. Advance online publication. DOI: 10.1016/0268-4012(89)90037-6

Becerra, A. (2018). *Generation Z: Social media, influencers and brand loyalty in entertainment* (Doctoral dissertation, University of Southern California).

Beguma, S., Siddiqueb, F. A., & Tiwaric, R. (2021). A Study for predicting heart disease using machine learning. Turkish Journal of Computer and Mathematics Education, 12(10), 4584–4592.

Beheshtinia, M. A., & Omidi, S. (2017). A hybrid MCDM approach for performance evaluation in the banking industry. *Kybernetes*, 46(8), 1386–1407. DOI: 10.1108/K-03-2017-0105

Bell, C. (2023). MySQL database service. MySQL Database Service Revealed. DOI: 10.1007/978-1-4842-8945-7_4

Benavente, S. L. (2017). 20% time in the classroom-bringing Google philosophy and the keys to motivation to your school. In *INTED2017 Proceedings* (pp. 1016-1020). IATED.

Berger, C. R., & Calabrese, R. J. (1975). "Some Functions of Communication in Interpersonal Relationships." Theories of Interpersonal Communication.

Berger, C.S and Messerschmidt, M.C. (2009). Babbling before banking? Online communities and pre-purchase information seeking. International Journal of Bank Marketing [e-journal] 2 (6).

Berger, A. N., & Mester, L. J. (2003). Explaining the dramatic changes in performance of US banks: Technological change, deregulation, and dynamic changes in competition. *Journal of Financial Intermediation*, 12(1), 57–95. DOI: 10.1016/S1042-9573(02)00006-2

Bhattacharyya, S. S., & Jha, S. (2015). Mapping micro small and medium enterprises from the resource-based view and dynamic capability theory perspectives and innovation classification. *International Journal of Entrepreneurship and Small Business*, 25(3), 331–350. DOI: 10.1504/IJESB.2015.069700

Big data and the supply chain: The big-supply-chain analytics landscape (Part 1). (2016, February 16). McKinsey & Company. https://www.mckinsey.com/capabilities/operations/our-insights/big-data-and-the-supply-chain-the-big-supply-chain-analytics-landscape-part-1

Bikker, J. A., & Haaf, K. (2002). Competition, concentration and their relationship: An empirical analysis of the banking industry. *Journal of Banking & Finance*, 26(11), 2191–2214. DOI: 10.1016/S0378-4266(02)00205-4

Biswas, S., & Joshi, N. (2023). A performance based ranking of initial public offerings (IPOs) in India. *Journal of Decision Analytics and Intelligent Computing*, 3(1), 15–32. DOI: 10.31181/10023022023b

Bley, K., Pappas, I. O., & Strahringer, S. (2021). Innovation Capability in Small Industrial Companies-a Set Theoretic Approach to Maturity Models. In ECIS.

Boeing, G. (2020b). Exploring Urban Form Through Openstreetmap Data. In *Urban Experience and Design*. DOI: 10.4324/9780367435585-15

Boeing, G. (2020a). A multi-scale analysis of 27,000 urban street networks: Every US city, town, urbanized area, and Zillow neighborhood. *Environment and Planning. B, Urban Analytics and City Science*, 47(4), 590–608. Advance online publication. DOI: 10.1177/2399808318784595

Bolek, M., Pietraszewski, P., & Wolski, R. (2021). Companies' growth vs. growth opportunity: Evidence from the regular and alternative stock markets in Poland. *Acta Oeconomica*, 71(2), 279–307. DOI: 10.1556/032.2021.00014

Boley, B. B., McGehee, N. G., & Hammett, A. T. (2017). Importance-performance analysis (IPA) of sustainable tourism initiatives: The resident perspective. *Tourism Management*, 58, 66–77. DOI: 10.1016/j.tourman.2016.10.002

Bonn, I., & Christodoulou, C. (1996). From strategic planning to strategic management. *Long Range Planning*, 29(4), 543–551. DOI: 10.1016/0024-6301(96)00046-5

Boopathi, S. (2022b). Cryogenically treated and untreated stainless steel grade 317 in sustainable wire electrical discharge machining process: A comparative study. *Springer :Environmental Science and Pollution Research*, 1–10.

Boopathi, S. (2022a). An investigation on gas emission concentration and relative emission rate of the near-dry wire-cut electrical discharge machining process. *Environmental Science and Pollution Research International*, 29(57), 86237–86246. DOI: 10.1007/s11356-021-17658-1 PMID: 34837614

Boopathi, S., Alqahtani, A. S., Mubarakali, A., & Panchatcharam, P. (2023). Sustainable developments in near-dry electrical discharge machining process using sunflower oil-mist dielectric fluid. *Environmental Science and Pollution Research International*, 31(27), 1–20. DOI: 10.1007/s11356-023-27494-0 PMID: 37199846

Bourdieu, P. (1984). *Distinction: A Social Critique of the Judgment of Taste*. Harvard University Press.

Bouzguenda, K. (2018). Emotional intelligence and financial decision making: Are we talking about a paradigmatic shift or a change in practices? *Research in International Business and Finance*, 44, 273–284. DOI: 10.1016/j.ribaf.2017.07.096

Bowers, J., & Khorakian, A. (2014). Integrating risk management in the innovation project. *European Journal of Innovation Management*, 17(1), 25–40. DOI: 10.1108/EJIM-01-2013-0010

Bowlby, J. (1969). Attachment and Loss: Vol. I. *Attachment*. Basic Books.

Bozkir, A. S., & Aydos, M. (2020). LogoSENSE: A companion HOG based logo detection scheme for phishing web page and E-mail brand recognition. In Computers and Security. Elsevier BV, 95. DOI: 10.1016/j.cose.2020.101855

Brand, J. E., & Davis, D. (2011). The Impact of College Education on Fertility: Evidence for Heterogeneous Effects. *Demography*, 48(3), 863–887. DOI: 10.1007/s13524-011-0034-3 PMID: 21735305

Brooks, C., & Thompson, C. (2017). Predictive modelling in teaching and learning. Handbook of learning analytics, 61-68. DOI: 10.18608/hla17.005

Bucciol, A., & Zarri, L. (2015). Does investors' personality influence their portfolios?.

Bucciol, A., Guerrero, F., & Papadovasilaki, D. (2021). Financial risk-taking and trait emotional intelligence. *Review of Behavioral Finance*, 13(3), 259–275. DOI: 10.1108/RBF-01-2020-0013

Bui, T. D., Tsai, F. M., Tseng, M. L., & Ali, M. H. (2020). Identifying sustainable solid waste management barriers in practice using the fuzzy Delphi method. *Resources, Conservation and Recycling*, 154, 104625. DOI: 10.1016/j.resconrec.2019.104625

Çakar, N. D., & Ertürk, A. (2010). Comparing innovation capability of small and medium-sized enterprises: Examining the effects of organizational culture and empowerment. *Journal of Small Business Management*, 48(3), 325–359. DOI: 10.1111/j.1540-627X.2010.00297.x

Calantone, R. J., Cavusgil, S. T., & Zhao, Y. (2002). Learning orientation, firm innovation capability, and firm performance. *Industrial Marketing Management*, 31(6), 515–524. DOI: 10.1016/S0019-8501(01)00203-6

Cao, Z., Zhou, X., Hu, H., Wang, Z., & Wen, Y. (2022). Toward a systematic survey for carbon neutral data centers. *IEEE Communications Surveys and Tutorials*, 24(2), 895–936. DOI: 10.1109/COMST.2022.3161275

Capozzoli, A., & Primiceri, G. (2015). Cooling systems in data centers: State of art and emerging technologies. *Energy Procedia*, 83, 484–493. DOI: 10.1016/j.egypro.2015.12.168

Cavallone, M., Magno, F., & Zucchi, A. (2017). Improving service quality in healthcare organisations through geomarketing statistical tools. *The TQM Journal*, 29(5), 690–704. Advance online publication. DOI: 10.1108/TQM-12-2016-0104

Ceylan, A., & Özarı, Ç. (2018). TOPSIS Yöntemiyle Benzer Sektörlerdeki Firmaların Finansal Performans Analizlerinin Karşılaştırılması: BİST 30 Endeksinde İşlem Gören Firmalar Üzerine Bir Araştırma. *Kesit Akademi Dergisi*, 16(16), 421–431. DOI: 10.18020/kesit.1514

Chan, D. Y., & Vasarhelyi, M. A. (2018). Innovation and practice of continuous Auditing1. In *Continuous Auditing* (pp. 271–283). Emerald Publishing Limited. DOI: 10.1108/978-1-78743-413-420181013

Chang, Y. C., Chang, H. T., Chi, H. R., Chen, M. H., & Deng, L. L. (2012). How do established firms improve radical innovation performance? The organizational capabilities view. *Technovation*, 32(7-8), 441–451. DOI: 10.1016/j.technova-tion.2012.03.001

Chaskalovic, J. (2009). Gravitation theory for mathematical modelling in geomarketing. *Journal of Interdisciplinary Mathematics*, 12(3), 409–420. Advance online publication. DOI: 10.1080/09720502.2009.10700633

Chaudhury, M., Karami, A., & Ghazanfar, M. A. (2022). Large-Scale Music Genre Analysis and Classification Using Machine Learning with Apache Spark. *Electronics (Basel)*, 11(16), 2567. DOI: 10.3390/electronics11162567

Chen, Y., Zheng, W., Li, W., & Huang, Y. (2021). Large group activity security risk assessment and risk early warning based on random forest algorithm. In Pattern Recognition Letters. Elsevier BV, 144. DOI: 10.1016/j.patrec.2021.01.008

Chen, C. F., & Kao, Y. L. (2010). Relationships between process quality, outcome quality, satisfaction, and behavioural intentions for online travel agencies - evidence from Taiwan. *Service Industries Journal*, 30(12), 2081–2092. DOI: 10.1080/02642060903191108

Chen, Y., Kang, Y., Zhao, Y., Wang, L., Liu, J., Li, Y., Liang, Z., He, X., Li, X., Tavajohi, N., & Li, B. (2021). A review of lithium-ion battery safety concerns: The issues, strategies, and testing standards. *Journal of Energy Chemistry*, 59, 83–99. DOI: 10.1016/j.jechem.2020.10.017

Chinowsky, P. S., & Meredith, J. E. (2000). Strategic management in construction. *Journal of Construction Engineering and Management*, 126(1), 1–9. DOI: 10.1061/(ASCE)0733-9364(2000)126:1(1)

Chiou, W. C., Lin, C. C., & Perng, C. (2011). A strategic website evaluation of online travel agencies. *Tourism Management*, 32(6), 1463–1473. DOI: 10.1016/j.tourman.2010.12.007

Choi, T., Wallace, S. W., & Wang, Y. (2018, October). Big Data Analytics in Operations Management. *Production and Operations Management*, 27(10), 1868–1883. DOI: 10.1111/poms.12838

Choudhury, M. M., & Harrigan, P. (2014). CRM to social CRM: The integration of new technologies into customer relationship management. *Journal of Strategic Marketing*, 22(2), 149–176. DOI: 10.1080/0965254X.2013.876069

Christenson, A. P.Jr, & Goldstein, W. S. (2022). Impact of data analytics in transforming the decision-making process. *BIT Numerical Mathematics*, XII(1), 74–82. DOI: 10.14311/bit.2022.01.09

Chronicle, D.(2023, September1). How does social media and its trends imoact gen z dating ideals. Retrieved February 19, 2024, from DeccanChronicle:[1] National Association of Software Companies.It is the software sector association in India

Chu, J., & Huang, X. (2021). *Research status and development trends of evaporative cooling air-conditioning technology in data centers*. Energy and Built Environment.

Cimpan, C., Maul, A., Wenzel, H., & Pretz, T. (2016). Techno-economic assessment of central sorting at material recovery facilities–the case of lightweight packaging waste. *Journal of Cleaner Production*, 112, 4387–4397. DOI: 10.1016/j.jclepro.2015.09.011

Činauskaitė-Cetiner, J. (2011). Namų ūkių finansinės gerovės kūrimo prielaidos Lietuvoje. Human Resources: The Main Factor of Regional Development, 4, 16–24. https://web.p.ebscohost.com/ehost/detail/detail?vid=0&sid=e05d18d1-5fee-4ab7 -84cba1ca0f235b2b%40redis&bdata=JnNpdGU9ZWhvc3QtbGl2ZQ%3d%3d#AN =67721867&db=bsh

Clark, J. S., Kulig, P., Podsiadło, K., Rydzewska, K., Arabski, K., Białecka, M., Safranow, K., & Ciechanowicz, A. (2023). Empirical investigations into Kruskal-Wallis power studies utilizing Bernstein fits, simulations and medical study datasets. *Scientific Reports*, 13(1), 2352. DOI: 10.1038/s41598-023-29308-2 PMID: 36759640

Columbus, L. (2014, October 21). 84% of enterprises see big data analytics changing their industries' competitive landscapes in the next year. Forbes. https://www.forbes.com/sites/louiscolumbus/2014/10/19/84-of-enterprises-see-big-data -analytics-changing-their-industries-competitive-landscapes-in-the-next-year/?sh =a61492417de1

Cormican, K., & O'Sullivan, D. (2004). Auditing best practice for effective product innovation management. *Technovation*, 24(10), 819–829. DOI: 10.1016/S0166-4972(03)00013-0

Cornwell, N., Bilson, C., Gepp, A., Stern, S., & Vanstone, B. J. (2022, February 27). The role of data analytics within operational risk management: A systematic review from the financial services and energy sectors. *The Journal of the Operational Research Society*, 74(1), 374–402. DOI: 10.1080/01605682.2022.2041373

Corsi, P., & Neau, E. (2015). *Innovation Capability Maturity Model. "A Method to Progress"*. John Wiley & Sons. DOI: 10.1002/9781119144335

Dadzie, K. K. E. (n.d.). Machine Learning-Based Classifi -cation Algorithms for the Prediction of Coronary Heart Disease, 14.

Dalbar, Inc. (2016). Dalbar is the financial community's leading independent expert for evaluating, auditing and rating business practices and customer performance since 1976. Dalbar.com. Boston, MA

Damayanti, S. M., Murtaqi, I., & Pradana, H. A. (2018). The importance of financial literacy in a global economic era. *The Business & Management Review*, 9(3), 435–441.

Damayanti, S. M., Raditya, T., Mambea, I. Y., & Putri, A. M. (2020). The determinants of point of sales system adoption perceived by micro small medium enterprises in West Java, Indonesia. *International Journal of Economic Policy in Emerging Economies*, 13(5), 483. DOI: 10.1504/IJEPEE.2020.110433

Dangolani, S. K. (2011). The Impact of information technology in banking system (A case study in Bank Keshavarzi IRAN). *Procedia: Social and Behavioral Sciences*, 30, 13–16. DOI: 10.1016/j.sbspro.2011.10.003

Das, M., & Mohanty, S. (2012). Spatial pattern of fertility transition in Uttar Pradesh and Bihar: A district level analysis. *Genus*, LXVIII, 81–106.

Dawar, S., Chatterjee, S., Hossain, M. F., & Malarvizhi, S. "Music Recommendation System Using Real Time Parameters," *2023 International Conference on Recent Advances in Electrical, Electronics, Ubiquitous Communication, and Computational Intelligence (RAEEUCCI)*, Chennai, India, 2023, pp. 1-6, DOI: 10.1109/RAEEUCCI57140.2023.10134257

De Almeida, L. B., Godoy, W., & Kovaleski, J. L. (1998, August). An authentication server in Java implementation of an encryption framework model and DES algorithm in Java. In *ITS'98 Proceedings. SBT/IEEE International Telecommunications Symposium (Cat. No. 98EX202)* (Vol. 2, pp. 627-631). IEEE.

de Reuver, M., & Ondrus, J. (2017). When technological superiority is not enough: The struggle to impose the SIM card as the NFC Secure Element for mobile payment platforms. *Telecommunications Policy*, 41(4), 253–262. DOI: 10.1016/j.telpol.2017.01.004

De Veirman, M., Cauberghe, V., & Hudders, L. (2017). Marketing through Instagram influencers: The impact of influencer marketing on consumer behavior. *International Journal of Advertising*.

Demir, F. (2018). A strategic management maturity model for innovation. *Technology Innovation Management Review*, 8(11), 13–21. DOI: 10.22215/timreview/1196

Deng, Y., Feng, C., Jiaqiang, E., Zhu, H., Chen, J., Wen, M., & Yin, H. (2018). Effects of different coolants and cooling strategies on the cooling performance of the power lithium ion battery system: A review. *Applied Thermal Engineering*, 142, 10–29. DOI: 10.1016/j.applthermaleng.2018.06.043

Desai, C., Bhadra, S., & Parekh, M. (2023). Music Recommendation System using Python. *International Journal for Research in Applied Science and Engineering Technology*, 11(7), 699–707. DOI: 10.22214/ijraset.2023.54740

Desai, N., & Kankonkar, S. (2019). Gen-Z's online buying involvement and decision style in buying fashion apparels. *Studies in Indian Place Name*, 40(26), 360–376.

Dewi, V. I. (2022). How do demographic and socioeconomic factors affect financial literacy and its variables? *Cogent Business & Management*, 9(1), 1. DOI: 10.1080/23311975.2022.2077640

Dhingra, S., Gupta, S., & Bhatt, R. (2022). Comparison of e-service quality of Indian e- commerce websites. *International Journal of Indian Culture and Business Management*, 26(3), 407–426. DOI: 10.1504/IJICBM.2022.124595

Dimiter, P., & Berghammer, C. (2007). Religion and fertility ideals, intentions and behaviour: A comparative study of European countries. *Vienna Yearbook of Population Research / Vienna Institute of Demography, Austrian Academy of Sciences*, 2007, 271–305. Advance online publication. DOI: 10.1553/populationyearbook2007s271

Dinçer, H., & Yüksel, S. (2019). An integrated stochastic fuzzy MCDM approach to the balanced scorecard-based service evaluation. *Mathematics and Computers in Simulation*, 166, 93–112. DOI: 10.1016/j.matcom.2019.04.008

Dincer, I. (2017). *Refrigeration systems and applications*. John Wiley & Sons. DOI: 10.1002/9781119230793

Dissanayake, K. (2021). Comparative Study on Heart Disease Prediction Using Feature Selection Techniques on Classification Algorithms. DOI: 10.1155/2021/5581806

Divya, P., Girija, P., Anuradha, M., Dinesh, M. G., & Aswini, J. (2023). Heterogeneous Ensemble Variable Selection To Improve Customer Prediction Using Naive Bayes Model. *International Journal on Recent and Innovation Trends in Computing and Communication*, 11(5s), 64–71. DOI: 10.17762/ijritcc.v11i5s.6599

Dolot, A. (2018). The characteristics of Generation Z. e-mentor, 74, 44–50. *Williams, K., Page, R., Petrosky, A., & Hernandez, E.(2010). Multi-Generational Marketing: Descriptions, Characteristics, Lifestyles, and Attitudes. Journal of Applied Business and Economics*

Dou, Y., & Sarkis, J. (2013). A multiple stakeholder perspective on barriers to implementing China RoHS regulations. *Resources, Conservation and Recycling*, 81, 92–104. DOI: 10.1016/j.resconrec.2013.10.004

Dreze, J., & Murthi, M. (2001). Fertility, Education, and Development: Evidence from India. *Population and Development Review*, 27(1), 33–63. DOI: 10.1111/j.1728-4457.2001.00033.x

DuffAgency. (n.d.). What is online engagement. Retrieved February 26, 2024, from Duff Agency Website: https://duffy.agency/insight/what-is-online-engagement/.

Easterlin, R. A. (1975). An Economic Framework for Fertility Analysis. *Studies in Family Planning*, 6(3), 54–63. DOI: 10.2307/1964934 PMID: 1118873

Ecer, F., Küçükönder, H., Kaya, S. K., & Görçün, Ö. F. (2023). Sustainability performance analysis of micro-mobility solutions in urban transportation with a novel IVFNN-Delphi-LOPCOW-CoCoSo framework. *Transportation Research Part A, Policy and Practice*, 172, 103667. DOI: 10.1016/j.tra.2023.103667

Ecer, F., & Pamucar, D. (2022). A novel LOPCOW-DOBI multi-criteria sustainability performance assessment methodology: An application in developing country banking sector. *Omega*, 112, 102690. DOI: 10.1016/j.omega.2022.102690

Elci, A., Abubakar, A. M., Ilkan, M., Kolawole, E. K., & Lasisi, T. T. (2017). The Impact of Travel 2.0 on Travelers Booking and Reservation Behaviors. *Business Perspectives and Research*, 5(2), 124–136. DOI: 10.1177/2278533717692909

Elgendy, N., & Elragal, A. (2016). Big data analytics in support of the decision making process. *Procedia Computer Science*, 100, 1071–1084. DOI: 10.1016/j.procs.2016.09.251

Ellison, N. B., Heino, R. D., & Gibbs, J. (2006). Managing impressions online: Self-presentation processes in the online dating environment. *Journal of Computer-Mediated Communication*, 11(2), 415–441. DOI: 10.1111/j.1083-6101.2006.00020.x

Elverdi, S., & Atik, H., (2020). Türkiye'de inovasyon ölçümüne yönelik bir değerlendirme. IBAD Sosyal Bilimler Dergisi, 695-712.

Erol, Y., & İnce, A. R. (2012). Rekabette Pozisyon Okulu Düşüncesi Ve Kaynak Tabanlı Görüşün Karşılaştırılması. Cumhuriyet Universitesi Journal of Economics & Administrative Sciences (JEAS), 13(1).

Essmann, H., & Du Preez, N. (2009). An innovation capability maturity model–development and initial application. *International Journal of Industrial and Manufacturing Engineering*, 3(5), 382–393.

Fahrurrozi, M. (2022). Evaluation of Educational Service Quality of Vocational High School (VHS) Based on Importance Performance Analysis (IPA) Quadrant. *Eurasian Journal of Educational Research*, 97(97), 27–42.

Faiayaz Waris, S. F., & Koteeswaran, S. (2021, January 19). WITHDRAWN: Heart disease early prediction using a novel machine learning method called improved K-means neighbor classifier in python. *Materials Today: Proceedings*. Advance online publication. DOI: 10.1016/j.matpr.2021.01.570

Fauziyah, A., & Ruhayati, S. A. (2016). Developing students' financial literacy and financial behaviour by students' emotional quotient in Proceedings of the 2016. In Global Conference on Business, Management and Entrepreneurship (pp. 65–69). DOI: 10.2991/gcbme-16.2016.10

Fazeli Burestan, N., Afkari Sayyah, A. H. A., & Taghinezhad, E. (2021). Prediction of some quality properties of rice and its flour by near-Infrared Spectroscopy (NIRS) analysis. *Food Science & Nutrition*, 9(2), 1099–1105. DOI: 10.1002/fsn3.2086 PMID: 33598193

Fernandes, B. B., Sacenti, J. A., & Willrich, R. (2017, October). Using implicit feedback for neighbors selection: Alleviating the sparsity problem in collaborative recommendation systems. In *Proceedings of the 23rd Brazillian Symposium on Multimedia and the Web* (pp. 341-348).

Finkel, E. J., Eastwick, P. W., Karney, B. R., Reis, H. T., & Sprecher, S. (2012). Online dating: A critical analysis from the perspective of psychological science. *Psychological Science in the Public Interest*, 13(1), 3–66. DOI: 10.1177/1529100612436522 PMID: 26173279

Fitriyani, N. L., Syafrudin, M., Alfian, G.-J., & Rhee, J.-T. (2020). HDPM: An Effective Heart Disease Prediction Model for a Clinical Decision Support System. https://doi.org/DOI: 10.1109/AC-CESS.2020.3010511

Fonte, C. C., Patriarca, J. A., Minghini, M., Antoniou, V., See, L., & Brovelli, M. A. (2019). Using OpenStreetMap to Create Land Use and Land Cover Maps: Development of an Application. In *Geospatial Intelligence* (Vol. 2). Concepts, Methodologies, Tools, and Applications., DOI: 10.4018/978-1-5225-8054-6.ch047

Forbes. (2024, February 6). Social Media Statistics. Retrieved February 15, 2024, from Forbes: https://www.forbes.com/advisor/in/business/social-media-statistics/#:~:text=Social%20Media%20Usage%20Statistics,-The%20average%20person&text=Interestingly%2C%20Indians%2C%20on%20average%2C,spent%20on%20social%20media%20platforms

Fornell, C., & Larcker, D. F. (1981). Evaluating structural equation models with unobservable variables and measurement error. *JMR, Journal of Marketing Research*, 18(1), 39–50. DOI: 10.1177/002224378101800104

Fox, J., Klüsener, S., & Myrskylä, M. (2018). Is a Positive Relationship Between Fertility and Economic Development Emerging at the Sub-National Regional Level? Theoretical Considerations and Evidence from Europe. *European Journal of Population = Revue Européenne de Démographie, 35*(3), 487–518. DOI: 10.1007/s10680-018-9485-1

Fox, J., Bailenson, J. N., & Tricase, L. (2016). The effect of online dating on sexual orientation and relationship quality. *Journal of Social and Personal Relationships, 33*(3), 452–470.

Fraczek, B., & Klimontowicz, M. (2015). Financial literacy and its influence on young customers' decision factors. *Journal of Innovation Management, 3*(1), 62–84. https://journalsojs3.fe.up.pt/index.php/jim/article/view/2183-0606_003.001_0007/166. DOI: 10.24840/2183-0606_003.001_0007

Francis, T., & Hoefel, F. (2018). True Gen': Generation Z and its implications for companies. *McKinsey & Company, 12*, 1-10. http://www.drthomaswu.com/uicmpaccsmac/Gen%20Z.pdf

Frantz, P. (2023, February 10). App Marketing: Dating Trends. Retrieved February 21, 2024, from Think with Google: https://www.thinkwithgoogle.com/future-of- marketing/management-and-culture/diversity-and-inclusion/app-marketing-dating-trends/

Freeman, R. E., Dmytriyev, S. D., & Phillips, R. A. (2021). Stakeholder theory and the resource-based view of the firm. *Journal of Management, 47*(7), 1757–1770. DOI: 10.1177/0149206321993576

Frost, J. (2019). "Regression Analysis: An Intuitive Guide". e-book. https://statisticsbyjim.com/regression/

Frye, M. (2022). Exploring inventory management's effects on a Company's profitability. https://dc.etsu.edu/honors/695 [Undergraduate Honors Thesis], paper 695.

Furnham, A., & Cheng, H. (2013). Factors influencing adult earnings: Findings from a nationally representative sample. *Journal of Socio-Economics, 44*, 120–125. DOI: 10.1016/j.socec.2013.02.008

Gallimberti, C. M., Marra, A., & Prencipe, A. (2013). Consolidation: Preparing and understanding consolidated financial statements under IFRS: Updated to the new IFRS 10 and 11. UK higher education business accounting.

Ganesh, N., Balamurugan, M., Chohan, J. S., & Kalita, K. (2024). Development of a grey wolf optimized-gradient boosted decision tree metamodel for heart disease prediction. *International Journal of Intelligent Systems and Applications in Engineering*, 12(8s), 515–522.

Garcia-Morales, V. J., Martín-Rojas, R., & Lardón-López, M. E. (2018). Influence of social media technologies on organizational performance through knowledge and innovation. *Baltic Journal of Management*, 13(3), 345–367. DOI: 10.1108/BJM-04-2017-0123

Garg, N., & Singh, S. (2018). Financial literacy among youth. *International Journal of Social Economics*, 45(1), 173–186. DOI: 10.1108/IJSE-11-2016-0303

Garson, G. D. (2012). *Testing statistical assumptions*. Statistical Associates Publishing.

Gatter, K. A., & Hodkinson, A. (2016). The effect of online dating on self-esteem and social anxiety. *Cyberpsychology, Behavior, and Social Networking*, 19(10), 657–662.

Ghosh, A., Bose, S., Maji, G., Debnath, N., & Sen, S. (2019, September). Stock price prediction using LSTM on Indian share market. In *Proceedings of 32nd international conference on* (Vol. 63, pp. 101-110).

Gibbs, J. L.. (2011). *Online dating: The relationship between the internet and the dating process*. New Directions in Psychology.

Giménez-Medina, M., Enríquez, J. G., & Domínguez-Mayo, F. J. (2023). A systematic review of capability and maturity innovation assessment models: Opportunities and challenges. *Expert Systems with Applications*, 213, 118968. DOI: 10.1016/j.eswa.2022.118968

Goffman, E. (1959). *The Presentation of Self in Everyday Life*. University of Edinburgh Press.

Goldscheider, C. (2006). *Religion, family, and fertility: What do we know historically and comparatively?* (pp. 41–57). DOI: 10.1007/1-4020-5190-5_3

Gonzalez, C.. (2020). Online dating during the COVID-19 pandemic: The role of social media in relationship development. *The Journal of Social Issues*, 76(4), 964–986.

Gowri, N. V., Dwivedi, J. N., Krishnaveni, K., Boopathi, S., Palaniappan, M., & Medikondu, N. R. (2023). Experimental investigation and multi-objective optimization of eco-friendly near-dry electrical discharge machining of shape memory alloy using Cu/SiC/Gr composite electrode. *Environmental Science and Pollution Research International*, 30(49), 1–19. DOI: 10.1007/s11356-023-26983-6 PMID: 37126160

Goyal, K. A., & Joshi, V. (2011). A study of social and ethical issues in banking industry. *International Journal of Economic Research*, 2(5), 49–57.

Goyal, K. A., & Joshi, V. (2012). Indian banking industry: Challenges and opportunities. *International Journal of Business Research and Management*, 3(1), 18–28.

Gracious, L. A., Jasmine, R. M., Pooja, E., Anish, T. P., Johncy, G., & Subramanian, R. S. (2023, October). Machine Learning and Deep Learning Transforming Healthcare: An Extensive Exploration of Applications, Algorithms, and Prospects. In 2023 4th IEEE Global Conference for Advancement in Technology (GCAT) (pp. 1-6). IEEE.

Graphical password authentication system based on persuasive cued Click-Points. (2018). International Journal of Recent Trends in Engineering and Research, 54–60. DOI: 10.23883/IJRTER.CONF.02180328.008.D09QI

Greenstein, S. (2021). Digital infrastructure. *Economic Analysis and Infrastructure Investment*, 28215, 409–447. DOI: 10.7208/chicago/9780226800615.003.0009

Guda, V., Shalini, K., & Shivani, C. (2020). Heart disease prediction using hybrid technique. Journal of Interdisciplinary Cycle Research, 12(6).

Gunkel, L. (2020). Dating apps and the emergence of new romantic norms: A qualitative study. *Journal of Social and Personal Relationships*.

Gupta, S., Mathew, M., Gupta, S., & Dawar, V. (2021). Benchmarking the private sector banks in India using MCDM approach. *Journal of Public Affairs*, 21(2), e2409. DOI: 10.1002/pa.2409

Gupta, S., Mathew, M., Syal, G., & Jain, J. (2021). A hybrid MCDM approach for evaluating the financial performance of public sector banks in India. *International Journal of Business Excellence*, 24(4), 481–501. DOI: 10.1504/IJBEX.2021.117648

Guskey, T. R., & Sparks, D. (1991). What to consider when evaluating staff development. *Educational Leadership*, 49(3), 73–76.

Hair, J. F., Ringle, C. M., & Sarstedt, M. (2011). PLS-SEM: Indeed a silver bullet. *Journal of Marketing Theory and Practice*, 19(2), 139–152. DOI: 10.2753/MTP1069-6679190202

Hamdan, S., Almajali, S., Ayyash, M., Salameh, H. B., & Jararweh, Y. (2023). An intelligent edge-enabled distributed multi-task learning architecture for large-scale IoT-based cyber–physical systems. *Simulation Modelling Practice and Theory*, 122, 102685.

Harari, T. T., Sela, Y., & Bareket-Bojmel, L. (2023). Gen Z during the COVID-19 crisis: A comparative analysis of the differences between Gen Z and Gen X in resilience, values and attitudes. *Current Psychology (New Brunswick, N.J.)*, 42(28), 24223–24232. DOI: 10.1007/s12144-022-03501-4 PMID: 35967492

Hasler, A., & Lusardi, A. (2017). The gender gap in financial literacy: A global perspective. *Global Financial Literacy Excellence Center, The George Washington University School of Business*.

Hazem, H., Awad, A., & Yousef, A. H. (2023). A distributed real-time recommender system for big data streams. *Ain Shams Engineering Journal*, 14(8), 102026. DOI: 10.1016/j.asej.2022.102026

Heidari, M., Seifi, B., & Gharebagh, Z. (2017). Nursing staff retention: Effective factors. *Annals of Tropical Medicine and Public Health*, 10(6).

Herfort, B., Lautenbach, S., Porto de Albuquerque, J., Anderson, J., & Zipf, A. (2023). A spatio-temporal analysis investigating completeness and inequalities of global urban building data in OpenStreetMap. *Nature Communications*, 14(1), 3985. Advance online publication. DOI: 10.1038/s41467-023-39698-6 PMID: 37414776

Hernandez-de-Menendez, M., Escobar Díaz, C. A., & Morales-Menendez, R. (2020). Educational experiences with Generation Z. [IJIDeM]. *International Journal on Interactive Design and Manufacturing*, 14(3), 847–859. DOI: 10.1007/s12008-020-00674-9

Hertig, L., & Maus, O. (1998). Geo-marketing solutions for the banking sector with emphasis on saving and cooperative banks [Geomarketing bei Banken und Sparkassen]. *Geo-Informations-Systeme, 11*(3).

Hilgert, M. A. (2003). JeanneM. *Hogarth, Sondra Baverly. Household Financial Management: The Connection between Knowledge and Behavior*.

Ho, C. I., & Lee, Y. L. (2007). The development of an e-travel service quality scale. *Tourism Management*, 28(6), 1434–1449. DOI: 10.1016/j.tourman.2006.12.002

Hoelter, J. W. (1983). The analysis of covariance structures: Goodness of fit indices. *Sociological Methods & Research*, 11(3), 325–344. DOI: 10.1177/0049124183011003003

Holmes, R. (2021). The impact of digital communication on romantic relationships in Gen Z. *Journal of Youth Studies*.

Hsu, C. L., Chang, K. C., & Chen, M. C. (2012). The impact of website quality on customer satisfaction and purchase intention: Perceived playfulness and perceived flow as mediators. *Information Systems and e-Business Management*, 10(4), 549–570. DOI: 10.1007/s10257-011-0181-5

https://www.businesswire.com/news/home/20221012005842/en/Global-Music -Streaming-Market-Report-2022-A-45-Billion-Industry-in-2026---Long-term -Forecast-to-2031-with-Amazon-Apple-Spotify-Gaana-SoundCloud-Dominating ---ResearchAndMarkets.com

https://www.cnet.com/tech/services-and-software/spotify-eclipses-205-million -subscribers-better-than-predicted/

https://www.deccanchronicle.com/lifestyle/sex-and-relationship/010923/how-does -social- media-and-its-trends-impact-genz-dating-ideals.html

https://www.statista.com/topics/6408/music-streaming/

https://www.wiwo.de/downloads/10773004/1/DTA_Report_neu.pdf

Hubspot. (n.d.). Instagram Marketing. Retrieved 22 2024, February, from Hubspot. com Website: https://www.hubspot.com/instagram-marketing

Hu, L., & Bentler, P. M. (1999). Cutoff criteria for fit indexes in covariance structure analysis: Conventional criteria versus new alternatives. *Structural Equation Modeling*, 6(1), 1–55. DOI: 10.1080/10705519909540118

Hult, G. T. M., Hurley, R. F., & Knight, G. A. (2004). Innovativeness: Its antecedents and impact on business performance. *Industrial Marketing Management*, 33(5), 429–438. DOI: 10.1016/j.indmarman.2003.08.015

Hu, R., Liu, Y., Shin, S., Huang, S., Ren, X., Shu, W., Cheng, J., Tao, G., Xu, W., Chen, R., & Luo, X. (2020). Emerging materials and strategies for personal thermal management. *Advanced Energy Materials*, 10(17), 1903921. DOI: 10.1002/aenm.201903921

Hurwitz, J. S., & Kirsch, D. (2020). *Cloud computing for dummies*. John Wiley & Sons.

Hussain, F., Hussain, R., Hassan, S. A., & Hossain, E. (2020). Machine learning in IoT security: Current solutions and future challenges. *IEEE Communications Surveys and Tutorials*, 22(3), 1686–1721. DOI: 10.1109/COMST.2020.2986444

Iddris, F. (2016). Innovation capability: A systematic review and research agenda. *Interdisciplinary Journal of Information, Knowledge, and Management*, 11, 235–260. DOI: 10.28945/3571

Ikhlayel, M. (2018). Development of management systems for sustainable municipal solid waste in developing countries: A systematic life cycle thinking approach. *Journal of Cleaner Production*, 180, 571–586. DOI: 10.1016/j.jclepro.2018.01.057

Ikram, S. (2023). Recipes and ingredients for ancient Egyptian mummification. *Nature*, 614(7947), 229–230. DOI: 10.1038/d41586-023-00094-1 PMID: 36725938

Illmeyer, M., Grosch, D., Kittler, M., & Priess, P. (2017). The impact of financial management on innovation. *Entrepreneurship and Sustainability Issues*, 5(1), 58–71. DOI: 10.9770/jesi.2017.5.1(5)

INEE. nter-agency N. for E. in E. (n.d.). *MIND THE GAP: The State of Girls' Education in Crisis and Conflict.* https://inee.org/resources/mind-gapstate-girls-education-crisis-and-conflict

Inghilleri, L., Solomon, M., & Schulze, H. (2010). *Exceptional service, exceptional profit: The secrets of building a five-star customer service organization.* AMACOM Books.

Inków, M. (2019). Measuring innovation maturity–literature review on innovation maturity models. *Informatyka Ekonomiczna*, 1(51), 22–34. DOI: 10.15611/ie.2019.1.02

Inoue, K., & Honjo, T. (2022). Differential-quadrature-phase-shift quantum digital signature. *Optics Express*, 30(24), 42933–42943. DOI: 10.1364/OE.468156 PMID: 36523003

Intelligence, M. (2023). *India Online Travel Market Size & Share Analysis - Growth Trends & Forecasts (2024 - 2029)*https://www.mordorintelligence.com/industry-reports/online-travel-market-in-india

Ishfaq, M., Nazir, M. S., Qamar, M. A. J., & Usman, M. (2020). Cognitive Bias and the Extraversion Personality Shaping the Behavior of Investors. *Frontiers in Psychology*, 11, 556506. DOI: 10.3389/fpsyg.2020.556506 PMID: 33178066

Iyengar, S. S., & Lepper, M. R. (2000). When choice is demotivating: Can one desire too much of a good thing? *Journal of Personality and Social Psychology*, 79(6), 995–1006. DOI: 10.1037/0022-3514.79.6.995 PMID: 11138768

Jadhav, S. S., & Thepade, S. D. (2019). Fake news identification and classification using DSSM and improved recurrent neural network classifier. In Applied Artificial Intelligence (Vol. 33, Issue 12, pp. 1058–1068). Informa Uk Limited, 33(12), 1058–1068. DOI: 10.1080/08839514.2019.1661579

Jakubowska, Z., Koza, K., Leder, W., Owczarczyk, A., Skorupka, Z., & Wróblewski, T. (2021). The Power of Fertility and Its Importance for the Concept of Sustainable Development. *Studia Ecologiae et Bioethicae*, 19(3), 25–35. DOI: 10.21697/seb.2021.19.3.03

Jamil, M. A., & Khanam, S. (2024). Influence of one-way ANOVA and Kruskal–Wallis based feature ranking on the performance of ML classifiers for bearing fault diagnosis. *Journal of Vibration Engineering & Technologies*, 12(3), 3101–3132. DOI: 10.1007/s42417-023-01036-x

Jangre, J., Prasad, K., & Patel, D. (2022). Analysis of barriers in e-waste management in developing economy: An integrated multiple-criteria decision-making approach. *Environmental Science and Pollution Research International*, 29(48), 72294–72308. DOI: 10.1007/s11356-022-21363-y PMID: 35696062

Jasper, M., & Crossan, F. (2012). What is strategic management? *Journal of Nursing Management*, 20(7), 838–846. DOI: 10.1111/jonm.12001 PMID: 23050617

Javeed, A., Rizvi, S., Zhou, S., Riaz, R., Khan, S. U., & Kwon, S. J. (2020). Heart Risk Failure Prediction Using a Novel Feature Selection Method for Feature Refinement and Neural Network for Classification. *Mobile Information Systems*, 2020, 8843115. Advance online publication. DOI: 10.1155/2020/8843115

Jayaraman, A., Mishra, V., & Arnold, F. (2009). The Relationship of Family Size and Composition To Fertility Desires, Contraceptive Adoption and Method Choice in South Asia. *International Perspectives on Sexual and Reproductive Health*, 35(01), 29–38. DOI: 10.1363/3502909 PMID: 19465346

Jiang, L. S., Tian, W. Y., & Zhu, X. F. (2011, July). Research on automatic detection of fake car-logo based on cloud-computing. In *2011 International Conference on Multimedia Technology* (pp. 5492-5494). IEEE.

Jiang, X., Sun, K., Ma, L., Qu, Z., & Ren, C. (2022). Vehicle logo detection method based on improved YOLOv4. *Electronics (Basel)*, 11(20), 3400. DOI: 10.3390/electronics11203400

Jie, X., Zhiwei, L., & Liang, X. (2019). Research on dynamic positioning accuracy evaluation method of GPS/Beidou dual mode navigation receiver 14th IEEE International Conference on Electronic Measurement y Instruments (ICEMI), 2019. DOI: 10.1109/ICEMI46757.2019.9101625

Jin, C., Bai, X., Yang, C., Mao, W., & Xu, X. (2020). A review of power consumption models of servers in data centers. *Applied Energy*, 265, 114806. DOI: 10.1016/j.apenergy.2020.114806

Jindal, R., Bharadwaj, M., & Mishra, V. (2022). IMPACT OF BIG DATA ON BUSINESS DECISIONS THROUGH THE VIEW OF DATA SCIENCE-BASED DECISION MAKING.

Jin, S. H., & Choi, S. O. (2019). The effect of innovation capability on business performance: A focus on IT and business service companies. *Sustainability (Basel)*, 11(19), 5246. DOI: 10.3390/su11195246

Jofre, S. (2011). Strategic Management: The theory and practice of strategy in (business) organizations.

Jokar Arsanjani, J., & Bakillah, M. (2015). Understanding the potential relationship between the socio-economic variables and contributions to OpenStreetMap. *International Journal of Digital Earth*, 8(11), 861–876. Advance online publication. DOI: 10.1080/17538947.2014.951081

Joshi, N. V., Gadgil, M., & Patil, S. (1996). Correlates of the desired family size among Indian communities. *Proceedings of the National Academy of Sciences of the United States of America*, 93(13), 6387–6392. DOI: 10.1073/pnas.93.13.6387 PMID: 11607687

Jou, R. C., & Day, Y. J. (2021). Application of revised importance–performance analysis to investigate critical service quality of hotel online booking. *Sustainability (Basel)*, 13(4), 2043. DOI: 10.3390/su13042043

Juliani, A. J. (2014). *Inquiry and innovation in the classroom: Using 20% time, genius hour, and PBL to drive student success*. Routledge. DOI: 10.4324/9781315813837

Kalita, K., Ganesh, N., Jayalakshmi, S., Chohan, J. S., Mallik, S., & Qin, H. (2023). Multi-Objective artificial bee colony optimized hybrid deep belief network and XGBoost algorithm for heart disease prediction. Frontiers in Digital Health, 5. *Frontiers in Digital Health*, 1279644, 1279644. Advance online publication. DOI: 10.3389/fdgth.2023.1279644 PMID: 38034907

Kamath, K. V., Kohli, S. S., Shenoy, P. S., Kumar, R., Nayak, R. M., Kuppuswamy, P. T., & Ravichandran, N. (2003). Indian banking sector: Challenges and opportunities. *Vikalpa*, 28(3), 83–100. DOI: 10.1177/0256090920030308

Kashem, S. B. A., Sheikh, M. I. B., Ahmed, J., & Tabassum, M. (2018, April). Gravity and buoyancy powered clean water pipe generator. In 2018 IEEE 12th International Conference on Compatibility, Power Electronics and Power Engineering (CPE-POWERENG 2018) (pp. 1-5). IEEE.

Katz, E., Blumler, J. G., & Gurevitch, M. (1973). Uses and Gratifications Research. *Public Opinion Quarterly*, 37(4), 509–523. DOI: 10.1086/268109

Kaur Harpreet, H., Keshri, R., & Sharma, A. (2020). Casualties caused by COVID-19 on education system. *International Journal for Research in Applied Sciences and Biotechnology*, 7(5), 125–133. DOI: 10.31033/ijrasb.7.5.18

Kavitha, C. R., Varalatchoumy, M., Mithuna, H. R., Bharathi, K., Geethalakshmi, N. M., & Boopathi, S. (2023). Energy Monitoring and Control in the Smart Grid: Integrated Intelligent IoT and ANFIS. In Arshad, M. (Ed.), (pp. 290–316). Advances in Bioinformatics and Biomedical Engineering. IGI Global., DOI: 10.4018/978-1-6684-6577-6.ch014

Keeter, S. (2020). *People financially affected by COVID-19 outbreak are experiencing more psychological distress than others* (Vol. 30). Pew Research Center.

Kelley, B. (2003). Innovation, Change and Digital Transformation. from Free Innovation Audit: Braden Kelley's 50 Question Innovation Audit: https:// bradenkelley .com/offerings/innovation-audit/ Date of access: 01.04.2024

Khalaj, A. H., & Halgamuge, S. K. (2017). A Review on efficient thermal management of air-and liquid-cooled data centers: From chip to the cooling system. *Applied Energy*, 205, 1165–1188. DOI: 10.1016/j.apenergy.2017.08.037

Khurshid, Z., Siddique, H., Waqas, A., & Sabir, S. (2019). Impact of Maternal Education on Child Mortality. *International Journal of Social Sciences and Management*, 6(4), 82–89. DOI: 10.3126/ijssm.v6i4.26221

Kietzmann, J. H., Hermkens, K., McCarthy, I. P., & Silvestre, B. S. (2011). Social media? Get serious! Understanding the functional building blocks of social media. *Business Horizons*, 54(3), 241–251. DOI: 10.1016/j.bushor.2011.01.005

Kim, D. J., Kim, W. G., & Han, J. S. (2007). A perceptual mapping of online travel agencies and preference attributes. *Tourism Management*, 28(2), 591–603. DOI: 10.1016/j.tourman.2006.04.022

Kim, M., Song, J., & Triche, J. (2015). Toward an integrated framework for innovation in service: A resource-based view and dynamic capabilities approach. *Information Systems Frontiers*, 17(3), 533–546. DOI: 10.1007/s10796-014-9505-6

King, B. (2010). *Bank 2.0: How customer behavior and technology will change the future of financial services*. Marshall Cavendish Business.

Kirchherr, J., Reike, D., & Hekkert, M. (2017). Conceptualizing the circular economy: An analysis of 114 definitions. *Resources, Conservation and Recycling*, 127, 221–232. DOI: 10.1016/j.resconrec.2017.09.005

Kiziloglu, M. (2015). The Effect of Organizational Learning on Firm Innovation Capability: An Investigation in the Banking Sector. *Global Business and Management Research*, 7(3).

Kluge, E.-H. W. (2020). *The nature of electronic health records*. The Electronic Health Record., DOI: 10.1016/B978-0-12-822045-0.00001-0

Ko, E., Kim, D., & Kim, G. (2022). Influence of emojis on user engagement in brand-related user-generated content. Computers in Human Behavior, 136. doi/. DOI: 10.1016/j.chb.2022.107387

Kopanakis, J. (2024, February 29). *5 Real-World Examples of How Brands Are Using Big Data Analytics*. Mentionlytics. https://www.mentionlytics.com/blog/5 -real-world-examples-of-how-brands-are-using-big-data-analytics/

Kortt, M. A., & Drew, J. (2019). Does Religion Influence Educational Attainment? *Religious Education (Chicago, Ill.)*, 46(4), 458–481. DOI: 10.1080/15507394.2018.1541694

Korzynski, P., & Protsiuk, O. (2024). What leads to cyberloafing: The empirical study of workload, self-efficacy, time management skills, and mediating effect of job satisfaction. *Behaviour & Information Technology*, 43(1), 200–211. DOI: 10.1080/0144929X.2022.2159525

Kovacs, P., Kuruczleki, E., Racz, T. A., & Liptak, L. (2021). Survey of Hungarian high school students' financial literacy in the last 10 years based on the econventio test. Pe´nz€ugyi Szemle/Public Finance Quarterly, 66(2), 175–194. DoI: https://doi.org/DOI: 10.35551/PFQ_2021_2_1

Kramer, S. (2021, September 21). Religious Composition of India. *Pew Research Center*. https://www.pewresearch.org/religion/2021/09/21/religious-composition -of-india/

Krstovski, K., Ryu, A. S., & Kogut, B. (2022). Evons: A dataset for fake and real news virality analysis and prediction (1st version). arXiv.

Kryvych, Y. M., & Goncharenko, T. (2020). Banking strategic management and business model: bibliometric analysis.

Kumar, M., Kumar, K., Sasikala, P., Sampath, B., Gopi, B., & Sundaram, S. (2023). Sustainable Green Energy Generation From Waste Water: IoT and ML Integration. In Sustainable Science and Intelligent Technologies for Societal Development (pp. 440-463). IGI Global.

Kumar, A., & Dixit, G. (2018b). An analysis of barriers affecting the implementation of e-waste management practices in India: A novel ISM-DEMATEL approach. *Sustainable Production and Consumption*, 14, 36–52. DOI: 10.1016/j.spc.2018.01.002

Kumari, A., & Singh, A. (2017). Impact of social media marketing on brand loyalty: A study with reference to State Bank of India. *International Journal of Applied Business and Economic Research*, 15(3), 363–374.

Kumar, V., Dudani, R., & Latha, K. (2021). The big five personality traits and psychological biases: An exploratory study. *Current Psychology (New Brunswick, N.J.)*, 42(8), 6587–6597. DOI: 10.1007/s12144-021-01999-8

Kumar, V., & L, M. (2018, July 16). Predictive Analytics: A Review of Trends and Techniques. *International Journal of Computer Applications*, 182(1), 31–37. DOI: 10.5120/ijca2018917434

Kumar, V., & Pradhan, P. (2016). Reputation management through online feedbacks in e-business environment. [IJEIS]. *International Journal of Enterprise Information Systems*, 12(1), 21–37. DOI: 10.4018/IJEIS.2016010102

Kumra, P., & Singh, M. (2018). Factors Influencing E-Service Quality in Indian Tourism Industry. *Research World*, 9(1), 99–110.

Kungu, G., Desta, I., & Ngui, T. (2014). An assessment of the effectiveness of competitive strategies by commercial banks: A Case of Equity Bank. *International Journal of Education and Research*, 2(12), 333–346.

Lai, I. K. W., & Hitchcock, M. (2015). Importance–performance analysis in tourism: A framework for researchers. *Tourism Management*, 48, 242–267. DOI: 10.1016/j.tourman.2014.11.008

Latour, B. (2005). *Reassembling the Social: An Introduction to Actor-Network-Theory*. Oxford University Press. DOI: 10.1093/oso/9780199256044.001.0001

Lawson, B., & Samson, D. (2001). Developing innovation capability in organisations: A dynamic capabilities approach. *International Journal of Innovation Management*, 5(03), 377–400. DOI: 10.1142/S1363919601000427

Lee, C. S., Cheang, P. Y. S., & Moslehpour, M. (2022). Predictive analytics in business analytics: Decision tree. *Advances in Decision Sciences*, 26(1), 1–29. DOI: 10.47654/v26y2022i1p1-29

Lewrick, M., & Raeside, R. (2010). Transformation and change process in innovation models: Start-up and mature companies. *International Journal of Business Innovation and Research*, 4(6), 515–534. DOI: 10.1504/IJBIR.2010.035711

Lewy, G. (2016). *Harmful and undesirable: Book censorship in nazi Germany*. Oxford University Press.

Li, Y. (2018). A Study on E-service Quality Dimensions for Online Travel Agencies. In *MATEC Web of Conferences* (Vol. 228, p. 05011). EDP Sciences. DOI: 10.1051/matecconf/201822805011

Liao, S. H., Chen, Y. J., & Lin, Y. T. (2011). Mining customer knowledge to implement online shopping and home delivery for hypermarkets. *Expert Systems with Applications*, 38(4), 3982–3991. Advance online publication. DOI: 10.1016/j.eswa.2010.09.059

Liebman, E., Saar-Tsechansky, M., & Stone, P. (2019). The Right Music at the Right Time: Adaptive Personalized Playlists Based on Sequence Modeling. *Management Information Systems Quarterly*, 43(3), 765–786. DOI: 10.25300/MISQ/2019/14750

Lin, C.-T. (2010). Examining e-travel sites: An empirical study in Taiwan. *Online Information Review*, 34(2), 205–228. DOI: 10.1108/14684521011036954

Liu, Q., Wan, H., & Yu, H. (2023, June 28). Application and Influence of Big data Analysis in Marketing Strategy. *Frontiers in Business. Economics and Management*, 9(3), 168–171. DOI: 10.54097/fbem.v9i3.9580

Li, Y., Shi, Q., Deng, J., & Su, F. (2017). Graphic logo detection with deep region-based convolutional networks. [VCIP]. *IEEE Visual Communications and Image Processing*, 1–4, 1–4. Advance online publication. DOI: 10.1109/VCIP.2017.8305065

Li, Y., Wen, Y., Tao, D., & Guan, K. (2019). Transforming cooling optimization for green data center via deep reinforcement learning. *IEEE Transactions on Cybernetics*, 50(5), 2002–2013. DOI: 10.1109/TCYB.2019.2927410 PMID: 31352360

Lookman, K., Pujawan, N., & Nadlifatin, R. (2022). Measuring innovative capability maturity model of trucking companies in Indonesia. *Cogent Business & Management*, 9(1), 2094854. DOI: 10.1080/23311975.2022.2094854

Lopes, P., Fonte, C., See, L., & Bechtel, B. (2017). Using OpenStreetMap data to assist in the creation of LCZ maps. *2017 Joint Urban Remote Sensing Event. JURSE*, 2017, 1–4. Advance online publication. DOI: 10.1109/JURSE.2017.7924630

Lu, J., & Hu, X. (2014). Novel three-bank model for measuring the systemic importance of commercial banks. *Economic Modelling*, 43, 238–246. DOI: 10.1016/j.econmod.2014.08.007

Lundberg, S., & Pollak, R. A. (2007). The American Family and Family Economics. *The Journal of Economic Perspectives*, 21(2), 3–26. DOI: 10.1257/jep.21.2.3

Lusardi, A. (2019). Financial literacy and the need for financial education: Evidence and implications. *Swiss Journal of Economics and Statistics*, 155(1), 1. Advance online publication. DOI: 10.1186/s41937-019-0027-5

Lusardi, A., Keller, P. A., & Keller, A. M. (2009). *New ways to make people save: A social marketing approach (No. w14715)*. National Bureau of Economic Research. DOI: 10.3386/w14715

Lusardi, A., Mitchell, O. S., & Curto, V. (2010). Financial literacy among the young. *The Journal of Consumer Affairs*, 44(2), 358–380. https://www.nber.org/papers/w15352. DOI: 10.1111/j.1745-6606.2010.01173.x

Luxen, D., & Vetter, C. (2011). Real-time routing with OpenStreetMap data. *GIS: Proceedings of the ACM International Symposium on Advances in Geographic Information Systems*. DOI: 10.1145/2093973.2094062

Madhani, P. M. (2010). Resource based view (RBV) of competitive advantage: an overview. Resource based view: concepts and practices, Pankaj Madhani, ed, 3-22.

Mahey, R., Gupta, M., Kandpal, S., Malhotra, N., Vanamail, P., Singh, N., & Kriplani, A. (2018). Fertility awareness and knowledge among Indian women attending an infertility clinic: A cross-sectional study. *BMC Women's Health*, 18(1), 177. DOI: 10.1186/s12905-018-0669-y PMID: 30373587

Mailund, T. (2020). *String algorithms in C: Efficient text representation and search*. Apress. DOI: 10.1007/978-1-4842-5920-7

Manimurugan, S., Almutairi, S., Aborokbah, M. M., Narmatha, C., Ganesan, S., Chilamkurti, N., Alzaheb, R. A., & Almoamari, H. (2022, January 9). Two-Stage Classification Model for the Pre -diction of Heart Disease Using IoMT and Artificial Intelligence. *Sensors (Basel)*, 22(2), 476. DOI: 10.3390/s22020476 PMID: 35062437

Mani, V., Delgado, C., Hazen, B., & Patel, P. (2017, April 14). Mitigating Supply Chain Risk via Sustainability Using Big Data Analytics: Evidence from the Manufacturing Supply Chain. *Sustainability (Basel)*, 9(4), 608. DOI: 10.3390/su9040608

Margate, A. M. N., Ravina, M. C. F., Pido, J. J. G., & Young, M. N. (2020, December). Seiton: A Mobile Inventory Management System Application for Micro, Small and Medium-sized Enterprise. In *2020 IEEE 7th International Conference on Engineering Technologies and Applied Sciences (ICETAS)* (pp. 1-5). IEEE.

Marq.com. (n.d.). 11 reasons your brand should use twitter marketing. Retrieved March 3, 2024, from Marq.com website: https://www.marq.com/blog/11-reasons -your-brand-should-use-twitter-marketing

Martilla, J. A., & James, J. C. (1977). Importance-performance analysis. *Journal of Marketing*, 10(1), 13–22.

Mattei, G., Canetta, L., Sorlini, M., Alberton, S., & Tito, F. (2019, June). Innovation maturity model for new product and services development: a proposal. In *2019 IEEE International Conference on Engineering, Technology and Innovation (ICE/ITMC)* (pp. 1-9). IEEE. DOI: 10.1109/ICE.2019.8792581

Matuszyk, P., & Spiliopoulou, M. (2017). Stream-based semi-supervised learning for recommender systems. *Machine Learning*, 106(6), 771–798. DOI: 10.1007/s10994-016-5614-4

Maxwell, J. C. (2017). *The Power of significance: How purpose changes your life.* Center Street.

Mayer, J., Caruso, D., & Salovey, P. (1999). Emotional Intelligence Meets Traditional Standards for Intelligence. *Intelligence*, 27(4), 267–298. DOI: 10.1016/S0160-2896(99)00016-1

McGuirk, M. (2021). Performing social media analytics with Brandwatch for Classrooms: A platform review. *Journal of Marketing Analytics*, 9(4), 363.

McKinsey. (2023, March 20). Mc Kinsey Explainers. Retrieved February 28, 2024, from Mc Kinsey: https://www.mckinsey.com/featured-insights/mckinsey-explainers/what-is- gen-z

McPherson, M., Smith-Lovin, L., & Cook, J. M. (2001). Birds of a Feather: Homophily in Social Networks. *Annual Review of Sociology*, 27(1), 415–444. DOI: 10.1146/annurev.soc.27.1.415

McQuillan, K. (2004). When Does Religion Influence Fertility? *Population and Development Review*, 30(1), 25–56. DOI: 10.1111/j.1728-4457.2004.00002.x

Mehta, R. (2023, December 23). How social media is playing an important role in Indian GDP. Retrieved 05 2024, January, from Times of India.

Mendoza-Silva, A. (2021a). Innovation capability: A sociometric approach. *Social Networks*, 64, 72–82. DOI: 10.1016/j.socnet.2020.08.004

Mendoza-Silva, A. (2021b). Innovation capability: A systematic literature review. *European Journal of Innovation Management*, 24(3), 707–734. DOI: 10.1108/EJIM-09-2019-0263

Messy, F. A., & Monticone, C. (2016). Financial education policies in Asia and the Pacific. https://doi.org/.DOI: 10.1787/20797117

Millar, N., McLaughlin, E., & Börger, T. (2019). The circular economy: Swings and roundabouts? *Ecological Economics*, 158, 11–19. DOI: 10.1016/j.ecolecon.2018.12.012

Mišanková, M., & Kočišová, K. (2014). Strategic implementation as a part of strategic management. *Procedia: Social and Behavioral Sciences*, 110, 861–870. DOI: 10.1016/j.sbspro.2013.12.931

Mishra, N. K. (2017). Population characteristics and fertility patterns of Saharsa district Bihar a geographical study. *University*. https://shodhganga.inflibnet.ac.in:8443/jspui/handle/10603/275267

Mishra, J. S., Gupta, N. K., & Sharma, A. (2024). Enhanced Heart Disease Prediction Using Machine Learning Techniques. *Journal of Intelligent Systems & Internet of Things*, 12(2).

Mittal, S., & Kumar, V. (2019). Study of knowledge management models and their relevance in organisations. Int. J. *Knowledge Management Studies*, 10(3), 322–335.

Moazamigoodarzi, H., Tsai, P. J., Pal, S., Ghosh, S., & Puri, I. K. (2019). Influence of cooling architecture on data center power consumption. *Energy*, 183, 525–535. DOI: 10.1016/j.energy.2019.06.140

Mohammed, M. E., Wafik, G. M., Jalil, S. G. A., & El Hassan, Y. A. (2016). The Effects of E-Service Quality Dimensions on Tourist's e-Satisfaction. *International Journal of Hospitality and Tourism Systems*, 9(1).

Momeni, M., Maleki, M. H., Afshari, M. A., Moradi, J. S., & Mohammadi, J. (2011). A fuzzy MCDM approach for evaluating listed private banks in Tehran stock exchange based on balanced scorecard. *International Journal of Business Administration*, 2(1), 80.

Mondal, T., & Department of Mathematics. (2022). "Distributive Lattices of λ-Simple Semirings." Iranian Journal of Mathematical Sciences and Informatics. Dr. Bhupendra Nath Duta Smriti Mahavidyalaya, Hatgobindapur, Burdwan. West. DOI: 10.52547/ijmsi.17.1.47

Mont, O., Plepys, A., Whalen, K., & Nußholz, J. L. (2017). Business model innovation for a Circular Economy: Drivers and barriers for the Swedish industry–the voice of REES companies.

Moraru, A. D., & Duhnea, C. (2018). E-banking and customer satisfaction with banking services. *Strategic Management*, 23(3), 3–9. DOI: 10.5937/StraMan1803003M

Moulasha, K., & Rao, G. R. (1999). Religion-Specific Differentials in Fertility and Family Planning. *Economic and Political Weekly*, 34(42/43), 3047–3051.

Mudgal, R. K., Shankar, R., Parvaiz, T., & Tilak, R. (2010). Modelling the barriers of green supply chain practices. *Int J Logist Syst Manag*, 7(1), 81–107. DOI: 10.1504/IJLSM.2010.033891

Müller-Prothmann, T., & Stein, A. (2011, Haziran). I²MM–İnovasyon yeteneğinin yalın değerlendirmesi için entegre inovasyon olgunluk modeli. XXII ISPIM Konferansında (12-15).

Mulliner, E., Smallbone, K., & Maliene, V. (2013). An assessment of sustainable housing afordability using a multiple criteria decision-making method. *Omega*, 41(2), 270–279. DOI: 10.1016/j.omega.2012.05.002

Mustapää, T., Tunkkari, H., Taponen, J., Immonen, L., Heeren, W., Baer, O., Brown, C., & Viitala, R. (2022). Secure exchange of digital metrological data in a smart overhead crane. *Sensors (Basel)*, 22(4), 1548. Advance online publication. DOI: 10.3390/s22041548 PMID: 35214455

Muthee, J. G., & Genga, P. (2019). Staff development and employee performance in Kenya Commercial Bank in Nyeri County, Kenya. *International Journal of Current Aspects*, 3(IV), 93–103. DOI: 10.35942/ijcab.v3iIV.50

Mutlu, Ü., & Özer, G. (2022). The moderator effect of financial literacy on the relationship between locus of control and financial behavior. *Kybernetes*, 51(3), 1114–1126. DOI: 10.1108/K-01-2021-0062

Muzakir, M., Bachri, S., Adam, R., & Wahyuningsih, W. (2021). The analysis of forming dimensions of e-service quality for online travel services. *International Journal of Data and Network Science*, 5(3), 239–244. DOI: 10.5267/j.ijdns.2021.6.010

Nada, N., Ghanem, M., Mesbah, S., & Turkyilmaz, A. (2012). İnnovation And Knowledge Management Practice in Turkish SMEs, Journal of Knowledge Management. *Economics and Information Technology*, 2(1), 248–265.

Nanmaran, R., Nagarajan, S., Sindhuja, R., Charan, G. V. S., Pokala, V. S. K., Srimathi, S., Gulothungan, G., Vickram, A. S., & Thanigaivel, S. (2020, December). Wavelet transform based multiple image watermarking technique. In IOP Conference Series. IOP Conference Series: Materials Science and Engineering (Vol. 993, No. 1, p. 012167). IOP Publishing, 993(1). DOI: 10.1088/1757-899X/993/1/012167

Nanmaran, R., Srimathi, S., Yamuna, G., Thanigaivel, S., Vickram, A. S., Priya, A. K., Karthick, A., Karpagam, J., Mohanavel, V., & Muhibbullah, M. (2022). Investigating the role of image fusion in brain tumor classification models based on machine learning algorithm for personalized medicine. *Computational and Mathematical Methods in Medicine*, 7137524, 1–13. Advance online publication. DOI: 10.1155/2022/7137524 PMID: 35178119

Nasir, J. A., Khan, O. S., & Varlamis, I. (2021). Fake news detection: A hybrid CNN-RNN based deep learning approach. In International Journal of Information Management Data Insights (Vol. 1, Issue 1, p. 100007). Elsevier BV, 1(1). DOI: 10.1016/j.jjimei.2020.100007

Nethravathy, J., & Maragatham, G. (2016). Malicious node detection in vehicle to vehicle communication. *International Journal of Engineering Trends and Technology*, 33(5), 248–251. DOI: 10.14445/22315381/IJETT-V33P249

Ngo, L. V., & O'cass, A. (2013). Innovation and business success: The mediating role of customer participation. *Journal of Business Research*, 66(8), 1134–1142. DOI: 10.1016/j.jbusres.2012.03.009

Nguyen, D. D., Nepal, S., & Kanhere, S. S. (2021). Diverse multimedia layout generation with multi choice learning. MM '21: ACM Multimedia Conference. *Academic Medicine*, ●●●, 218–226. DOI: 10.1145/3474085.3475525

Nickols, F. (2016). Strategy, strategic management, strategic planning and strategic thinking. *Management Journal*, 1(1), 4–7.

Niewöhner, N., Lang, N., Asmar, L., Röltgen, D., Kühn, A., & Dumitrescu, R. (2021). Towards an ambidextrous innovation management maturity model. *Procedia CIRP*, 100, 289–294. DOI: 10.1016/j.procir.2021.05.068

Nishanth, J., Deshmukh, M. A., Kushwah, R., Kushwaha, K. K., Balaji, S., & Sampath, B. (2023). Particle Swarm Optimization of Hybrid Renewable Energy Systems. In *Intelligent Engineering Applications and Applied Sciences for Sustainability* (pp. 291–308). IGI Global. DOI: 10.4018/979-8-3693-0044-2.ch016

Nithya, T., Kumar, V. N., Gayathri, S., Deepa, S., Varun, C. M., & Subramanian, R. S. (2023, August). A comprehensive survey of machine learning: Advancements, applications, and challenges. In *2023 Second International Conference on Augmented Intelligence and Sustainable Systems (ICAISS)* (pp. 354-361). IEEE. DOI: 10.1109/ICAISS58487.2023.10250547

Niu, Y. (2022). Collaborative Filtering-Based Music Recommendation in Spark Architecture. *Mathematical Problems in Engineering*, 2022, 2022. DOI: 10.1155/2022/9050872

Norton, S., & Tomal, A. (2009). Religion and Female Educational Attainment. *Journal of Money, Credit and Banking*, 41(5), 961–986. DOI: 10.1111/j.1538-4616.2009.00240.x

Nunes, A., Santana, C., Bezerra, F., & Sobral, N. (2014). Knowledge Acquisition Based on Geomarketing Information for Decision Making: A Case Study on a Food Company. *International Journal of Innovation, Management and Technology*, 5(6), 422–427. Advance online publication. DOI: 10.7763/IJIMT.2014.V5.552

OECD. (2013).Financial literacy and inclusion: Results of OECD/ INFE survey across countries and by gender. *Financial Literacy & Education, Russia, jun.*

OECD. (2020). InternationalSurvey of Adult Financial Literacy. Paris: OECD Publishing. https://www.oecd.org/financial/education/launchoftheoecdinfeglobalfinancialliteracysurveyreport.htm

OECD. (2022), OECD/INFE Toolkit for Measuring Financial Literacy and Financial Inclusion 2022, www.oecd.org/financial/education/2022-INFE-Toolkit-Measuring-Finlit-Financial-Inclusion.pdf

Okamoto, S., & Komamura, K. (2021). Age, gender, and financial literacy in Japan. *PLoS One*, 16(11), e0259393. DOI: 10.1371/journal.pone.0259393 PMID: 34788283

Omidipoor, M., Jelokhani-Niaraki, M., & Samany, N. N. (2019). A Web-based geo-marketing decision support system for land selection: A case study of Tehran, Iran. *Annals of GIS*, 25(2), 179–193. Advance online publication. DOI: 10.1080/19475683.2019.1575905

Onağ, O., & Tepeci, M. (2016). Örgütsel öğrenme kabiliyetinin örgütsel yenilikçilik araciliğiyla yeni ürün ve işletme performansina etkisi. *Isletme Iktisadi Enstitüsü Yönetim Dergisi*, (80), 50.

Ongondo, F. O., Williams, I. D., & Cherrett, T. J. (2011). How are WEEE doing? A global review of the management of electrical and electronic wastes. Waste management, 31(4), 714-730.

Oró, E., Depoorter, V., Garcia, A., & Salom, J. (2015). Energy efficiency and renewable energy integration in data centres. Strategies and modelling review. *Renewable & Sustainable Energy Reviews*, 42, 429–445. DOI: 10.1016/j.rser.2014.10.035

Özemre, M., & Kabadurmus, O. (2020, May 26). A big data analytics based methodology for strategic decision making. *Journal of Enterprise Information Management*, 33(6), 1467–1490. DOI: 10.1108/JEIM-08-2019-0222

Pajila, P. B., Sudha, K., Selvi, D. K., Kumar, V. N., Gayathri, S., & R. S. (2023, July). A Survey on Natural Language Processing and its Applications. In 2023 4th International Conference on Electronics and Sustainable Communication Systems (ICESC) (pp. 996-1001). IEEE.

Pal, C., Kushwaha, S., Tanwar, P., & Sharma, S. (2022). Analysis of graphical password systems-recognition based GPS and recall based GPS International Conference on Computer Communication and Informatics (ICCCI), 2022. DOI: 10.1109/ICCCI54379.2022.9740899

Pamikatsih, T. R., Lusia, A., Rahayu, A. S., Maisara, P., & Farida, A. (2022). THE INFLUENCING FACTORS FOR FINANCIAL BEHAVIOR OF GEN Z. *International Conference of Business and Social Sciences, 2*(1), 440–449. Retrieved from https://debian.stiesia.ac.id/index.php/icobuss1st/article/view/196

Panda, P., Mishra, A. K., & Puthal, D. (2022). A novel logo identification technique for logo-based phishing detection in cyber-physical systems. *Future Internet*, 14(8), 241. DOI: 10.3390/fi14080241

Pangestu, S., & Karnadi, E. B. (2020). The effects of financial literacy and materialism on the savings decision of generation Z Indonesians. *Cogent Business & Management*, 7(1), 1743618. DOI: 10.1080/23311975.2020.1743618

Papatya, N. (2013). Çokuluslu şirketlerin kaynak-tabanlı biyo-politik üretiminde rekabetçi gücün diyalektiği-eleştirel ve bütünsel bakış. *Süleyman Demirel Üniversitesi İktisadi ve İdari Bilimler Fakültesi Dergisi*, 18(3), 1–23.

Park, H., & Martin, W. (2022). Effects of risk tolerance, financial literacy, and financial status on retirement planning. *Journal of Financial Services Marketing*, 27(3), 167–176. DOI: 10.1057/s41264-021-00123-y

Park, S. (2018). A review on the role expansion of German federal office for information security(Bundesamt für Sicherheit in Der Informationstechnik, BSI) in 2017. *Journal of Security Engineering*, 15(2), 69–80. DOI: 10.14257/jse.2018.04.01

Park, Y. A., & Gretzel, U. (2007). Success factors for destination marketing web sites: A qualitative meta-analysis. *Journal of Travel Research*, 46(1), 46–63. DOI: 10.1177/0047287507302381

Parson, A. (2013). How Does Social Media Influence the Buying Behavior of Consumers? https://yourbusiness.azcentral.com/social-media-influence-buying-behavior-consumers-17017.html (Accessed 24 January 2024).

Pašiušienė, I., Podviezko, A., Malakaitė, D., Žarskienė, L., Liučvaitienė, A., & Martišienė, R. (2023). Exploring Generation Z's Investment Patterns and Attitudes towards Greenness. *Sustainability (Basel)*, 16(1), 352. DOI: 10.3390/su16010352

Patil, S. K., & Kant, R. (2014). A fuzzy AHP-TOPSIS framework for ranking the solutions of Knowledge Management adoption in Supply Chain to overcome its barriers. *Expert Systems with Applications*, 41(2), 679–693. DOI: 10.1016/j.eswa.2013.07.093

Paul, S., Chatterjee, A., & Guha, D. (2019). Study of smart inventory management system based on the internet of things (IOT). *International Journal on Recent Trends in Business and Tourism*, 3(3), 27–34.

Peñarubia-Zaragoza, M. P., Simancas-Cruz, M., & Forgione-Martín, G. (2019). An application of geomarketing to coastal tourism areas. *Tourism & Management Studies*, 15(4), 7–16. Advance online publication. DOI: 10.18089/tms.2019.150401

Petrides, K. V. (2011). *Ability and trait emotional intelligence. The Wiley-Blackwell Handbook of Individual Differences* (1st ed.). Blackwell Publishing Ltd.

Petty, R. E., & Cacioppo, J. T. (1986). *Communication and Persuasion: Central and Peripheral Routes to Attitude Change*. Springer-Verlag. DOI: 10.1007/978-1-4612-4964-1

Pew Research Center. (2020). "The state of dating in 2020."

Pham, L., Limbu, Y. B., Bui, T. K., Nguyen, H. T., & Pham, H. T. (2019). Does e-learning service quality influence e-learning student satisfaction and loyalty? Evidence from Vietnam. *International Journal of Educational Technology in Higher Education*, 16(1), 1–26. DOI: 10.1186/s41239-019-0136-3

Philippas, N. D., & Avdoulas, C. (2021). Financial literacy and financial well-being among generation-Z university students: Evidence from Greece. In *Financial Literacy and Responsible Finance in the FinTech Era* (pp. 64–85). Routledge., DOI: 10.4324/9781003169192-5

Pilot, S. (2024, April 6). Facebook Statistics. Retrieved April 10, 2024, from Social Pilot.co: https://www.socialpilot.co/facebook-marketing/facebook-statistics

Pinitjitsamut, K., Srisomboon, K., & Lee, W. (2021). Logo detection with artificial intelligent 9th International Electrical Engineering Congress (iEECON), 2021 (pp. 408–411). DOI: 10.1109/iEECON51072.2021.9440236

Podsakoff, P. M., MacKenzie, S. B., Lee, J. Y., & Podsakoff, N. P. (2003). Common method biases in behavioral research: A critical review of the literature and recommended remedies. *The Journal of Applied Psychology*, 88(5), 879–903. https://psycnet.apa.org/doi/10.1037/0021-9010.88.5.879. DOI: 10.1037/0021-9010.88.5.879 PMID: 14516251

Polchinski, J. (2005). String theory." https://ui.adsabs.harvard.edu/abs/2005stth .book.....P/abstract

Polidano, C. (2000). Measuring public sector capacity. *World Development*, 28(5), 805–822. DOI: 10.1016/S0305-750X(99)00158-8

Porter, M. E. (1996). *What is strategy?* Harvard Business School Publishing Corporation.

Powell, T. C. (2002). The philosophy of strategy. *Strategic Management Journal*, 23(9), 873–880. DOI: 10.1002/smj.254

Prasad, S. (2021). Analysis of the Existing model of Financial Inclusion of poor people in Jharkhand.

Prasanth, N. N., & Devi, K. V. (2023). *Fundamental Of Data Science And Big Data Analytics*. Academic Guru Publishing House.

Primack, B. A.. (2017). Use of multiple social media platforms and symptoms of depression and anxiety: A nationally-representative study among U.S. young adults. *Depression and Anxiety*, 34(11), 1094–1100.

Pujitha, U., & Vickram, A. S. (2023, November). Implementation and comparison of proportional (P), integral derivative (ID) control technique for pacemaker design to regulate heart rate for patients with Bradycardia. In AIP Conference Proceedings. AIP Publishing, 2822(1). DOI: 10.1063/5.0173205

Purnomo, M. (2021). Brain Tumor Classification in MRI Images Using En-CNN. International Journal of Intelligent Engineering and Systems, 437–451. DOI: 10.22266/ijies2021.0831.38

Puspitasari, N. B., Purwaningsih, R., Fadlia, N., & Rosyada, Z. F. (2021). Driving Factors of the Intention to Purchase Travel Products through Online Travel Agent (OTA). In *Proceedings of the International Conference on Industrial Engineering and Operations Management* (pp. 1729-1731). DOI: 10.46254/SA02.20210641

Quinn, J. F., & Wilemon, D. (2009, August). Emotional intelligence as a facilitator of project leader effectiveness. In *PICMET'09-2009 Portland International Conference on Management of Engineering & Technology* (pp. 1267-1275). IEEE. DOI: 10.1109/PICMET.2009.5262022

Rahamathunnisa, U., Subhashini, P., Aancy, H. M., Meenakshi, S., & Boopathi, S. (2023). Solutions for Software Requirement Risks Using Artificial Intelligence Techniques. In *Handbook of Research on Data Science and Cybersecurity Innovations in Industry 4.0 Technologies* (pp. 45–64). IGI Global.

Rahimi Bourestan, N., Nematollahzadeh, A., Parchehbaf Jadid, A., & Basharnavaz, H. (2020). Chromium removal from water using granular ferric hydroxide adsorbents: An in-depth adsorption investigation and the optimization. *Chemical Physics Letters*, 748, 137395. Advance online publication. DOI: 10.1016/j.cplett.2020.137395

Rai, R., Tiwari, M. K., Ivanov, D., & Dolgui, A. Rahul Rai and Manoj Kumar Tiwari and D. Ivanov and Alexandre Dolgui,"Machine learning in manufacturing and industry 4.0 applications,". (2021). In International Journal of Production Research, 59(16), 4773–4778. : DOI: 10.1080/00207543.2021.1956675

Raj, N., & Priya, P. (2023). Sustainable and Inclusive Strategies for Tribal Development in Jharkhand. *International Journal of Social Science & Management Studies*, 9(7), 2454–4655.

Ramirez-Hurtado, J. M. (2017). The use of importance-performance analysis to measure the satisfaction of travel agency franchisees. *RAE*, 57(1), 51–64. DOI: 10.1590/s0034-759020170105

Rani, N., & Bansal, A. (2020). Implementation of Heart Disease Pre -diction using Machine Learn -ing with data analytics. Aegaeum Journal, 8(9).

Rao, P. K., & Shukla, A. (2023). Sustainable strategic management: A bibliometric analysis. *Business Strategy and the Environment*, 32(6), 3902–3914. DOI: 10.1002/bse.3344

Rao, P. K., & Shukla, A. (2024). Strategic sustainability in Indian banking industry: A performance analysis. *International Journal of Productivity and Performance Management*, 73(6), 2016–2034. DOI: 10.1108/IJPPM-04-2023-0199

Reddy, K. V. V., Elamvazuthi, I., Aziz, A. A., Paramasivam, S., Chua, H. N., & Pranavanand, S. (2021). Heart Disease Risk Prediction Using Machine Learning Classifiers with Attribute Evaluators. *Applied Sciences (Basel, Switzerland)*, 11(18), 8352. DOI: 10.3390/app11188352

Rezwan, S., Ahmed, W., Mahia, M. A., & Islam, M. R. (2018). IoT based smart inventory management system for kitchen using weight sensors, LDR, LED, Arduino Mega and node MCU (ESP8266) wi-fi module with Website and app Fourth International Conference on Advances in Computing, Communication y Automation (ICACCA), Subang Jaya, Malaysia, 2018 (pp. 1–6). DOI: 10.1109/ICACCAF.2018.8776761

RGI releases Census 2011 data on Population by Religious Communities. (2021). https://pib.gov.in/newsite/printrelease.aspx?relid=126326

Rhee, K.-N., Olesen, B. W., & Kim, K. W. (2017). Ten questions about radiant heating and cooling systems. *Building and Environment*, 112, 367–381. DOI: 10.1016/j.buildenv.2016.11.030

Rizos, V., Behrens, A., Van der Gaast, W., Hofman, E., Ioannou, A., Kafyeke, T., Flamos, A., Rinaldi, R., Papadelis, S., Hirschnitz-Garbers, M., & Topi, C. (2016). Implementation of circular economy business models by small and medium-sized enterprises (SMEs): Barriers and enablers. *Sustainability (Basel)*, 8(11), 1212. DOI: 10.3390/su8111212

Robinson, S., & Gillis, A. S. (2023, November 17). *5V's of big data*. Data Management. https://www.techtarget.com/searchdatamanagement/definition/5-Vs-of-big -data#:~:text=The%205%20V's%20of%20big%20data%20%2D%2D%20velocity %2C%20volume%2C%20value,innate%20characteristics%20of%20big%20data

Romijn, H., & Albaladejo, M. (2002). Determinants of innovation capability in small electronics and software firms in southeast England. *Research Policy*, 31(7), 1053–1067. DOI: 10.1016/S0048-7333(01)00176-7

Rosenfeld, M. J., & Thomas, R. J. (2012). Searching for a mate: The rise of the Internet as a social intermediary. *American Sociological Review*, 77(4), 523–547. DOI: 10.1177/0003122412448050

Rosu, L., Blageanu, A., & Iacob, I. (2013). Geomarketing -A New Approach in Decision Marketing : Case Study – Shopping Centres in Iasi. *Lucrările Seminarului ..., January.*

Roy, R., & Patil, S. (May 7, 2021). Fake product monitoring system using artificial intelligence. SSRN Electronic Journal. Proceedings of the 4th International Conference on Advances in Science and Technology, (ICAST2021). DOI: 10.2139/ssrn.3867602

Rumelt, R. P., Schendel, D., & Teece, D. J. (1991). Strategic management and economics. *Strategic Management Journal*, 12(S2), 5–29. DOI: 10.1002/smj.4250121003

Saggaf, M. S., Aras, M., Akib, H., Salam, R., Baharuddin, A., & Kasmita, M. (2018). *The Quality Analysis of Academic Services Based on Importance Performance Analysis.* IPA.

Sakti, S. M., Laksito, A. D., Sari, B. W., & Prabowo, D. "Music Recommendation System Using Content-based Filtering Method with Euclidean Distance Algorithm," *2022 6th International Conference on Information Technology, Information Systems and Electrical Engineering (ICITISEE)*, Yogyakarta, Indonesia, 2022, pp. 385-390, DOI: 10.1109/ICITISEE57756.2022.10057753

Saleh, B., Saeidi, A., Al-Aqbi, A., & Salman, L. (2020). Analysis of Weka Data Min -ing Techniques for Heart Disease Prediction System. International Journal of Medical Reviews, 7(1), 15–24. DOI: 10.30491/ijmr.2020.221474.1078

Sanz, J. L. C., & Zhu, Y. (2021). *Toward scalable artificial intelligence in finance.* IEEE Publications., DOI: 10.1109/SCC53864.2021.00067

Saranya, G., Arulanandhaguru, I., Pandiyan, A. M., Dharshan, K., & Anandh, S. (2021). IoT based engineering calculator using BOLT IoT module 5th International Conference. DOI: 10.1109/ICECA52323.2021.9676062

Saunila, M. (2020). Innovation capability in SMEs: A systematic review of the literature. Journal of Innovation & knowledge, 5(4), 260-265.

Schultz, M., Voss, J., Auer, M., Carter, S., & Zipf, A. (2017). Open land cover from OpenStreetMap and remote sensing. *International Journal of Applied Earth Observation and Geoinformation*, 63, 206–213. Advance online publication. DOI: 10.1016/j.jag.2017.07.014

Shabbir, M. Q., & Gardezi, S. B. W. (2020, July 8). Application of big data analytics and organizational performance: The mediating role of knowledge management practices. *Journal of Big Data*, 7(1), 47. Advance online publication. DOI: 10.1186/s40537-020-00317-6

Shafiq, A., Ahmed, M. U., & Mahmoodi, F. (2020, July). Impact of supply chain analytics and customer pressure for ethical conduct on socially responsible practices and performance: An exploratory study. *International Journal of Production Economics*, 225, 107571. DOI: 10.1016/j.ijpe.2019.107571

Shaik, K., Ramesh, J. V. N., Mahdal, M., Rahman, M. Z. U., Khasim, S., & Kalita, K. (2023). *Big data analytics framework using squirrel search optimized gradient boosted decision tree for heart disease diagnosis. Applied Sciences. MDPI, 13(9).* DOI: 10.3390/app13095236

Shaitura, S. V., Feoktistova, F. M., Minitaeva, A. M., Olenev, L. A., Chulkov, V. O., & Kozhaev, Y. P. (2020). Spatial geomarketing powered by big data. *Revista Turismo Estudos & Práticas*, S5, 13.

Shankar, N., Vinod, S., & Kamath, R. (2022). Financial well-being–A Generation Z perspective using a Structural Equation Modeling approach. *Investment Management and Financial Innovations*, 19(1), 32–50. DOI: 10.21511/imfi.19(1).2022.03

Shaverdi, M., Akbari, M., & Fallah Tafti, S. (2011). Combining fuzzy MCDM with BSC approach in performance evaluation of Iranian private banking sector. *Advances in Fuzzy Systems*, 2011(1), 148712. DOI: 10.1155/2011/148712

Sherwani, R. A. K., Shakeel, H., Awan, W. B., Faheem, M., & Aslam, M. (2021). Analysis of COVID-19 data using neutrosophic Kruskal Wallis H test. *BMC Medical Research Methodology*, 21(1), 1–7. DOI: 10.1186/s12874-021-01410-x PMID: 34657587

Shi-Nash, A., & Hardoon, D. R. (2017). Data analytics and predictive analytics in the era of big data. Internet of things and data analytics handbook, 329-345.

Sholevar, M., & Harris, L. (2020). Women are invisible?! A literature survey on gender gap and financial training. *Citizenship. Social and Economics Education*, 19(2), 87–99. DOI: 10.1177/2047173420922501

Shonubi, A. O. (2020). The perceived effect of staff development on organisational performance in selected First Banks in Lagos State, Nigeria. *Inkanyiso: Journal of Humanities and Social Sciences*, 12(1), 56–71.

Siddiqui, S., & Singh, T. (2016). Social media its impact with positive and negative aspects. *International Journal of Computer Applications Technology and Research*, 5(2), 71–75. DOI: 10.7753/IJCATR0502.1006

Singh, A., Kumar, K., Kumar Pathak, P., Kumar Chauhan, R., & Banerjee, A. (2017). Spatial Patterns and Determinants of Fertility in India. *Population (English Edition, 2002-)*, 72(3), 505–526.

Singh, P., Singh, S., & Pandi-Jain, G. S. (2018). Effective heart disease prediction system using data mining techniques. International Journal of Nanomedicine, 13, 121–124. DOI: 10.2147/IJN.S124998

Singh, S. A. D. H. V. I., & Sarkar, A. K. (2020). Index of Financial Inclusion (IFI) and banking penetration in Jharkhand. Purakala, 31(12), 749-757.

Singh, S., Shekhar, C., Bankole, A., Acharya, R., Audam, S., & Akinade, T. (2022). Key drivers of fertility levels and differentials in India, at the national, state and population subgroup levels, 2015–2016: An application of Bongaarts' proximate determinants model. *PLoS One*, 17(2), e0263532. DOI: 10.1371/journal.pone.0263532 PMID: 35130319

Siva Subramanian, R., Maheswari, B., Nikkath Bushra, S., Nirmala, G., & Anita, M. (2023). Enhancing Customer Prediction Using Machine Learning with Feature Selection Approaches. In Inventive Computation and Information Technologies [Singapore: Springer Nature Singapore.]. *Proceedings of ICICIT*, 2022, 45–57.

Song, C. L., Pan, D., Ayub, A., & Cai, B. (2023). The Interplay Between Financial Literacy, Financial Risk Tolerance, and Financial Behaviour: The Moderator Effect of Emotional Intelligence. *Psychology Research and Behavior Management*, 16, 535–548. DOI: 10.2147/PRBM.S398450 PMID: 36860350

Song, Y. (2023). How do Chinese SMEs enhance technological innovation capability? From the perspective of innovation ecosystem. *European Journal of Innovation Management*, 26(5), 1235–1254. DOI: 10.1108/EJIM-01-2022-0016

Sprecher, S., & Schwartz, P. (2021). The role of dating apps in modern relationships: A critical review. *Journal of Social and Personal Relationships*, 38(2), 453–470.

Statista. (2023). *Online travel market size in India in financial year 2020, with an estimate for 2025, (in billion U.S. dollars)*https://www.statista.com/statistics/1344430/india-online-travel-market-size-by-type/

Statista. (2023, February 11). Online dating: Worldwide Statistics. Retrieved February 27, 2024, from Dating services: https://www.statista.com/outlook/dmo/eservices/dating- services/online-dating/worldwide

Su, H., Zhu, X., & Gong, S. (2018). Open logo detection challenge (3rd version). arXiv.

Subashini, R. (2016). A review of service quality and customer satisfaction in banking services: Global scenario. *Journal of Internet Banking and Commerce*, 21(S5), 1.

Subramanian, R. S., Maheswari, B., Bushra, S. N., Nirmala, G., & Anita, M. (2023). Enhancing Customer Prediction Using Machine Learning with Feature Selection Approaches. Inventive Computation and Information Technologies: Proceedings of ICICIT 2022, 563, 45. DOI: 10.1007/978-981-19-7402-1_4

Sudha, K., Balakrishnan, C., Anish, T. P., Nithya, T., Yamini, B., Subramanian, R. S., & Nalini, M. (2024). Data Insight Unveiled: Navigating Critical Approaches and Challenges in Diverse Domains Through Advanced Data Analysis. Critical Approaches to Data Engineering Systems and Analysis, 90-114.

Suler, J. (2004). The Online Disinhibition Effect. *Cyberpsychology & Behavior*, 7(3), 321–326. DOI: 10.1089/1094931041291295 PMID: 15257832

Sullivan, R. N. (2011). Deploying financial emotional intelligence. *Financial Analysts Journal*, 67(6), 4–10. DOI: 10.2469/faj.v67.n6.6

Sumter, S. R., Vandenbosch, L., & Ligtenberg, L. (2017). The role of mobile dating apps in the dating process. *Computers in Human Behavior*, 66, 86–92.

Sundbo, J. (1997). Management of innovation in services. *Service Industries Journal*, 17(3), 432–455. DOI: 10.1080/02642069700000028

Sun, J. (2022). Personalized music recommendation algorithm based on spark platform. *Computational Intelligence and Neuroscience*, 2022, 2022. DOI: 10.1155/2022/7157075 PMID: 35222633

Sutejo, B. S., Sumiati, S., Wijayanti, R., & Ananda, C. F. (2024). Do Emotions Influence the Investment Decisions of Generation Z Surabaya Investors in the Covid-19 Pandemic Era? Does Financial Risk Tolerance Play a Moderating Role? *Scientific Papers of the University of Pardubice, Series D. Faculty of Economics and Administration*, 31(2), 1755. DOI: 10.46585/sp31021755

Syamala, M., Komala, C., Pramila, P., Dash, S., Meenakshi, S., & Boopathi, S. (2023). Machine Learning-Integrated IoT-Based Smart Home Energy Management System. In *Handbook of Research on Deep Learning Techniques for Cloud-Based Industrial IoT* (pp. 219–235). IGI Global. DOI: 10.4018/978-1-6684-8098-4.ch013

Tabachnick, B. G., Fidell, L. S., & Ullman, J. B. (2007). *Using multivariate statistics* (Vol. 5, pp. 481-498). Boston, MA: pearson.

Tajudeen, F. P., Jaafar, N. I., & Ainin, S. (2018). Understanding the impact of social media usage among organizations. *Information & Management*, 55(3), 308–321. DOI: 10.1016/j.im.2017.08.004

Tamer Cavusgil, S., Calantone, R. J., & Zhao, Y. (2003). Tacit knowledge transfer and firm innovation capability. *Journal of Business and Industrial Marketing*, 18(1), 6–21. DOI: 10.1108/08858620310458615

Tan, D., & Zahdjuki, D. A. (2023). The Compliance of Limited Liability Companies to Conduct Annual General Meeting of Shareholders. *Journal of Judicial Review*, 25(1), 51–70. DOI: 10.37253/jjr.v25i1.7736

Taryadi, A. R., & Miftahuddin, M. A. (2021). The Role of Mediation Electronic Word of Mouth (E-wom) in Relationship Quality of Services and Tourism Products against Visiting Decisions. *Journal of Economics Research and Social Sciences*, 5(1), 64–76. DOI: 10.18196/jerss.v5i1.10948

Taylor-Sakyi, K. (2016). Big data: Understanding big data. arXiv preprint arXiv:1601.04602.

Teece, D. J. (2019). A capability theory of the firm: An economics and (strategic) management perspective. *New Zealand Economic Papers*, 53(1), 1–43. DOI: 10.1080/00779954.2017.1371208

The Advantages of Data-Driven Decision-Making | HBS Online. (2019, August 26). Business Insights Blog. https://online.hbs.edu/blog/post/data-driven-decision-making

Thibaut, J. W., & Kelley, H. H. (1959). *The Social Psychology of Groups*. Wiley.

Times, E. (2023, February 10). Dating patterns of 2023: Millenials and Gen Z. Retrieved February 24, 2024, from Economic Times: https://economictimes.indiatimes.com/magazines/panache/dating-patterns-of-2023- millennials-find-ghosting-immature-genz-wants-to-explore-before-getting-serious- reveals-study/articleshow/98181137.cms?from=mdr

Tinder. (2023, May 21). Welcome to a renaissance in dating driven by authenticity. Retrieved February 24, 2024, from Tinder News Room: https://www.tinderpressroom.com/2023-05-22-WELCOME-TO-A-RENAISSANCE-IN- DATING,-DRIVEN-BY-AUTHENTICITY

Tiwari, S., Lane, M., & Alam, K. (2019). Do social networking sites build and maintain social capital online in rural communities? *Journal of Rural Studies*, 66, 1–10. DOI: 10.1016/j.jrurstud.2019.01.029

Tkhorikov, B., Kazybayeva, A., Gerasimenko, O., & Zhakypbek, L. (2020). *Theoretical and Methodological Approaches and Stages of Formation Concept Geomarketing*. DOI: 10.2991/aebmr.k.201215.055

Tkhorikov, B. A., Klimova, T., Gerasimenko, O., Titova, I. N., & Ozerova, M. M. (2020). Geomarketing—A new concept or an applied business tool? *Bulletin of Tomsk State University.Economy*, 49, 199–213.

Toma, C. L., & Hancock, J. (2013). What's in a picture? Photographic, and emotional cues in online dating. *Computers in Human Behavior*, 29(1), 16–22.

Trigun, V. (2020, October 28). Determinants of Fertility Preference in Bihar: An Analysis from National Family Health Survey. *Journal of University of Shanghai for Science and Technology*. https://jusst.org/determinants-of-fertility-preference-in -bihar-an-analysis-from-national-family-health-survey/

Trivani, G., & Soleha, E. (2023). The Effect of Financial Literacy, Income and Self Control on Financial Behavior Generation Z (Study on Generation Z Financial Behavior in Bekasi Regency). *Economic Education Analysis Journal*, 12(1), 69–79. DOI: 10.15294/eeaj.v12i1.67452

Tsai, W. H. S., & Lin, Y. H. (2020). Online dating behavior: The effect of physical appearance, profile information, and relationship expectations. *International Journal of Human-Computer Interaction*, 36(4), 388–399.

Tsao, W. C., & Hsieh, M. T. (2012). Exploring how relationship quality influences positive eWOM: The importance of customer commitment. *Total Quality Management & Business Excellence*, 23(7-8), 821–835. DOI: 10.1080/14783363.2012.661137

Turner, C. (2021). Strategic Decision Making: The Effects of Big Data. *International Journal of Operations Management*, 1(2), 38–45. DOI: 10.18775/ijom.2757-0509.2020.12.4005

Turrin, R., Condorelli, A., Cremonesi, P., Pagano, R., & Quadrana, M. (2015). Large scale music recommendation. In *Workshop on Large-Scale Recommender Systems (LSRS 2015) at ACM RecSys*.

Twenge, J. M. (2019). iGen: Why Today's Super-Connected Kids Are Growing Up Less Rebellious, More Tolerant, Less Happy—And Completely Unprepared for Adulthood.

Ugandar, R. E., Rahamathunnisa, U., Sajithra, S., Christiana, M. B. V., Palai, B. K., & Boopathi, S. (2023). Hospital Waste Management Using Internet of Things and Deep Learning: Enhanced Efficiency and Sustainability. In Arshad, M. (Ed.), (pp. 317–343). Advances in Bioinformatics and Biomedical Engineering. IGI Global., DOI: 10.4018/978-1-6684-6577-6.ch015

Ujwary-Gil, A., & Potoczek, N. R. (2020). A dynamic, network and resource-based approach to the sustainable business model. *Electronic Markets*, 30(4), 717–733. DOI: 10.1007/s12525-020-00431-6

Ullah, S. S., Hussain, S., Uddin, M., Alroobaea, R., Iqbal, J., Baqasah, A. M., Abdelhaq, M., & Alsaqour, R. (2022). A Computationally Efficient Online/Offline Signature Scheme for Underwater Wireless Sensor Networks. *Sensors (Basel)*, 22(14), 5150. Advance online publication. DOI: 10.3390/s22145150 PMID: 35890830

Uyar, M. (2018). Muhasebe Denetimi ve İç Kontrol Sisteminin İşletmelerde İnovasyon Yapma Yeteneğine Etkileri Üzerine Ampirik Bir İnceleme. İstanbul Gelişim Üniversitesi Sosyal Bilimler Dergisi, 5(1), 149-168.

Uyguçgil, H., & Atalık, Ö. (2017). Geomarketing As A Tool For Health Service Business: Private Hospital Application. *Journal of Business Research - Turk, 9*(1). DOI: 10.20491/isarder.2017.252

Van Cauwenbergh, A., & Cool, K. (1982). Strategic management in a new framework. *Strategic Management Journal*, 3(3), 245–264. DOI: 10.1002/smj.4250030306

Van Dongen, G., & Van den Poel, D. (2020). Evaluation of stream processing frameworks. *IEEE Transactions on Parallel and Distributed Systems*, 31(8), 1845–1858.

Van Kleef, J. A., & Roome, N. J. (2007). Developing capabilities and competence for sustainable business management as innovation: A research agenda. *Journal of Cleaner Production*, 15(1), 38–51. DOI: 10.1016/j.jclepro.2005.06.002

Van Le, D., Liu, Y., Wang, R., Tan, R., Wong, Y.-W., & Wen, Y. (2019). Control of air free-cooled data centers in tropics via deep reinforcement learning. *Proceedings of the 6th ACM International Conference on Systems for Energy-Efficient Buildings, Cities, and Transportation*, 306–315. DOI: 10.1145/3360322.3360845

Vashisht, P., & Gupta, V. (2015, October). Big data analytics techniques: A survey. In *2015 International Conference on Green Computing and Internet of Things (ICGCIoT)* (pp. 264-269). IEEE. DOI: 10.1109/ICGCIoT.2015.7380470

Venkateswaran, N., Kumar, S. S., Diwakar, G., Gnanasangeetha, D., & Boopathi, S. (2023). Synthetic Biology for Waste Water to Energy Conversion: IoT and AI Approaches. In Arshad, M. (Ed.), (pp. 360–384). Advances in Bioinformatics and Biomedical Engineering. IGI Global., DOI: 10.4018/978-1-6684-6577-6.ch017

Verhaeghe, A., & Kfir, R. (2002). Managing innovation in a knowledge intensive technology organisation (KITO). *Research Management*, 32(5), 409–417.

Vidhyalakshmi, R., & Kumar, V. (2016). Determinants of cloud computing adoption by SMEs. *International Journal of Business Information Systems*, 22(3), 375–395.

Viederyte, R., & Abele, L. (2020). Innovations audit of industrial clusters: process and main trends of development. International Multidisciplinary Scientific Geo-Conference: SGEM, 20(4.2), 43-54.

Vinod-Prasad, P. (2016). A novel algorithm for string matching with mismatches. In *Proceedings of the 5th International Conference on Pattern Recognition Applications and Methods*, 638–644. DOI: 10.5220/0005752006380644

Vlăduţ, G., Tănase, N. M., Caramihai, M., & Purcărea, A. A. (2018). Innovation Audit for business excellence. In *Proceedings of the international conference on business excellence* (Vol. 12, No. 1, pp. 1026-1037). DOI: 10.2478/picbe-2018-0092

Vlašić, G., Keleminić, K., & Šubić, R. (2022). Understanding drivers of consumer loyalty in the banking industry: A comparative study of generation z individuals exhibiting high vs. low financial literacy. *Management*, 27(1), 213–235. DOI: 10.30924/mjcmi.27.1.12

Wagner Mainardes, E., Ferreira, J. J., & Raposo, M. L. (2014). Strategy and strategic management concepts: are they recognised by management students?.

Walker, A. (2011). 'Creativity loves constraints': The paradox of Google's twenty percent time. *Ephemera*, 11(4).

Wang, L., & Song, T. (2016). An improved digital signature algorithm and authentication protocols in cloud platform IEEE International Conference on Smart Cloud (SmartCloud), 2016. DOI: 10.1109/SmartCloud.2016.46

Wang, L. (2022). Collaborative filtering recommendation of music MOOC resources based on spark architecture. *Computational Intelligence and Neuroscience*, 2022, 2022. DOI: 10.1155/2022/2117081 PMID: 35295283

Wang, X., & Dass, M. (2017). Building innovation capability: The role of top management innovativeness and relative-exploration orientation. *Journal of Business Research*, 76, 127–135. DOI: 10.1016/j.jbusres.2017.03.019

Waqar, M., Dawood, H., Dawood, H., & Ma, N. (2021). An Efficient SMOTE-Based Deep Learning Model for HeartAttack Prediction. *Scientific Programming*, 2021, 6621622. Advance online publication. DOI: 10.1155/2021/6621622

Watson, W. E., Johnson, L., & Merritt, D. (1998). Team orientation, self-orientation, and diversity in task groups: Their connection to team performance over time. *Group & Organization Management*, 23(2), 161–188. DOI: 10.1177/1059601198232005

Weber, P., & Haklay, M. (2008). OpenStreetMap: User-generated street maps. *IEEE Pervasive Computing*, 7(4).

Wee, L. L. M., & Goy, S. C. (2022). The effects of ethnicity, gender and parental financial socialisation on financial knowledge among Gen Z: The case of Sarawak, Malaysia. *International Journal of Social Economics*, 49(9), 1349–1367. DOI: 10.1108/IJSE-02-2021-0114

Wen, I. (2012). An empirical study of an online travel purchase intention model. *Journal of Travel & Tourism Marketing*, 29(1), 18–39. DOI: 10.1080/10548408.2012.638558

Whitty, M. (2021). The online dating revolution: What psychology tells us. *Psychology Today*.

Why you should be marketing on LinkedIn right now. (2023, July 6). Retrieved February 20, 2024, from Linkedin.com: https://www.linkedin.com/business/marketing/blog/linkedin-ads/why-you-should-be-marketing-on-linkedin-right-now

Wichmann, J. R. K., Scholdra, T. P., & Reinartz, W. J. (2023). Propelling International Marketing Research with Geospatial Data. *Journal of International Marketing*, 31(2), 82–102. DOI: 10.1177/1069031X221149951

Wilson-VanMeter, A., & Courtney, L. (2019). *The electronic health record, electronic medical record, and personal health record*. Fast Facts in Health Informatics for Nurses., DOI: 10.1891/9780826142269.0006

Wong, E., Rasoolimanesh, S. M., & Sharif, S. P. (2020). Using online travel agent platforms to determine factors influencing hotel guest satisfaction. *Journal of Hospitality and Tourism Technology*, 11(3), 425–445. DOI: 10.1108/JHTT-07-2019-0099

Wong, M. S., Hideki, N., & George, P. (2011). The use of importance-performance analysis (IPA) in evaluating Japan's e-government services. *Journal of Theoretical and Applied Electronic Commerce Research*, 6(2), 17–30. DOI: 10.4067/S0718-18762011000200003

Woods, R. (2020). "Understanding the role of emotional intelligence in dating among Gen Z." Journal of Emotional Intelligence.

Worokinasih, S., Nuzula, N. F., Damayanti, C. R., & Sirivanh, T. (2023). The resilience of youth entrepreneur: The role of social capital, financial literacy, and emotional intelligence on SME performance in Indonesia. *BISMA (Bisnis dan Manajemen)*, 1-28. https://doi.org/.DOI: 10.26740/bisma.v16n1.p1-27

Wu, H. Y., Tzeng, G. H., & Chen, Y. H. (2009). A fuzzy MCDM approach for evaluating banking performance based on Balanced Scorecard. *Expert Systems with Applications*, 36(6), 10135–10147. DOI: 10.1016/j.eswa.2009.01.005

Wu, J., He, C., Xie, J., Liu, X., & Zhang, M. (2022). Twin-field quantum digital signature with fully discrete phase randomization. *Entropy (Basel, Switzerland)*, 24(6), 839. Advance online publication. DOI: 10.3390/e24060839 PMID: 35741559

Wulandari, D. A., Akmal, M., Gunawan, Y., & others. (2020). *Cooling improvement of the IT rack by layout rearrangement of the A2 class data center room: A simulation study.*

Wu, W., Wang, S., Wu, W., Chen, K., Hong, S., & Lai, Y. (2019). A critical review of battery thermal performance and liquid based battery thermal management. *Energy Conversion and Management*, 182, 262–281. DOI: 10.1016/j.enconman.2018.12.051

Xia, G., Cao, L., & Bi, G. (2017). A review on battery thermal management in electric vehicle application. *Journal of Power Sources*, 367, 90–105. DOI: 10.1016/j.jpowsour.2017.09.046

Xuechao, Y. (2023). Recommender Systems: Collaborative Filtering and Content-based Recommender System. *Applied and Computational Engineering*, 2(1), 346–351. DOI: 10.54254/2755-2721/2/20220658

Yadav, P. K., Burks, T., Frederick, Q., Qin, J., Kim, M., & Ritenour, M. A. (2022). Citrus disease detection using convolution neural network generated features and softmax classifier on hyperspectral image data. *Frontiers in Plant Science*, 13(December), 1043712. DOI: 10.3389/fpls.2022.1043712 PMID: 36570926

Yamini, B., Ramana, K. V., Nalini, M., Devi, D. C., & Maheswari, B. (2024). Customer churn prediction model in enterprises using machine learning. *International Journal of Advanced Technology and Engineering Exploration.*, 11(110), 94–107.

Yam, R. C., Guan, J. C., Pun, K. F., & Tang, E. P. (2004). An audit of technological innovation capabilities in Chinese firms: Some empirical findings in Beijing, China. *Research Policy*, 33(8), 1123–1140. DOI: 10.1016/j.respol.2004.05.004

Yang, J., Zhang, X., Zhang, X., Wang, L., Feng, W., & Li, Q. (2021). Beyond the visible: Bioinspired infrared adaptive materials. *Advanced Materials*, 33(14), 2004754. DOI: 10.1002/adma.202004754 PMID: 33624900

Yar Muhammad, M. T., Hayat, M., & Chong, K. T. (2020). Early and accurate detection and diagnosis of heart disease using intelligent computational model. *Scientific Reports*, 10(1), 19747. DOI: 10.1038/s41598-020-76635-9 PMID: 33184369

Yaseen, R. (2023, June 29). Post Grad Gen Z online daing drwbacks. Retrieved February 24, 2024, from WashingtonPost: https://www.washingtonpost.com/opinions/2023/06/29/post-grad-gen-z-online-dating- drawbacks

Yu, Y., Yao, H., Ni, R., & Zhao, Y. (2020). Detection of fake high definition for HEVC videos based on prediction mode feature. In Signal Processing. Elsevier BV, 166. DOI: 10.1016/j.sigpro.2019.107269

Yuan, X., Zhou, X., Pan, Y., Kosonen, R., Cai, H., Gao, Y., & Wang, Y. (2021). Phase change cooling in data centers: A review. *Energy and Building*, 236, 110764. DOI: 10.1016/j.enbuild.2021.110764

Yukalang, N., Clarke, B., & Ross, K. (2017). Barriers to effective municipal solid waste management in a rapidly urbanizing area in Thailand. *International Journal of Environmental Research and Public Health*, 14(9), 1013. DOI: 10.3390/ijerph14091013 PMID: 28869572

Zaim, D., & Bellafkih, M. (2016). Bluetooth Low Energy (BLE) based geomarketing system. *SITA 2016 - 11th International Conference on Intelligent Systems: Theories and Applications*. DOI: 10.1109/SITA.2016.7772263

Zawislak, P. A., Cherubini Alves, A., Tello-Gamarra, J., Barbieux, D., & Reichert, F. M. (2012). Innovation capability: From technology development to transaction capability. *Journal of Technology Management & Innovation*, 7(2), 14–27. DOI: 10.4067/S0718-27242012000200002

Zhang, Q., Meng, Z., Hong, X., Zhan, Y., Liu, J., Dong, J., Bai, T., Niu, J., & Deen, M. J. (2021). A survey on data center cooling systems: Technology, power consumption modeling and control strategy optimization. *Journal of Systems Architecture*, 119, 102253. DOI: 10.1016/j.sysarc.2021.102253

Zhao, H., Tong, X., Wong, P. K., & Zhu, J. (2005). Types of technology sourcing and innovative capability: An exploratory study of Singapore manufacturing firms. *The Journal of High Technology Management Research*, 16(2), 209–224. DOI: 10.1016/j.hitech.2005.10.004

Zhao, Q., Tsai, P. H., & Wang, J. L. (2019). Improving financial service innovation strategies for enhancing china's banking industry competitive advantage during the fintech revolution: A Hybrid MCDM model. *Sustainability (Basel)*, 11(5), 1419. DOI: 10.3390/su11051419

Zhou, K. Z., Brown, J. R., & Dev, C. S. (2009). Market orientation, competitive advantage, and performance: A demand-based perspective. *Journal of Business Research*, 62(11), 1063–1070. DOI: 10.1016/j.jbusres.2008.10.001

Zsoter, B. (2017). Personality, attitude and behavioural components of financial literacy: A comparative analysis. *Journal of Economics and Behavioral Studies*, 9(2 (J)), 46–57. DOI: 10.22610/jebs.v9i2(J).1649

About the Contributors

Kanak Kalita is a prominent researcher in Computational Engineering, acknowledged among the Top 2% of scientists by Elsevier-Scopus and Stanford University's citation analysis. He earned his M.E and PhD in Applied Mechanics from the Indian Institute of Engineering, Science & Technology, Shibpur, India in 2014 and 2019 respectively. He currently holds the position of Associate Professor in the Department of Mechanical Engineering at Vel Tech University, Chennai. He is also a visiting professor at the VSB-Technical University of Ostrava, Czech Republic and Jadara University, Jordan. With over 10 years of experience, Dr. Kalita has authored 160+ SCOPUS articles including 90+ SCI articles. He has written 1 book, edited 10 books, and accumulated around 2700 citations with an h-index of 30. He has delivered 20+ expert lectures/keynote addresses/invited lectures and serves as the Editor of esteemed journals, like "Scientific Reports", SCI journal by Springer-Nature; "Discover Applied Science", WOS-SCOPUS journal by Springer-Nature and "Frontiers in Mechanical Engineering" WOS-SCOPUS journal.

Diego Oliva (Senior Member, IEEE) received a B.S. degree in Electronics and Computer Engineering from the Industrial Technical Education Center (CETI) of Guadalajara, Mexico, in 2007 and an M.Sc. degree in Electronic Engineering and Computer Sciences from the University of Guadalajara, Mexico, in 2010. He obtained a Ph. D. in Informatics in 2015 from the Universidad Complutense de Madrid. Currently, he is an Associate Professor at the University of Guadalajara in Mexico. He has the National Researcher Rank 2 distinction by the Mexican Council of Science and Technology. Currently, he is a Senior member of the IEEE. His research interests include evolutionary and swarm algorithms, hybridization of evolutionary and swarm algorithms, and computational intelligence. He is the Associate Editor of the following journals, IEEE Access, Q1, IF = 4.098; IEEE Latin America Transaction, Q2, IF=0.804; Mathematical Problems in Engineering, Q2, IF = 1.009 and Plos One, Q1, IF = 2.740.

Xiao-Zhi Gao is an esteemed academic with an extensive background in technology and computing. He commenced his academic journey at Harbin Institute of Technology, China, where he earned both his B.Sc. and M.Sc. degrees. Dr. Gao further advanced his education at the Helsinki University of Technology, now known as Aalto University, Finland, where he obtained his Ph.D. degree in 1999. With over 22 years of experience in teaching and research, Dr. Gao has established himself as a leading figure in the field. Since 2018, he has been a Professor od Data Science at the University of Eastern Finland, Kuopio, Finland, where he continues to contribute significantly to the academic community. Dr. Gao's editorial roles are remarkable. He serves as chief editor, associate editor, and a member of the editorial board for several prominent soft-computing journals, including Swarm and Evolutionary Computation, Information Sciences, and Applied Soft Computing. His scholarly output is impressive, with over 500 technical papers published in refereed journals and international conferences, and more than 400 SCI/SCOPUS research articles to his name. In addition to his extensive list of articles, Dr. Gao has authored 2 books and edited 4 books for renowned publishers such as Springer and IGI Global. His research is particularly focused on nature-inspired computing methods, with applications spanning optimization, prediction, data mining, signal processing, control, and industrial electronics. This breadth of interest underscores his deep understanding and innovative approach to complex technological challenges. Dr. Gao's academic achievements are further highlighted by his impressive Google Scholar H-index of 44, reflecting the widespread influence and high citation rate of his work. His dedication to advancing the frontiers of knowledge in computing and technology makes him a vital asset to the global academic and scientific community. His ORCID is 0000-0002-0078-5675.

Rishi Dwivedi is currently working as an Assistant Professor in the Department of Finance, XISS, Ranchi. He has obtained his PhD degree from Jadavpur University, Kolkata after completing MBA degree with specialization in Finance from IBS Business School, Kolkata. Dr Rishi has obtained his Bachelor's degree in Mechanical Engineering from Sikkim Manipal Institute of Technology, Rangpo, Sikkim. Before joining XISS, Ranchi, Dr Rishi has worked as an Assistant Professor in Management Department at Central University of Jharkhand. He has also almost one year of corporate experience as an Assistant Manager at ICICI Bank Limited, Kolkata, West Bengal. In that role, he was accountable for the complete credit granting process, including consistent application of a credit policy, periodic credit reviews of existing customers and assessment of the creditworthiness of potential customers, with the goal of maximizing customer profitability and minimizing bad debt losses. During his corporate career, he evaluated the credit proposals of various SME and MSME clients, through incisive financial statement analysis, industry performance, economic analysis and management quality. Dr Rishi is regular reviewer of many international journals of high repute like, International Journal of Production Research, Journal of Cleaner Production, OPSEARCH etc. His research interests include development of integrated activity based costing and quality function deployment models for various industries in order to attain competitive edge. Of late he is also interested in exploring the ways in which MCDM model can be applied to achieve sustainable advantage for assorted industries. Dr. Rishi has been awarded with esteemed UGC-BSR Research Fellowship in Science for Meritorious Students. He has published several research papers in well renowned international journals as well as presented papers in international conferences. He has carried out collaborative research with professionals from Indian Institute of Technology and National Institute of Technology.

***

Pooja is presently working as an Assistant Professor at Xavier Institute of Social Service, Ranchi. She completed her PhD from Birla Institute of Technology, Mesra, Ranchi in the year 2018. She holds an MBA degree with specialization in Human resources and Marketing. She has several papers to her credit in both national as well as international journals indexed in prestigious databases. She has worked with academic institutions of repute as a faculty member prior to joining Xavier Institute of Social Service, Ranchi. She is also an appointed member of editorial board and reviewer for journals of repute. Her areas of specialization are Organizational Behaviour, Human Resource Management and Leadership. She is also life time member of National Human Resource Development Network (NHRD) and Indian Society for Training and Development (ISTD).

R. Gnanjeyaraman, B.E., M.E., Ph.D., Professor of the Department of Applied Machine Learning, Institute of Artificial Intelligence and Machine Learning. He is a Life Member of ISTE chapter and ACEEE, IDEAS, UACEE, Global Member – Internet Society. He has 19+ years of teaching experience in UG & PG Engineering courses. He has published 34 papers in well reputed international journals, 15 papers in international conferences and 8 papers in national conferences. His current research interests are Network Security, Cryptography & Block chain, Medical Imaging & Analytics, Bio Medical Image Processing, and AI & Machine Learning.

Sudhair Abbas Bangash, Professor and HoD Department of Pharmacy, Sarhad University of Science and Information Technology, Peshawar. I am Ph. D. (UoP) with specialization in Pharmacology and B. Pharmacy (Pak), engaged in Teaching and Research in the universities for more than last 17 years. Produces about 12 MS.

Scholars and published more than 90 research articles in journals of National and international repute. I did also MBA from Abasyn University, Peshawar and MS in Management Sciences from Abasyn University, Peshawar. I am Now enrolled in PhD management Sciences and Published about 14 papers in Management Sciences.

Munir Ahmad is a seasoned professional in the realm of Spatial Data Infrastructure (SDI), Geo-Information Productions, Information Systems, and Information Governance, boasting over 25 years of dedicated experience in the field. With a PhD in Computer Science, Dr. Ahmad's expertise spans Spatial Data Production, Management, Processing, Analysis, Visualization, and Quality Control. Throughout his career, Dr. Ahmad has been deeply involved in the development and deployment of SDI systems specially in the context of Pakistan, leveraging his proficiency in Spatial Database Design, Web, Mobile & Desktop GIS, and Geo Web Services Architecture. His contributions to Volunteered Geographic Information (VGI) and Open Source Geoportal & Metadata Portal have significantly enriched the geospatial community. As a trainer and researcher, Dr. Ahmad has authored over 50 publications, advancing the industry's knowledge base and fostering innovation in Geo-Tech, Data Governance, and Information Infrastructure, and Emerging Technologies. His commitment to Research and Development (R&D) is evident in his role as a dedicated educator and mentor in the field.

Maher Ali Rusho is currently employed as a Research Associate in Human-Computer Interaction (HCI) at Brain-Station 23 PLC. Beyond that, he also founded his own software company, UntieAI, in Canada. He has an impressive research background, which includes nine design patents and numerous scholarly articles in high-impact journals (SCI index, Q1/Q2). In addition to his entrepreneurial and research activities, Rusho served as an adjunct faculty member at an Argentine university last year, where he coauthored a book on machine learning with a researcher from Harvard University. He has collaborated with many prominent scientists, including those ranked among the top 2% in the world by Stanford University and Elsevier. Rusho's achievements have also been recognized by Forbes magazine, where he was featured for his significant contributions to his field.

B. Yamini (Bhavanishankar Yamini) has completed her Bachelor of Engineering in Computer Science and Engineering from Mailam Engineering College, in the year 2003. She pursued her Master of Technology in Information Technology from Sathyabama University, Chennai in the year 2007. She was awarded the Doctor of Philosophy in Computer Science and Engineering from Sathyabama Institute of Science and Technology, Chennai in the year 2020. She has published papers in various International and National Conferences and Journals. She is currently working at SRM Institute of Science and Technology, College of Engineering and Technology as Associate Professor in the Department of Networking and Communications. Her areas of interests include Network Security, Cyber Forensics, Image Processing, and Information Retrieval system, Machine Learning, Deep Learning and Cloud Computing.

Srijon Ghosh Student from TISS pursuing data analytics, interested in researching both macro and micro level data. Passionate about understanding complex patterns and making data-driven decisions.

Ayush Gupta was born in 2002 in Kanpur, Uttar Pradesh. Ayush Gupta has completed his undergrad studies as a part of IPM (Integrated Programme in Management) at IIM Bodhgaya. His research interests lie in data analytics, strategy, HRM, OB, well-being, mental health, and mindfulness.

Sudipta Halder is a Full Stack Web Developer from Bengaluru with expertise in front-end (React, Angular) and back-end (Node.js, Express) frameworks. Holding a B.E. in Computer Science from *Atria Institute of Technology, she has worked as a **Web Developer Intern* at *Business Web Solutions* and *Bhargawa InfoTech Solutions*, where she expanded her skills into AI and machine learning. Her portfolio features projects like an *E-Commerce site, a **blogging platform, and a **chatbot* utilizing *IBM Watson's AI. Known for her problem-solving and leadership abilities, Sudipta holds certifications from **IBM, **Google Cloud, and **Udemy*. Passionate about community service, she volunteers with organizations like *AICTE* and the *Robin Hood Army, and serves as a **Community Lead* at Atria. Always eager to learn and collaborate, Sudipta is open to exploring new opportunities in tech and beyond.

K. Sivakumar is the Associate Professor and Head of the Department of Information Technology at Nehru Institute of Engineering and Technology. He leads academic and research initiatives within the department, focusing on advancements in IT education. With his leadership, the department fosters innovation and excellence in preparing students for the evolving tech industry.

Arana Kausar is an Assistant Professor in the Financial Management Programme at XISS,Ranchi. She teaches courses onBusiness Law, Managerial Economics, Organizational Behaviour, Insurance & Risk Management, Strategic Management and Business Ethics. She has completed her B.Com Hons from Aligarh Muslim University. In order to pursue higher studies, she did her Post Graduate Diploma in Business management from KIIT School of Management-University at Bhubaneswar with Finance as her major area and Systems as minor area of specialization.To hone her skills further, she completed her Masters in Commerce with specialization in International Business. Thereafter, she completed her Ph.D from the Faculty of Commerce, Ranchi University. She is currently pursuing her Masters in Business Law from National Law School of India University, Bangalore. She has got her research papers published in various National and International journals of high repute. She has also presented her research papers in various International Seminars. She is also a Life time member of the Indian Commerce Association.

Dinesh Kumar, PhD, is an Assistant Professor in the Department of Production and Industrial Engineering, National Institute of Technology, Jamshedpur, Jharkhand, India. He completed his PhD. from IIT Roorkee in 2016 in supply chain management. He has authored more than 30 papers in reputed journals. His areas of expertise are perishable inventory theories, operations management, supply chain sustainability, circular economy, and system dynamics. Dr. Kumar has guided three Ph.D.s and eight master's theses with his research acumen. He has authored various book chapters in several international editions. He has edited three books of reputed international publishers. He is the reviewer of various reputed international journals, including Operations Management Research, International Journal of Logistics Research and Applications, Computers and Industrial Engineering Environmental Science and Pollution Research etc. He is also a life member of the Operations Research Society of India (ORSI).

Shailendra Mishra Completed my PhD thesis entitled "Brain Tumor Classification By The Combination of Different Wavelet Transforms And Support Vector Machine" in 2021. I have done my Post Graduate degree (M.Tech) from SRM University, Kattankulathur Chennai, Tamilnadu, india. The author became a IEEE Senior Member (SM) in may 2024. I have Worked as Assistant Professor in Vel Tech Rangarajan Dr. Sagunthala R&D Institute of Science and Technology, Chennai, from 27th June 2013 to 26th December 2021. I am involved in designing and executing theory courses and laboratory experiments for undergraduate students for more than ten years. My research Interest lies in the field of Image Processing, IoT, AI & ML and Antenna Design. As of now, from the research work I have published more than twenty five papers in reputed journals and conferences. Dr. Shailendra Kumar Mishra, Associate Prof. REVA University, is a member of various professional societies such as IAENG, TERA, ICSES.

Sabyasachi Pramanik is a professional IEEE member. He obtained a PhD in Computer Science and Engineering from Sri Satya Sai University of Technology and Medical Sciences, Bhopal, India. Presently, he is an Associate Professor, Department of Computer Science and Engineering, Haldia Institute of Technology, India. He has many publications in various reputed international conferences, journals, and book chapters (Indexed by SCIE, Scopus, ESCI, etc). He is doing research in the fields of Artificial Intelligence, Data Privacy, Cybersecurity, Network Security, and Machine Learning. He also serves on the editorial boards of several international journals. He is a reviewer of journal articles from IEEE, Springer, Elsevier, Inderscience, IET and IGI Global. He has reviewed many conference papers, has been a keynote speaker, session chair, and technical program committee member at many international conferences. He has authored a book on Wireless Sensor Network. He has edited 8 books from IGI Global, CRC Press, Springer and Wiley Publications.

Kanika Prasad is working as Assistant Professor in Production and Industrial Engineering Department of National Institute of Technology, Jamshedpur. She graduated in Mechanical Engineering from Sikkim Manipal Institute of Technology, Sikkim in 2010 and completed her Master of Engineering in Production Engineering from Jadavpur University, Kolkata in 2013, earning distinction in both degrees. She earned prestigious DST INSPIRE fellowship to pursue her doctoral research from Jadavpur University. She has been awarded with Ph.D. (Engg.) degree from Jadavpur University in 2016. She has worked with Sikkim Manipal Institute of Technology as an Assistant Professor for almost a year and taught various undergraduate and post graduate subjects, like Operations Research, Quality Control Assurance and Reliability, Manufacturing Planning and Control, Manufacturing Process etc. She has published several papers in peer reviewed international journals. With many publications in journal and conferences of international repute so early in her academic career, much is expected of her research career. She specializes in application of quality function deployment technique and multi-criteria decision-making to develop expert systems for selection and design problems in manufacturing. Of late sustainability and waste management domain interests her and she is working in that area. She has guided several UG and PG dissertations. She is also a regular reviewer of several journals of international repute.

Siva Subramanian R. is an Associate Professor in the Department of Computer Science and Engineering, RMK College of Engg and Tech, Chennai, India. He received her B.E. in Computer Science and Engineering from Anna University, Chennai in 2009 and M.Tech. in Computer Science and Engineering from Bharath University, Chennai, India in 2013. He has 10 years teaching experience. His research interests include Data Mining, Machine Learning, Big Data Analytics and Networking. He has published many articles in reputed Journals.

R. Bhuvanya is an Assistant Professor at Sri Ramachandra Faculty of Engineering and Technology, part of the Sri Ramachandra Institute of Higher Education and Research in Porur, Chennai. She specializes in engineering education and contributes to research and academic development within the institution. With a commitment to academic excellence, she plays a pivotal role in shaping future engineers and researchers.

P Kritee Rao is a research scholar at National Institute of Technology Jamshedpur. Her research interests include strategic management, sustainable performance, sustainable strategic management and multi-criteria decision making (MCDM).

Asma Sayyad Student from TISS pursuing data analytics, interested in researching both macro and micro level data. Passionate about understanding complex patterns and making data-driven decisions.

Akanksha Shukla is an Assistant Professor at National Institute of Technology Jamshedpur. Her research interests include marketing management, entrepreneurship, strategic management and corporate social responsibility.

Amar Eron Tigga is the Dean Academics at XISS Ranchi and Professor in the area of Marketing Management. He is also the Chief Placements Coordinator of XISS and works for strengthening the Corporate and Alumni Relations. He received his Ph.D. and B.Tech. from IIT(ISM) Dhanbad and PGDM from IIM Calcutta. He also completed a course on Advance Marketing Management from IIM Lucknow. He teaches subjects in Marketing domain namely, Brand Management, Sales Management, Customer Relationship Management and B2B Marketing. His has interest in technology and teaches Management Information System also for Marketing students. He also works in developing, training and mentoring entrepreneurs. He is also coordinating the Doctoral Programme of XISS called Fellow Programme in Management (FPM). His research areas include Brand Management and Sales Management. He has presented several research papers in national and international conferences and published articles in journals of repute. He is also attached with various corporate and development organizations for training and projects implementation. His research interests are also in Educational Institution Branding, especially B-Schools. He is also involved in XISS UNICEF Project which aims for Child Protection, Covid Appropriate Behaviour etc. in the selected districts of Jharkhand. He has delivered training to Block Program Officers of Jharkhand Education Project Council (JEPC), Ranchi. He has trained many youths for getting associated as franchisee of Jharkhand Electricity Board as a project of Rural Electrification Corporation (REC). Prior to joining XISS, Prof.

Amar worked with Punjab National Bank as a Sr. Manager Marketing and worked for bank's business development and marketing of various products. He also served as mining engineer in Pyrites, Phosphates and Chemicals Ltd., Dehradun. He is an Independent Director for Ranchi Smart City Corporation Ltd. (RSCCL) and a member of Board of Governors of various institutions like Indian Institute of Coal Management (IICM), Ranchi, Xavier Institute of Social Service (XISS), Ranchi and Indian Institute of Information Technology (IIIT), Ranchi. He is also a Trustee of Maruti Suzuki XISS Awanish Kumar Dev Memorial Trust. He also served the Institute (XISS) as an Acting Director from 1st Aug 2019 to 15th June 2020. He strongly believes in "Giving Back to the Society". He believes in Hard Work, Integrity, Sincerity and God.

Sathya V is a faculty member at Vel Tech Rangarajan Dr. Sagunthala R&D Institute of Science and Technology. She is committed to teaching and research, focusing on advancing scientific knowledge and innovation.

V. M. Gobinath is a faculty member in the Department of Mechanical Engineering at Rajalakshmi Institute of Technology, Chennai. He is dedicated to teaching and mentoring students in mechanical engineering while contributing to academic research. His work focuses on developing engineering skills and knowledge to meet industry standards.

Saikonda Vaishnavi was born in 2003 in Bangalore, India. Saikonda Vaishnavi has completed her undergrad studies as a part of IPM (Integrated Programme in Management) at IIM Bodhgaya. Her research interests lie in data analytics, strategy, leadership and Organisational Behavior.

Index

A

Alternating Least Squares 176, 177, 180, 186
AMOS 55, 59, 61, 63, 64, 65, 73
ANOVA tests 333, 345, 352
Artificial Intelligence 9, 11, 38, 46, 99, 213, 214, 232, 235, 236, 237, 238, 249, 250, 254, 256, 259, 265, 367

B

banking industry 39, 101, 283, 319, 321, 322, 323, 324, 325, 326, 327, 328, 329, 331, 332
Barriers 157, 158, 159, 160, 161, 162, 163, 165, 167, 168, 169, 170, 171, 172, 245
Big Data 1, 3, 4, 5, 6, 21, 29, 30, 31, 32, 33, 34, 35, 36, 37, 38, 41, 42, 43, 44, 45, 46, 47, 48, 49, 50, 51, 153, 155, 188, 219, 233
Bihar 263, 277, 333, 334, 335, 336, 339, 340, 341, 343, 344, 345, 346, 347, 348, 349, 350, 351, 352

C

Case Studies 20, 32, 34, 41, 359, 360
Chi-square tests 333, 342, 352, 353
Circular Economy 157, 171, 172
Cloud Computing 102, 204, 369, 370, 371, 372, 373, 377, 378
Comparison of Companies 103
cooling in data centers 235, 237, 243, 244, 249, 250, 260
customer engagement 86, 87, 89, 91, 99, 135, 142, 151, 152

D

Data 1, 2, 3, 4, 5, 6, 7, 8, 9, 10, 11, 12, 13, 14, 15, 16, 17, 18, 19, 20, 21, 22, 23, 24, 25, 26, 27, 28, 29, 30, 31, 32, 33, 34, 35, 36, 37, 38, 39, 40, 41, 42, 43, 44, 45, 46, 47, 48, 49, 50, 51, 55, 59, 60, 63, 64, 65, 66, 78, 85, 92, 93, 99, 103, 120, 128, 133, 134, 135, 136, 137, 138, 139, 140, 141, 142, 143, 144, 145, 146, 147, 148, 149, 150, 151, 152, 153, 154, 155, 156, 159, 163, 170, 175, 176, 177, 178, 179, 180, 181, 182, 183, 184, 185, 186, 188, 193, 195, 199, 201, 205, 206, 207, 208, 212, 214, 215, 216, 217, 218, 219, 220, 221, 222, 223, 224, 226, 227, 230, 232, 233, 235, 236, 237, 238, 240, 242, 243, 244, 245, 246, 247, 248, 249, 250, 251, 252, 253, 254, 255, 256, 257, 258, 259, 260, 268, 269, 270, 277, 285, 297, 298, 303, 304, 305, 312, 322, 324, 325, 326, 327, 333, 335, 336, 340, 341, 348, 351, 353, 354, 355, 357, 358, 359, 360, 361, 362, 364, 365, 369, 370, 371, 375, 376, 377, 379
Data Analytics 1, 2, 3, 4, 5, 6, 13, 17, 18, 19, 20, 21, 22, 23, 24, 25, 28, 29, 30, 31, 32, 34, 35, 36, 37, 38, 41, 42, 43, 45, 46, 47, 48, 49, 50, 51, 137, 153, 186, 232, 233, 370
Data-Driven Decision-Making 14, 22, 23, 24, 28, 35, 51, 359
Dating apps 285, 286, 287, 288, 290, 291, 292, 293, 294, 295, 296, 299, 315, 316
Decision Making 2, 3, 10, 13, 22, 24, 29, 41, 50, 51, 144, 155, 158, 263, 265, 266, 267, 278, 321, 324, 359
Development 2, 3, 4, 9, 11, 24, 28, 32, 41, 56, 76, 85, 91, 104, 106, 108, 109, 121, 125, 127, 128, 129, 130, 131, 134, 136, 138, 146, 148, 153, 154, 160, 164, 171, 172, 177, 179, 186, 212, 231, 242, 252, 257, 258, 265, 266, 277, 278, 279, 285, 289, 306, 311, 315, 319, 320, 321, 324, 325, 326, 327, 329, 330, 331, 333, 334, 335, 341, 347, 348, 349, 350, 351, 352, 360, 366
Digital 5, 12, 24, 28, 42, 47, 86, 87, 89, 97, 99, 105, 123, 126, 153, 154, 204,

Printed in the United States
by Baker & Taylor Publisher Services